OCCUPATIONS AND THE SOCIAL STRUCTURE

richard h. hall
university of minnesota

OCCUPATIONS AND THE SOCIAL STRUCTURE

prentice-hall, inc.
englewood cliffs, n.j.

prentice-hall sociology series
neil j. smelser, editor

13–629352–2

Library of Congress Catalog Card No.: 69–14434

Current printing (last number):
10 9 8 7 6 5 4 3 2 1

Printed in the United States of America

Prentice-Hall International, Inc., *London*
Prentice-Hall of Australia, Pty. Ltd., *Sydney*
Prentice-Hall of Canada, Ltd., *Toronto*
Prentice-Hall of India Private Ltd., *New Delhi*
Prentice-Hall of Japan, Inc., *Tokyo*

to ed and tom

preface

This book is written with three purposes in mind. The first is to analyze the manner in which the occupational system articulates with the balance of the social system. From this analysis it will be clear that occupations serve as a major link between the individual and the larger society. The obvious relationship between occupations and social status, the less obvious but equally important relationships between occupations and education, political involvement, and family life, and the reciprocal relationships between general social change and changes in the occupational system all indicate the centrality of occupations in the social structure. Conflict between occupations and the social system comprises a significant part of the total relationship and is, thus, an important component of this analysis.

The second purpose of this book is to describe and analyze the various types of occupations as they exist in the social system. The basic theme of this description and analysis is change. Change affects occupations from every direction. The societal demands for a particular occupation's services, the educational prerequisites for entry, and the organizational settings in which occupational duties are performed can be approached only from the perspective of change.

The book is also designed, as a third purpose, to serve as a text for courses in occupational sociology or as a supplement to courses in complex organizations, industrial sociology, or general social organization.

I became interested in the sociology of occupations first when my research and thought about the nature of complex organizations indicated that organizational phenomena cannot be fully understood without taking the kinds of occupations found in organizations into account and second when, after teaching a course in occupational sociology for a number of years, it became evident that there was a need for additional thought and writing in the area.

This book is not oriented around the individual, either in terms of his occupational choice or his reactions to his occupation. Both topics are touched on briefly, but the basic theme remains the relationships between occupations and the social system.

My general intellectual debts will become evident as the reader scans the footnotes. Much of the general analytical framework has its origins in Theodore Caplow's *The Sociology of Work*. I hope the present work extends this approach into a number of useful areas. At the more practical level I would like to thank James Clark and Neil Smelser for their thoughtful criticism of an early version of this manuscript and Cordelia Thomas of Prentice-Hall for her work on the book's and my behalf. Casandra Mihalchick provided cheerful and thoughtful assistance in the preparation of the manuscript. My classes at Indiana University and the University of Minnesota are also due thanks as they survived the development of the ideas in the book. Finally, I would like to thank my wife, Sherry, for her cheerfulness and love throughout this project.

contents

ix

OCCUPATIONS AND THE SOCIAL STRUCTURE

PART I

OCCUPATIONS:
THE CONTEXT
AND THE
INDIVIDUAL

chapter 1

definitions
and distinctions

The centrality of an individual's occupation to his life is a fact that requires little verification. During the adult years work is rivaled only by sleep as a routine activity. Much of the time before and after the working period of life is related to work. The pre-occupational period is typically spent in acquiring skills that can be used in the occupational world. Postoccupational life or retirement is related to work by income received through pension plans or national old-age-insurance plans. More importantly, perhaps, this period is also one in which an individual looks back to his work as a major reference point for his retirement. Thus, regardless of the level of satisfaction or intrinsic interest a person has in his job, work is a central part of life. These remarks apply to both men and women, since the latter are, of course, employed outside the home, and the work performed inside the home can legitimately be called an occupation.

While the relationships described above are perhaps obvious, the same cannot be said for the relationships between occupations and the social structure. Though there is general agreement that occupations and social status are highly associated, there is less agreement as to why this is so. Similarly, the reasons for the growing dependence of employing organizations on the educational system are not clear. Developments in work technology are affecting the work itself, but again the extent and directions of the effects are not clear. Even more subtle are the relationships between a person's background, in terms of both the characteristics associated with his position in the social structure and the related personality variables, and his motivation to work or not to work.

This book is an attempt to relate occupations to the broader social structure. It assumes that the relationships are somewhat stable and can thus be analyzed in a somewhat static fashion. At the same time, the existence of "deviant cases," such as unemployment and dissatisfactions with work, will also be examined. The very important factors of social and technological change and their effects on the equilibrium will, similarly, be discussed. The approach to be taken is that the basic, systematic relationship between occupations and the social structure remains stable, although its specific forms undergo continual alterations.

the definition problem

The obvious first step in any analysis is to define the subject matter. In the case of occupations many definitions are available, but Nels Anderson's point, that "definitions of work tell us little about it, and apparently the making of such definitions has never given man much concern,"[1] is probably close to the truth. The reason for the lack of concern is undoubtedly the fact that the term "occupation" has a very real meaning for almost all people. Nevertheless, a definition is needed, and it must be inclusive in two ways. It must, first, include the great variety of activities that can legitimately be called occupations and, second, suggest the fact that an occupation has multiple consequences for the individual and society.

On the latter ground, definitions that stress only the financial rewards to the individual would appear to be too limited. Robert Dubin, for example, in defining work states, "By work we mean continuous employment, in the production [sic] of goods and services, for remuneration."[2] Besides whatever questions might be

[1] *Dimensions of Work* (New York: David McKay Co., Inc., 1964), p. 1.
[2] *The World of Work* (Englewood Cliffs, N.J.: Prentice-Hall, Inc., © 1958), p. 4.

raised in regard to production, since many kinds of work (occupations) cannot be realistically said to be part of the production process, the concentration on remuneration is unfortunate because remuneration, though important, is only a part of the outcome for the individual of his occupation.

A slightly broader perspective is offered by Arthur Salz, who notes that "occupation may be defined as that specific activity with a market value which an individual continually pursues for the purpose of obtaining a steady flow of income. This activity also determines the social position of the individual."[3] While the emphasis on remuneration remains, the inclusion of the additional idea of determining social position suggests the centrality of occupations for both the individual and the social structure. This is especially true when social position is taken to mean more than position in an organizational hierarchy or stratification system. Thus the occupation determines the individual's relationships with and to other individuals in the same and other occupations because the positions themselves are related.

Everett Hughes also sees the meaning of occupation in broad terms; he states that "an occupation, in essence, is not some particular set of activities; it is the part of an individual in any ongoing set of activities. The system may be large or small, simple or complex."[4] Hughes emphasizes the social relationships surrounding an occupation, not in order to minimize the financial side, but to keep it in perspective as part of a more inclusive set of social relationships. Similarly, Anne Roe defines an occupation as "whatever an adult spends most of his time doing . . . the major focus of a person's activities and usually of his thoughts."[5] This definition suggests the importance of an occupation to the individual. It also, therefore, suggests that this major focus is transmitted into the social process and thus means that occupations are a major component of the social structure.

With these considerations in mind, a definition of occupations can be offered that encompasses the variety of activities and outcomes that must be taken into account in the analysis of occupations. *An occupation is the social role performed by adult members of society that directly and/or indirectly yields social and financial*

[3]"Occupations: Theory and History," *Encyclopedia of the Social Sciences* (New York: The Macmillan Company, Publishers, 1944), XI, 424.

[4]"The Study of Occupations," in *Sociology Today*, ed. R. K. Merton, L. Broom, and L. S. Cottrell (New York: Harper & Row, Publishers, 1965), p. 445.

[5]*The Psychology of Occupations* (New York: John Wiley & Sons, Inc., 1956), p. 3.

consequences and that constitutes a major focus in the life of an adult.

The limitation to the adult years in the definition is in recognition of the fact that schooling and occupational experiences prior to this period are essentially preparations for the occupational role of an adult. Delbert Miller and William Form have suggested that the work career can be separated into five parts: the preparatory, initial, trial, stable, and retirement periods.[6] For the purposes of this definition the preparatory and initial periods are not included in what is being labeled an occupation. The initial period includes summer and part-time jobs that a person may have as he passes through adolescence. While these jobs may be important in developing work habits and attitudes, they are not truly an occupation since they are recognized as temporary.

The definition recognizes the multiplicity of outcomes of occupations for the individual and society without minimizing the centrality of financial rewards. Rather obviously, the degree to which the financial aspect of the occupational contribution is important to the individual varies with the individual's own outlook toward his work, as will be discussed later. The inclusion of the idea of indirect consequences is intended to recognize the fact that a number of roles that have the characteristics of occupations do not confer direct financial or social rewards. The housewife, for example, does not receive pay for her work. Her work does, however, have important indirect yields, particularly if part of her husband's career depends upon her success in the housewife's role. By the same token, the role of the graduate- or professional-school student has indirect (future) yields. In terms of this definition it can legitimately be called an occupation, even though it is usually of limited duration.[7] It can be argued that graduate or professional students approach their work in the same way their contemporaries not in the educational system do. The centrality to life on the one hand and the hours spent at "work" on the other suggest that this interpretation is not inappropriate, even though the period is preparatory for another occupation. The role of this type of student is similar to that of a "junior executive" or a new member of a large law firm during the first years of employment in its preparatory and temporary nature, although its financial and social yield lies in the future.

[6]*Industrial Sociology* (New York: Harper & Row, Publishers, 1964), pp. 541–45.

[7]While this particular role is designed to serve as a preparation for a career, it appears to involve more than the preparatory phase discussed by Miller and Form.

One further distinction should be noted before leaving this definition. For the purposes of this analysis, *work* will be considered the activity that is performed in the occupational role. Work and occupation are often used synonymously with little loss in clarity. The term occupation seems preferable when it is used in the broader context discussed previously. "What is your occupation?" implies a title that in turn implies some social valuation about that role. On the other hand, "What kind of work do you do?" requests information about the specific activity performed in the occupation. This distinction is of course not always followed, but it does appear to be useful for the purposes of this analysis.

plan of the book

The rather broadly based definition we have adopted suggests that an occupation has ramifications for both the individual and society. The major focus of this analysis will be on the latter point, the interrelationships between occupations and the social structure. At the same time, some attention will be given to the impact of occupations on the individual, principally with regard to *why* people work and *what kinds* of satisfactions, rewards, dissatisfactions, and stresses they experience in their work.

The procedure to be followed in this analysis is first to examine briefly the antecedents of contemporary occupations. The current composition of the labor force will then be examined, with particular emphasis on significant shifts both in the nature and location of occupations. Next will come an analysis of the individual's responses to work, his motivations, his satisfactions, and his dissatisfactions. In order to analyze the relationships between occupations and the social structure, it will be necessary to subdivide the broad range of occupations into reasonably homogeneous categories, since different occupations have widely varied meanings and rewards. While no perfect typology of occupations is available, the categorization developed by the U.S. Bureau of the Census will be utilized as a heuristic device, as it does group occupations into categories sufficiently homogeneous for this analysis.[8] At the same time, variations within the categories will be noted, since it is clear that such broad types as professionals contain wide variations in performance,

[8]Department of Commerce, Bureau of the Census, *Census of the Population: 1960* (Washington, D.C.: Government Printing Office, 1960), Table D 72–122, p. 74.

outlook, training, and reward patterns. These steps will serve as the background for the more intensive analysis of occupations as they are categorized by the Census. These categories are:

1. Professionals
2. Managers, proprietors, and officials
3. Clerical and kindred workers
4. Skilled workers and foremen
5. Semiskilled workers
6. Unskilled workers (Including farm and nonfarm workers)

While the occupations are categorized in this manner primarily for convenience, it should be evident that this categorization corresponds to a rough approximation of the social stratification system. It is important to note that the amounts of information available about the work areas outlined above are not equal. Professionals, for example, have been examined much more intensively than any of the other groups, and there is a surprising lack of adequate information about managers, executives, and farm employees. For this reason the treatment of the different types of occupations will vary both in length and, unfortunately, in substantive knowledge.

The balance of the book will be concerned with the relationships between occupations and the wider social structure. Here the first area to be analyzed will be the connection between the social-stratification system and occupations, the importance of which is implied in the typology of occupations suggested above. Included in this will be discussions of the interrelated factors of mobility and career patterns. The analysis will then shift to the relationships between occupations and the familial, political, educational, and technological systems and to the effects of technological change. While technology is not an "institution" in the same manner as the other areas discussed, the interactions among the producers of changing technology—essentially the research and development complex in education, industry and government—appear well enough developed to at least suggest that it can be treated as one of the institutional areas. Unemployment as an occupational phenomenon will also be treated in this section, partly because there is a relationship between it and technological change and partly for convenience.

summary and conclusions

This chapter has been devoted to the development of a definition of occupations. The definition (the social role performed by adult members of society that directly and/or indirectly yields social and financial consequences and that constitutes a major focus in the life of an adult) will serve as the basis for the analysis in the balance of this book. In the chapters that follow, the historical roots of contemporary occupations will be traced. The individual's orientations toward, and reactions to, his occupation will be discussed. The various types of occupations will then be analyzed in order to provide an understanding of the heterogeneity of occupations found in the system. The final section of the book will discuss the manner in which occupations are related to the balance of the social system. As will be seen, this relationship is not one of total harmony. Both the integrative and conflictual patterns of interaction between occupations and the social structure will be considered.

chapter 2

occupations in their historical and contemporary context

Obviously work is different in an urbanized, industrialized society from what it was in the past, but the nature of the differences and the changes that have led to the broad spectrum of contemporary occupations are probably less evident. The purpose of this chapter is to explore the nature of, and reasons for, these changes, which provide at least a partial basis for the examination of the relationships between occupations and the social structure. While these changes are an accomplished fact, they can yield insights into the present. These are especially important in that some of the current relationships are not ones of equilibrium. That is, strains that exist between certain aspects of contemporary occupations and institutions, such as the family or educational system, are, at least in part, historically based.

Two perspectives on the history of work will be taken. Besides examining the changes that have occurred in the relations between work and other aspects of society, we will also examine the changed values or meanings that men have applied to their work.[1] One of the

[1]Such factors as the removal of work from the home and the impact of changing technology on occupations have identifiable historical roots.

lasting intellectual debates has been whether changes in the social structure have led to changes in values or whether value changes must occur before the structure can change.[2] While this is an interesting, if unsettled, issue, it would appear to be fruitless to attempt its resolution here. Instead, the assumption will be made that the changes are concurrent, without suggesting a priority. In a rather simple way, it does not matter which came first, since changes in both structure and values have occurred that have an impact on contemporary occupations. The changes are more important for the present analysis than any causal relationships which happen to exist among them. With this in mind, structural changes will be considered first, primarily because shifts in the orientation toward work can probably be more easily understood if the shifts in the nature of work are first discussed.

structural changes

Before beginning the analysis of changes in the structure of occupations, it would be useful to look briefly at two major characteristics of modern work that have evolved from the historical context. The first is that work is something done as a separate activity, apart from the rest of a person's life. The phrase "go to work" exemplifies this characteristic. Work is carried on outside the home. More importantly, modern occupations involve activities that are distinctly different from those activities that are carried on in nonwork or leisure time.[3] The skills and social relationships of modern occupations are not just those that are learned as one becomes socialized into adulthood. Instead, they are specific to the occupation, often are not transferable to other occupations, and in the case of social relationships, are not transferable if the location of the occupation shifts.

The second major characteristic of modern occupations is that

[2]The classical development of these structural approaches is Marx's insistence on the priority of economic (structural) factors in social change. See Karl Marx, *Capital*, trans. Samuel Moore and Edward Aveling, ed. Frederick Engels (London: George Allen & Unwin, Ltd., 1946). Weber, on the other hand, took the position that value changes (religion) precede structural developments. See Max Weber, *The Protestant Ethic and the Spirit of Capitalism*, trans. Talcott Parsons (London: George Allen & Unwin, Ltd., 1935), pp. 35–78.

[3]See Sigmund Nosow and William H. Form, *Man, Work and Society* (New York: Basic Books Inc., Publishers, 1962), p. 11 and Anderson, *Dimensions of Work*, p. 3.

they are carried out in organizational settings.[4] The movement of work away from individualized settings has accelerated until some 85 per cent of the labor force now work as employees. Organizational employment is a characteristic of the total labor force; even occupations that retain the image of individualism, such as the professions, have been considerably affected by this trend. Much of what is called private practice in the professions is carried out in organizations, such as law firms or medical clinics, which, as will be discussed later, are in many ways similar to other kinds of organizations.[5] This movement to organizations amplifies the effects of the separation of work from the rest of life, not only because occupations are physically located in organizations, but also because the organizational arrangements themselves produce requirements and social relationships that are not found when work is carried out by the solo worker or the worker in the small, usually family, grouping.

If these are the dominant characteristics of modern occupations and if they are rather recent in their evolution, then what were the earlier conditions of work?

The change that is most often noted is the shift from craft production to factory production. This shift involved a great deal more than just the change in technologies of work. As Anderson points out, "each craft had its place in the community and each worker had his place in some craft."[6] A man's craft thus directly tied him to the social structure, with the crafts having distinctive social rankings. The entire socialization process prepared one for taking his ascribed place in the community. Not only was a man's occupation set, but also, apparently, he had no aspiration for other types of work. This period was one of relative social stability, although the stability was clearly short-lived. The stereotyped image that we have of the craft era is one of happy workers dedicated to their work without thoughts of, or desires for, different occupations.

This stereotype is probably, like most others, inaccurate. We can deduce this from the rather simple fact that changes have occurred. Changes occur because of the infusion of different ideas into a social system, and these different ideas come about, at least partially, as a consequence of dissatisfaction with the existing system. Another inaccuracy of the stereotype is that during this

[4]See Theodore Caplow, *The Sociology of Work* (Minneapolis: University of Minnesota Press, 1954), pp. 20–21 and Robert Presthus, *The Organizational Society* (New York: Alfred A. Knopf, Inc., 1962), pp. 59–92.

[5]See Erwin O. Smigel, *The Wall Street Lawyer* (New York: The Free Press of Glencoe, Inc., 1964).

[6]*Dimensions of Work*, p. 5.

period crafts were not the dominant occupation. The society was predominantly agrarian.[7] While farming and the crafts share a number of characteristics, such as the total involvement of the individual in his work and the integration of work with the rest of life, the important fact remains that farming as an occupation involves a greater variety of skills and activities and less control of the work environment than do the crafts. But despite the danger of utilizing too simple a picture of the craft era, many of the changes in the occupational world can be analyzed using the crafts as a starting point. Some of the important changes have been examined by Reinhard Bendix, who states:

> In practice, the workers were managed by a reliance upon the traditions of craftmanship and of the master-servant relationship. However important these traditions were for industrialization, they were not always compatible with the requirements of industrial production. Traditionally, skilled work was performed at a leisurely pace or in spurts of great intensity, but always at the discretion of the individual worker. In modern industry work must be performed above all with regular intensity. Traditionally the skilled worker was trained to work accurately on individual designs; in modern industry he must adapt his sense of accuracy to the requirements of standardization. In handicraft production, each individual owned his own tools and was responsible for their care; by and large this is not true in modern industry, so that care of tools and machinery is divorced from the pride of ownership. Traditionally, skills were handed down from generation to generation and, consequently, were subject to individual variations. In industry the effort has been to standardize the steps of work performance as much as possible.[8]

Another view of this transition is offered by Thorstein Veblen, who notes that the initial shift took place in craft industries, such as brewing or tanning, that were rather easily transformed into group work and then into larger industrial complexes. As this occurred, the worker increasingly began to keep pace with the work process, rather than the reverse. Thus the industrial worker began to be tied inexorably to the machinery of the work process. The requirements for becoming a worker also changed. Veblen suggests that at this

[7]While the occupational distribution of this era cannot be analyzed through census data, it is obvious that agricultural occupations have been numerically dominant until only very recently.

[8]*Work and Authority in Industry* (New York: John Wiley & Sons, Inc., 1956), pp. 203–4.

point increased training on the part of prospective workers became essential, thus making the schooling demanded for general preparation "unremittingly more exacting."[9]

The paradox of the simpler work in the machine era requiring a greater amount of education than the more exacting craft work is more apparent than real. The worker in the craft era did not need formal education; he simply "grew up" in the craft, learning the skills and behaviors necessary for such a craftsman as part of the normal socialization process in the home. The industrial worker, on the other hand, did not have this type of learning environment. More importantly, he did not have the family based ties to the work process or to the authority system of the factory. School provided, as it does today, exposure to training in mental and mechanical skills *and* to the impersonal discipline inherent in the industrial-work setting.

The shift from craft work has been the change most widely noted in occupational literature, since it appears to symbolize other similar shifts. A change of perhaps equal importance, which developed at about the same time, was the movement of work into organizations. Organizations themselves were not, of course, a new phenomenon. Military, religious, and public bureaucracies existed in the majority of developed societies before these developments in Western Europe.[10] The important factor in the industrial revolution was therefore not the emergence of organizations but rather the relationship between the individual and the organization. Workers at all levels in the emerging industrial and later governmental organizations appear to have had a fundamentally different orientation to the employing organization than that which existed in the past.

A useful way of viewing this change is to apply, *ex post facto*, Amitai Etzioni's typology of organizations to the changes occurring during this era.[11] Etzioni suggests three major organizational types, each characterized by a distinct power structure and manner of involvement on the part of the lower participants. The first type is the *coercive* organization, which uses coercion as the major

[9]*The Instinct of Workmanship* (New York: The Macmillan Company, Publishers, 1914), p. 309.

[10]See Max Weber, *The Theory of Social-Economic Organization*, trans. A. M. Henderson and Talcott Parsons (New York: The Free Press of Glencoe, Inc., 1947), pp. 341–82, for an analysis of the forms and consequences of organizational arrangements in the pre-industrial period.

[11]*A Comparative Analysis of Complex Organizations* (New York: The Free Press of Glencoe, Inc., 1961), pp. 12–40.

means of control over lower participants, who, in turn, feel alienated from the organization. The second type is the *normative* organization, in which normative power (belief in the goals of the organization) serves as the major source of control over lower participants, who are characterized by high commitment to it. The conscription based military forces of the period and the religious organizations of the era are examples, respectively, of these two types of organizations.

The third type of organization, the *utilitarian*, uses remuneration as the basis for control, with the lower participants of the organization tied to the organization by a calculative orientation. This type of organization undoubtedly existed throughout history in such systems as the Chinese, Egyptian, or Roman public bureaucracies. What is significant is that it became the dominant organizational form during and after the industrial revolution. Workers and management alike came into the organizations because they perceived that they could get something (remuneration) out of it. While family loyalties and/or tradition played, and in some cases continue to play, a role in occupational selection in such a system, the emergent industrial organizations were rather clearly utilitarian.

Anderson provides a somewhat related approach to the same phenomena; he notes that the earlier era could be characterized by an *ascription orientation*, in which the worker and his occupation were closely associated.[12] Anderson suggests that in this type of system the person's occupation was often symbolized by his appearance, dress, or other appointments that he maintained off the job. A type of hat or cap, a particular kind of jacket, a particular kind of walk (bowlegs among cowboys) were signs of a person's occupation. Just as important, according to Anderson, was the fact that the occupation was passed on from father to son in the majority of the cases. The contrasting type of system, characterized by an *achievement orientation*, is based on accomplishment rather than inheritance and on separation of life from work. This system of course, is highly typical of modern occupations.

Before leaving this discussion of structural shifts, it should be noted that just as the occupational structure of the preindustrial era was not solely the craft system, the movement to the industrial-organizational era was not uniform, intra- or internationally. Agricultural and craft pursuits have remained and have been maintained

[12]*Dimensions of Work*, p. 3.

in some areas. Nevertheless, work as a separate activity and the movement to the organizational setting are the distinctive characteristics of modern work, as will be further demonstrated.

The most comprehensive overview of the meanings attached to work through different historical eras is provided by Adriano Tilgher.[13] In the Greek era work was viewed as a curse, at least insofar as it involved manual as opposed to intellectual labor. The source of this curse was the gods, who hated man. According to Tilgher, the Romans held a very similar view of work. He notes that Cicero believed that the only worthy occupations for a free man were agriculture and business, if the latter led to a situation of retirement and rural peace. The Hebrew view of work was essentially similar, but with the additional rationale that work was drudgery because it was the way in which man could atone for the original sin. At the same time, work received a slightly higher meaning in that it was a way by which spiritual dignity could be captured.

As might be expected, early Christianity differed little from its Hebrew antecedents. One additional meaning was attached to work in that the fruits of one's labor could legitimately be shared with the less fortunate. The doctrine that idleness was akin to sinfulness also appeared during this era. But, Tilgher points out, despite this new interpretation work as such had no intrinsic meaning; rather it was a means to other, loftier ends. This interpretation of work was apparently maintained through the Middle Ages, with the idea growing that work was appropriate for all people as a means of spiritual purification. The coming of the Reformation saw little change in this basic attitude, except for a small, but vital, reinterpretation. Luther saw work as a form of serving God. Whatever a person's occupation, if the work were performed to the best of one's ability, it had equal spiritual value with all other forms of work.

A more significant shift in the meaning of work occurred with the advent of Calvinism. Calvin built upon the older traditions of work as the will of God and the need for all men to work. To this he added the idea that the results of work, profits, had only one legitimate use, to finance new ventures for additional profit and thus

[13]*Work: What It Has Meant to Men Through the Ages*, trans. Dorothy C. Fisher (New York: Harcourt, Brace & World, Inc., 1930).

for additional investment. This concept, of course, is totally compatible with the rise of capitalism, as Weber so forcefully argued. An additional, important aspect of Calvinist doctrine was that man had an obligation to God to attempt to achieve the highest possible and most rewarding occupation. Thus striving for upward mobility is morally justified.

The development of socialism gave an additional interpretation to work. It was viewed, not as a form of expiation, but rather as something that man wants to do as the normal way of living. Each was to receive value equal to his work, and drudgery would be reduced by scientific advances, allowing more time for nonwork activities.

Tilgher notes that the "religion of work," so basic to capitalism, may be beginning to falter in the twentieth century as a new orientation toward recreation and leisure develops. Nevertheless, there is strong evidence that work still occupies a central place in the lives of at least most American workers. Nancy Morse and R. S. Weiss have shown, for example, that eighty per cent of the employees in the labor force would continue working even if they were given the opportunity to maintain their style of life without work.[14] This particular study also points out a major consideration in the discussion of the values and meanings of work, that work does not mean the same things to all people. Without going into great detail at this time about the substance of the Morse-Weiss study, it is evident that there are clear differences in the perceptions of the meaning of work that are related to the position of the worker in the status hierarchy—a point reinforced by the work of Joseph Kahl.[15] These findings suggest that Tilgher's work must be taken as a general description of the modal intellectual values attached to work, as expressed in the written evidence, and not as descriptive of the meanings attached to work by the entire population.

A thorough analysis of the contemporary meanings and values attached to occupations is directly related to the rewards men derive from their work and to the stresses and strains with which it confronts them. Therefore, further examination of these subjective reactions to the occupational situation will be postponed until the chapter that deals specifically with this topic. For the present, we may note that Tilgher's evidence, as well as the arguments developed by Weber in regard to the Protestant ethic, suggests that the

[14]"The Function and Meaning of Work and the Job," *American Sociological Review*, XX, 2 (April, 1955), 192.
[15]*The American Class Structure* (New York: Holt, Rinehart & Winston, Inc., 1957), pp. 184–219.

values surrounding work change over time; whether or not these value changes precede or follow from the changes in the occupational structure cannot be definitively answered at this time, and, indeed, may be little more than an interesting mental exercise. At least in the historical context, the best substantiated conclusion, which can be reached, is that the values have in fact changed.

the contemporary occupational context

The two major shifts in the occupational structure, which have been previously noted, the movement of occupations away from the home setting into organizations and the separation of work from the rest of life, occurred in the context of a significant shift of the basic economy of Western society from agricultural to industrial domination. As Table 2.1 indicates, the employment rates in farm as opposed to industrial work have reversed themselves. This reversal has occurred in the overall context of the industrialization and urbanization of Western society. Later it will be argued that a movement from the industrial era into a new era may be occurring. For the moment, however, an analysis of the meaning of the shifts indicated in Table 2.1 will provide some understanding of the contemporary context of the occupational structure.

As Phillip Hauser points out, "although the data have many limitations, it is clear that the predominant proportion of the work force in the United States, about 72 per cent, [was] farm workers in 1820. By 1900, the proportion of workers engaged in farm occupations had shrunk by almost 50 per cent and was at a level of approximately 37 per cent. By 1960 only 6.3 per cent of the labor force was in agriculture."[16]

This does not, of course, suggest that there has been less agricultural production but rather that the smaller proportion of workers has been able to produce more through technological and organizational innovations. If current projections are accurate, the decline in agricultural employment will continue until such time as agricultural production falls below the demand level, when an upturn in this type of employment could be anticipated. Whether or not such a period will be reached is at present in the realm of conjecture.

The shift away from agriculture work was initially accompa-

[16]"Labor Force," in *Handbook of Modern Sociology*, ed. Robert E. L. Faris (Chicago, Ill.: Rand McNally & Company, 1964), p. 182.

Table 2.1.   Major Occupation Group of Experienced Labor Force for the United States, 1900-1960 (Per Cent Distribution)

Major Occupation Group	Both Sexes							Males			Females		
	1900	1910	1920	1930	1940	1950	1960	1900	1950	1960	1900	1950	1960
Total	100.0	100.0	100.0	100.0	100.0	100.0	100.0	100.0	100.0	100.0	100.0	100.0	100.0
White Collar	17.6	21.4	25.0	29.4	31.1	36.6	42.2	17.6	30.5	35.4	17.8	52.5	56.3
Professional, technical, and kindred workers	4.3	4.7	5.4	6.8	7.5	8.6	11.4	3.4	7.2	10.4	8.2	12.2	13.3
Managers, officials, proprietors, except farm	5.9	6.6	6.6	7.4	7.3	8.7	8.5	6.8	10.5	10.8	1.4	4.3	3.8
Clerical and kindred workers	3.0	5.3	8.0	8.9	9.6	12.3	14.9	2.8	6.4	7.2	4.0	27.4	30.9
Sales workers	4.5	4.7	4.9	6.3	6.7	7.0	7.4	4.6	6.4	7.0	4.3	8.6	8.3
Service	9.1	9.6	7.9	9.8	11.7	10.5	11.8	3.1	6.2	6.5	35.5	21.5	22.8
Private household workers	5.4	5.0	3.3	4.1	4.7	2.6	2.8	0.2	0.2	0.2	28.7	8.9	8.4
Other service workers	3.6	4.6	4.5	5.7	7.1	7.9	8.9	2.9	6.0	6.3	6.8	12.6	14.4
Manual	35.8	38.2	40.2	39.6	39.8	41.1	39.7	37.6	48.4	49.7	27.8	22.4	19.1
Craftsmen, foremen, and kindred workers	10.6	11.6	13.0	12.8	12.0	14.2	14.3	12.6	19.0	20.6	1.4	1.5	1.3
Operatives and kindred workers	12.8	14.6	15.6	15.8	18.4	20.4	19.9	10.4	20.6	21.2	23.8	20.0	17.2
Laborers, except farm and mine	12.5	12.0	11.6	11.0	9.4	6.6	5.5	14.7	8.8	7.8	2.6	0.9	0.6
Farm	37.5	30.9	27.0	21.2	17.4	11.8	6.3	41.7	14.9	8.5	19.0	3.7	1.9
Farmers and farm managers	19.9	16.5	15.3	12.4	10.4	7.4	3.9	23.0	10.0	5.5	5.9	0.7	0.6
Farm laborers and foremen	17.7	14.4	11.7	8.8	7.0	4.4	2.4	18.7	4.9	3.0	13.1	2.9	1.3

SOURCE: Philip M. Hauser, "Labor Force," in Handbook of Modern Sociology, ed. Robert E. L. Faris (Chicago: Rand McNally & Company, 1964), p. 183. Derived from 1900-1950: U.S. Bureau of the Census, Historical Statistics of the United States, Colonial Times to 1957 (Washington, D.C.: Government Printing Office, 1960), Table D 72-122, p. 74. 1960: U.S. Bureau of the Census, U.S. Census of Population: 1960, General Social and Economic Characteristics, U.S. Summary (Washington, D.C.: Government Printing Office), Final Report PC (1)-1C.

nied by an increase in the proportion of the labor force engaged in industrial production, as the data on craftsmen, foremen, and kindred workers and operatives and kindred workers suggest. This increase was quite slight, however, and the stabilization or slight downturn in employment in these categories in recent decades indicates that the same factors of technological and organizational innovations evident in the agricultural system are operative. Thus, though the industrial era was entered, the effect on the labor force has been relatively slight in terms of the per cent of persons actually engaged in industrial production. As will be suggested below, the industrial era might well have been entered and then left in a relatively short period of time.

As is evident from the data contained in Table 2.1, the most significant increase in the labor force has occurred in the white-collar category. This has, of course, not simply been a transfer of people from agricultural employment to white-collar work. While there may have been some such movement in terms of the clerical or sales categories, the movement of people into the higher-level white-collar occupations has undoubtedly come from the contiguous categories of lower white-collar and upper blue-collar occupations. Despite the source of the growth, its occurrence suggests that three related phenomena have occurred. The first is the aforementioned movement to organizational work, with the greater need for managers and clerks. An interesting question here is whether the growth in managerial personnel has in fact been required or whether it has happened because of the perpetuation of the idea that a certain number of managers are needed for organizations of particular sizes. But this question is not central to the present analysis and will be dealt with at a later time. Meanwhile, we may note that while the category of managers, proprietors, and officials increased in the 1950–60 decade, the self-employed managers, proprietors, and officials declined from 4.3 to 2.9 per cent of the labor force; this suggests, of course, an even greater increase in the proportion of organizationally based officials.

The second trend of major importance is the growth in the proportion of the labor force in the professional, technical, and kindred workers category. This fact suggests that there has been a growing demand for such highly trained, specialized occupations within every segment of the society. The needs of advancing technology and the complexity of legal, social, educational, medical, and scientific developments apparently have created a situation wherein this occupational category is witnessing a truly phenomenal growth. Additionally, some of the occupations that are traditionally considered under the managers category in the census may themselves be attempting to professionalize, so that the category under discussion may in fact be experiencing a growth above that indicated in the census data.

The third important factor here is that the growth of professional workers, which is indicated by the census data, has occurred within the organizational world. The proportion of self-employed professional workers has actually declined, as this type of worker is being employed increasingly by organizations. In addition, many of the professionals who are traditionally thought of as being self-employed, such as physicians or lawyers, are increasingly being found in large medical clinics or law firms. While the arrangements are such that a semblance of self-employment remains, the fact is that these organizations are in many ways similar to other large scale bureaucracies.[17]

Two trends that are evident in the census data and indicative of an important shift in the occupational structure are the increase in the proportion of service workers and the decrease in the proportion of manual workers. Advances in production technology and the greater affluence of the majority of the population have apparently led to this development; due to automation and general technological advancement fewer man-hours are now needed to produce a given amount of goods. This is true across industrial subdivisions, with relatively few exceptions. The exceptions are chiefly in those industries that produce goods directly affected by changes in consumer demands and tastes. The following summary from a U.S. Department of Labor report on technological trends in American industries clearly suggests the direction of the impact of changing technologies:

Some Implications of Technological Change
Prospective technological developments suggest a number of implications for manpower trends and adjustments.

1. *All industries will be affected, to some degree, by prospective changes in equipment, methods of production, materials, and products.* Industries where extensive change will occur include steel, textiles, electric machinery, synthetic materials, aluminum, telephone, water transportation, air transport, electric power, insurance, and banking. Competition from other materials and from foreign producers, greater complexity in production and

[17]See Smigel, *The Wall Street Lawyer*, for a discussion of this tendency.

defense requirements, increasing volume of business, and technological breakthroughs from research and development are some factors that foster the introduction of new techniques in these industries.

In other industries, technological changes will continue to be limited. Among these are apparel, furniture, footwear, foundries, and dairy. Consumer taste, preference for frequent style changes, custom nature of the work, job lot production, and dominance of small firms with little capital tend to retard the rate of mechanization.

Technological changes take place within a complex network of interrelated industries. All industries are affected not only by changes from within but also by changes that occur among purchasers of their output and suppliers of materials for processing. The substantial curtailment of ingot casting implicit in the growth of continuous casting in the steel industry, for example, will curtail demand for ingot molds, one of the large tonnage products of the foundry industry.

2. *"Automation," as technically defined, will become increasingly important in many industries, but changes along past lines of technological development will remain highly significant.* Computers, automatic controls, and transfer machines are being introduced gradually in many industries. Their application, as in the case of other technological changes, depends on an assessment of costs relative to possible future returns. Economic feasibility remains the governing consideration.

Continuing improvements in existing processes or products in some cases limit the introduction of more radical technological changes. In electric power, for example, reduction in the cost of coal through improved transportation tends to delay the introduction of nuclear power generation. The appearance of manmade materials for making shoes is stimulating leather producers to improve their competitive position. Because of such competition, the timing of many changes is often difficult to predict, and changes in one field often have unforeseen and far-reaching effects in others.

3. *Employment prospects in the industries studied are generally favorable.* The table [Table 2.2] shows the changes expected by 1970. Of the 40 industries, employment is expected to rise in 17, with about 26 million workers or about 77 per cent of all employees in those industries covered by the study.

The prospects are less promising in 13 industries

Table 2.2. Employment in 1957 and 1964 and Prospects for 1970

Industry	Employment 1957 (Thousands)	1964 (Thousands)	Per Cent Change
Industries Where Employment by 1970 Will Probably Be Higher			
Air transportation	148.4	190.8	28.6
Apparel	1,210.1	1,302.0	7.6
Banking	602.9	764.4	26.8
Concrete, gypsum, and plaster products	[1]140.1	172.1	22.8
Contract construction	2,923.0	3,056.0	4.6
Electrical machinery, equipment, and supplies	1,343.8	1,548.4	15.2
Federal government	2,217.0	2,348.0	5.9
Foundries	306.5	286.3	−6.6
Furniture and fixtures	374.0	406.0	8.6
Glass containers	54.3	60.4	11.2
Instruments and related products	342.1	369.3	8.0
Insurance carriers	[1]813.6	895.2	10.0
Motor freight	804.2	919.8	14.4
Printing and publishing	870.0	950.5	9.3
Pulp, paper, and board	226.4	220.9	−2.4
Synthetic materials and plastics products	[1]244.2	354.0	45.0
Wholesale and retail trade	10,886.0	12,132.0	11.4
Industries Where Employment by 1970 Will Probably Be Lower			
Bakery products	302.5	289.9	−4.1
Bituminous coal	229.8	136.0	−40.8
Dairy products	[1]319.1	288.6	−9.6
Flour and other grain mill products	27.1	21.9	−19.2
Hydraulic cement	41.6	34.5	−17.1
Lumber and wood products	655.3	602.5	−8.1
Malt liquors	77.4	61.9	−20.0
Meat products	333.1	313.6	−5.8
Petroleum refining	153.9	113.9	−26.0
Railroads	985.0	665.0	−32.5
Textile mill products	981.1	891.1	−9.2
Tobacco products	71.5	62.9	−12.0
Water transportation	[2]231.7	222.3	−4.0

Table 2.2.   (continued)

Industry	Employment		
	1957 (Thousands)	1964 (Thousands)	Per Cent Change
Industries Where Employment by 1970 Will Probably Be Only Slightly Changed Or Is Uncertain			
Aircraft, missiles, and space vehicles	[1]848.0	790.6	−6.8
Aluminum	65.0	76.4	17.5
Copper ore mining	32.3	27.1	−16.1
Crude petroleum and natural gas	344.0	289.4	−15.9
Electric power and gas	581.8	575.9	−1.0
Footwear (except rubber)	235.0	213.3	−9.2
Iron and steel	719.9	629.4	−12.6
Motor vehicles and equipment	769.3	755.4	−1.8
Telephone communication	768.2	706.1	−8.1
Tires and inner tubes	96.9	85.8	−11.5

[1] 1958
[2] 1959

where employment by 1970 will probably be lower than in 1964. Increasing demand in these industries will not compensate for the reduction in unit-labor requirements, and even with higher output, employment may decline. This group of industries employs about 3.7 million.

Projections for a third group, with about 4.1 million employees or 12 per cent of the employment covered, show only a slight decline or a slight increase in employment by 1970, or the outlook is uncertain.

4. *Prospective technological changes will continue to reduce the proportion of jobs involving primarily physical and manual ability and to increase the need for jobs requiring ability to work with data and information.* No attempt was made to quantify these changes in this report, but several broad trends can be described.

The proportion of the labor force engaged in materials handling will continue to be reduced. A few operators of mechanized handling equipment or conveyors can often do the work done by a number of manual materials handlers.

Among operatives, faster and larger automatic machinery reduces the number employed per unit of output in jobs involving direct, step-by-step manual manipulation, loading and unloading, or tending of equipment. Increasingly, the function of the factory operative is to patrol a number of automatic machines and to be responsive to signals indicating breakdown.

In process industries, the typical operator will monitor a wide panel of control instruments and record information for interpretation. The control operator performs as a skilled watchman, with duties demanding patience, alertness to malfunctioning, and a sense of responsibility for costly equipment.

In many industries, maintenance and repair work is becoming increasingly important or is being changed as new types of equipment are introduced. Complex electronic equipment, such as numerical controls and computers, require specially trained electronic maintenance workers. On the other hand, routine maintenance on new equipment is often reduced by means of devices for automatic lubrication of machinery.

Technological advances may also result in new requirements for some skilled craftsmen. Instrumentation, for example, requires the flour miller to supplement his "rule of thumb" methods with a knowledge of more scientific procedures. New materials and processes require construction craftsmen, printers, and power-plant operators to learn new skills and update their knowledge.

Electronic data processing (EDP) will reduce the relative proportion of routine office jobs, especially in repetitive manual record-keeping work, but will require new and higher-grade jobs to plan, program, and operate such systems.

The narrowing of opportunities in low-skilled work and the trend toward greater knowledge requirements in many fields of work underscore the importance of broad education and training as preparation for work. With the prospect of marked changes in jobs over his working life, the American worker will have great need for adaptability and flexibility in the years ahead.

5. *This study indicates the inevitability and pervasiveness of technological change and underscores the importance of developing adequate plans to facilitate manpower adjustment.* Management and labor have adopted a great diversity of measures, ranging from on-the-job retraining to comprehensive programs for job security. The coverage and scope of these measures vary from industry to industry depending on economic and other conditions. The government's training, counseling, and

placement services, together with the Nation's educational system, remain the focus of efforts to prepare young persons who are entering the labor market and to assist unemployed adults to meet the requirements of advancing technology. Measures to maintain a high rate of employment remain the basic condition for the success of adjustment programs.[18]

The growth of service-based occupations can probably be largely attributed to the growing affluence of the society. More financial resources and time are available for recreational and travel activities and personal services. At the same time, more personnel are available due to the changed technology in the production processes. A significant aspect of the service organizations is that they are less likely to be affected by technological changes of the sort that is affecting the production process. Since much of the work in such organizations is concerned directly with dealing with people, it seems that the replacement of personnel by automated or computerized equipment would have only a minimal effect. Indicative of the growth of these service organizations is the increase in the numbers and proportion of the labor force employed by state and local governments. This has been the largest growth area of the labor force, as Table 2.3 indicates. While much of the data processing and general clerical work in such organizations has been and will be affected by changes in the technological base of work, the person-to-person relationships basic to the service function will remain.

An important issue in this shift toward service occupations is whether or not the growth in this area will in fact be sufficient to absorb those people who normally would enter or are already employed in production based occupations. Rather clearly, the skills involved are somewhat different. The data thus far available suggest that employment rates have not declined with advancing technology in the production process. While this issue will be discussed in detail in the chapter on technology, it would appear that the overall rate of unemployment will probably not increase, though specific types and clusters of workers may be adversely affected. The data thus far available do not suggest that the consequences of the changes discussed will be dire for the society as a whole.

Two additional trends, evident in the data, should be noted before the implications of the changing labor force composition are discussed. First is the evident decline of manual laborers, which has

[18]U.S. Department of Labor, Bureau of Labor Statistics, *Technological Trends in Major American Industries* (Washington, D.C.: Government Printing Office, 1966), pp. 7–9.

Table 2.3. Change in Civilian Employment,[1] by Major Industry Group, Selected Periods and Projected 1965-1970

Major Industry Group	Selected Periods 1957-1965	Selected Periods 1957-1963	Selected Periods 1963-1965	Projected 1965-1970 3 Per Cent Unemployment Basic Model	Projected 1965-1970 4 Per Cent Unemployment Basic Model	Projected 1965-1970 4 Per Cent Unemployment High Durables	Projected 1965-1970 4 Per Cent Unemployment High Services
			Aggregate Change				
Total	6,184	2,721	3,463	8,633	7,423	7,423	7,423
Agriculture	−1,637	−1,276	−361	−505	−505	−505	−505
Mining	−201	−192	−9	−38	−44	−40	−46
Construction	296	37	259	633	589	714	436
Manufacturing	797	−190	987	899	692	1,136	473
Durable	527	−243	770	508	396	826	194
Nondurable	270	53	217	391	296	310	279
Transportation	−167	−234	67	78	49	60	39
Communications and public utilities	−36	−104	68	4	−15	−41	−5
Trade	1,648	830	818	1,604	1,421	1,665	1,260
Finance, insurance, and real estate	568	398	170	525	467	294	475
Services and miscellaneous	2,325	1,630	695	2,400	2,207	1,604	2,585
Government	2,430	1,609	821	2,637	2,216	2,190	2,365
Federal	162	141	21	145	131	118	129
State and local	2,268	1,469	799	2,492	2,085	2,072	2,236
Private households	160	212	−52	396	346	346	346
Addendum							
Total	6,184	2,721	3,463	8,633	7,423	7,423	7,423
Government	2,430	1,609	821	2,637	2,216	2,190	2,365
Private	3,753	1,111	2,642	5,996	5,207	5,233	5,058
Goods producing industries	−745	−1,621	876	989	732	1,305	358
Goods related industries[2]	1,481	596	885	1,682	1,470	1,725	1,299
Service industries	3,017	2,136	881	3,325	3,005	2,203	3,401

[1] Covers wage and salary employees, self-employed, and unpaid family workers.
[2] Trade and transportation; part of the latter is for transportation of persons.

Table 2.3.   (continued)

Major Industry Group	Selected Periods			Projected 1965-1970			
				3 Per Cent Unemployment	4 Per Cent Unemployment		
	1957-1965	1957-1963	1963-1965	Basic Model	Basic Model	High Durables	High Services
	Average Annual Rate of Change[3]						
Total	1.1	0.7	2.4	2.2	1.9	1.9	1.9
Agriculture	−3.8	−3.8	−3.8	−2.3	−2.3	−2.3	−2.3
Mining	−3.3	−4.1	−0.6	−1.2	−1.4	−1.2	−1.4
Construction	1.0	0.2	3.4	3.0	2.8	3.3	2.1
Manufacturing	0.6	−0.2	2.8	1.0	0.7	1.2	0.5
Durable	0.6	−0.4	3.9	0.9	0.7	1.5	0.4
Nondurable	0.4	0.1	1.4	1.0	0.7	0.8	0.7
Transportation	−0.8	−1.4	1.2	0.6	0.4	0.4	0.3
Communications and public utilities	−0.3	−1.2	2.3	0.1	−0.2	−0.6	−0.1
Trade	1.5	1.0	2.8	2.0	1.8	2.1	1.6
Finance, insurance, and real estate	2.3	2.2	2.6	2.9	2.6	1.7	2.7
Services and miscellaneous	3.0	2.9	3.3	4.0	3.7	2.7	4.2
Government	3.5	3.2	4.4	4.8	4.1	4.0	4.3
Federal	0.9	1.0	0.5	1.2	1.1	1.0	1.1
State and local	4.5	4.1	5.6	5.8	4.9	4.9	5.3
Private households	0.8	1.4	−1.0	2.9	2.5	2.5	2.5
Addendum							
Total	1.1	0.7	2.4	2.2	1.9	1.9	1.9
Government	3.5	3.2	4.4	4.8	4.1	4.0	4.3
Private	0.8	0.3	2.1	1.8	1.6	1.6	1.5
Goods producing industries	−0.3	−1.0	1.6	0.7	0.5	0.9	0.3
Goods related industries[2]	1.1	0.6	2.6	1.8	1.6	1.9	1.4
Service industries	2.2	2.1	2.4	3.3	3.0	2.3	3.4

[1] Covers wage and salary employees, self-employed, and unpaid family workers.

[2] Trade and transportation; part of the latter is for transportation of persons.

[3] Compound interest rates based on terminal years.

NOTE: Because of rounding, sums of individual items may not equal totals.

SOURCE: U.S. Department of Labor, *Projections 1970* (Washington, D.C.: Government Printing Office, 1966), p. 121, Table VI-2.

been taking place since 1910. This is, of course, a consequence of changing technology and is related to the growth of the more mental types of employment previously discussed. The second trend is the decline in the labor force engaged in farming activities. As agriculture moves toward even more mechanized, scientifically based operations, the productivity per man engaged in this kind of work will probably continue to increase, although not at a precipitous rate. In many ways, agriculture will probably increasingly resemble industrial-production operation in terms of size and the organizational structures involved, as smaller farms become less profitable and farming operations take place on a larger scale. Many of the comments which will follow in regard to the organizational environment of work will probably be applicable to agriculture.

the changing organizational environment

Two overriding themes in the changing occupational structure are the growing importance of the manipulation of ideas, as evidenced by the increases in professional and managerial employment, and the fact that work is increasingly "people oriented." That is, much of work is concerned with face-to-face interactions with customers, clients, and organizational members, as seen in the growth of sales and service personnel, and also of those managerial and professional personnel whose activities include dealing with people.

Evidence from organizational research strongly suggests that both of these trends will result in "de-bureaucratization" of organizational structures. One type of evidence is based on the fact that organizations totally or partially composed of personnel engaged in working with ideas or people are in fact less bureaucratic than their more product-oriented counterparts.[19] In organizations which deal in activities oriented toward products, ideas, and people, the latter two are found in departments or segments that are less bureaucratized than the more product-oriented balance of the organization.[20]

A second type of evidence derives from analyses of manage-

[19]For a discussion of the factors involved in this structural differentiation see Talcott Parsons, *Structure Process in Modern Society* (New York: The Free Press of Glencoe, Inc., 1960), p. 70 and Eugene Litwak, "Models of Organization Which Permit Conflict," *American Journal of Sociology*, LXVII (September, 1961), 177–84.

[20]Richard H. Hall, "Intra-Organizational Structure Variation: Application of the Basic Model," *Administrative Science Quarterly*, VII (December, 1962), 295–308.

ment techniques which repeatedly suggest that less formalized and routinized supervisory principles are required in the idea and people sectors of the organization.[21] While both sets of evidence are persuasive, it is not clear whether or not the less bureaucratized form of organization is either applicable or desirable for the segments of organizations involved in more traditional activities. Nevertheless, organizations of the present and of the future are apt to present different working environments from their counterparts of the recent past.

the changing social environment

Less easily documented is a major shift in the society from what has been called the industrial era into what might be called the services-human resources era. The statistical trends within the labor force already discussed will serve as the basis for the discussion that follows.[22]

It is quite clear that preceding and during the beginning of the twentieth century, the United States moved from an agriculturally based to an industrially based society. This movement was more than a simple reorientation of the economic structure. It also involved a major redistribution of the population from towns into urban areas, alterations of the family structure from the extended to the nuclear pattern, the development of secular rather than sacred orientations toward the world, and all the other aspects of the industrialization and urbanization movement. At the same time, the nature of the agricultural enterprise itself had begun changing. Farming began to mature into a production, rather than a subsistence activity, and farmers began to produce more than they could consume, thus allowing the phenomenal growth of the city. In this sense, the problems of agricultural production as a major societal concern were conquered.

As industry developed, a phenomenon similar to that occurring in agriculture took place; organizational and technological developments began to allow industry to produce sufficient goods for the bulk of the domestic and part of the foreign population. Thus industry essentially began to achieve the same position which the agricultural system had attained somewhat earlier. As the data have suggested, less and less of the labor force is directly engaged in the

[21]For example, see Rensis Likert, *New Patterns of Management* (New York: McGraw-Hill Book Company, 1961).
[22]See particularly Table 2.2.

production process. And while the industrial system has been developing, the agricultural system has reorganized yet further, utilizing the organizational and technological developments of industry, which has thus had a reflexive effect on the system whose development preceded its own.

If, as seems very likely, these trends continue, an era, which has been labelled the services-human resources period, is now emergent. This implies that these activities are beginning to dominate the occupational structure and, as noted before, problems of both agricultural and industrial productivity have been largely overcome. This concept is, of course, very similar to A. H. Maslow's higher level of needs concept applied to the societal level.[23] This approach also ignores the evident fact that neither sustinence (agricultural) nor comfort (industrial) needs have been satisfied for all members of the society. Nevertheless, the evidence suggests that the United States and much of Western society are moving or have moved into a situation which is based more on the services-human resources orientation than on either agricultural or industrial production.

Just as industrial growth was built upon and then contributed to the continued development of agriculture, the new configuration very evidently is contributing to the agricultural and industrial periods. Research and development (human resources) are playing an increasingly important role in both agricultural and production organizations, and concern with human relations has been well documented in at least the industrial world.

This three-era formulation is undoubtedly an oversimplification of many significant changes which have occurred in the occupational and the larger social structure. But there is strong evidence, at least in terms of the changing distribution within the labor force, that agricultural work and physical production work are declining in proportional representation as occupations increasingly become oriented toward people and ideas. If this trend continues, as it appears that it will, the interpretation presented may well be essentially correct.

a note on unemployment

The movement into the industrial era from agrarian-craft era had an impact above and beyond the changing occupational patterns, which have been discussed. The concept of unemployment did

[23]"A Theory of Human Motivations," *Psychological Review*, L, 4 (1943), 370–96.

not exist until the industrial era, since relatively few workers were employed. That is, the ascription based work of the earlier era precluded layoffs or depressions as they are known today. While periods of severe economic and social hardship undoubtedly existed, the person still had a job in the sense that his craft or agricultural work could still be performed. The movement into the organizational-industrial situation established a new relationship that allowed a person to be separated from his job or not to be hired or not to be able to find work in the first place.

Unemployment has both personal and social consequences; as Hauser suggests, "unemployment is probably among the more catastrophic and critical experiences both of the person and family."[24] At the societal level the fact that unemployment is most likely to be severe among the young, the aged, women, minority groups, and those persons who have been laid off because of technological change is indicative of their lack of integration into the occupational structure and, if the thesis of this volume is correct, into the total social structure. While the severe consequences of unemployment indicate that the system, which has been described, is not "perfect," in the sense that both personal and social needs are not optimally met, the impact of unemployment is not the major concern of this analysis. Rather, it will be used to provide further support for the analysis of social/occupational change.

summary and conclusions

The changes in the occupational system and attitudes toward work, which have been traced in this chapter, are an example of the importance and limitations inherent in a strictly historical analysis. On the positive side knowledge of the characteristics of the agrarian and industrial eras provides insights into the contemporary occupational structure. Behavior and values are carried over from the past into the present. At the same time the contemporary occupational system differs from those of the past. Reliance upon old understandings inhibits a full understanding of the present.

The dominant theme in this chapter has been social change as it affects the occupational structure and the distribution of people therein. The current situation of work as a separate, organizationally based activity emerged from the agrarian and craft era. Within the contemporary framework a change from the industrially based

[24]"Labor Force," p. 185.

system to one that has been labelled the services and human resources system appears to be taking place. If this analysis is correct,
contemporary occupations will increasingly be concerned with ideas
as opposed to objects. Direct interactions with people may become
proportionally more important, both in the provision of services
and, within the occupational system itself, in an ever wider array of
jobs. Despite this movement, the production of agricultural and
industrial goods will not diminish in importance but will probably
involve less of the occupational structure. The changes, which have
been discussed, will probably not be as revolutionary as those that
transpired during the industrialization process, when work emerged
as a separate activity and when the organizational bases of contemporary occupations were laid. With these changes, however, different work motivations, rewards, and stresses will probably evolve, as
the next chapter will indicate.

chapter 3

occupations
and the
individual

In this section three related issues will be discussed. First is the general area of motivations or incentives to work. The major concern is with questions such as why people work in the first place; what keeps people engaged in occupations; and the differences in motivation, if any, for people at different levels of the occupational hierarchy or for people from different social origins. The second issue to be discussed is the nature of the rewards that a person gains as a result of his occupation. The emphasis here is on the positive "feedback" from his job that the individual receives. As will be noted, these rewards are related to, but not necessarily the same as, his original motivations to work. The final area to be discussed is the negative aspect of occupations—those stresses and conflicts that are occupationally based. The purpose of this analysis is to provide a survey of the reactions of the individual to his occupation.

work motivation

The simplest answer to the question of why people work is that they generally both have to and want to work. While this is a simple answer, it is also rather correct, even though not specific enough for utilization in any careful analysis. It is clear that, for the overwhelming majority of the population, work is necessary for subsistence. At the same time, this overwhelming majority also believes in work for its own sake, at least in some way. Occupations thus serve two kinds of needs for the individual. But the "subsistence need" has evolved from the necessity of some kind of work for mere survival to a state wherein the definition of subsistence is highly relative. The line between basic maintenance of life and the pursuit of greater comforts and luxuries in the "subsistence area" (food and shelter) has been crossed for the majority of occupations. But even if the subsistence need at this level of greater affluence is no longer related to survival, the motivation to work and the subsequent kinds of activities are designed to assure the individual the level of comfort he has learned to expect in the subsistence area. A person thus has to work in order to maintain what he considers to be his level of subsistence. This does not imply, of course, that everyone who is employed earns enough to live at this higher level.

There is strong evidence to suggest that among those who are unemployed, for whatever reasons, the desire to work is present. Among those regularly employed, the belief in the desirability of working persists to a high degree. This desirability is above and beyond concern with subsistence. Morse and Weiss, for example, found that some 80 per cent of a national sample of employed men would continue to work even if confronted with the hypothetical situation of having inherited enough money to live comfortably without working.[1] Even more interesting in this particular study was the fact that this attitude was strongest among the younger respondents. This suggests that the feeling that work is important for its own sake is part of the socialization process and is systematically inculcated in the young as they are formally and informally socialized.

Data from the Morse and Weiss study also provide some indications of the various motivations for and meanings of work for the individual. As Table 3.1 suggests, more positive than negative reasons for continuing work were cited. These data also suggest the importance of social, as opposed to economic, motivations for work. The importance of the occupation for maintaining personal identity, some pattern to life, and ties to the wider social structure through interpersonal ties are demonstrated in these findings. These can be viewed as learned expectations about life in general and about the place of an occupation in a person's life in particular.

[1]"The Function and Meaning of Work and the Job," p. 192.

Table 3.1.   Reasons for Continuing Work

Question: "Why Do You Feel That You Would Work?"

	Number	Per Cent
Positive Reasons		
Enjoy the kind of work	27	9
To be associated with people	4	1
To keep occupied (interested)	93	32
Justifies my existence	14	5
Gives feeling of self-respect	13	5
Keeps individual healthy,		
good for person	30	10
Other	4	1
Total Positive Reasons	185	63
Negative Reasons; Without Work, Would		
Feel lost, go crazy	42	14
Feel useless	5	2
Feel bored	11	4
Not know what to do with my time,		
can't be idle	29	10
Habit, inertia	17	6
To keep out of trouble	3	1
Other	2	0
Total Negative Reasons	109	37
Total responding	294	100
Not ascertained	20	
Total would work	314	
Total would not work	79	
Not ascertained	8	
Total Sample	401	

SOURCE: Nancy C. Morse and R.S. Weiss, "The Function and Meaning of Work and the Job," *American Sociological Review*, XX, 2 (April, 1955), Table 2, 192.

Before proceeding to a more systematic analysis of the reasons why people work, an observation regarding the relative importance of economic as opposed to noneconomic or social factors is appropriate. Studies, such as the Morse and Weiss research and much of the literature on business and organizational administration, indicate the importance of noneconomic motivations in the occupational setting which might suggest that sheerly economic motivations are in reality less important than social motivations. But the research that leads to this conclusion, though generally sound, tends to ignore a vital aspect of the economic-reward structure. Economic motivations and rewards are themselves the socially approved motivational and reward system. Economic rewards are sought for the same reasons as social rewards, at least above the subsistence level. People are socialized into the belief that economic rewards are not only desirable but are also within the general framework of moral and social values. In this sense, then, the kinds of social motivations for working that have been discussed, are supplemental to economic motivations. The relative position of economic versus social motivations for particular occupations is a research question that has not been systematically investigated.[2]

An additional consideration in this discussion is the fact that financial rewards also have important social connotations, such as the person's relative worth in relation to others in his reference group, his family's welfare, and his position within the social-stratification system.[3] The point here is not that financial rewards are necessarily more important than social, but that economic motivations and rewards should not be underemphasized. In reality, economic and social motivations are probably so intertwined that they cannot be definitively separated. Ideally, it would be useful to be able to determine the extent to which each type of motivation is operative for a particular occupation, but since such information is not available at present, the mixture of these factors must be assumed.

Victor Vroom provides a useful overview of the various factors which are important as work motivations. He notes, first of all, that wages, including all of the various sorts of financial remunerations associated with the term fringe benefits, are an "indisputable source of the desire of people to work."[4] Fringe benefits include retirement and insurance programs, as well as miscellaneous inducements such as meals, educational programs, and recreational opportunities. One small college, for example, offers a free membership in the local country club as a faculty recruitment device. As discussed

[2]For a general discussion of the relationships between the approaches utilized by economists and sociologists in regard to this issue, see Neil J. Smelser, *The Sociology of Economic Life* (Englewood Cliffs, N.J.: Prentice-Hall, Inc., 1965), especially pp. 22–35. Smelser does not resolve the issue of the relative importance of economic versus more social factors but correctly implies that this is a question that must be dealt with through further research.

[3]Miller and Form, *Industrial Sociology*, pp. 433–35.

[4]*Work and Motivation* (New York: John Wiley & Sons, Inc., 1964), p. 30.

previously, these financial rewards contain connotations for one's social status and general style of life and are more than simple subsistence. Vroom notes that while the salary provided by an occupation is important, it is certainly not the sole source of motivation.

A second motivational basis for work is the expenditure of physical and/or mental energy.[5] Vroom notes that while most theories of behavior are based on the assumption that a person will try to avoid the expenditure of energy, or at least select behavior patterns involving a minimum of such expenditure, good evidence suggests that some energy expenditure is satisfying rather than dissatisfying. Obvious examples of this phenomenon are the recreational patterns of people who are desk-bound while on the job. Golf courses and tennis courts are generally filled by people who feel the need for exercise after a work week of physical inactivity. Alfred C. Clarke's analysis of the leisure patterns within the various social classes is instructive in this regard.[6] As Table 3.2 indicates, there are distinct differences between classes, as determined by occupational prestige ratings in this case, in terms of the type of leisure activity. For our purposes, the important point here is that for all the prestige levels, the leisure activities involve energy expenditure.

While one might argue that television watching and spending time in taverns is at best a passive activity, except for some slight arm movement, in general these activities involve the use of mental energy. The other forms of leisure rather clearly require both mental and physical energy expenditure. A legitimate question in the area of leisure patterns is the extent to which the person engages in the various activities because he wants to or because he feels that he is expected to do so. Regardless of the reasons, nonwork or leisure time does take the form of energy usage. Human beings thus do not remain inert when not confronted with occupational role requirements. If this form of activity is rewarding to the individual, then it can at least be inferred that energy expenditure on the job also serves as part of the complex of motivations.

Vroom also notes that some recent research has suggested that animals will engage in activity as a consequence of activity deprivation. He proposes that energy expenditure up to some point has positive consequences, but beyond that point such expenditure becomes a negative factor. The analysis of animals focused on physiological needs for activity; when one adds to this the importance of

---

[5] *Work and Motivation*, p. 32.
[6] Alfred C. Clarke, "Leisure and Occupational Prestige," *American Sociological Review*, XXI, 3 (June, 1956), 301–7.

Table 3.2. Leisure Activities by Prestige Level Participating Most Frequently

Activity	Prestige Level Participating Most Frequently I	II	III	IV	V	Level of Significance
Attending theatrical plays	X					.001
Attending concerts	X					.001
Attending special lectures	X					.001
Visiting a museum or art gallery	X					.001
Attending fraternal organizations	X					.001
Playing bridge	X					.001
Attending conventions	X					.001
Community service work	X					.001
Reading for pleasure	X					.001
Studying	X					.001
Entertaining at home	X					.01
Attending motion pictures	X					.05
Out-of-town weekend visiting (overnight)		X				.001
Attending football games		X				.001
Attending parties		X				.001
Playing golf			X			.001
Working on automobile				X		.01
Watching television					X	.001
Playing with children					X	.001
Fishing					X	.001
Playing card games other than bridge and poker					X	.001
Playing poker					X	.01
Driving or riding in car for pleasure					X	.01
Attending auto theater					X	.01
Spending time in tavern					X	.01
Spending time at zoo					X	.05
Attending baseball games					X	.05

SOURCE: Alfred C. Clarke, "The Use of Leisure and Its Relation to Levels of Occupational Prestige," *American Sociological Review*, XXI, 3 (June, 1956), Table 2, 304.

the learned need to work and to be active, the case is further strengthened. Vroom cites Weber's analysis that the Protestant ethic contributed to the kinds of activity which allowed capitalism to develop, since the proposition that it is moral to be active can serve as a powerful work motivation.[7] Gerhard Lenski's recent work also generally affirms the Weberian analysis, in that it shows that those persons who believe in the Protestant ethic (Protestants or not) tend to have stronger advancement aspirations.[8] Thus the need for activity probably has both a physiological and a learned basis, though the interplay between these two factors has not yet been examined systematically. For our purposes such an examination would be desirable but is not necessary, since the need for activity serves as at least a partial source of work motivations. As will be suggested below, the importance of energy expenditure itself varies in relationship to the other sources of motivation.

The third motivational basis for work, according to Vroom, is the production of goods and services and involves the intrinsic satisfaction a person derives from successfully manipulating some part of his environment.[9] Vroom cites evidence from experimental and general psychology to demonstrate that tasks are carried on without external rewards, for their own sake. Rather obviously, some occupations allow more satisfactions of this sort than others. An additional aspect of this motivational base is the fact that the performance of the work role can produce a moral satisfaction for the individual. Saving souls, defending the accused, advancing the frontiers of knowledge, and broadening students' intellectual horizons serve the moral commitments of many clergymen, attorneys, scientists and teachers. Here, again, the importance of this motivational basis varies from occupation to occupation.

A fourth motivational basis is social interaction.[10] Most work roles involve interactions, whether with customers, clients, or members of an identifiable work group as part of the expected behavior. Components of this motivational base include having influence over others, being liked by others, and being controlled by others. These components, which vary among themselves in terms of their importance in particular occupations, function as inducements to engage in work. A person can derive his most gratifying social interactions on the job, whatever his basis of gratification might be.

[7] Work and Motivation, pp. 36–37.
[8] The Religious Factor (New York: Doubleday & Company, Inc., 1963), pp. 89–92.
[9] Work and Motivation, p. 37.
[10] Vroom, Work and Motivation, p. 39.

The final basis for work motivations, according to Vroom, is social status.[11] As will be discussed later in some detail, occupations are perhaps the single best determinant of social status. They function at both the popular and scientific level. Thus one is often asked his occupation on meeting another person for the first time, in order to provide the other with a labelled category in which to place him. Scientifically, the relationship between occupational status and social status has been well documented. As a motivational force, for most segments of the social structure, social status is gained simply by working. If social status is important to the individual, in the sense that he wishes to hold his own in the system or improve his position, then it will be an important component of his motivational system; and if social status is important to a large segment of society, then it will be important throughout the system.

These various bases of motivations to work undoubtedly assume different configurations for different people and occupations. Social interaction may loom large for some people, with status considerations playing a lesser role. For others, financial motivations may be dominant. At the same time, the over-all amount of motivation to work would also appear to be subject to variation. For example, the man who works a 60-hour week voluntarily, or because he feels that there is a tremendous amount of work to be accomplished, would have more motivation to work than the man who is trying to work less than the traditional 40-hour week.

At the risk of oversimplifying, this point can be illustrated by using hypothetical people in real occupations, as in Fig. 3.1.

If this interpretation is correct, in terms of both the over-all amount of motivation and the internal variations among the motivational bases, then the incentives offered to various occupations in the wide variety of settings must also vary to coincide with the motivations. By the same token, job satisfaction and occupational stress will also be directly related to the original motivations to work. This approach to work motivations stresses the fact that motivations vary, both in amount and type. Just as it is naive to believe that all people want to advance as rapidly as possible and earn as much money as they can, it is equally naive to assume that particular classes of people have no motivation to work. At the same time, the internal variations within the over-all motivations suggest that a view of man based solely on the assumption that he is an "economic animal" is as absurd as one which sees him as seeking only social interaction on the job. The mixture of these various types of

[11]*Work and Motivation*, p. 41.

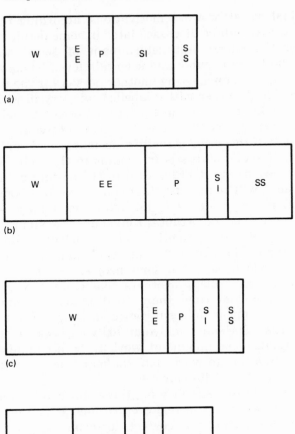

Fig. 3.1. (a) Secretary, 22, Pretty. (b) Lawyer, Married, 45, Ambitious. (c) Auto Worker, Married, 25, Four Children. (d) Professional Football Player, Single, 23, Quarterback. W = Wages, EE = Energy Expenditures, P = Production of Goods or Services, SI = Social Interaction, SS = Social Status.

motivations varies with the occupation and the individual. Through research, central tendencies in particular occupations with particular sets of workers can undoubtedly be identified.

Another approach to motivations to work is taken by Dubin.[12]

[12]*The World of Work,* pp. 226–28.

He notes that there are various forms of incentives to induce workers to maintain their participation in the system. The forms are essentially similar to those discussed above, with Dubin's distinction essentially being between economic and noneconomic rewards. In addition to the specific incentive that is designed to coincide with the original motivation for the individual, Dubin notes that a person responds subjectively to any existing incentive system, thus providing additional motivations in a number of directions. For example, a person can respond positively to the present system and attempt to assure the continuance of its pleasures. The person who feels that he has found a real social niche for himself will probably be motivated to try to continue the existing relationships with the individuals presently involved. His subjective response to this particular motivational base, if it is important to him, will be to try to maintain it, thus providing further motivational bases for work.[13]

A second type of subjective response is based upon felt dissatisfactions with the existing situation, wherein a person wants more of one of the various motivational bases as translated into incentives. For example, if a person is dissatisfied with the amount of income he is receiving, this may be translated into working harder, changing jobs, or assuming an additional job (moonlighting) ; if he feels his creativity (mental-energy expenditure) is being stifled in a particular position, he may either try to change his position or to alter the conditions surrounding the present one. Whichever path is followed, motivations to work are enhanced or at least maintained.[14]

The third type of subjective response, according to Dubin, is a feeling that the "work organization . . . provides its members with functional equivalents of services or rewards that can also be secured on a private basis."[15] By this, Dubin means that the individual feels that the employing organization has taken over his responsibilities for security in the form of pension plans, insurance packages, and job tenure, and also at times provides recreational or cultural facilities that would otherwise have to be purchased privately. If these are meaningful to the individual, he will continue to be motivated to participate in the organization.

A person is thus motivated to work by his subjective reactions to such objective bases as wages or social interaction. For example, a person earning five, ten, twenty, or fifty thousand dollars a year may feel that he is worth more and react by being motivated to seek employment elsewhere or to engage in individual or collective efforts

[13]Dubin, *The World of Work*, p. 227.
[14]Dubin, *The World of Work*, p. 227.
[15]*The World of Work*, p. 227.

at improvement of his position in the existing context. The same would be true for the other motivational bases discussed.

When the question of why people work is viewed from a more general perspective, a number of conclusions can be drawn. First, the individual brings with him a set of expectations regarding what he should get out of his work. These expectations are a result of his previous socialization, which has also developed within him motivations to work, and both motivations and expectations can vary widely. The variations in the over-all amount of motivation and in the kinds of motivations and expectations, which a person has, are present when the person enters an occupation. The experiences in the occupation can strengthen, modify, completely change, or essentially have no impact on them; or the interaction of the original motivations and the occupation itself may produce a new set of expectations and motivations, which the person carries forward with him on the job. If his expectations are insufficiently met and he has the opportunity to do so, he will change jobs in an attempt to satisfy these expectations more completely. In many cases, of course, he may be unable to make a change and may work in a state of prolonged dissatisfaction. On the positive side, the occupation and his motivations and expectations may coincide well, leading to a continued state of satisfaction. In any event, the meaning of work to an individual at any point in time is a cumulative result of his previous socialization, before beginning the occupation, and the on-going socialization that occurs on the job. Motivations to work and the meanings derived from work are thus part of a dynamic process.

In order to illustrate this point, two studies will be examined briefly. The first is an analysis of differing educational-aspiration levels among a sample of working-class high-school students. Educational aspirations are related to work motivations in two ways. In a general sense, educational aspirations, like work motivations, are expectations about a significant phase of life. More specifically, educational aspirations contribute to work motivations in that the level of education desired and achieved is a component of the over-all socialization process, which itself leads to particular motivational types and levels. In this particular study, by Irving Krauss, the well-known relationship between social-class position and plans for attending college was again documented.[16] Of the middle-class youths in the sample, 64 per cent planned to attend college, whereas only 41 per cent of the working-class youths had such aspirations. An intensive examination of the working-class youths revealed

[16]"Sources of Educational Aspirations Among Working Class Youth," *American Sociological Review*, XXIX (December, 1964), 867–79.

systematic reasons for the differing aspiration levels. First was the existence of a status discrepancy between the parents of those having higher (college-attendance plans) aspirations. The important status discrepancy was in the direction of the mother having higher status than the father in terms of her job and/or her education. Mothers in this position apparently push their children toward higher aspirations. While the exact dynamics of this situation are not examined because data are unavailable from this study, Krauss suggests that the mothers may be aware of, and instill in their children, the idea that there are horizons beyond a working-class life. In some cases, of course, a "don't be like your father" syndrome might operate.

Other factors that contribute to differences among aspiration levels are the presence of other family members and friends who have college experience, participation in extracurricular activities in high school with peers who plan to attend college, and fathers who hold positions in the higher levels of the working class, such as foremen or skilled craftsmen. But for our purposes, the specific nature of the sources of differing aspirational levels is not the central issue; what is important is the fact that the home and school environment, together with later experiences, contribute to distinctly different aspirational (motivational) levels within the same class and between classes. Aspirational levels are, of course, only a part of the over-all set of motivations to work, but the process whereby differing background experiences contribute to work motivations is probably similar in all aspects of the work motivations discussed.

When the focus is changed to an examination of the reactions of individuals to their occupational environment, the work of Robert Presthus is instructive.[17] Presthus examined the manner in which employees react to their life in large organizations and identified three major types of adaptation. The first type is the "upwardly-mobile."[18] A person who adapts in this way, typically an executive, is characterized by high morale, strong identification with the organization, and acceptance of the legitimacy of the organizational demands on the individual. The upwardly mobile individuals internalize the organization's values, stress good interpersonal relations, dislike controversy and those who dissent from the general organizational direction, and are strongly oriented toward action. A major motivating force for a person of this type is the improvement of his status. He will probably become a joiner of organiza-

[17]*The Organizational Society* (New York: Alfred A. Knopf, Inc., 1962).
[18]Presthus, *The Organizational Society*, pp. 164–204.

tions that will enhance his opportunities for advancement in stressing the acceptance of the organization as the legitimate source of power and morality. The person who adapts in this way is in some senses a captive of the organization, but the question of individual autonomy notwithstanding, the adaptation is, of course, useful for the organization and for the individual. In the terms that we have been using, an adaptation of this sort coincides with the expectations and motivations that the person has brought with him to the job and serves to reinforce them. Since the opportunities for advancement in status are limited, real stress may occur for this type of individual if his advancement is temporarily or permanently blocked.[19]

The second type of adaptation to the organization is what Presthus characterizes as the indifferent response.[20] The indifferent worker withdraws from competition for the rewards the organization has to offer. Presthus believes that this response characterizes the majority of the wage and salary earners in large organizations. Their interests are directed toward off-the-job pursuits, with only lip service paid to the goals of the organization. Presthus believes that this response is encouraged by the bureaucratic conditions in large organizations, and, although most characteristic of the blue-collar and lower white-collar workers, can be found among those professionals and executives who become disenchanted with organizational life.

The final adaptive mode, according to Presthus, is the ambivalent.[21] He notes:

> In both personal and organizational terms, the ambivalent's self-system is generally dysfunctional. Creative and anxious, his values conflict with bureaucratic claims for loyalty and adaptability. While the upward mobile finds the organization congenial, and the indifferent refuses to become engaged, the ambivalent can neither reject its promise of success and power, nor can he play the roles required to compete for them.[22]

The ambivalent is likely to be introverted, with limited interpersonal abilities. He is likely to be a specialist with ties to his specialist (professional) colleagues as a reference group. Bureau-

[19]See Dero A. Saunders, "Executive Discontent," *Fortune*, LIV, 4 (October, 1956), 154–56, 244, 245, 250–51 for an analysis of the stress induced when upward mobility is perceived to be blocked.
[20]*The Organizational Society*, pp. 205–56.
[21]*The Organizational Society*, pp. 257–86.
[22]*The Organizational Society*, p. 257.

cratic hierarchical standards, as such, are likely to be an anathema to him, even when they are legitimate. He tends to view the world through glasses ground to his own individualized prescription, and thus cannot accept the standards of success with which the organization confronts him; at the same time, he wants success as he himself has defined it. This type of orientation tends to lead to a worsening of interpersonal relations for the ambivalent, since others do not conform to his individual standards. Presthus suggests that this type of response creates a dysfunctional form of anxiety for both the individual and the organization. He does not suggest that this is the modal pattern among specialists or scientists within large organizations, but he does seem to imply that it is likely to occur in this employee group. Though it will be suggested that large, bureaucratic organizations need not confront the professional person with a working environment that is different from that which he finds in the normal professional environment, the antiorganizational response that Presthus describes is undoubtedly common. If the trend toward greater specialization and the increasing emphasis on advanced scientific and technological training within the labor force in general continues, then this response might become still more prevalent, as more of these highly trained types are found in various organizations. On the other hand, the extremely individualized and antiorganizational response may become less prevalent as the socialization of scientists and specialists begins to include formal and informal introductions to the facts of organizational life, with the result that the individual may be better able to balance his personal and organizational demands. Unfortunately data are not available to determine if this antiorganizational response is increasing or decreasing.

This analysis of Presthus' work has been designed to demonstrate that the motivations that a person brings to his occupation interact with the conditions of the occupation, leading to a variety of responses to the work situation. Whether the Presthus formulation is inclusive of all such responses is not the major issue. The responses are based on a person's previous socialization and the current situation. With this in mind, it is now time to turn to the positive rewards a person derives from this interaction process.

job satisfactions

The most evident fact about job satisfaction is that it varies, in terms of the over-all amount of satisfaction, directly with a person's position in the occupational hierarchy. Alex Inkeles has demonstrated that this is true across national lines in Western industrialized nations, as Table 3.3 indicates.[23] While the international differences are interesting, they cannot be taken as conclusive, given the fact that different questions were asked in each setting, but the major point is the consistency of the hierarchical relationship. Indeed, in light of what was said earlier about motivations to work, we might expect those occupations that have a higher status to be most likely to return positive reinforcements to the individual for his motivations. As might be expected, there are variations in the amount and types of satisfactions at, as well as between, the various hierarchical levels, as will be discussed below. But, again following Inkeles' work, findings from the Soviet Union and the United States are congruent in terms of what workers at varying levels value about their jobs, as Table 3.4 indicates. The importance of pay and security is inversely related to hierarchical level, while interesting work varies directly with the worker's level.

Further insights into these relationships can be attained by examining the components of job satisfaction among two diverse occupations. The first, the automobile-assembly-line worker, was intensively examined by Ely Chinoy,[24] who found that the auto worker works in a situation where the work itself is largely meaningless, with little opportunity to gain intrinsic satisfactions. Even the satisfaction of earning money is somewhat blunted by the fact that the pay differentials between jobs are so slight that an increase in pay, while rewarding, cannot set a particular worker apart from his fellows. Instead of being a satisfaction as such, his wages are apparently viewed as a normal expectation from putting in a certain amount of time on the job. This is not to suggest that money and the secondary pleasures that it can bring are unimportant to the auto worker. Rather, the satisfaction derived from the money earned is not from the work itself, but from pleasures that his wages afford in the "real world" for the worker. Thus, as this perhaps overly simplified view of the auto worker suggests, he does not actually derive satisfactions from his wages as part of his job. They are part of life's satisfactions, but not of the job's.

Although auto work is probably not the best example of blue-collar or semiskilled work, the boredom and monotony of it leads to the conclusion that job satisfactions in this type of work must be

[23]"Industrial Man: The Relation of Status to Experience, Perception, and Value," *American Journal of Sociology*, LXVI (July, 1960), 1–31.
[24]*Automobile Workers and the American Dream* (New York: Doubleday & Company, Inc., 1955).

Table 3.3. National Comparisons of Job Satisfaction, by Occupation

Percentage Satisfied[1]

U.S.S.R.		U.S.		Germany		Italy		Sweden		Norway	
Administrative, professional	77	Large business	100								
		Small business	91								
Semiprofessional	70	Professional	82	Professional	75			Upper class	84	Upper class	95
White collar	60	White collar	82	Upper white collar	65						
				Civil servants	51						
				Lower white collar	33			Middle class	72	Middle class	88
Skilled worker	62	Skilled manual	84	Skilled worker	47	Skilled worker	68	Working class	69	Working class	83
Semiskilled	45	Semiskilled	76	Semiskilled	21	Artisan	62				
Unskilled	23	Unskilled	72	Unskilled	11	Unskilled	57				
Peasant	12			Farm labor	23	Farm labor	43				

[1] U.S.S.R.—percentage answering "Yes" to: "Did you like the job you held in 1940?" (Soviet-refugee data, Russian Research Center, Harvard University). U.S.—percentage answering "Yes" to: "Are you satisfied or dissatisfied with your present job?" (Richard Centers, "Motivational Aspects of Occupational Stratification," *Journal of Social Psychology*, XXVII (1948), 100). Germany—percentage who would choose present occupation in response to: "If you were again 15 years old and could start again, would you choose your present occupation or another one?" (from German poll data, courtesy of S.M. Lipset). Italy—those "satisfied" or "fairly satisfied" with work (*Doxa Bolletineo*). Sweden and Norway—percentage giving "satisfied" in response to question: "Are you satisfied with your present occupation, or do you think that something else would suit you better?" (Hadley W. Cantril, ed., *Public Opinion, 1935-1946* (Princeton, N.J.: Princeton University Press, 1951), p. 535).

SOURCE: Reprinted from Alex Inkeles, "Industrial Man: The Relation of Status to Experience, Perception, and Value," *American Journal of Sociology*, LXVI, 1 (July, 1960), p. 6, by permission of The University of Chicago Press. Copyright 1960 by The University of Chicago.

Table 3.4.   Quality Most Desired in a Work Situation, in Percentages By Country and Occupations

Preferences of Sample of Soviet Refugees[1]

Occupation	Adequate Pay	Interesting Work	Free of Fear	All Others	N
Intelligentsia	8	62	6	24	95
White collar	23	31	13	33	62
Skilled workers	22	27	15	36	33
Ordinary workers	48	20	13	19	56
Peasants	57	9	17	17	35

Preferences of Sample in United States[2]

Occupation	High Pay	Interesting Work[3]	Security	Independence	Other
Large business	6	52	2	7	33
Professional	3	50	3	12	32
Small business	6	41	5	22	26
White collar	7	42	12	17	22
Skilled manual	4	36	13	22	25
Semiskilled	6	20	26	24	24
Unskilled	8	19	29	15	29
Farm tenant and laborer	12	21	20	18	29

[1] Based on coding of qualitative personal interviews from the Harvard Project on the Soviet Social System.

[2] Based on R. Centers, "Motivational Aspects of Occupational Stratification," *Journal of Social Psychology,* XXVIII (November, 1948), 187-218, Table 11.

[3] Includes: "A very interesting job" and "A job where you could express your feelings, ideas, talent, or skill."

SOURCE: Reprinted from Alex Inkeles, "Industrial Man: The Relation of Status to Experience, Perception, and Value," *American Journal of Sociology,* LXVI, 1 (July, 1960), p. 10, by permission of The University of Chicago Press. Copyright 1960 by The University of Chicago.

derived from interpersonal relations or from those rewards available off the job. Chinoy notes some auto workers spend time dreaming about other kinds of work; they are able to pass the time and utilize their minds, if they so desire, in these off the job kinds of activities. The direct job satisfactions are at the best quite limited.

In another study of automobile assembly line workers, Charles Walker and Robert Guest arrived at essentially the same conclusions as did Chinoy.[25] They note that for the majority of the workers, the pacing and repetitiveness of the work limits the direct satisfactions that can be derived from it. For some workers, however, the assembly line appears to offer a source of competition. The worker does not expect to win the competition but may derive pleasure in at least breaking even. Walker and Guest quote the following comments:

> I do my job well. I get some satisfaction from keeping up with a rapid-fire job. On days when the cars come off slowly, I sometimes get bored.

> I get satisfaction from doing my job right and keeping up with the line.

> It makes you feel good . . . when the line is going like hell and you step in and catch up with it.[26]

While these are comments of the minority, they do suggest that machine pacing does not provoke rebellion or criticism among all who are confronted with it. By the same token, the repetitiveness of the work also can be linked to satisfactions for a minority of the workers, as these comments suggest:

> I keep doing the same thing all the time, but it doesn't make any difference to me.

> I like doing the same thing all the time. I'd rather stay right where I am. When I come in in the morning, I like to know exactly what I'll be doing.

> I like to repeat the same thing, and every car is different anyway. So my job is interesting enough.[27]

In these cases of positive satisfactions, as well as in those of dissatisfaction, which will be touched on later, the major factor is the mix between the workers' expectations (personality) which he brings to the job and the characteristics of the job. In the case of the men who find assembly-line work both challenging and satisfying, their expectation level is such that a position which appears to be more challenging to an outside observer might create a high level of anxiety and dissatisfaction for them.

In contrast to the auto worker, the executive generally experiences more job satisfaction, however it is measured. This greater

[25]"The Man on the Assembly Line," *Harvard Business Review*, XXX (May–June, 1962), 71–88.
[26]"The Man on the Assembly Line," p. 77.
[27]Walker and Guest, "The Man on the Assembly Line," pp. 77–78.

satisfaction results from the fact that the job itself offers the individual a wider range of activities of the sort he has learned to expect. This is not to suggest that all executives are happier or better adjusted than all assembly-line or blue-collar workers. The stresses on a particular executive may be more real and more severe than on a particular blue-collar worker, but at the same time the general relationship between hierarchical level and amount of job satisfaction remains a rather systematically documented phenomenon. One could ask whether or not the executive, having learned to expect more satisfaction, reports a higher level thereof in order to protect his self-image, but this is not our major concern. Similarly, one could question the biases of researchers in the area of job satisfaction since they also are white-collar professionals and might be looking for the aspects of an occupation that are satisfying to themselves. Thus they would tend to find that executives have the same kinds of satisfactions while blue-collar workers do not. But even if this were the fact, as it might well be, it is not particularly important. The executive perceives himself to be more satisfied with his work than the blue-collar worker, and even if he is fooling himself and the researcher, he still acts on the basis of how he feels about the situation. For him (note the assumption that he is a he) the job satisfies a number of needs.

For examples of the kinds of needs which an executive has and which are generally met by his work, Lyman Porter's article is instructive.[28] Porter asked executives in a number of organizations of varying sizes what their occupational desires were. They responded by noting, first, a desire for security in the sense that their employment would not be terminated. A second type of need was social; they wanted to develop close friends on the job and also help other people. A third type of need was status or esteem in the organization and in the wider community, as well as self-esteem. A fourth need category was autonomy, by which they meant possessing authority, having an opportunity for independent thought, and participating in setting the goals for the organization and the methods and procedures of obtaining them. The final need category was self-actualization, which involves feelings of personal growth and development, of fulfillment through the utilization of skills, and of accomplishment. It is interesting to note that financial desires are not included in this list, except by inference in the security area. This is probably a consequence of having sufficient incomes, so that

---

[28]"Job Attitudes in Management: Perceived Importance of Need on a Function of Job Level," *Journal of Applied Psychology*, XLVII, 2 (December, 1963), 141–48.

this issue becomes less crucial; or perhaps it results from a feeling on the part of the researcher or the executives themselves that money is less central than the more socially based needs which were mentioned.

These needs, of course, become the bases for the satisfactions that the executives feel. Porter found that the needs were generally more sufficiently met as the hierarchy was ascended. An interesting exception to this finding was that lower and lower-middle managers in small corporations were happier than those in larger organizations. Thus there are variations in job satisfaction within the executive category, as well as between executives and workers at lower levels in organizations. Porter also notes that executives in larger organizations have more social needs and that these can probably be met if the work units are kept moderately small.

This discussion of job satisfactions has been intended to provide an overview of the kinds of positive rewards a person derives from his occupation. They are congruent with the kinds of motivations outlined in the previous section and apparently are sufficient to keep people on the job. The alternatives to working must be less rewarding to the individual than working is. The kinds of satisfactions that a person derives are also clearly related to the kind of work he is doing, as are the stresses, conflicts, and dissatisfactions that he faces.

stresses, tensions, and alienation

Just as particular kinds of occupations and their settings provide particular kinds of satisfactions, an analysis of the other side of the coin suggests that conflict and tension ensue from particular configurations of personal and nonpersonal factors within the occupational setting. In the following discussion the same two general types of occupations, factory work and executive, will serve as the basis for the discussion.

the factory worker

Besides less job satisfaction than those higher in the occupational hierarchy, the factory worker generally experiences more occupationally based strains, tensions, and feelings of alienation. Karl Marx, for example, spoke of the alienation of the working masses.[29] According to Marxian analysis, the worker has no power

[29]See Erich Fromm, *Marx's Concept of Man* (New York: Frederick Ungar Publishing Co., Inc., 1961), pp. 44–58.

over the production process and becomes little more than another machine, isolated from the production system even though a part of it. In a later analysis, Simone Weil, took a similar view of the worker:

> All or nearly all factory workers, even the most free in their bearing, have an almost imperceptible something about their movements, their look, and especially the set of the lips, which reveals that they have been obliged to consider themselves as nothing.[30]

Georges Friedman suggests that the extreme specialization in factory work is oppressive and leads to dissatisfactions on the part of workers.[31] On the basis of their analysis of the auto worker, Walker and Guest conclude: "It seems to us significant that the average worker appeared to be oppressed by this sense of anonymity *in spite of the fact that he declared himself well satisfied with his rate of pay and the security of his job.*"[32] These authors and others tend to view factory workers as a rather homogeneous group, who share common background characteristics and reactions to their jobs.

The view of the factory worker or blue-collar worker as dissatisfied is not uncommon. Whether it is correct or not is a question that can at least be partially answered by an analysis of Robert Blauner's investigation of industrial workers' reactions to their occupational situation.[33] His particular focus is on the amount and kinds of alienation that workers exhibit on the job. Blauner's approach to alienation is similar to the contemporary approach to the concept, which is to analyze its component parts.[34] Unlike some analysts, Blauner uses the concept of alienation as a research device, rather than as a polemically based attack on contemporary or historical conditions.

Four aspects of alienation are considered. First is *powerlessness*.[35] A powerless person is an object controlled and

[30]"Factory Work," in *Politics*, trans. F. Giovaelli, III, 11 (December, 1946), 370; reprinted in Nosow and Form, *Man, Work and Society*, p. 453.

[31]*The Anatomy of Work* (New York: The Free Press of Glencoe, Inc., 1961).

[32]"The Man on the Assembly Line," p. 83.

[33]*Alienation and Freedom* (Chicago: University of Chicago Press, 1964).

[34]For an analysis of the various meanings of the concept of alienation and some of the techniques used in their measurement, see Melvin Seeman, "On the Meaning of Alienation," *American Sociological Review*, XXIV, 6 (December, 1959), 783–91 and Dwight Dean, "Alienation: Its Meaning and Measurement," *American Sociological Review*, XXVI, 5 (October, 1961), 753–58. 753–58.

[35]Blauner, *Alienation and Freedom*, pp. 16–22.

manipulated by others or by an impersonal system, such as technology. He cannot assert himself as an agent of change or modify the conditions of his domination. He reacts rather than acts. The opposite of this condition is freedom and control over his own life. Blauner points out that the modern worker, at all levels, is separated from ownership, and that the vast majority of all workers, at all levels, are separated from the decision-making process. At the same time, an indirect source of control over the conditions of his employment is available to him through unionization and a growing amount of industrial democracy found in many employment situations. Thus while there are factors that operate to increase the amount of powerlessness a person experiences, counter trends are also evident.

Blauner's main concern, however, is not with these conditions, which are to some extent removed from the workers' immediate situation, important as they may be. The amount of control an individual has over his immediate situation is his dominant concern. Blauner therefore examines a person's freedom of physical movement, his freedom to make choices, his freedom from constraints regarding the pace of his work, his control over the quantity and quality of his work, and his freedom to select his own work techniques and routine. The basic assumption is the more freedom a person has, the less alienation.

The second component of alienation is *meaninglessness*, the situation when a person experiences the lack of a sense of purpose in his work.[36] He feels no connection between the parts (his own work) and the whole (the complete product or service). Meaninglessness comes about with standardized production techniques and with division of labor, which reduces the size of the individual worker's contribution to the total product. Blauner suggests that in small factories, in situations where team production was utilized, and where the technology is such that the work is highly integrated there would be less meaninglessness than under conditions where a worker is concerned with a single small unit and where he cannot see the relationship between his unit and the whole.

The third component is social alienation or *isolation*,[37] a feeling of not belonging to effective social units. The individual has little chance for self-expression. The presence of informal work groups would, of course, reduce the likelihood of this form of alienation, but as Blauner suggests, not all factory work allows the emergence of these work groups. Some workers are physically isolated from others, while in other situations the noise level might preclude the

[36]Blauner, *Alienation and Freedom*, pp. 22–24.
[37]Blauner, *Alienation and Freedom*, pp. 24–26.

development of such groups. Widely diverse backgrounds on the part of the workers might also operate to produce alienation if the diversity prevents the development of meaningful social relations on the job.

The final component of alienation to be considered is *self-estrangement*,[38] the alienation of a person from himself. The worker is depersonalized and detached. Self-estrangement would be most evident when the individual feels a need for exercising control and initiative but cannot because of the conditions of his work. Work that is boring and monotonous is most likely to cause this form of alienation. The self-estranged worker is detached from his work, viewing it as a means to an end and having no sense of pride in what he is doing nor any feeling of intrinsic satisfaction from it.

Blauner's primary purpose is to delineate those conditions under which the various forms of alienation are most likely to occur. In the course of so doing he points out the rather obvious, but often ignored, fact that although the majority of research on industrial work has been concentrated on the auto worker, who appears in most analyses as the archetype of the alienated man, assembly-line work, as characterized by the auto worker, comprises only five per cent of all industrial work. Industrial work is, in fact, highly varied. This variation, according to Blauner, should be and is accompanied by variations in the types and degrees of alienation present among the workers.

The first source of this variation is the type of technology in the industry. By technology Blauner means the complex of physical objects and technical operations, both mechanical and manual, regularly employed in turning out the goods and services produced by an industry. The type of technology is affected by the over-all state of the industrial arts, the economic and engineering resources of the specific firms involved, and the nature of the product being manufactured.[39] The impact of these sources of technological differentiation can be seen in the types of industries which Blauner considers in his analysis. The printing industry is characterized by a craft technology that has been minimally affected by technological change. At the same time, the product is unique for each day's work as the material to be printed changes. The textile industry, in which machine tending is a major component of the production process, has a more advanced technology and a more standardized product. The auto industry is characterized by standardized products and great variety in the production process, which itself is rather

[38] Blauner, *Alienation and Freedom*, pp. 26–31.
[39] Blauner, *Alienation and Freedom*, p. 6.

technologically advanced. Finally, the industrial-chemicals and petroleum-refining industries are highly advanced technologically with continuous flow production. These industries engage in continual research to improve the production process. The product here is also standardized in terms of the batches of particular substances which are refined.

The second major source of variation is the nature of the division of labor within a particular organization.[40] While this is clearly affected by the technology involved in the production process, it also varies independently according to the manner in which the particular organization assigns the men and machines at its disposal to the individual tasks. The division of labor can vary from high differentiation, in which each man and machine combination works only on a minute part of the whole, to situations in which both systematically contribute to a wider portion of production. The attempts at job enlargement, which have been noted at organizations such as International Business Machines, exemplify the ways in which the division of labor can be altered within an industry.

The social organization of the particular industry itself provides the third source of variation.[41] This involves the degree to which either traditional or bureaucratic standards are employed in organizational operations. By this, Blauner means the degree to which rules are present and enforced, the amount of emphasis on following standard operating procedures, and the extent to which personal considerations are rejected. Organizations can vary from highly bureaucratic to highly traditional along the various sub-dimensions of bureaucratization.

The final source of variation is in the economic structure of the industry.[42] Blauner points out that marginal industries with smaller profit margins generally push their workers harder and engage in tighter supervisory practices.

These sources of variation affect the settings from which the various forms of alienation may emerge. As will be noted below, there are variations among and within the four major industries to be analyzed. Some organizations within the textile industry, for example, are probably less bureaucratic than others and have a more advanced technology, a less intensive division of labor, and a more secure economic position. Although further analyses of these intra-industry variations would be profitable, our concern, at the present time, will be focused on the broader patterns of differences among

---

[40]Blauner, *Alienation and Freedom*, p. 6.
[41]Blauner, *Alienation and Freedom*, p. 6.
[42]Blauner, *Alienation and Freedom*, p. 10.

the various industries. An additional point, which should be added before Blauner's findings in this regard are considered, is that the workers in the various industries bring expectations with them to the job; their backgrounds affect their reactions to the diverse situations that confront them on the job.

The diversity of the industrial settings becomes very evident as the types and extent of alienation among the workers are analyzed. The printer works in a craft industry with a craft technology. He feels little powerlessness since he can set his own work pace, can move about, and is relatively free from supervisory control. The constantly changing product and the readily seen results make his work meaningful. Since a printer is part of a strong occupational community, he has few feelings of isolation. Similarly, he is not self-alienated because of his pride in his work and his involvement in what he is doing. The printer is thus not alienated in his industrial work. This is not to suggest that he does not suffer dissatisfactions on the job. Doing a poor job or working with people whom he finds unpleasant certainly would yield dissatisfactions, but he is relatively free from alienation as the term is being used.[43]

The textile worker provides some contrast to the printer. His work is essentially that of tending looms; a weaver can tend from forty to sixty. He thus is controlled in terms of the degree to which he can move about; though he has to move to tend the looms, he has little or no opportunity to go beyond specific locations. The rhythm and pace of his work are also controlled, and he is tightly supervised both by his immediate superior and by the nature of the work itself. As a consequence he experiences a rather high degree of powerlessness. He feels somewhat less meaninglessness because he can see the finished product and understand the processes designed to produce it. Since there is little variety in his work, some meaninglessness is, however, present. The setting of the particular textile workers studied, a small town in the South, coupled with some company pride and homogeneity of backgrounds of the workers, created a situation in which isolation was not felt. It was eliminated by a common residential and cultural community rather than by an occupational community, such as was evident among the printers. The backgrounds of the workers also affected the degree of self-alienation; being from the rural South, with little education, and placing minimal emphasis on self-expression, they experienced minimal self-alienation.[44]

When the auto worker is considered, the level of all four types

43Blauner, *Alienation and Freedom*, pp. 35–37.
44Blauner, *Alienation and Freedom*, pp. 58–88.

of alienation is found to be high. Blauner concentrates on the assembly line worker in his analysis, noting that not all of the work in automobile factories shares the characteristics he discusses. Powerlessness is high for the auto worker. The assembly line keeps moving with a constant flow of work designed to keep him busy all the time. The quantity, quality and techniques of the work are predetermined and are not under his control. There is little freedom of movement from the line. The worker is controlled quite impersonally, the assembly line itself becoming a control mechanism. The auto worker has, and feels that he has, little power.

He also experiences a high degree of meaninglessness. His work is only a small part of the whole. Furthermore, there are other workers doing exactly the same thing that he is; as Blauner points out, a person cannot be *the* left hubcap assembler. While the worker may know a lot about automobiles from his leisure activities, his level of meaninglessness is still high. The heterogeneity of backgrounds reduces the chances for the development of a cohesive occupational or residential community, which would reduce the feeling of isolation. The factories are large, contributing to a person's feeling "like a number." Further contributors to the feeling of isolation are the compressed wage and skill distributions in the plant and the fact that there is little chance for advancement. Self-estrangement is also present, because of the monotony of the work and the lack of challenge on the job. Money becomes the principal work motivation. While the auto worker is perhaps the classical alienated man, it should again be noted that his type of work comprises only a small fraction of all industrial work.[45]

The final type of worker to be considered is the chemical operator who works in the continuous-process chemical refinery. Most of the work is skilled maintenance, involving mental and visual, rather than manual, skills. The worker is responsible for the smooth and continued flow of the product and usually must move about as part of the job. Blauner suggests that the management of chemical and other such continuous-flow production organizations is usually progressive, with few ties to traditional management practices. The chemical operator experiences little powerlessness because of his freedom of movement and control over the quality of production. He is able to set his own pace of work and, to some degree, the order in which some procedures are followed. Since the work is largely team work and the workers understand the contribution each makes to the total process, little meaninglessness is felt.

[45]Blauner, *Alienation and Freedom*, pp. 89–123.

Similarly, little isolation is experienced because of the closely-knit work groups. The supervision is relatively loose, and there are enough status differentials to make the possibility of advancement a reality for most of the workers. The opportunity to experiment with new jobs and the level of involvement in the work lead to little self-estrangement.[46]

Blauner's conclusions are supported by a number of other studies. In a study of the mental health of the industrial worker, Arthur Kornhauser found the mental health of the worker directly related to the skill level of his job.[47] Kornhauser goes further than Blauner in attributing good mental health among workers to on the job situations. Blauner, it may be remembered, suggested that the background of the worker in the community, as in the case of the textile workers, was a key factor affecting the amount of aliena-tion experienced. Although their central concerns are different, Kornhauser's evidence suggests that such factors are not really central. He states: "Differences in mental health are not accounted for by the amount of education or other prejob characteristics of the men in different job categories."[48]

An interesting side issue here is the degree to which previous experiences predispose a person to experience job satisfactions or dissatisfactions. Blauner, Presthus, and others take the position that background characteristics are quite important, while Kornhauser's evidence suggests they are less important than the job situation itself. While there is an unfortunate lack of correspondence in the kinds of data the various authors have used, the evidence seems to suggest that background and personality factors interact with the work situation to yield reactions to the work. The relative weight of background, personality, and situational factors in bringing about particular responses is an issue that is not yet resolved. Kornhauser himself, however, while generally discounting the importance of the background and personality variables, notes:

> Generally advantageous or disadvantageous social and economic influences in childhood exert effects on personal development and self-feelings that carry over directly as determinants of subsequent mental health. Later condi-tions of work and life provide gratifications and impose frustrations in relation to established wants and expecta-tions in a manner that fosters or impairs self-esteem and

[46]Blauner, *Alienation and Freedom*, pp. 124–42.
[47]*Mental Health of the Industrial Worker* (New York: John Wiley & Sons, Inc., 1965).
[48]*Mental Health of the Industrial Worker*, p. 261.

overall mental health. Disparity between aspiration and achievement, with resultant sense of failure, is one important aspect of this total process.[49]

What Kornhauser appears to be saying is that background and personality factors are important but that they only make a difference in the context of the actual work situation and that particular types of work situations are more likely to lead to good mental health or to feelings of alienation. Given a particular work situation, in other words, healthy or alienative responses will probably ensue, regardless of the particulars of a person's background. This position is strengthened by Arthur G. Neal and Salomon Rettig's findings in regard to alienation among manual and nonmanual workers.[50] They find little relationship between the mobility values (the expressed amount of desire to advance in the stratification system) of their subjects and their feelings of alienation. They suggest that the opportunity structure, career history, and place of a person in an organization are the key factors leading to differing degrees of alienation. Along the same lines, Leo Meltzer and James Salter suggest that job satisfaction is related to freedom on the job, lack of close supervision, opportunity to use one's own abilities, etc.[51] Both of these studies reinforce the idea that background and personality factors interact with the work situation to yield the varying levels of satisfaction or alienation. The crucial variable is the work situation, in the sense that the personal factors would not matter at all unless they were placed in a work situation, and because the research evidence indicates that similar work situations yield similar responses.

Before examining an approach to occupational stresses and tensions among executives, an additional point about alienation should be made. Although the concept has most often been applied to the blue-collar worker, it is evident that alienation can be experienced at all levels of the occupational structure. Michael Aiken and Jerald Hage, for example, found that relatively high levels of alienation are present among a professional group (social workers) when the organizational environment in which they work is characterized by high degrees of centralization and formalization.[52] High centralization and formalization lead to a lack of participation in

[49]*Mental Health of the Industrial Worker*, pp. 154–55.
[50]"Dimensions of Alienation Among Manual and Non-manual Workers," *American Sociological Review*, XXVIII (August, 1963), 599–608.
[51]"Organizational Size and Performance and Job Satisfaction," *American Sociological Review*, XXVII (August, 1962), 351–62.
[52]"Organizational Alienation: A Comparative Analysis," *American Sociological Review*, XXXI (August, 1966), 497–507.

62   occupations and the individual

decision making and an absence of discretionary power on the part of the persons involved, who are confronted with a situation in which their expectations are not met, causing a high level of alienation. Approaching the problem from a different perspective, one might expect that job satisfaction for social workers would be higher in those agencies where centralization and formalization are low. This assumes, of course, that the desire for autonomy and decision making power is relatively high throughout the various agencies.

executives and white-collar workers

That executives and other white-collar workers are not immune to tensions and conflict in their occupations is evident from the works of Presthus and Saunders, which were mentioned earlier. A systematic overview of both the types and sources of conflict for white-collar workers is provided by Robert Kahn et al. in their analysis of the stresses confronting the personnel employed in large organizations.[53] A basic assumption in this study is that many persons are continually engaged in a quest for identity, which is congruent with the earlier discussion of work motivations in that identity can be achieved through achievement of status, the production of goods or services, or rewards from social interaction. The authors of this study contend that, while the quest for identity may be central for many persons, the organization confronts a person with conditions of ambiguity and conflict rather than clarity and harmony. This is not meant as an attack on the large organization but rather as a statement of the facts of modern organizational life as they perceive them.[54]

The basic model in this analysis is that of the role set, following the lead developed by Robert K. Merton.[55] This model begins with the idea that a person (the focal person) has his own perceptions of his role. At the same time the members of his role set also have expectations regarding his behavior. The role set is composed of those persons with whom he systematically interacts; his superiors, peers, and in many cases, his subordinates. Their role expectations take the form of sent roles that are transferred to the focal person in the form of role pressures, which can be legitimate or illegitimate and which can vary in strength, direction, specificity, and in the

[53]Robert Kahn et al., *Organizational Stress* (New York: John Wiley & Sons, Inc., 1964).
[54]Kahn et al., *Organizational Stress*, pp. 4–6.
[55]*Social Theory and Social Structures* (2nd ed.) (New York: The Free Press of Glencoe, Inc., 1957), pp. 368–80.

range of conditions under which they are applicable. A person's behavior is thus based on the interaction of his role perceptions and the pressures from the members of his role set.

When role pressures and a person's own role perceptions coincide, ambiguity and conflict will not be present. As might be expected, this coincidence occurs only in the minority of occupational situations. Kahn *et al.* state that a national survey shows that only one-sixth of the labor force reported being free from tension on the job,[56] and some thirty-five per cent of the labor force experienced real ambiguity in their roles.[57] This conflict and tension result in felt tensions on the part of the organizational members and in less effective work on their part, thus affecting the organizational output. While not all conflict has negative consequences, in this case the conflict and ambiguity are rather clearly detrimental to the organization and the individuals involved.

A series of factors contribute to the conflict and ambiguity experienced. In the first place, many organizations contain built-in conflict. Subsystems or departments may be engaged in activities that are incompatible unless the coordination of the total organization approaches perfection. For example, personnel, production, purchasing, sales, and research and development departments often are in conflict because of the nature of their activities. The personnel and production departments often work most effectively by maintaining equilibrium, while sales, purchasing, and research and development departments often are sources of change for the organization.[58] Another such source of built-in conflict exists in those situations where subsystems of the organization are engaged in essentially the same functions and utilize essentially the same facilities. The various automotive divisions of some of the major manufacturers are an example of this, as are the various departments within a university. Conflict arises over the allocation of scarce resources within the organization. This conflict can be viewed as conflict between sub-systems, but also as conflict that affects the individuals within those subsystems.[59] The reward system established by the organization can serve as an additional source of built-in conflict. When the status system is rather rigidly defined, groups or individuals with entrenched positions are in conflict with those who believe the system should be altered to enhance their own positions. Whether or not the entrenched status system is rational or

[56]*Organizational Stress*, p. 55.
[57]*Organizational Stress*, p. 74.
[58]Kahn *et al.*, *Organizational Stress*, p. 99.
[59]Kahn *et al.*, *Organizational Stress*, p. 100.

the demands of those who wish to alter it are legitimate is actually irrelevant, since the conflict will exist in any case.[60] These built-in conflicts affect the individuals in that part of their role expectations, from others and usually from themselves, is to support the subsystem of which they are a part.

In addition to these types of conflicts, the organization itself contributes to conflict and ambiguity on the part of individuals through the job descriptions (role expectations) that are formally or informally developed from particular positions. One type of position within the organization that is particularly susceptible to such conflict is the "boundary position," which entails contacts with persons or groups outside the organization or in other parts of it. According to Kahn *et al.*, the holders of such positions are prone to experience chronic conflict because of the differing role pressures on them from the multiple sources of pressure with which they must deal.[61] Those in innovative roles in the organization, such as in research and development departments, many engineering departments, and in situations such as converting hand operations into computer-based operations, face conflicts between themselves, the new guard, and the old guard, who have vested interests in the maintenance of the *status quo*. Similarly, those whose roles demand creativity often are in conflict with those whose role expectations are to maintain routine procedures.[62]

An additional organizational basis of stress is the status of the person in the organization. As noted earlier, those of higher status are likely to experience greater job satisfaction and greater tension. Higher status roles usually involve both boundary relationships and demands for innovativeness. In addition, the organizational demands on such individuals are greater in terms of the quantity of expectations. Those in middle management may also face tensions engendered by their own mobility aspirations. The same factors that contribute to job satisfaction and that are a part of the original motivation to work thus contribute to these occupationally related tensions and conflicts.[63]

In addition to these organizationally based situations, the nature of the interpersonal relationships on the job can also contribute to stress situations. Members of the focal person's role set exert direct pressures on him to conform to their expectations. The closer the relationships, the greater the pressures become. The very facts

[60]Kahn *et al.*, *Organizational Stress*, p. 100.
[61]*Organizational Stress*, pp. 102–24.
[62]Kahn *et al.*, *Organizational Stress*, pp. 125–36.
[63]Kahn *et al.*, *Organizational Stress*, pp. 137–49.

of organizational life, the presence of superiors, peers, and subordinates, suggests that incompatible expectations from these people are almost built into the situation.[64]

Similarly, the focal person's own personality can contribute to felt conflicts, tensions, and ambiguities. Kahn *et al.*, for example, suggest that the introverted individual may experience tensions because his tendency to withdraw from interpersonal relations leads to antagonisms on the part of members of his role set. In addition, many organizations appear to expect some degree of extroversion among their employees. In terms of flexibility and rigidity, the authors found that the flexible person is subject to more tensions because he tends to reach out for more role expectations as he attempts to expand his own range of activities. He can thus experience what could be termed "role overload." Similarly, the person who is highly motivated to increase his expertise or his status is liable to face high levels of conflict and tension as these needs are not constantly met. The more security-minded individuals will experience less such tension, in that they will tend to withdraw from the competition and be satisfied with somewhat blunted role relationships.[65]

summary and conclusions

In this chapter, the reactions of the individual to his occupation have been examined. The most general point that has been made is that a person reacts to his occupation on the basis of his learned expectations. The need for money is learned, as are those regarding the more social aspects of work motivations. By the same token, the satisfactions derived and the tensions felt are also based on these learned motivations. These are modified during the course of involvement in an occupation, but the modifications themselves serve as the source of continued motivations, satisfactions, and tensions.[66] A second major point is that the personal expectations interact with the situation as it is perceived by the individual, as the Blauner

[64]Kahn *et al.*, *Organizational Stress*, pp. 185–222.
[65]Kahn *et al.*, *Organizational Stress*, pp. 225–333.
[66]Frank Friedlander and Eugene Walton, "Positive and Negative Motivations Toward Work," *Administrative Science Quarterly*, IX, 2 (September, 1964), 194–207, suggest that positive satisfactions are related to elements in the work process itself, while dissatisfactions are based on more peripheral elements, such as promotion and pay, living conditions, etc., in the work context. The expectations and reality of the work process and context again are the important factors in satisfaction or dissatisfaction.

work illustrates. A person is continually confronted with an objective situation, which he interprets on the basis of his own learned perceptual framework. As we have seen, the objective situation itself, in terms of a person's status in an organization or within the occupational structure, also affects the reactions of the individual to his work. With this in mind, the analysis will now shift to an examination of the various types of objective situations or of occupations, which comprise the occupational structure.

PART II

TYPES OF OCCUPATIONS

It is obvious to even the most untrained observer that occupations assume many different forms. Less obvious are some of the reasons for the differences. The purpose of this section is to examine the occupational system in terms of broad categories in order to describe it and to analyze the reasons for occupational differentiation. The basic emphasis will be on those characteristics of the wider social structure, such as the increasing amount of work in organizations, technological changes, and increasing educational demands, which affect the nature of the types of occupations. At the same time, changes and variations within the broad categories will be discussed and explained. In order to analyze these occupational types, it is necessary to describe them, and thus in the chapters that follow we will first describe the occupations and then analyze the reasons for variations and changes within each type in order to provide an overview of the occupational system.

A basic problem in this analysis is the lack of a good typology of occupations. One could, for example, divide the occupational universe into categories based on whether a person utilized manual, mental, or social skills. But, while a few occupations might exclusively utilize one of these skill types, most use a combination of them. Simple dichotomies, such as blue-collar versus white-collar or professional versus nonprofessional are too broad and contain categories that actually are not mutually exclusive. Other groupings based on such criteria as the amount and kind of education required or the amount of responsibility or authority found in the occupation might be very relevant, but the fact is that such categorizations are not available.

As an heuristic device we shall use the categories developed by the U.S. Bureau of the Census in its analyses of the labor force. This categorization corresponds to a general ranking of occupations on the basis of socio-economic status, the purpose for which it was intended, although it does appear to group the occupational system into relatively homogeneous categories. It should be stressed that the categories to be used here are chosen on the basis of availability, but since occupations are central to socio-economic status, they also relate to a significant aspect of the social structure.

The categories, and the chapters corresponding to them, are :[1]

1. Professionals
2. Managers, Proprietors, and Officials

[1]This categorization is based on Theodore Caplow's slight rearrangement of the Bureau of the Census classification. See Caplow, *The Sociology of Work*, p. 23.

3. Clerks and Kindred Workers
4. Skilled Workers and Foremen
5. Semiskilled Workers
6. Unskilled Workers (Including farm and nonfarm workers)

chapter 4

the professions

Profession is probably the most widely used and commonly known occupational category and refers to the occupational class most readily identified as a type of occupation by the public at large. From the sociologist's perspective, it and many similar "types" are misused at times. For example, the fact that an athlete is no longer an amateur, in the sense that his payments are larger and more open, does not make him a professional in the limited sense the term implies here. The "world's oldest profession," prostitution, similarly would not qualify from the perspective of the sociologist. At the outset, then, it should be clear that an occupation is not a profession simply because its members are being paid. The concept of profession has come to have a rather specific meaning, which allows determination of the degree to which a specific occupation can be considered a profession.

Before proceeding with the discussion of the exact nature of professions, the reasons for the prominence of this occupational type should be explored. An obvious point is that many professions have high status; doctors and lawyers have high visibility and images which are consistently developed and reinforced through literature and the mass media. They are also very close to being true professionals from the technical standpoint. A second point is that the growing number of persons in the professional category and the growing number of occupations which have become, or are attempting to become, professions are increasing occupational specialization. A member of an occupation which becomes specialized as he carries on his work will increasingly identify with and share the values and behaviors of his fellow specialists. An occupational community will develop, fostering solidarity among its members and excluding those who are not part of it.[1] Concomitant with specialization is the greater amount of training needed to become a specialist; persons undergoing training in a particular area tends to increase solidarity among those with a similar experience. And as more knowledge becomes available in most areas of human endeavor, more extensive and intensive training is needed for even minimal competence. Those who undergo this training become experts and, at least in one sense, professionals.

In addition to this rather general social change, some occupationally generated factors, both selfish and altruistic, contribute to the growth of the professions. On the selfish side, the motive of groups to improve their status within the occupational structure is served by their becoming regarded as professions, since the label has an honorific connotation. At the same time, the occupations' economic position can often be strengthened by the bargaining position of a united group of practitioners. A profession also can often exclude persons who are deemed unqualified, which allows control over the labor market, thus again enhancing the group's position. On the altruistic side, there is an evident desire on the part of many occupations to improve the services and performance levels of their members. This can be accomplished by the establishment of stricter entrance requirements, ethical codes, and certification statutes. The exact degree to which either selfish or altruistic factors operate in specific cases is subject to empirical determination, but in a real sense, it does not matter which type of motivation is dominant in the drive toward professionalization, for both selfish and altruistic motives yield occupationally beneficial consequences.

A point made earlier should be re-emphasized. As Western society becomes more services-human resources oriented, the demand for professional services and abilities will increase. The

[1]See William J. Goode, "Community Within a Community: The Professions," *American Sociological Review*, XXII, 2 (April, 1957) 194–200 for a discussion of the communitylike aspect of the professions.

demand for more and better educational, health, and social services will create demands for more personnel in the professions associated with them, and the scientific-technological base of productive and service industries will require the skills of professionals. Thus the overall social structure is ripe for a further increase of professionalization.

the professional model

Most analyses of the profession begin with a consideration of the professional model, a series of attributes, the exact content of which depends on the particular analysis. The model is designed to allow assessment of the degree to which an occupation possesses the characteristics of the model, and thus serves the function of an ideal-type formulation. It is generally assumed that if an occupation contains the characteristics of the professional model, it can be considered a profession. While there is some evidence that this is not necessarily the case, any variations will be considered at a later time. With so many occupations attempting to professionalize, the efforts are usually in the direction of attempting to make ,the occupation fit the professional model. As it succeeds, it typically begins to label itself as a profession.

The components of this model have been approached somewhat differently by different authors, but there is a strong thread of common ideas throughout. A. M. Carr-Saunders and P. A. Wilson suggest that the major criterion for professional status is the presence of an intellectual technique, acquired by special training, which performs a service for society and is unavailable to the laity.[2] In their analysis of the historical development of the professions, Carr-Saunders and Wilson note that licensing, by the profession itself or by the state with the profession establishing the criteria, follows the development of this intellectual technique. This allows the profession to determine if potential members have in fact acquired the specified training and intellectual techniques. The term intellectual techniques raises an important question, since technique suggests an application of knowledge, while intellectual connotes a more theoretically oriented approach. Talcott Parsons recognizes the apparent incompatibility of these two terms when he points out that professions such as medicine are primarily applied, while scientific disciplines, such as sociology or biochemistry, are prima-

[2]"Professions," *Encyclopedia of the Social Sciences* (New York: The Macmillan Company, Publishers, 1944), XXII, 476–80.

rily dedicated to the advancement and transmission of empirical knowledge, with only a secondary emphasis on its utilization.[3]

Parsons' definition of a profession makes this point explicit:

> I conceive a profession to be a category of occupational role which is organized about the mastery of and fiduciary responsibility for any important segment of a society's cultural tradition, including responsibility for its perpetuation *and* for its future development. In addition, a profession may have responsibility for the application of its knowledge in practical situations.[4]

The stress on intellectual techniques and important segments of cultural tradition runs through every definition of the professions and can perhaps be restated by saying that professions are organized around bodies of knowledge. Whether this knowledge is gathered and transmitted in the form of a scientific discipline, or is applied in the form of a service is not the central issue at this time. The issue of pure (scientific inquiry) versus applied knowledge can become important within particular professions, but, for our purposes, an occupation involved in either or both can be considered a profession if it meets certain other criteria.

The characteristics discussed thus far are probably central to the nature of the professions, but they are also rather general; additional criteria or attributes of professionalism should be added to clarify further the nature of this occupational type. Ernest Greenwood has suggested five major professional attributes.[5] First, as might be expected from the previous discussion, is the presence of systematic theory. Ernest Greenwood also notes that this can be intellectual as well as practical, and adds that it is based on research.[6] This is, of course, congruent with Parsons' emphasis on the perpetuation and development of a profession's knowledge base. Greenwood's emphasis on research appears to overlook a minor, but interesting, point. While most professions in fact rely upon research as a contribution to the base of knowledge, two of the most easily identified professions, the law and ministry, apparently do not. Their knowledge base depends on lore rather than on science. Various sources of knowledge are available for the development of the systematic theory that underlies a profession. While most professions do rely on research, other approaches are feasible.

[3]"Some Problems Confronting Sociology as a Profession," *American Sociological Review*, XXIV, 4 (August, 1959), 547.

[4]"Some Problems Confronting Sociology as a Profession," p. 547.

[5]"Attributes of a Profession," *Social Work*, II, 3 (July, 1957), 45–55.

[6]"Attributes of a Profession," pp. 46–47.

A second professional attribute, according to Greenwood, is professional authority.[7] The professional can dictate what is good or bad for his client, who gives him this authority in the belief that the professional's knowledge will enable him to make the correct judgment in matters affecting the client's life. Professional-client relationships will require more extended discussion at a later point, but at present they can be taken as a regular professional attribute.

Greenwood's third attribute is formal and informal community sanction of the profession, its powers and privileges.[8] Formal approval can be seen in the manner in which the profession itself is given the power to determine the appropriate character and curriculum of the training process. While state accreditation and licensing procedures may follow the training period, the standards are set by the profession itself, since the state or its functionaries do not have the knowledge to set standards. Another aspect of the sanctions given to professions is in the area of professional confidence; the information given to a professional by his client is privileged communication, thus protecting the rights of the client but also reaffirming the authority of the professional.

Another attribute is a regulative code of ethics, in the form of codified statements of the appropriate behavior of the professional toward his clients and toward fellow professionals.[9] These ethical codes are both formally and informally enforced, through censure, removal from the professional association, or ostracism from interaction systems. There is some indication that increased specialization within professions leads to difficulties in the enforcement of ethical codes and that these codes are violated in practice. It is clear, however, that occupations which are aspiring to be known as professions usually develop ethical codes as part of what they envision as the process of professionalization.

Greenwood's final attribute is a professional culture, which involves norms governing membership in professional associations, organizations which are qualified to provide training, and appropriate sites for professional practice.[10] In addition, the professional culture contains the language and symbols of the profession. A professional culture is a means of differentiating between professionals and outsiders, since only insiders are privy to the meanings of the symbolic system of the profession. It could be hypothesized that the greater the development of the professional culture, the greater the social distance between the profession and the laity.

[7]"Attributes of a Profession," pp. 47–48.
[8]"Attributes of a Profession," pp. 48–49.
[9]Greenwood, "Attributes of a Profession," pp. 49–51.
[10]"Attributes of a Profession," pp. 51–54.

Greenwood's set of attributes is largely concerned with the way an occupation is linked to the social structure. If an occupation has these characteristics, according to this type of formulation it can be considered a profession. A profession's knowledge base is part of the wider society, its ethical codes are utilized by the wider society as the means of controlling professional behavior, and its power and authority are granted to it by the community. However, in a sense whether or not an occupation is a profession depends on the way in which it is viewed by society. It may have all the other attributes thus far discussed, but if it is not given community sanction, it will not be considered, and cannot operate as, a profession.

Further insights into the nature of the professions are provided by Edward Gross.[11] While some of the characteristics to be treated below are similar to those already discussed, Gross adds another dimension to the professional characteristics. Some of the attributes, which he discusses, are clearly attitudinal. That is, the characteristics appear as the direction and strength of the orientations of the persons involved, rather than as structural characteristics which may be present or absent. For example, a central characteristic in this formulation is the degree of personality involvement.[12] The professional is characterized by a high level of involvement, which is transmitted to his clients in the form of their belief that he will consistently act in their best interests. The professional also has a well developed sense of obligation to his art; he wants to do the best job he possibly can. Gross notes that the professional "is not supposed to be interested in sordid money."[13] While this supposition is probably unwarranted in practice, the point is that the professional is thought to be one who would work just for the intrinsic rewards of his occupation. Another attitudinal component is the closeness with which the professional identifies with his colleagues through formal and informal professional associations.[14] This close identification is a source of attitudes governing his own orientations as well as a source of control over his behavior.

In addition to these attitudinal components, Gross notes some of the same general structural characteristics which have already been discussed. For example, the professional is viewed as working with an unstandardized product.[15] His knowledge is applied to solving particular problems, each of which, though unique, fits

[11]*Work and Society* (New York: Thomas Y. Crowell Co., 1958), 77–82.
[12]Gross, *Work and Society*, p. 78.
[13]*Work and Society*, p. 79.
[14]Gross, *Work and Society*, pp. 79–80.
[15]*Work and Society*, pp. 77–78.

within his general body of theoretical knowledge. Related to this is the idea that the source of the professional's power is his knowledge. Since the client is usually ignorant in the field of the professional's competence, the professional has power over him through his advice and suggestions. In this sense, the idea of community sanctions, suggested by Greenwood, is given further support, since the wider community itself is similarly ignorant and must give the professional the right to make decisions in important areas of life.

A final characteristic, again related to those being discussed, is that the service provided by the professional is essential to the health and welfare of the individual and of society.[16] It is clearly very difficult to determine exactly why one service is more essential than another, but the implication here is that there is some societal consensus in this regard. Even if there were no consensus, the fact is that the laity does not have the prerequisite knowledge to replace the professional; thus the professional is able to attain and maintain his position by an essentially monopolistic control over the knowledge. Obviously, this knowledge must be considered important for individuals or society, or the monopoly would have no impact, since a monopoly of trivia would not be too marketable.

Another sociologist, William J. Goode, has suggested some additional characteristics of professions, which provide further insights into the nature of this occupational type. In addition to some of the points already noted, Goode suggests that the student of a profession undergoes a more far-reaching adult socialization process than the person learning other occupations.[17] By this, Goode suggests that professional training not only consumes more time in the formal school setting but also involves socialization into appropriate attitudes and behaviors. While Howard S. Becker and Blanche Geer suggest that the major impact on the medical student is from his peers, with the faculty having a lesser role in the formation of professional attitudes, the crucial point is that an attitudinal consensus is achieved.[18] Such a consensus is a hallmark of professionalism, regardless of its source.

Although the extensive socialization brings about common sets of knowledge and attitudes, it should not be assumed that graduates of professional training are a totally homogeneous group who march through life in a sort of conceptual lockstep. As will be demon-

[16]Gross, *Work and Society*, p. 80.
[17]"Encroachment, Charlatanism, and the Emerging Profession: Psychology, Sociology, and Medicine," *American Sociological Review*, XXV, 6 (December, 1960), 903.
[18]Howard S. Becker and Blanche Geer, "The Fate of Idealism in Medical School," *American Sociological Review*, XXIII, 1 (February, 1958), 50–56.

strated later, wide variations in performance and attitude exist within any profession. Nevertheless, professions appear to have more homogeneity than most other occupational types.

Goode also suggests that the profession is a powerful force in society and over the individual, in that most legislation concerning the profession is generated by the profession itself.[19] This relates to Gross's point about the ignorance of the general public, including legislators, of the work of the professional, so that legislative efforts must be turned over to the profession in the absence of alternative sources of knowledge. Goode also suggests that the norms developed by professional groups to govern their conduct are more stringent than those with a legal basis.[20] Thus, the real source of control over an individual professional lies in the hands of the profession, with society's (legal) control being weaker. This mechanism allows the profession to maintain its autonomy.

A final point made by Goode is that a profession is typically the terminal occupation for members.[21] The trained professional does not leave the profession in contrast to many occupations in which a change in jobs is quite normal. The professional has both a financial and temporal investment in the occupation. Additionally, the long socialization has made him, in many ways, incapable of changing occupations, since both his skills and his attitudes are relatively fixed.

Thus far the discussion has been concerned with the development of a set of attributes characterizing professions. Before proceeding to an analysis of the interrelations among these attributes, it would be useful to introduce certain distinctions among the terms which are being used. In their book, *Professionalization*, Howard Vollmer and Donald Mills note:

> In our discussion of the readings, for example, we avoid the use of the term "profession," except as an "ideal type" of occupational organization which does not exist in reality, but which provides the model of the form of occupational organization that would result if any occupational group became completely professionalized. In this way, we wish to avoid discussion of whether or not any particular group is "really a profession," or not. In accord with Hughes' experience, we feel that it is much more

[19] "Encroachment, Charlatanism, and the Emerging Profession: Psychology, Sociology, and Medicine," p. 903.
[20] "Encroachment, Charlatanism, and the Emerging Profession: Psychology, Sociology, and Medicine," p. 903.
[21] "Encroachment, Charlatanism, and the Emerging Profession: Psychology, Sociology, and Medicine," p. 903.

fruitful to ask "how professionalized," or more specifically "how professionalized in certain identifiable respects" a given occupation may be at some point in time.
We suggest, therefore, that the concept of "profession" be applied only to an abstract model of occupational
organization, and that the concept of "professionalization" be used to refer to the dynamic *process* whereby
many occupations can be observed to change certain crucial characteristics in the direction of a "profession,"
even though some of these may not move very far in this
direction. It follows that these crucial characteristics
constitute specifiable criteria of professionalization.[22]

The authors further specify that the term professionalism be
used to refer to the ideology found in many occupational groups in
the process of professionalization. Although professionalism may
not lead an occupation very far down from the professionalization
in every instance, it is an integral part of the process. Further
distinctions are that professional groups are those associations of
colleagues found in occupational contexts in which a high degree of
professionalization has occurred. The noun professional refers to
those who "are considered by their colleagues to be members of
professional groups."[23] These distinctions should add clarity to the
discussions that follow and also suggest, as Vollmer and Mills
intended, that professionalization is a dynamic process, linked to the
wider social structure and to the occupational groups themselves.

professional attributes: structural and attitudinal

The array of attributes of professionalization discussed above
can be divided into two types. First are the structural attributes.
This label is attached because the attributes become part of the
social structure in the form of professional training schools and
organizations. These attributes are thus part of the ongoing social
system and part of the smaller social structure of which the professional is a member. In a useful article, which synthesizes much of
the earlier literature, Harold L. Wilensky has suggested that they
form a set of sequential stages through which occupations pass in
the process of professionalization.[24] These stages are:

22Howard M. Vollmer and Donald L. Mills, eds., *Professionalization*
(Englewood Cliffs, N.J.: Prentice-Hall, Inc., 1966), pp. vii–viii.
23Vollmer and Mills, eds., *Professionalization*, p. 8.
24"The Professionalization of Everyone?" *American Journal of Sociology*,
LXX, 2 (September, 1964), 137–58.

1. Creation of a full time occupation. This involves the performance of functions that may have been performed previously as well as new functions and can be viewed as a reaction to needs in the wider social structure.

2. The establishment of a training school. This reflects both the knowledge base of a profession, central to most considerations of the nature of professions, and the efforts of early leaders in the field to improve the lot of the occupation. In the occupations further along in the process of professionalization, the move is then followed by affiliation of the training school with established universities. In occupations that have begun the process of professionalization more recently, the establishment of professional training schools and university affiliation tends to occur simultaneously.

3. Formation of professional associations. The formation of such associations is often accompanied by a change in the occupational title, attempts to define more clearly the exact nature of the professional tasks, and efforts to eliminate practitioners who are deemed incompetent by the emergent professionals. Local associations will unite into national associations after a period of political manipulation. As stronger associations are formed, political agitation, in the form of attempts to secure licensing laws and protection from competing occupations, becomes an important associational task.

4. Formation of a code of ethics. These ethical codes are concerned with both internal (colleague) and external (client and public) relations. They are designed to be enforced by the professional associations themselves and, ideally, are given legal support.

This formulation is very similar to Caplow's, except that the order of events is slightly altered. Caplow suggests that the formation of a professional association, a change of occupational title, the development of a code of ethics, political agitation, and the emergence of training facilities is the more typical process.[25] Wilensky's evidence suggests that his formulation is a more accurate descrip-

[25]"Sequential Steps in Professionalization," in Vollmer and Mills, eds., *Professionalization*, pp. 20–21.

tion, however. Despite the disagreement as to sequence, the components of the two approaches are very similar. Both have apparently caught the essence of the professionalization process insofar as structural characteristics are concerned.

Wilensky identifies four occupational types on the basis of his analysis, which is based on the degree to which the occupation proceeds through the sequence discussed above without "errors or ties."[26] Errors occur when stages are reached in the sequence out of the suggested order, while ties occur when stages are reached simultaneously. The first type of occupation, with the fewest errors or ties, is the established profession. The types of occupations included are accounting (CPA), architecture, civil engineering, dentistry, law, and medicine. The ministry, one of the oldest organizations thought to be a profession, was not included. The second category is labeled "others in process, some marginal." This group includes library science, nursing, optometry, pharmacy, school teaching, social work, and veterinary medicine. The next category is the "new" professions, including city management, city planning, and hospital administration. The last category is "doubtful," and includes advertising and funeral direction. The proportion of errors in the process of professionalization increases with each category, thus yielding a nominal scale of the degree of professionalization of the groups involved. Other occupations could be considered, using the same format.

It should be noted that this type of formulation leads to a bias against occupations that are attempting to professionalize, since they could well meet the criteria for professionalization, but would meet them in such a close time span that many ties or errors would occur, causing them to be rated as doubtful or marginal. Since the components of professionalization are well known to occupational groups that are aspiring to become known as professions, they can rather easily establish training schools, associations, and ethical codes within a short period of time. Another criticism of this formulation is that it tends to ignore an important component of the relationship between an occupation and the wider social structure, namely, recognition by society that the occupation is in fact a profession.[27] It is conceivable that an occupation could have all the components of professionalization, but, for one reason or another, not be recognized as a profession. Nevertheless, the Wilensky formulation remains a useful device for summarizing the nature and

---

[26]"The Professionalization of Everyone?" p. 143.

[27]Vollmer and Mills stress the importance of societal recognition in *Professionalization*, pp. 26–27.

order of the structural components. As noted before, it also is useful as a crude means of determining the degree to which various occupations professionalize in regard to the various structural components.

An important component of professionalization, which has both structural and attitudinal aspects, is professional autonomy. The structural aspect of autonomy is indirectly subsumed under the efforts of professional associations to exclude the unqualified and to provide for the legal right to practice; but autonomy is also part of the work setting, in that the professional is expected to utilize his professional judgment with at least relative confidence that only other professionals will be in any position to question it. This particular component is a critical one, in as much as threats to professional autonomy, such as organizational rules that might take precedence over professional norms, can create real conflict for the professional, as will be discussed in more detail below.[28] In a very real sense, autonomy can be considered the key element of professionalization, since the knowledge basis, community sanction, and colleague control of behavior are all elements of autonomy. If these factors are present in a work environment that does not allow the exercise of autonomy, then an individual or group cannot utilize their professional abilities. If they are strongly oriented to the professional role, obvious frustrations and tensions could ensue.

Autonomy, considered in terms of the professional's attitude, is related to his feeling that he is free to exercise his judgment and discretion. In a sense, this attitudinal aspect may be the most crucial of all, since the individual reacts to his perception of the situation and his attitude reflects the manner in which he perceives his work. As it is generally assumed that attitudes influence behavior, professional attitudes should be correspondingly related to professional behavior. If this assumption is correct, attitudes comprise an important part of the components of professionalization. The attitudinal attributes of professionalization that appear to be crucial are:

1. The use of the professional organization as a major reference. Both the formal organization, such as a bar association, and informal colleague groupings can be the major source of ideas and judgment for the professional in his work.
2. A belief in service to the public. This component

---

[28]For discussions of the importance of autonomy see William Kornhauser, *Scientists in Industry* (Berkeley: University of California Press, 1963) and Simon Marcson, *The Scientist in American Industry* (New York: Harper & Row, Publishers, 1960).

includes the idea that the occupation is indispensable and that it benefits both the public and the practitioner.

3. Belief in self-regulation. This involves the belief that, since the persons best qualified to judge the work of the professional are his fellows, colleague control is both desirable and practical.

4. A sense of calling to the field. This attitude reflects the dedication of the professional to his work and his feeling that he would probably want to continue in the occupation even if fewer extrinsic rewards were available.

5. Autonomy. This involves the feeling that the practitioner ought to be allowed to make his own decisions without external pressures from clients, from others who are not members of his profession, or from his employing organization.

The combination of the structural and attitudinal components serves as the basis for the professional model. It is generally assumed that both aspects are present to a high degree in highly professionalized occupations and to a lesser degree in those occupations that are less professionalized. It is also commonly thought that the structural and attitudinal attributes will vary together.

In order to test that assumption, the author recently undertook an examination of both aspects of the professional model, using a variety of occupations as the basis for the study.[29] After developing attitude scales for each of the professional attitudes discussed above, the scales were administered to groups of physicians, nurses, accountants, teachers, lawyers, social workers, stockbrokers, librarians, engineers, personnel managers, and advertising executives. All the groups except personnel managers and stockbrokers were considered by Wilensky in his study, thus allowing rather easy comparisons. In this case, the two new occupations were placed in Wilensky's "doubtful" category because of the patterning of their structural characteristics.

This study suggests that the assumption of concomitant variation between structural and attitudinal components of professionalization is incorrect. For example, with regard to use of the professional organization as a reference group, one group of stockbrokers emerged as highest on this attitude while another group of stockbrokers was quite low (see Table 4.1). The highly professionalized group

[29]Richard H. Hall, "The Components of Professionalization," (paper read at the meetings of the American Sociological Association, San Francisco, August, 1967).

Table 4.1. Ranks on Professionalism Scales by Occupational Group[1]

Occupational Group	Scale A Professional Organization as Reference	B Belief in Service to Public	C Belief in Self-Regulation	D Sense of Calling to Field	E Feeling of Autonomy
Accountant					
CPA firm 1	12	18	15	18.5	19
CPA firm 2	16	10	20	10.5	6
Acct. dept. 1	2.5	6	24.5	4	3
Acct. dept. 2	1	1	2.5	1	1
Advertising Exec.					
Ad. agency 1	8	4	9	15	20
Ad. agency 2	20	23	7	20	23
Engineer					
Engineering dept.	4	9	2.5	5	11
Lawyer					
Law firm 1	22	16	19	10.5	14
Law firm 2	13	14	22	7	22
Law firm 3	23	12.5	18	13	15
Legal dept. 1	26	11	23	8.5	10
Legal dept. 2	9	24	14	2.5	25
Legal dept. 3	11	5	4	2.5	26
Librarian					
Public library	21	15	11	25	4.5
Nurse					
Nursing division 1	10	20.5	16	18.5	4.5
Nursing division 2	14	19	27	24	2
Personnel Mngr.					
Per. dept. 1	7	2	5.5	8.5	7.5
Per. dept. 2	5.5	7.5	9	22	13
Physician					
Med. dept. 1	19	3	17	21	21
Med. dept. 2	5.5	7.5	9	16	12
Social Worker					
Private agency 1	17	17	12	17	9
Private agency 2	18	22	21	27	16
Public agency 1	25	20.5	5.5	26	17
Stock Broker					
Firm 1	2.5	12.5	24.5	6	24
Firm 2	27	25	26	23	27

Table 4.1.   (continued)

Occupational Group	Scale				
	A	B	C	D	E
	Professional Organization as Reference	Belief in Service to Public	Belief in Self-Regulation	Sense of Calling to Field	Feeling of Autonomy
Teacher					
Elem. school	24	26	13	14	7.5
High school	15	27	1	12	18

[1] Lower rank indicates lower degree of professionalization.

SOURCE: Richard H. Hall, "The Components of Professionalization," paper presented to the American Sociological Association, San Francisco, August, 1967.

in fact spends a great deal of time in professional organizational meetings off the job. Since there is not a training school, as such, for this occupation, the learning of this attitude probably must occur on the job. Thus, in this occupation, the employing organization itself would appear to have a strong impact on the professional attitude, since it can promote or inhibit such extraorganizational efforts. Other groups that exhibit high degrees of this attitude are the physicians and some of the lawyers studied.

On the variable dealing with belief in service to the public, the teachers emerge as the group with the strongest attitude in this regard, suggesting that they firmly believe that they are important for society. This can be attributed to the rather intense socialization into the profession both in schools of education and in school systems. It is also perhaps a reflection of the stress placed on education in the mid-twentieth century. Teachers apparently believe what everyone else has been saying. Another possible interpretation of this finding is that the belief in service to the public serves as some form of compensation for the relatively low pay and status of teachers in relation to the other occupations. This interpretation is strengthened when the data in regard to social workers and nurses are analyzed. They are also relatively high on this attitude and rather poorly rewarded. The fact that these are traditionally women's occupations may also be relevant to both the lower rates of compensation and the belief that the public is being served. These latter points are simply interpretations, since data are not available for their support.

At the other end of this particular scale are the physicians. This occupation's members in this study felt least that they were of service to the public. Both groups of physicians included in the study were in institutional settings, a university student health service and a government hospital, which may have influenced the findings. Another factor may be some kind of decline of idealism, such as has been noted among medical students.[30] Although these students tend to become more idealistic as they are ready to leave medical school, idealism could again decline once medical practice is begun. Another possible interpretation is that these doctors are simply not trying to demonstrate their collective self-importance to themselves or to others by continuously claiming that they provide a most vital service to the public.

On the belief in self-regulation, no clear patterns emerge. Both stockbroker groups were strongly professional, as was one group of nurses and almost all the lawyers. The teachers and physicians emerge as rather weak on this attitude, although the variations in this attitude were rather slight. Among the teachers, this may reflect the fact that the professional organizations themselves have not been very successful in their attempts to gain the power of self-regulation. This would not be the case among the physicians, however. It might be that nonoccupational factors are operative here, such as the nature of the work setting, types of clients, or structure of the employing organization.

The most professional groups in regard to their sense of calling to the field are the librarians, nurses, and social workers. This variable is similar in many ways to belief in service to the public, with dedication perhaps substituting for compensation. The teachers do not fit this pattern, however, which may reflect the fact that many women appear to enter teaching simply because it is something that college-educated women do and because it allows the woman to work but does not tie her to one location if her family moves. A subjective impression is that many women choose teaching because it is a "safe" occupation for women who have no real sense of calling and who anticipate early marital or family obligations. A major in education will allow them to enter and leave and perhaps re-enter the occupation with relative ease. It is interesting to note that the lawyers are also relatively weak on this professional attribute, perhaps because late choice of law as a career characterizes many lawyers and law students. The physicians, with their rather programmed premedical training and longer periods of postgraduate work, have this attitude to a much higher degree.

[30]See Becker and Geer, "The Fate of Idealism in Medical School."

On the feeling of autonomy variable, the stockbrokers are again very professional. These men are quite autonomous in their day to day work, with direct client relationships and the expectation that they can make decisions and suggestions on their own. William M. Evan has suggested that the commission basis for earnings for stockbrokers and the general profit orientation of brokerage firms make it difficult for this group to be really considered as a profession,[31] but the evidence here is that they have a number of professional attitudes present to a high degree. Whether or not they act on the basis of these attitudes is, of course, another question. The lawyers also emerge as quite autonomous, while the nurses are the least autonomous of the groups. This latter finding is not surprising given the position of nurses in the hospital setting and their rather distinctive subordination to the medical staff. Few other patterns emerge on this variable.

When a more direct comparison is made between an occupation's position on the attitudinal components and its position in terms of Wilensky's structural formulation, it becomes even more clear that the attitudinal and the structural attributes do not necessarily vary together. For the purposes of this analysis, Wilensky's established, process, and doubtful categories were utilized, with the stockbrokers and personnel managers placed in the doubtful category. The other occupations were left in the categories suggested by Wilensky (see Table 4.2).

On the attitudinal variable of the professional organization as a reference group, the established professions were slightly more professional in their attitudes than the process group, which was in turn slightly more professional than the doubtful group. While this relationship is in the expected direction, it is weak and enough variations exist within each group to preclude a conclusion of correspondence of attitudinal and structural characteristics. On the belief in service to the public variable, the findings are in the direction which would be expected from the previous discussion: the process group, containing the teachers, social workers, and librarians, is the most professional, followed by the doubtful, and then the established. As noted previously, the fact that the process group is largely composed of women's occupations may contribute to the strength of this attitude. In light of the traditional role expectation that the woman's place is in the home, those who deviate from this expectation, at least to the degree that they have outside employment, might need a higher level of dedication to their occupation as

[31]"Status-Set and Role-Set Conflicts of the Stockbroker: A Problem in the Sociology of Law," *Social Forces*, XLV, 1 (September, 1966), 80–82.

Table 4.2. Ranks on Attitude Scales and Type of Profession (With One Way Analysis of Variance)[1]

	Average Rank	Type of Profession		
		Established	Process	Doubtful
1. Professional organization as reference group		19	12	5
		10	14	17
		20	15	1
		24	18	25
		6	22	4
		9	21	3
		8	7	
		16	11	
		13	2	
		23		
	$H = 2.44$ $P < .30$	14.8	13.6	9.2
2. Belief in service to the public		14	25	4
		12	15	21
		10.5	20	10.5
		9	13	23
		22	18.5	1
		16	24	6
		5	18.5	
		3	17	
		8	7	
		2		
	$H = 5.60$ $P < .10$	10.2	17.6	10.9
3. Belief in self-regulation		13.5	1	7.5
		18	10	6
		21	20	23
		17	9	24
		22	4.5	4.5
		13.5	11	7.5
		3	15	
		16	25	
		19	2	
		12		
	$H = 2.19$ $P < .40$	15.5	10.8	12.1

Table 4.2.   (continued)

	Average Rank	Type of Profession		
		Established	Process	Doubtful
4. Sense of calling to the field		8.5	10	13
		5	15	18
		11	25	4
		6.5	23	21
		1.5	24	5.5
		16.5	12	20
		1.5	22	
		19	3	
		8.5	16.5	
		14		
	$H = 5.20$	9.2	16.7	13.7
	$P <$ .10			
5. Feeling of autonomy		12	16	18
		20	8	21
		13	14	22
		9	2.5	25
		23	2.5	5.5
		17	15	11
		24	5.5	
		19	1	
		4	9	
		10		
	$H = 5.76$	15.1	8.2	17.1
	$P <$ .10			

[1] Lower rank indicates lower degree of professionalization.

a motivational source. Another important consideration here is the fact that these occupations are in the process of becoming known as professions. Their self-conscious effort to improve the status and conditions of the profession apparently leads to continual emphasis on professionalization on the part of training schools and professional organizations. This in turn is probably reflected in the strength of the attitudes expressed.

The patterns found on the belief in self-regulation and sense of calling to the field variables are similar to those on the professional organization as a reference group on belief in service to the public, respectively. With regard to the autonomy attitudinal variable, an interesting pattern emerges. The doubtful group is the most professional, followed closely by the established professions. The strength of the doubtful group is due to the presence of the advertising and brokerage occupations, which do in fact operate autonomously in their day-to-day work, with this being reflected in their attitudes, while the other occupations in this category express less autonomous attitudes. The established professions can and do operate on the basis of their professional judgments. The position of the process group as the weakest on this variable is undoubtedly based on their general subordination to other persons and other rules, which was discussed above. These findings suggest that the doubtful group might be able to achieve higher professionalization more readily than the process group, if the latter remains in a relatively subordinate position in its actual work situation.

The most obvious conclusion, which can be drawn from these results, is that the attitudinal and structural variables discussed do not necessarily vary together; the more professionalized occupations structurally are not always the most professionalized attitudinally. This has two implications. First, two of the attitudinal variables may actually have little to do with the process of professionalization, even though they are often cited as important to that process.[32] Belief in service to the public and a sense of calling to the field may be nice, but they appear to have little relevance to the position of an occupation in the over-all occupational structure. On the other hand, the use of the professional organization as a major reference, the belief in self-regulation, and the degree of autonomy appear to be quite central to professionalization, since they give the individual practitioner or the group some power in decision making and some

---

[32]Howard W. Vollmer and Donald L. Mills, "Some Comments on 'The Professionalization of Everyone?'" *American Journal of Sociology*, LXX, 4 (January, 1965), 481, note that the professional ideology may or may not be associated with the professionalization process.

protection from outside constraints. The professional can utilize judgment sources indigenous to his occupation, rather than relying on outside influences. The second implication of these findings is that the process of professionalization probably is based on much more than what the occupation does in trying to professionalize itself. A key, but often neglected, element of the whole process would appear to be public (community) acceptance of the occupation as a profession.[33] No level of attitudes nor set of prerequisites for entry will automatically place an occupation into the established or even the doubtful category of professionalization. Although it is not clear exactly what leads to such public acceptance, it is probably some combination of performance and public relations. If the latter is important, then the attitudinal characteristics may be important insofar as they are translated to clients and to the public. If an occupation can convince the public that it both acts and thinks according to professional standards, then its path to acceptance is probably shortened. An obvious problem with this sort of analysis is that the public remains amorphous and undefined. It is clear from such things as public opinion polls, however, that the public has opinions and that these opinions change; it would appear, therefore, that the attitudes and behavior of an occupational group could influence these opinions and thus affect the degree to which an occupation is considered a profession.

The second conclusion, which can be drawn from these findings, is that occupations vary in two ways from the professional model. Interprofession variations occur in that the occupations differ in their degree of professionalization on both the structural and attitudinal attributes. But intraprofession variations are even more important to understanding of the nature of the professions.[34] Even among the established professions, members and groups of members vary in the degree to which they conform to both aspects

[33]Marie R. Haug and Marvin B. Sussman suggest that public opinion is a critical element in professionalization and that the question of public opinion may best be approached through using segments of the public in determining public acceptance. These segments would be composed of colleagues and clients of the occupation being assessed and thus would be knowledgeable about it. This is suggested because of the intense specialization of the labor force. Haug and Sussman, "Professionalism and the Public," paper read at the meetings of the American Sociological Association, San Francisco, California, August, 1967.

[34]See Rue Bucher and Anselm Strauss, "Professions in Process," *American Journal of Sociology*, LXVI, 4 (January, 1961), 325–34 and Jack Ladinsky and Joel B. Grossman, "Organizational Consequences of Professional Consensus: Lawyers and Selection of Judges," *Administrative Science Quarterly*, XI, 1 (June, 1966), 79–106, for a discussion of this type of variation.

of the professional model. The sources of these variations will be examined in detail in the sections which follow.

sources of professional variation and differentiation

The findings suggest that the variations described undoubtedly have multiple sources. Certainly the socialization process during professional training has an impact, in addition to other individual and collective background factors. From the evidence presented, the setting of a profession or employment in or out of an organization probably will have a strong impact. With this in mind, the various settings for professional work will be analyzed.

the settings of professional work

The work of the occupations we are considering is carried out in three basic settings. The first is that of the individual practitioner. This setting often serves as the major model in discussions of the nature of professions. In this setting the professional is seen as a free, autonomous individual. The country doctor heeding the call of the sick or working in his laboratory, the individual lawyer searching for support for his client's position, or the architect developing original and controversial designs have been discussed and celebrated in fact and fiction. Although central to many conceptualizations of the nature of professional work, this type of setting is in actuality a disappearing phenomenon and, in addition, may contain elements dysfunctional for the professionals involved.

A second basic setting is the professional organization, such as the law firm, medical clinic, social work agency, or library. This type of setting is probably that of the majority of the occupational groups being considered. It should be divided into two subtypes, on the basis of W. Richard Scott's suggestion.[35] He notes that, on the one hand, there are autonomous professional organizations, in which the members of the profession determine the norms governing their behavior, with administrative tasks, which are of course necessary for the operation of any organization, essentially separate from professional tasks. The architectural firm, law firm, or medical clinic

[35]"Reactions to Supervision in a Heteronomous Professional Organization," *Administrative Science Quarterly*, XX, 1 (June, 1965), 65–81.

are examples of this subtype. The second subtype, according to Scott, is the "heteronomous" professional organization, in which the professional employees are at least partially subordinated to an externally imposed administrative framework. Examples are public schools, libraries, and social work agencies. These externally imposed norms, which often have a legislative origin, serve as a set of general or specific guidelines within which the professionals must operate, thereby lessening the amount of professional autonomy. Obvious examples of reduction of autonomy are the legal stipulations of welfare eligibility or the statewide selection of textbooks for schools. In both cases, the individual professional or the professional group as a whole has greatly diminished authority to determine their own clients or work materials.

The third basic setting is the professional department within a larger organization, such as engineering, legal, or research and development departments. In this setting the professional and his department are merely a part of a larger organization. It is often assumed that this setting confronts the professional with many situations in which organizational and bureaucratic norms conflict with professional standards. Scott, for example, has suggested that there are four basic sources of professional-organizational conflict.[36] The professional desiring to utilize his own internalized normative system may resist bureaucratic rules because they constrain the methods normally used to solve problems. A second source of conflict is the professional's resistance to bureaucratic standards. For example, a physician in an industrial setting may be asked by his employer to minimize time lost by getting workers back on the job as quickly as possible, but his professional standards demand a time consuming complete diagnosis and treatment of each case. A third source of conflict is the professional's resistance to bureaucratic supervision. In this case the professional is asked to subordinate himself to a system in which his superiors are likely not to have expertise in his specialty. In reality, it would probably be impossible for a person in a position of authority over a group of professionals to have competence in all areas in which his subordinates are operating. As Scott suggests, when "professionals enter bureaucratic organizations conflicts in the area of authority relations are widespread if not ubiquitous."[37] These same kinds of conflicts could conceivably be present in the two types of professional organizations previously discussed.

[36]"Professionals in Bureaucracies—Areas of Conflict," in *Professionalization,* eds. Vollmer and Mills, pp. 265–75.
[37]"Professionals in Bureaucracies—Areas of Conflict," in *Professionalization,* eds. Vollmer and Mills, p. 274.

The final source of conflict is the professional's conditional loyalty to the bureaucracy. If he uses his professional organization as a major reference, he is likely to view his employing organization simply as one of many potential employing organizations. If conditions arise that make his present situation undesirable, he will seek employment elsewhere, using his professional colleague group as a means of locating a new position. The employing organization is thus a means to an end. But Scott notes that, although a number of studies have shown professionally oriented workers to have low loyalty to their employing organization, the organization itself often has a reward system based upon successive advances within the organization. Thus for the organization advancement depends on the employee's not changing organizations. The "visible" professional, however, can advance within or without a particular organization.

While the existence of such professional-organizational conflict is indisputable, it is not clear whether professionals in the organizational setting experience more conflict than those in the other two kinds of settings. Furthermore, most of the analyses of the conflict appear to assume that the professionals are the "good guys" and that the organization blocks the "higher ideals" of professionalism, an assumption which would be most difficult to substantiate.

Regarding the relative potentials for conflict within the various types of settings, the author found that, while the autonomous professional organizations, discussed above, tended to be less bureaucratic than the heteronomous professional organizations or the professional departments within large organizations, the reverse was sometimes true on particular bureaucratic dimensions and within particular organizations.[38] For example, some legal departments were less bureaucratic than some law firms, which suggests that the potential for conflict for lawyers is at least as great within some law firms as it is within some legal departments. In this study it was also found that professional departments tended to be less bureaucratic than the heteronomous professional organizations. It would thus appear that those professionals in larger organizations do not necessarily confront situations that contain inherently more conflict potential than their colleagues in other types of settings.

One further point on professional-organizational conflict is relevant. While the kinds of conflicts that Scott and others have described have some negative consequences for both the organization and the professionals involved, there is no clear evidence

[38]Hall, "Professionalization and Bureaucratization," *American Sociological Review*, XXXIII, 1 (February, 1968), 92–104.

suggesting that the consequences are wholly negative. Lewis A. Coser, for example, has suggested that conflict per se may be positively functional in terms of creating solidarity within the conflicting groups while the conflict persists and of opening communications channels during its resolution.[39] For these reasons, it will not be assumed in the discussions that follow that a professional person or group experiences more conflict or more gratification in any one type of setting. With this in mind, the settings themselves will be more intensively examined.

the individual practitioner

While the individual, "free" professional appears to be the ideal type and has served at times as a sort of cultural hero, relatively little is actually known about his type of professional work. At best, perhaps, much of the data available is in the form of impressions about the individual practitioner, with only a few empirical studies to serve as points of departure. The general conclusion, which will be drawn in this analysis, is that this type of professional may in fact not be as professionalized as his counterparts in other settings; an even broader conclusion, which will be reached at the conclusion of the analysis of the work of professionals in the various settings, is that the professional model is not fully realized in practice by any of the groups involved.

Most of the occupations involved in individual practice fall in Wilensky's "established" category. The architect, lawyer, dentist, or physician in practice by himself is a clear example of this. At the same time, some of the occupations in the "process" category, such as optometrists, pharmacists, or veterinarians can and do operate on an individual basis, although there is a strong tendency for pharmacists to work under the auspices of large, multipurpose drug-store chains. Relatively few of the "new" or "doubtful" occupations are found in individual practice. Some funeral directors operate their own establishments, but the trend toward larger organizations is evident here. Marriage counseling, where it is carried out as a separate occupation, is often done on an individual basis. Other professionalizing occupations also appear at times in the individual-practice setting, but the previously noted trend toward organizational work appears to be a major factor operating against individ-

[39]*The Functions of Social Conflict* (New York: The Free Press of Glencoe, Inc., 1956), pp. 72–148.

ual practice. The place of scientists of various kinds along the professionalization continuum is still somewhat unclear, but if scientists are considered professionals to any degree, they are almost totally employed by industry, government, or academic institutions. The lone scientist working in (and blowing up) his basement is a product of literary imagination.

If the ranks of individual practitioners are thinning in comparison to those of professionals in other settings, the question remains, what are the unique characteristics of the solo practitioner? Does he vary in terms of his background? Are there any special characteristics about the kinds of work he does? Where does he fit into the overall professional structure?

Among the various occupations found in this setting, lawyers have been the most intensively examined. In *Lawyers on Their Own*, Jerome Carlin analyzed a sample of individual practitioners in Chicago.[40] Carlin points out that over half of all lawyers are in individual practice, regardless of the size of the community in which they practice. Since the majority of lawyers are found in cities with populations in excess of 200,000, this study can be taken as at least partially representative of the majority of individual practitioners, although the Chicago situation may be somewhat unique. Later studies in Detroit and New York, to be noted below, seem to confirm the Carlin findings regarding the characteristics of the urban individual practitioner.

The most striking finding in the Carlin study is that the individual practitioner is separated, both in terms of the kinds of legal work performed and in terms of social status, from the rest of the legal profession. Part of the reason for this is the background of lawyers in individual practice. They tend to be self-made men, who have risen the hard way from lower- or working-class backgrounds and immigrant parents.[41] Their rise is into the ranks of a profession, even though their status within the profession is quite low. The majority of this group did not attend full-time law schools but received their legal training in Catholic night law schools or proprietary law schools, which have no university affiliations and are sometimes operated for profit.[42] At the time these lawyers attended them, the part-time schools were clearly inferior to the full-time, university-affiliated law schools; entrance often demanded little more than a high-school diploma, and a much smaller percentage of

[40]*Lawyers on Their Own* (New Brunswick, N.J.: Rutgers University Press, 1962).
[41]Carlin, *Lawyers on Their Own*, p. 3.
[42]Carlin, *Lawyers on Their Own*, pp. 6, 18.

the graduates passed the bar exam. Nevertheless, the lawyers who made it through such schools and passed the bar exam have all the rights and privileges of other lawyers, at least at the formal level.

The background of these lawyers reveals another interesting fact. Many of them entered the field of law by default; originally wanting to pursue another professional career, they found the training too difficult or too expensive or thought that their background would serve as a basis for discrimination against them. They thus did not have a sense of calling to the field, but rather a sense of calling to become a professional person.

Despite the high hopes they often had for their careers as professionals, many of these lawyers engage in the most marginal areas of the law, such as personal-injury cases, collections, rent cases, and evictions. One of their major problems is simply getting business, as direct and severe competition from other occupations is beginning to undermine their work in many areas. Thus accountants and real-estate brokers are increasingly able to handle the tax and real-estate work, traditionally done by the solo practitioner. Carlin notes that the pressures to earn a livelihood may force the solo lawyer to submit to pressures to violate legal ethics[43] and in a later study, to be discussed below, suggests that this is in fact the case. The financial incentive may also force the individual lawyer to become a middleman or broker between clients and other lawyers in order to receive referral fees. The decision to refer a case is often not based on the best interests of the client but on the lawyer's desire to obtain the largest settlement or recovery, and hence the largest commission. The solo lawyer thus may become a businessman rather than a lawyer, defeating his own purpose in becoming a professional in the first place.

Carlin summarizes his findings by stating:

> In considering the work of the individual lawyer in Chicago, one is drawn to the conclusion that he is rarely called upon to exercise a high level of professional skill. This arises in part from the generally low quality of his professional training, but even more from the character of the demands placed upon him by the kinds of work and clients he is likely to encounter. Most matters that reach the individual practitioner—the small residential closing, the simple uncontested divorce, drawing up a will or probating a small estate, routine filings for a small business, negotiating a personal-injury claim, or collecting on a debt—do not require very much technical knowledge, and

[43]*Lawyers on Their Own*, p. 209.

what technical problems there are are generally simplified by use of standard forms and procedures.[44]

This pessimistic conclusion about the solo practitioner says little about the way the individuals in this type of work feel about their own existence. Carlin notes that these lawyers tend to deny their low status by stressing their independence and the fact that they are in the general practice of all facets of the law. This feeling of autonomy, however, does not overcome the fact that these lawyers also feel insignificant in the over-all legal structure and are frustrated because their high ambitions have not been realized, even though they are professionals. Carlin suggests that these individual practitioners, like general practitioners in medicine, are "most likely to be found at the margin of [their] profession, enjoying little freedom in choice of clients, type of work, or conditions of practice."[45] Furthermore, their verbalizations of autonomy do not correspond to the facts, and they appear to realize that individual practitioners have little freedom. They only get the business that comes their way or that they can bring in. Their cases usually are in one type of legal practice, such as personal injury or small-business taxation, and they are generally geographically limited to their immediate neighborhoods.

This picture of the individual lawyer is strengthened by Jack Ladinsky's findings regarding a sample of lawyers in Detroit.[46] These data reveal that solo lawyers come from minority religious and ethnic backgrounds, have parents of entrepreneurial or small business status, and receive qualitatively and quantitatively inferior educations more often than the lawyers in law-firm practice included in the study.[47] Ladinsky suggests that these lawyers select this role for themselves, to a degree, in that the minority background of many of them has taught them to expect discrimination in the hiring policies of firms and to avoid it by entering individual practice. At the same time, overt discrimination is a reality, and the lawyer with this type of background who tries to get into firm practice will have a difficult time. Ladinsky suggests that discrimination and self-selection interact to perpetuate the situation. Like Carlin, he also suggests that the work of the solo practitioner is being eroded by outside agencies, such as automobile clubs, insurance and real-estate companies, abstracting firms, banks and sav-

[44]*Lawyers on Their Own*, pp. 206–7.
[45]*Lawyers on Their Own*, p. 206.
[46]"Careers of Lawyers, Law Practice, and Legal Institutions," *American Sociological Review*, XXVIII, 1 (February, 1963), 47–54.
[47]"Careers of Lawyers, Law Practice, and Legal Institutions," p. 49.

ings-and-loan associations, and accounting firms. Thus, the "minority lawyer, then, inoculated with the ethic of entrepreneurship, goes solo to remain 'free'—only to discover that freedom to practice the rounded kind of law he desires has eluded him."[48] Though he may work outside of bureaucratic organizations, he finds that organizations not belonging to the profession have taken over many of his functions.

One further note about the metropolitan individual practitioner should be made. Carlin, in following up some leads from his earlier work, examined the degree to which a sample of lawyers in New York accepted and conformed to ethical norms.[49] He found that the individual practitioner was the most likely to violate these norms, with the nature of the client and type of case being important contributing factors in the violations. Both Carlin and Ladinsky suggest that their findings have real importance for the practice of law. Since these lawyers often represent individuals, as opposed to corporations, which are represented by the larger law firms, the quality of the lawyers involved adversely affects the legal representation, which many individuals receive. Since these lawyers are often from minority groups, minority clients are the ones who are adversely affected. Furthermore, many of the larger, more prestigious and more ethical firms will not accept the kinds of cases the solo practitioner confronts and, in fact, refer these cases to him, so that the organization of the bar is such that ethical violations and ineffective legal practice are almost built into certain situations.

The discussion thus far has concentrated on the metropolitan bar. Certainly many of the findings would be inapplicable to the legal profession in smaller cities and towns, although Carlin suggests that even here the individual practitioner is at a disadvantage. Spatial isolation from research centers often puts a professional at a disadvantage in terms of access to new developments in his field, and the problem is intensified if he is in private practice. But the solo practitioner in these settings is unlikely to be a minority group member and is probably no more or less likely to be unethical than members of small firms in the same setting.

Rather obviously, everyone has known individual practitioners in law or medicine in either smaller or larger communities who are dedicated to their field, its ethics, and their clients and who try, despite the difficulty, to keep up with the rapid developments in their field. What is being suggested here is that such factors as the growth

[48]Ladinsky, "Careers of Lawyers, Law Practice, and Legal Institutions," p. 54.
[49]*Lawyers' Ethics* (New York: Russell Sage Foundation, 1966).

of group practice of various sorts, limited access to communication processes and to financial rewards, and the growing complexity of the professions themselves militate against the solo practitioner. For most fields, therefore, individual practice is probably just an image of the past, and like many such images, revered, but somewhat irrelevant.

Some professions, both established and otherwise, such as dentistry and optometry, still appear to be largely practiced individually. But the trend toward organizational work may involve professions such as these when the desirability of specialization, leading to a need for a coordinated group of specialists in the clinic setting, and the financial and temporal advantages of group practice become more apparent. A higher volume of clients can probably be handled in group practice, and the practitioners can rotate the time allotted for being "on call," thus leaving more time free for other activities. This is not meant to suggest that group, firm, or organizational practice is a panacea for professional problems or that problems in the areas of ethics and the place of the individual client in the system can be solved by a more organized kind of practice. Extensive changes toward more organized practice would presuppose that discrimination on grounds other than professional competence would be eliminated, since one of the key factors in keeping people out of group practice, at least among the lawyers, seems to be actual or perceived discrimination on the basis of race, religion, or ethnicity. Since the total elimination of such discrimination is rather unlikely, the solo practitioner will probably remain in the system as a minority professional. Even if discrimination were to be limited to professional competence, with those who are less competent not admitted to organized practice, the persons discriminated against might still filter down to individual practice, thus maintaining its low status.

Two additional and somewhat related points should be raised before turning to an examination of the professional in the organized setting. In the discussion of the reasons for the relatively low quality of the solo lawyer, the role of the inferior part-time law school in producing such lawyers was mentioned. The part-time law school is a type of professional training institution that is unique to the legal profession, although many students attend graduate schools on a part-time basis. It has served as a means of social mobility for many persons who do not have the financial resources for full-time study or who prefer to work and study part-time. Thus, though these schools have given inferior training when compared with full-time schools, they appear to serve an important function.

One obvious solution to this dilemma is to improve the quality of the part-time schools, thus maintaining a source of legal training for those who would otherwise be unable to acquire any, while providing them with training that would be at least roughly comparable to that received from full-time schools. This, of course, is more easily said than done.

The second point is related to the place of the person seeking good legal representation within the legal system. If Carlin is correct in his assertion that law firms tend to deal with corporate clients, which seems to be the case at least in metropolitan areas, trends toward even more such organized practice in law, as well as in the other professions, may create a situation in which the individual has little access to professional services. This would appear to be particularly true in situations wherein a client must be understood on more than the basis of particular legal, medical, or social symptoms. The recurring concern of the medical profession about the disappearing general practitioner and the steps it has taken to create a "family physician" specialty exemplify this trend. Here again, the development of techniques to deal with these individualized problems is probably up to the professional organizations involved, since as we have seen, they tend to exercise the major control over the profession. Organized professional practice need not be concerned with highly specialized problems, even though this has been the tendency, as will be seen in the next section.

the autonomous professional organization

As previously stated, the autonomous professional organization is one in which the members of the profession determine its structure. Consequently, norms and sanctions are established in keeping with the expectations of the professionals involved. Decisions in regard to type of practice, criteria for selection and advancement of members, distribution of income, etc. are made by the professionals in the organization. The organizational structure is thus in a sense imported from the outside in terms of the norms of the profession itself. The organization is designed to accomplish the goals of the profession.

In the discussion of the individual practitioner it was apparent that his type of professional practice contains elements leading to deviations from the ideal-type professional model. The autonomous organizational setting also contains such elements, although they take a very different form and produce correspondingly different results. The autonomous setting is most clearly exemplified by the law or architectural firm or the medical clinic, which are organized around established professions. Organizations such as advertising agencies, management-consultant firms, or marriage-counseling clinics are also autonomous professional organizations, but their professional basis is less well developed in terms of traditions or acceptance. They appear to lack the normative base that the established professions have. Unfortunately, comparative data are not available to assist in the analysis of the differences between types of autonomous professional organizations. Data are available regarding some such organizations, however, and the contrasts with individual practice can easily be seen.

One of the most thorough analyses of the autonomous professional organization is Erwin O. Smigel's *Wall Street Lawyer*. The legal profession has perhaps been the most comprehensively examined profession because of its centrality to the wider social structure. Although the Wall Street law firm is not typical of the majority of law firms in the United States, because of its size and type of practice, the contrast between this type of legal practice and that previously discussed illustrates the immense diversity within the legal profession and suggests that such intraprofessional differentiation is not unique to the law.

The law firms studied by Smigel perform a number of functions.[50] First and foremost, they are spokesmen for much of big business in the United States. Not only do they represent business, but many members of the firms serve as members of the boards of directors of the corporations they represent. While such membership might be viewed as an impediment to professional judgment, it is generally assumed that the Wall Street law firm will serve as the legal conscience for the corporations. These lawyers also develop much of the business law in the United States through their intellectual and financial resources. Smigel suggests that many judges rely upon the briefs prepared by respected firms as the bases for their own decisions.

A second major function of these firms is that of recruiting centers for government service. Members of the firms are appointed to important governmental positions and seek national political offices; prominent examples are Adlai Stevenson, John Foster Dulles, Thomas E. Dewey, and Senator Clifford Case of New Jersey.

[50]The following material is a condensation of the material in Erwin O. Smigel, *The Wall Street Lawyer* (New York: The Free Press of Glencoe, Inc., 1964), pp. 1–14, 38–40, 47–100, 296–307, and 343–50.

Many other members of the firms are active in various capacities for national, state, and local governmental agencies. Wall Street lawyers also participate in civic and philanthropic activities, such as the Metropolitan Opera, various art museums, and other cultural and charitable affairs. Here again the national impact is great, since many of these orgnizations and activities have a scope much wider than the New York metropolitan area. The Wall Street law firms also are important in international relations, since many of their corporate clients deal extensively with foreign governments. The Wall Street lawyer is thus an important figure not only as a type of professional, for the purposes of this analysis, but also in his own right. Smigel's analysis is concerned primarily with how the law firms operate and the impact this has on the individuals involved and the legal profession. Our concern is similar, with particular emphasis on the effect of this kind of organizational setting on the idealized professional model.

These law firms are large, the smallest one considered having 50 lawyers on the staff and the largest having 125. Smigel had some difficulty in gaining entree into the firms because most of the lawyers felt that professional and organizational ethics would be violated when clients and their cases were discussed. Many also felt that the profession itself was rather sacred and should not be investigated. Gradually Smigel was able to persuade most of the firms that his research would not threaten them or their clients and that the results might well be beneficial to the profession.

The lawyers involved have personal backgrounds that are in direct contrast to those of the solo practitioners. The most striking fact is that over 70 per cent of the lawyers had attended Harvard, Yale, or Columbia law school—in most assessments the elite schools of the nation—and were top students. The Wall Street law firms actively recruit these top men and would prefer all their lawyers to have these credentials. The firms also look for the "correct" family background, which is viewed as being important in the development of the proper social graces and for contacts to bring business in the future. The recruit should also have the type of personality that fits with those of the members of the firm.

Lawyers with this set of credentials, which the potential recruit should have, are obviously in short supply. Since competition among the firms is keen and there is increasing competition for top law-school graduates from firms outside of New York and from various governmental units, the firms are being forced to look beyond the Ivy League schools for their recruits. They are apparently hiring Jewish graduates more frequently, a practice which was rare in the very recent past. As more and more Jewish students are able to enroll in the prestige law schools, and as the performance level of these students puts them near the top of the class, the trend will probably increase. Relatively few Catholic lawyers are found in the Wall Street firms, because of what are considered to be lower class origins, poorer education, and, often, immigrant parents. Since few Negroes attend Ivy League undergraduate or law schools, the pool of potential candidates here is low. Additionally, it is thought that the Negro lawyer would not "fit in" in dealing with most clients. As Smigel suggests, from the point of view of the law firms themselves, this seems rational. As might be expected, there are very few women attorneys in the Wall Street firms. Smigel notes that there is greater discrimination against women than against Jewish recruits. The law firms believe that clients would object to women lawyers and that the women are likely to get married and leave. In addition to these reasons for the exclusion of women, which seem rational from the point of view of the firm, an antiwomen bias is also evident in many firms. Smigel notes that one firm "still elects to employ male stenographers when it can get them."[51]

The differences in background between these Wall Street lawyers and their colleagues in individual practice is so great that the term colleague itself is probably inapplicable. The Wall Street lawyer has a superior education, both quantitatively and qualitatively. The individual practitioner often is a member of a minority group, a fact which has no effect on his ability to practice law but which puts him into contact with minority, hence less powerful, clients, while the Wall Street lawyer deals with the corporate and governmental seats of power. As will be seen below, the kind of law practiced is also clearly different.

Before turning to an examination of the work of the Wall Street lawyer, it should be pointed out that not every graduate of the prestige law schools desires this type of practice. An additional fact the firms have to face is that they do not always appear to be the most desirable places to work for law students. Many potential employees believe that the specialization in the large law office is so great that they would soon become limited in their abilities. Others feel that they would be lost in such a setting and would have a greater chance for advancement elsewhere. The hiring practices of some firms are hindered by having, for one reason or another, the reputation of being cold and unfriendly "law factories." Since the firms are competing for the same men, they try to build their images

[51] *The Wall Street Lawyer*, p. 47.

as good places to work. They try to de-emphasize their departmentalization and emphasize the opportunities to work at all phases of the organization's activities. They also stress the excellent training the graduate will receive in the firm. Many graduates in fact look upon experience in a Wall Street firm as an excellent post-graduate training period, which will serve as a basis for future positions in industry or government. The competition between firms is a controlled competition in the sense that there are unwritten rules regarding the kinds of inducements offered, with all firms offering the same starting salaries and other benefits; but they compete strongly at the symbolic level of the attractiveness of working in one firm as opposed to another. The hiring process has become routinized to the extent that specific persons are designated as "hiring partners," whose function is to seek out top prospects and to screen applicants. These men become personnel men as well as lawyers, with visitations to the law schools and routinized interview procedures.

The selection process for the Wall Street firms in reality is highly structured and programmed. Minority lawyers, graduates of less desirable law schools, and poor performers are automatically excluded. The combination of the proper preparatory school, undergraduate college, and law school puts a candidate, who is interested in this type of practice, into contention for an associate position in a Wall Street firm. As the competition becomes more severe for these people, the requirements themselves will probably change, with more minority lawyers being considered, if they are the "right type," and a broader range of law schools being regarded as appropriate.

The careers of the men who join a Wall Street firm are not locked into a set pattern once the hiring process is completed. Several career patterns can be identified. Some graduates plan to use the Wall Street firm solely as post-graduate training for positions in big business. The pay offered by corporations is a great deal more than the relatively low pay that beginning firm lawyers receive. Thus some men who did not intend to go into corporate practice do so because of the financial inducements. This, of course, is a slight, but normal, variation from the idealized professional person, who is dedicated to his work and has relatively little interest in the material advantages it can bring. Others who leave the Wall Street firm after a relatively short internship do so for family reasons, finding the time demands from the firm too severe for their wives and children. Smigel notes that the firms actually encourage such "dropping out," since they do not want lawyers who are not devoted to this type of practice.

Another interesting pattern is found among those lawyers who realize that they will not be chosen for partnership in the firms. For some, this constitutes a form of failure, even though they take rewarding and important jobs in industry or in smaller firms. Failure is thus a highly relative thing, since these failures are professionally and financially in much stronger positions than the solo practitioners discussed above. Others who are not accepted into partnership remain with the firms as permanent associates, a position which is usually viewed by incoming associates as another form of failure. The permanent associates are typically specialists in particular areas who are secure in their positions. They are important to the law firms, despite their lack of success by the firms' standards.

For the incoming associate, the patterns discussed above are discernible career paths, and if the new associate has a strong desire to move into a partnership position in the firm, they are paths to be avoided. For such a person, competition with his cohorts is very strong. Smigel discusses the various systems of cues by which the associates can judge their progress. These cues range from the amount of responsibility and the difficulty of the assignments given to the associate to the relative size of his end-of-the-year bonus. The average amount of time spent at the associate level for those who become partners is eight and one-half years, but, as some men move up to the partnership level as early as the sixth year, the period of real tension for the aspiring associate begins rather early in his career. The competition, though keen, is gentlemanly; the associate is judged on the basis of his ability and personality. If he is perceived as pushing too hard, this will operate against him. Both partners and associates stress the fact that hard and good work are the keys to advancement into the partnership position.

Definite patterns exist in the kind of work performed by the lawyers at particular phases of their careers. The beginning associate is viewed as having limited skills, even with his elite education, and is put to work preparing briefs and engaging in legal research under the supervision of a partner or a senior associate. Since the cases handled by these firms are usually very complex, the associate works on only a small segment of the over-all problem. As he is doing this, he learns legal and social skills. His interactions with the various partners to whom he is assigned have a great deal to do with his future in the firm.

As his tenure with the firm continues, he is given more and more responsibility. He begins to have contact with clients. While his work is still specialized, his area of responsibility in particular cases is broadened. As associates move toward partnership positions, some assume supervisory positions over beginning associates. Once partnership is achieved, even more client contacts are maintained. The new partner still performs specialized work, but as time passes he assumes broadened responsibilities over cases. The senior partner is an advisor and administrator; he does little research on his own but is very knowledgeable about the entire range of the particular cases he is handling. Smigel suggests that the senior partner becomes a general practitioner in the area of business law. He manages and coordinates the work of his subordinates, and his role of advisor is based upon his knowledge and experiences.

The Wall Street law firm is somewhat unique in that it specializes in business law. At the same time, Smigel notes that its organization and practices are very similar to those of other large law firms, whether in New York or elsewhere. If this is the case, the large law firm, like solo practice, creates conditions which are clearly deviant from the idealized professional model. In the first place, the associate is an employee rather than a free professional; he works on a salaried basis and is thus rewarded like any other employee. He takes orders and works under supervision. Indeed, this is an additional reason for some associates' decisions to leave this type of practice. While the legal profession as a whole places a high value on disputation, the associate is expected to dispute tactfully and only up to the point a partner expects. He is in fact not autonomous. In addition, strict, but unwritten, standards of dress and decorum are upheld.

The partner does not escape from this deviation. A great amount of his time is spent in bringing in and maintaining business for the firm. With large overhead expenses, the firms must maintain a dollar volume in order to survive. Since they do, the efforts of the partners must be viewed as successful, but at the expense of the practice of the profession. In addition, the complexity of the cases involved requires the specialization and coordination discussed above. The partner thus becomes a caller of committee meetings, further dissipating the amount of time devoted to legal practice.

Despite these variations from the professional model, Smigel suggests that the Wall Street firm contains elements essential to the model. Extremely high ethical standards are maintained. The emphasis on performance as the basis for advancement is central to a rational profession. Specialization itself is required when complex issues are confronted, for without specialization, the answers to complex problems could not be found.

Smaller law firms in and out of metropolitan areas have not been systematically investigated. It would appear that these smaller firms and their members escape some of the problems of specialization and lack of autonomy noted previously. At the same time, similar pressures to bring in business operate. Also, these lawyers probably, although not necessarily, have received inferior training, both in law school and in practice. If they are in the general practice of law, their knowledge base and facilities, such as libraries, appear to be inferior.

But the concern of this chapter is not with lawyers per se, and the problems confronting the practice of law in the various settings thus far discussed appear not to be unique to this profession. If we take the Wall Street firm as the elite of its profession, as Smigel believes we can, then it is clear that the autonomous professional organization, like solo practice, confronts the professional with a setting in which the ideal form of professional practice cannot be achieved.

Freidson and Rhea's analysis of a large medical clinic provides additional insights into the nature of professional practice in the autonomous setting and into an important issue in the general area of professionalization.[52] This study was concerned with the self-regulation of professionals. Freidson and Rhea note:

> Professionals have the special privilege of freedom from the control of outsiders. Their privilege is justified by three claims. First, their work entails such a high degree of skill and knowledge that only fellow professionals can make accurate assessments of professional performance. Second, a high degree of selflessness and responsibility characterizes professionals, so they can be trusted to work conscientiously. Third, in those rare instances in which individual professionals do not perform with skill or conscientiousness, their colleagues may be trusted to take the proper regulatory action.[53]

These claims and the privilege that they support were verbalized by many of the lawyers interviewed by Smigel. The issue of self-regulation is also central to Carlin's analysis of lawyers' ethics. He suggests that the large firm is better able to enforce ethical standards on its members than is the bar itself on its individual and group members. But Freidson and Rhea's findings suggest that, while group practice may enhance the level of adherence to ethical and performance standards, the self-regulation system in such a setting is less than perfect.

[52]See Eliot Freidson and Buford Rhea, "Knowledge and Judgment in Professional Evaluation," *Administrative Science Quarterly*, X, 1 (June, 1965), 107–24.

[53]"Knowledge and Judgment in Professional Evaluation," pp. 107–8.

Many of the doctors in the clinic studied were unable to rate some of their colleagues' competence levels. The rating process in the clinic was structured according to specialties; those specialties which do not refer clients to each other (pediatrics and ophthamology, for example) have very little knowledge about each other. The knowledge level was relatively high, however, within specialties. Systematic differences also appeared in the competence rating according to age and length of tenure in the clinic. Younger doctors consistently gave lower ratings to their colleagues. Newcomers to the clinic are rated lower than oldtimers, regardless of their age. Other aspects of the organizational structure also affect the rating process. For example, physicians in obstetrics-gynecology were rated as quite competent by pediatricians, but as having much less competence by specialists in internal medicine. As the authors point out, the pediatricians only see the successful products of the obstetricians' work—healthy babies. The physicians in internal medicine, on the other hand, share the gynecologists' problems.[54]

Freidson and Rhea suggest that their findings indicate that the "prerequisites for regulation do not seem well enough developed to allow an extensive and coherent process of professional regulation."[55] Despite the fact that the process is less than perfect, gross or potentially dangerous misconduct would be rather quickly handled, in the opinion of these authors. The lack of information about colleagues does not appear to affect evaluations on serious matters. Nevertheless, these findings suggest that this type of autonomous professional organization does not lend itself to a comprehensive evaluatory system. This clinic, like the Wall Street law firm, relies upon the records of its recruits as evidence of competence, and a person, once admitted, is assumed to be competent. The question that remains unanswered concerns the manner in which self-regulation occurs for professionals outside the rather elite establishments discussed. If the communications processes contain blockages in the organized setting, they are undoubtedly also present in other types of practice.

the heteronomous professional organization

The autonomous professional organization is characterized by many elements that allow the professionals operating in it to exer-

[54]Freidson and Rhea, "Knowledge and Judgment in Professional Evaluation," pp. 116–20.
[55]"Knowledge and Judgment in Professional Evaluation," p. 122.

cise a great deal of personal and collective autonomy. Professional judgment is maximized, and the individual is expected to reach his own conclusions regarding the appropriate disposition of the various issues he confronts. Despite the conformity of dress and decorum demanded of the Wall Street lawyer, he is expected to remain "creatively conformist" in his thoughts. The conformity is limited to certain generally accepted legal and firm-based standards. In the heteronomous type organization,

> professional employees are clearly subordinated to an administrative framework, and the amount of autonomy granted professional employees is relatively small. An elaborate set of rules and a system of routine supervision control many if not most aspects of the tasks performed by professional employees, so that it is often difficult, if not impossible, to locate or define an arena of activity for which the professional group is responsible individually or collectively.
>
> Examples of professional organizations often corresponding to this type include many public agencies—libraries, secondary schools, social welfare agencies—as well as some private organizations such as small religious colleges and firms engaged in applied research.[56]

In his development of the nature of the heteronomous professional organization, Scott does not attempt to explain why these external constraints are present in these organizations. He suggests that, in general, the stronger professions, such as medicine and law, enjoy mandates allowing them greater autonomy. This argument is weakened by the existence of autonomous organizations, such as advertising or management consulting, among the less professionalized occupations. He also notes that a majority of the occupations found in the heteronomous setting are composed largely of women, a fact which apparently hinders professionalization. But, while these factors are certainly operative, two additional considerations appear to be of even greater importance.

In their book, *Formal Organizations*, Peter M. Blau and W. Richard Scott develop an organizational typology based on the principle of *cui bono*—who benefits? This typology is designed to demonstrate that the nature of the public served by an organization has a strong impact on the kinds of problems it confronts. The four basic types are the "mutual benefit" organizations, in which the

[56]Scott, "Reactions to Supervision in a Heteronomous Professional Organization," p. 67.

membership is the prime beneficiary; the "business" concerns, in which the owners are the prime beneficiaries; "service" organizations, in which the client group receives the major benefits; and "commonweal" organizations, in which the public at large is the prime beneficiary.[57] Blau and Scott argue that organizations that fit the heteronomous category are service organizations, since the client group, such as the student or the welfare case, is the prime beneficiary of the services provided. While the clients hopefully do benefit from the services, a strong case can be made for labeling these organizations as commonweal types. The public at large benefits from the educational process, and in fact is highly dependent upon it. It also benefits, socially and financially, from the work of social welfare agencies. Since the public has such a stake in the results of the work of these organizations, it is understandable that it also wants a role in their operation. Obviously, the extent to which the public, through controlling boards, should control such organizations is difficult to determine. Many teachers and social workers would suggest that lack of professional knowledge on the part of the controlling public actually is detrimental to the operation of such organizations. Nevertheless, the fact remains that these organizations are at least partially "commonweal" in their outputs and orientations.

This is related to the second factor which probably exerts pressure toward external controls on the professionals in the heteronomous organizations. The general public, in addition to having a stake in the operation of the organization, also has strong opinions and a belief in its own knowledge about the actual work done by the professionals involved. Most parents, for example, believe that they know their children better than the teachers and many probably feel that they would be effective teachers. Social welfare programs are controversial for many reasons; many lay people obviously believe that their own solutions to the problems of the indigent and the unemployed would be superior to those of the social workers trained in the area. In short, the public appears to believe that the professionals do not have any particular knowledge that is not available to the general masses.[58] Critics of the education of teachers have probably added fuel to this argument by their insistence that teacher education itself is not intellectually demanding.

For whatever reasons, the heteronomous professional organi-

[57]Blau and Scott, *Formal Organizations* (San Francisco, Chandler Publishing Company, 1962), pp. 45–57.
[58]In Everett C. Hughes' terms, these professionals have neither "licence nor the mandate" sufficient to command the amount of public respect necessary for them to carry out their own judgments. See Hughes, *Men and Their Work* (New York: The Free Press of Glencoe, Inc., 1958), pp. 78–87.

zation has externally imposed rules and standards. These can range from legislatively developed laws regarding welfare eligibility or child adoption procedures to the selection of textbooks by state boards of education. The professional person in such an organization cannot exercise professional discretion in any area where these external norms prevail. If he does so, he violates the norms and is potentially subject to censure. As Harold L. Wilensky and Charles N. Lebeaux note in regard to public welfare workers,

> public welfare programs are framed in law, and the agency operates in a "goldfish bowl." The basic law setting up a program is usually brief; administration of the program requires an endless flow of regulations which comprise the everchanging "Manual." Operation in the glare of publicity may create an atmosphere of insecurity which . . . tends to foster rigidity and proceduralism.[59]

In some ways, less conflict for the professionals in such settings would be generated if they held weaker ideals of professionalism or professional attitudes. Blau and Scott, for example, found that the professionally oriented social workers in the agency they studied were much more likely to be critical of the agency and the laws and procedures governing it than were the less professionally oriented workers.[60] Scott's further analysis of data from the same study found that the professionally oriented workers were also more likely to be critical of their supervisors and the overall organizational system.[61]

In his analysis of the role of the teacher, Ronald G. Corwin suggests:

> Teachers have virtually no control over their standards of work. They have little control over the subjects to be taught; the materials to be used; the criteria for deciding who should be admitted, retained, and graduated from training schools; the qualifications for teacher training; the forms to be used in reporting student progress; school boundary lines and the criteria for permitting students to attend; and other matters that affect teaching. Teachers have little voice in determining who is qualified to enter teaching. Nonprofessionals control the state boards which set standards for teaching certificates.[62]

[59]*Industrial Society and Social Welfare* (New York: The Free Press of Glencoe, Inc., 1965), p. 246.

[60]*Formal Organizations*, pp. 71–74.

[61]"Reactions to Supervision in a Heteronomous Professional Organization," p. 81.

[62]*A Sociology of Education* (New York: Appleton-Century-Crofts, 1965), p. 241.

In his own research Corwin found that teachers who are highly professionally oriented are usually militant in their professionalism. They want to change the system. At the same time these teachers experience the most numerous and intense conflicts in the schools, as evidenced by heated discussions or major incidents. They are the most dissatisfied with the system. Teachers who accept the status of an employee, as opposed to that of a professional, are likely to be satisfied with the system.[63] Here again, a high level of professionalism is dysfunctional for the smooth operation of the organizations involved. If it is assumed, however, that a high level of professionalism is beneficial for the client groups and for the public, then the external controls found in the heteronomous organizations are what is dysfunctional. These organizations are thus in an extremely difficult dilemma. Public control and accountability are probably necessary and worthwhile, as is a high level of professionalism. Procedures have yet to be developed that will allow the maximization of both sources of control. It is probably possible to devise a system where both can be optimized, but the centrality of the services performed make it appear unlikely that the public would want to relinquish its role in the control process. It could be hypothesized, however, that increased demonstration of professionalization on the part of occupations involved would yield them greater controls.

An additional aspect of the heteronomous professional organization is that it is a rather "flat" organization; the professional members usually have exactly the same title, with relatively minor pay differentials if the qualifications for employment are enforced. If a person is to advance, he must do so by leaving the profession; that is, he must take a supervisory position in which he no longer engages in professional practice. While advancement in the autonomous type of organization does not involve a change in title (once a lawyer, a person remains a lawyer even though he may move up from associate to partner), the differentials in pay and status are wide and recognizable. In the heteronomous professional organization, this is not the case.

The heteronomous professional organization confronts its members with conditions far from optimal in terms of individual or collective professional advancement. While the individual can certainly improve his skills and knowledge, the organizational structure tends to prevent their effective utilization and may even provide a source of real stress for the professional. It would seem that if

[63]Corwin, *A Sociology of Education*, pp. 258–63.

an occupation as a whole increases its degree of professionalization, employment in heteronomous organizations would lead to collective frustration. Maximal use of professional skills and knowledge appears to be contingent upon a work setting which allows their utilization. Therefore, increased professionalization should be accompanied by reduced external controls. Whether this is possible is difficult to assess, given the previously discussed lay concerns about the operations of such organizations.

the professional department

As mentioned above, the professional department is generally thought to be the setting wherein the professional is likely to be confronted with the most frequent and severe conflicts between professional and organizational norms and values. Occupations at various degrees of professionalization are found in larger organizations. The medical or legal staffs of private and public organizations, libraries in business firms or universities, or advertising or personnel departments exemplify the diversity of professionals found in this setting.

In an analysis of scientists in an industrial setting, William Kornhauser found that there are built-in strains between organizational and professional values. While such values may not be crucial in the professionalization process, they are important factors in everyday work situations.[64] Kornhauser suggests that there are four areas in which professional and organizational values are in basic conflict. The first is the nature of the goals sought. The professional scientist seeks excellence and adherence to scientific standards. The organization also seeks excellence, but wants its scientists to come up with profitable developments in a regular fashion. But the nature of science is such that the developments may not only fail to be profitable but also may not occur with any temporal regularity. It is important to note that both sets of goals are legitimate, but both cannot always be realized at the same time.[65]

[64]*Scientists in Industry*, pp. 12–13. The professional in the organization is not, of course, the only type of professional who faces conflicting value systems. The professional in the other types of settings may have clients who oppose his value system. The professional himself may hold conflicting values, as in the case of a person who wants to improve his economic position but also maintain the highest professional standards. These values may not always be incompatible, but at times they are.

[65]Kornhauser, *Scientists in Industry*, pp. 17–41.

The second area, involving several types of conflict, lies in the source of control over the scientists' work. The recruitment of new personnel and personnel policies in general operate on different premises. The organization wants to select persons it believes will benefit the organization in the long run. It may, for example, desire personnel who have potential to move into management positions. The sciences, on the other hand, demand that selection be based on scientific ability, and these skills are not necessarily the same. In addition, the organization may have personnel procedures inapplicable or inappropriate for scientists or other professionals.[66] Simon Marcson has noted that civil service regulations impede recruitment in a governmental research setting.[67] The actual organization of work groups is another example of conflicts over controls. Scientists desire work groups to be organized around scientific specialties, since this facilitates intensive investigations into specific areas of interest. The organization, on the other hand, prefers that work groups be organized around particular tasks, which involves mixing different types of scientists and engineers for the solution of a particular problem or the development of a particular product.[68]

Supervision is another problem within the general control area. Organizations rely upon legitimate hierarchical authority as the means of control; scientists and other professionals rely on expertise as the major control mechanism. Although movement up the hierarchy in an organizational setting is typically based on expertise, the kinds of expertise demanded for advancement in the hierarchy may not be the same as those demanded by science. In addition, as a scientist is placed in a supervisory position his ability as a scientist is likely to suffer, since he will have less time to spend on keeping up with his field. Also, those in supervisory positions are likely to be supervising scientists and engineers whose specialties are different from their own. In this case, expertise cannot be expected. Communications pose an additional problem. One of the strongest values of the scientific community is free communication among scientists in order to facilitate further developments. The organization, on the other hand, has a strong value of maintaining company secrets. A new product or process is no longer a secret once it is produced, but businesses like to achieve any competitive edge they can; thus they do not want their scientists to communicate significant findings if they are in any way a threat to secrecy.[69]

[66]Kornhauser, *Scientists in Industry*, pp. 49–50.
[67]*Scientists in Government* (New Brunswick, N.J.: Rutgers University Press, 1966), pp. 12–24.
[68]Kornhauser, *Scientists in Industry*, pp. 50–56.
[69]Kornhauser, *Scientists in Industry*, pp. 56–80.

A third major area of value conflicts derives from the kinds of incentives sought. The scientist operates in a community that transcends organizational or geographical boundaries and is known by his contributions to this community. He is rewarded by the recognition that he has made contributions to knowledge. The organization uses advancement within it as its primary reward system. As discussed above, this creates conflict with continued scientific advances. The organization expects its members to be local in orientation, with loyalty to the organization and its purposes, but the scientist is cosmopolitan in that his rewards and references are in the wider scientific community. For the cosmopolitan, advancement in the local organization may not be an attractive incentive.[70]

The final conflict area concerns the matter of influence; Who has the ultimate power in decision making? Since the organization assumes the risks for its actions, it has the last word in deciding which course of action to pursue. In this sense, the hierarchy has ultimate power over professional expertise, which puts the scientist in a rather awkward position. If he remains detached from the decision making process, he has little impact on organizational matters. If he becomes involved in organizational matters, he in reality becomes part of the organization and moves out of the scientist role. His expertise does not give him influence except in his own limited area. Since everyone in the organization who is not in his specialized area does not understand his expertise, it has no influence over them unless they have requested his specialized knowledge.[71]

While these areas of value conflict are probably inherent in the situation, conflict need not result from them, either for the professional or the organization. Kornhauser points out that the organization adjusts to the presence of professionals. He states:

> In sum, the strain between professional autonomy and bureaucratic control is accommodated by the creation of new roles for research administration. Administrative matters are controlled on the basis of hierarchical principles of authority, while matters regarded by professionals as the primary responsibility of the individual are more subject to multilateral determination through colleague relations. Thus organizational controls are relied upon to a greater extent in the sphere of general policy, in research areas close to operations, and by top research directors,

---

[70]Kornhauser, *Scientists in Industry*, pp. 117–55. See also Barney G. Glaser, *Organizational Scientists: Their Professional Careers* (Indianapolis: The Bobbs-Merrill Co., Inc., 1964).

[71]Kornhauser, *Scientists in Industry*, pp. 158–91.

whereas professional controls are used more extensively in research assignments and procedures, in more basic research areas, and by first-line research supervisors.[72]

The accommodation of the organization to the presence of professionals is accompanied by accommodations on the part of the professionals. Multiple career lines develop for these people as some remain in research, some become research administrators, and some move into the higher levels of management. Kornhauser notes that these multiple career lines allow the research oriented person to receive more pay and freedom of investigation and those who choose the organizational route to receive more pay and new ranks. But, since not all professionals or organizations are willing to make these accommodations, the potential for conflict remains. Kornhauser's own data suggest that organizations vary rather widely in their adaptations to professional employees. A study by Todd R. La Porte suggests that accommodative mechanisms are generated within the organization as it seeks to maximize the research contributions of its scientists. In the organization he examined, La Porte found that the existing causes of strain and conflict came from sources external to the organization, in areas such as procurement and budgetary procedures.[73]

While the kinds of accommodations which Kornhauser and La Porte describe are important means of ameliorating some of the conflicts between organizational and professional norms and values, it is clear that such amelioration does not take place at all times and in all situations. Kornhauser notes that the organizations he examined varied in their success in accommodating the conflicts. The nature of accommodation itself is such that the bases of the conflicts remain, even though they may not always be in the open. The organization still maintains its purposes and the professionals still have their values. As will be suggested later, changes in the organization or among the professionals can alter an accommodative balance, thus creating new conflicts or demanding new accommodative techniques.

Conflict is not the only condition of imbalance between professional and organizational values. Ambiguities also are present, which can result in conflicts for the individuals involved. John D. Donnell, in a study which utilized the conceptual framework of Kahn *et al.* as discussed in Chapter 3, noted a series of ambiguities

[72]Kornhauser, *Scientists in Industry*, pp. 201–2.
[73]"Conditions of Strain and Accommodation in Industrial Research Organizations," *Administrative Science Quarterly*, XX, 1 (June, 1965), 21–38.

in the role of the corporate lawyer. The number of lawyers employed by corporations has increased greatly in recent years. In the 12 years between 1951 and 1963, the number of lawyers in industry increased 127 per cent, while there was only a 13 per cent increase in the number of lawyers in private practice.[74] Donnell notes that the large organization is the most likely to have a legal department. Since most organizations are increasing in size, the trend toward increased use of corporate legal departments will probably continue. Like the scientists discussed before, corporation lawyers are caught between their professional norms and those of the organization. Donnell views this as resulting in ambiguity, rather than conflict. The probable reason for this difference in outcome results from the nature of the professions involved. The law tends to operate on the basis of past precedent, while science is in the business of developing new knowledge. In this sense, law is conservative, while science is radical. The conservatism of the law would appear to coincide rather closely with the purposes of corporations, while the radicalism of science may or may not so coincide. My impression is that the backgrounds of lawyers also would lead them to believe in the goals of business, while the same might not be true for scientists.

Despite the more moderate nature of the outcome of the professional-organizational relationship in the case of lawyers, the ambiguities, which Donnell notes, have an impact on the professional services performed. These ambiguities have three sources. The first is that the role of the lawyer in private practice is itself ambiguous. Donnell states that the "only activity of a lawyer in private practice which is exclusively his is to represent a client in a court."[75] Other activities overlap with other occupations and agencies, such as the services which realtors, bankers, and accountants provide which could be and at times are performed by lawyers. Lawyers themselves provide services that are in the province of other occupations, such as marriage counseling or business management. This ambiguity does not end when the lawyer enters the corporation, although the potential range of his activities is greatly diminished, since he now is a specialist in business law. In reality, the lawyer who enters the corporation undoubtedly had this specialty beforehand, as Smigel's evidence on Wall Street lawyers suggests, but there was a potential for him to practice in other areas of the law.

This general ambiguity is made specific for the corporate

[74]Donnell, "The Corporate Counsel: A Role Study," (DBA thesis, Harvard University, 1966), p. 61.
[75]"The Corporate Counsel: A Role Study," p. 63.

counsel by the fact that he is likely to perceive most of the actions of the corporation as involving potential legal problems. An absence of criteria for determining priorities among the legal issues which arise makes it difficult for the lawyer to determine just where and how he should act. Donnell states that even if such criteria were available, a large amount of time and energy must be devoted to an investigation into a potential corporate action to determine the potential legal problem involved and then rank this problem in the hierarchy of priorities. The lawyers resolve this dilemma by attempting to be on top of everything or by only giving advice when it is solicited.

The second source of ambiguity is similar to one faced by the organizational scientist. The lawyer must come to grips with the issue of whether he is a lawyer or a businessman.[76] He must often balance legal risks and business risks, since his job demands that he be familiar with each. The scientist, asked to come up with profitable developments, is in the same position in that he must weigh the merits of the development for his employer against the demands of his scientific discipline. As in the case of the scientist, appropriate legal actions may or may not be appropriate business actions. The lawyer also is often in the position where his knowledge of the business almost demands he give business advice when he believes that an incorrect decision is about to be made, although it may be legally appropriate. If he gives the advice, he becomes a businessman; if he does not and acts exclusively as a lawyer, his employer is liable to lose money and this part of his knowledge is being wasted. If he chooses the businessman role, it may later be difficult to separate it from the lawyer role, thus limiting his effectiveness in his position. The latter role, if played exclusively, limits his effectiveness as an officer of the corporation. This particular dilemma is resolved in some instances by polarization at either extreme, but in most cases the lawyers attempt to play both roles, separating them where necessary and possible.

The third source of ambiguity is tied to the traditional role of the lawyer as an officer of the court. The lawyer is expected to uphold the law but at the same time to contribute to the profit making of the corporation. In most cases, corporate policy is to obey the law, incidents of white-collar crime notwithstanding. There are times, however, when actions of corporate personnel may come into conflict with the law. The lawyer may decide to act as a policeman, a role that involves knowing what the intended actions are to be and

[76]"The Corporate Counsel: A Role Study," pp. 64–65.

then acting to prevent them. This choice involves some betrayal of confidential information that the potential law violator, in many ways the lawyer's client, has provided the lawyer. This is in clear violation of general professional standards of confidentiality. If the lawyer does not attempt to prevent the illegal act, he is not serving the corporate interests, even though he keeps the information confidential. Another facet of this problem is that if the lawyer does decide to play the role of policeman and does reveal the potentially illegal action, his future relationships with other executives may suffer, in that they may be unwilling to reveal the exact nature of their plans for fear the lawyer will both pass information on to their superiors and prevent actions they view as organizationally beneficial.[77]

Additional insights into the problems confronted by lawyers in the corporate setting are provided by Quintin Johnstone and Dan Hopson, Jr. They note that some executives would like corporate counsel to act as a rubber stamp for their ideas.[78] When the lawyer, or any professional, is put in this position and acts according to the executives' expectations, he no longer operates as a professional. These instances are in the minority, but the potential for this kind of expectation is heightened by the pyramidal hierarchy of most business organizations. The corporation is likely to have a finely developed organization chart, with the relative positions in the hierarchy of professional and nonprofessional staffs clearly indicated. Johnstone and Hopson point out that corporate legal departments are likely to be highly differentiated in terms of multiple levels and corresponding job titles. If an executive at a higher level in the hierarchy approaches a lawyer at a lower level, this type of relationship has a higher probability of existing. In most cases, however, relationships between lawyers and clients (executives in this case) appear to be among equals in the organizational hierarchy. The problem of rubber stamping appears not to be limited to members of professional departments. Smigel suggests that the younger associates in Wall Street law firms generally will dispute a point of law only to the extent of the expectations of partners with whom they are dealing.[79] The young lawyer soon learns when he is expected to cease disputation and yield to his superior. The Wall Street lawyer is disputing with other lawyers, but the structured form of the expectations is not dissimilar to that of the executive

[77]"The Corporate Counsel: A Role Study," pp. 65–66.
[78]Johnstone and Hopson, *Lawyers and Their Work* (Indianapolis: The Bobbs Merrill Co., Inc., 1967), p. 205.
[79]*The Wall Street Lawyer*, pp. 322–29.

lawyer. In both cases, hierarchical factors can outweigh potential expertise.

An interesting facet of corporate legal practice discussed by Johnstone and Hopson is the tendency toward very low turnover rates. While this indicates satisfaction with the work and a stable situation for the organization itself, the authors suggest that it may also indicate that the "minimum tolerable level of performance is rather low."[80] While their evidence is rather weak, there is some suggestion that corporate lawyers do in fact operate somewhat below the highest standards of the profession. This, of course, is the same thing that Carlin and Ladinsky have suggested about the individual practitioners, while Smigel suggests the opposite in regard to the Wall Street lawyer. Good comparative data would be needed before firm conclusions could be drawn in this area.

Another problem for corporate counsel is that they are likely to handle only a narrow range of legal problems. This, according to most people concerned about the legal profession, is not as it should be, since lawyers should be familiar with both the practice and implications of a wide range of legal problems. Here again, however, the picture of the corporate counsel is not clearly differentiated from that of the solo practitioner or the Wall Street lawyer who also specializes to a fairly high degree. Again, good comparative data is needed for any conclusive analysis of the extent and consequences of extreme specialization.

The Johnstone and Hopson research indicates that the legal departments studied varied rather widely in the stress placed upon professional (bar) activities. They also varied in the degree to which they were hierarchically organized. The corporations themselves varied in the kinds of expectations they held for the departments. These findings raise an important issue for the general discussion of professionalization—the role of the setting of professional work on the behavior of the professionals involved. Four distinct settings of professional work have been discussed, the solo practitioner, the autonomous professional organization, the heteronomous professional organization, and the professional department. Each of these settings confronts the professional with a different working environment with differing sources of norms, career patterns, problems, and rewards. At the same time, the common characteristics, discussed before, exist in the variety of settings.

A major source of both the variations and the common characteristics is the organizational setting in which the professional is employed. Since the solo practitioner is not subject to this type of

[80]Johnstone and Hopson, *Lawyers and Their Work*, p. 235.

work structure, he will be ignored in this analysis. Any of the three types of organizational setting discussed may vary to the extent that professional behavior and values are affected. My analysis of the degree of bureaucratization of a group of professional organizations provides some indication of the manner in which professional work settings do vary and of the relationship between the setting and professional values and attitudes. In this discussion, the importance of varied professional training and of differing degrees of professionalization among the occupations involved in affecting behavior and values is not considered, even though these are undoubtedly important factors. The concentration on the setting assumes that differences in socialization in professional schools and differing levels of professionalization of the occupations involved do make a difference but that the effect of these variations will be randomly distributed among the occupational groups analyzed. The professions involved are the same as those discussed in the earlier section on the structural and attitudinal components of professionalization.

In this phase of the research, the organizational settings were analyzed by determining the degree to which they were bureaucratized.[81] The bureaucratization of the organizations involved was approached from a dimensional perspective, which involves the assumption that organizations will vary in their degree of bureaucratization along several dimensions of bureaucratization. Previous research in this area has suggested that organizations do not necessarily exhibit the same degree of bureaucratization on all of the dimensions, but this is not the central issue at this time. What is of interest here is the determination of the relationships between the degree of bureaucratization, as the measure of the organizational structure, and the degree of professionalism, as measured by the attitudinal scales of professionalism discussed in previous sections.

The components of the bureaucratic model used here are:

1. Hierarchy of authority is the extent to which the locus of decision-making is prestructured by the organization and the extent to which it follows hierarchical principles. (Decisions of varying types are made at different levels in the organization with the assumption that decision-making ability and power are directly related to hierarchical position.)

[81]See Richard H. Hall, "Professionalization and Bureaucratization," pp. 95–104, for additional discussions of the techniques used and of the findings reported here.

2. Division of labor is the extent to which work tasks are subdivided into functional specialization as determined by the organization.

3. Presence of rules is the degree to which the behavior of organizational members is subject to organizational control.

4. Procedural specifications refers to the extent to which organizational members must follow organizationally defined techniques in dealing with the variety of situations they face.

5. Impersonality describes the extent to which both organizational members and outsiders are treated without regard to individual qualities. (All people are treated the same way without consideration of individual differences.)

6. Technical competence is the extent to which organizationally defined universal standards are utilized in the selection of personnel and in the advancement process.

In the research under discussion, these dimensions were measured by asking the professionals involved to respond to a series of statements about their organization. Their responses were tabulated to develop a score for each dimension. The average score for the respondents in a particular organization was then taken as the degree of bureaucratization on a particular dimension. The relationships between the scores on the bureaucratic dimensions test and the scores on the professional attitude scales were then determined as indicated in Table 4.3.

The most obvious general finding is that there is an inverse relationship between degree of bureaucratization and level of professional attitude. This implies, of course, that a highly bureaucratic organization tends to impede the development of strong professional attitudes. At the same time, an organization whose members hold strong professional values may be difficult to bureaucratize, a point which will be discussed later.

When the specific relationships are examined, some interesting patterns emerge. With regard to the use of the professional organization as a reference group, there is a relatively small negative relationship between this variable and the presence of a rigid hierarchy of authority. It would thus appear to make little difference if there is extensive reliance upon such a hierarchy in professional organizations. The findings of Peter M. Blau, Wolf V. Heydebrand, and Robert E. Stauffer support this conclusion, which

Table 4.3.   Rank Order Correlation Coefficients Between Professionalism Scales and Bureaucracy Scales

	Professional Organization Reference	Belief in Service to Public	Belief in Self-Regulation	Sense of Calling to Field	Feeling of Autonomy
Hierarchy of authority	−.029	−.262	−.149	.148	−.767[2]
Division of labor	−.236	−.260	−.234	−.115	−.575[2]
Rules	−.144	−.121	−.107	.113	−.554[2]
Procedures	−.360[2]	−.212	−.096	.000	−.603[2]
Impersonality	−.256	−.099	−.018	−.343[1]	−.489[2]
Technical competence	.593[2]	.332[1]	.420[2]	.440[2]	.121

[1] $= p < .05$
[2] $= p < .01$

suggests that the presence of such a hierarchy may facilitate the work of professionals if they serve coordination and communication functions.[82] This would be the case particularly when the hierarchy is recognized as legitimate. The professional may thus recognize and essentially approve of the fact that certain decisions must be made by particular positions in the hierarchy. Since many decisions are based on the suggestions of the professionals involved, this would further tend to minimize feelings that the hierarchical principals are in opposition to professional values. Conflict probably exists only in those cases where the decisions made in some way disagree with either the professional's own judgment or adversely affect his own work. As will be seen below, such hierarchies are not limited to professional departments, since relatively bureaucratic hierarchies are found in other types of organizations.

A stronger negative relationship is found on the division of labor dimension. If the division of labor is very intense, forcing the professional to work in only a limited area, the person may be forced

[82]"The Structure of Small Bureaucracies," *American Sociological Review*, XXXI, 2 (April, 1966), 179–91.

away from his broader professional ties. This finding confirms the suggestion noted above by Johnstone and Hopson about extreme specialization among lawyers. It is clear that professionals can be highly specialized in their work. The issue here is the source of the specialization. If the source is organizational, professional identification is weakened; if the source is within the profession itself, such identification might not be affected.

The presence of the rules dimension is, to a limited degree, inversely related to the professional attitude. Organizationally developed rules about the behavior of members appear not to intrude too strongly on this or the other professional attitudes. It would appear that these rules are not too stringent in the organizations analyzed. A strong negative relationship exists between the procedural specifications dimension and the attitude of the professional organization as a reference group. This is expected, since strong professional orientations appear to be basically incompatible with organizationally developed techniques of dealing with work situations—the more procedures developed by the organization, the less room for professional discretion. This area would thus be a real source of conflict for professionals if they work in such procedure-laden environments. The presence of professionals in an organization in many ways demands that the organization not develop its own procedures, since one of the major elements in the nature of professions is professional judgment based upon the criteria of the profession.

The relatively strong negative relationship between this professional attitude and the impersonality dimension is not unexpected. The more professional groups apparently do not need or utilize impersonality in their organizational arrangements. If the organization itself stresses impersonality and contains a highly professionalized group, conflict again can ensue.

The strong positive relationship between the use of the professional organization as a reference group and the organizational emphasis on technical competence is, of course, predictable. Organizations that employ professionals by definition utilize competence criteria, rather than selecting personnel by nepotistic or particularistic means.[83] It is not clear, on the basis of this research, whose criteria of competence are being utilized. From the previous discussions it is evident that if the organization determines the criteria for personnel policies and if these policies contain elements inconsistent

[83]Since this bureaucratic dimension is so strongly related to most of the professional attributes, it might even serve as an informal indicator of the level of professionalization of the members of an organization if other such indicators are not available.

with the standards of the profession involved, a strong potential for conflict exists. This would be a strong possibility in the cases of the heteronomous organization and the professional department. In the research being discussed, the ratings of the degree of bureaucratization and the measures of the professional attitudes were gathered from the same persons. It would thus appear that such conflict is minimal in the organizations being examined here.

The findings concerning belief in service to the public, belief in self-regulation, and sense of calling to the field are essentially the same as those just discussed. The areas of congruence and conflict, which might emerge, also appear to be quite similar.

Strong negative relationships exist between the autonomy variable and the first five bureaucratic dimensions. This suggests, of course, that increased bureaucratization would threaten professional autonomy. It is in this set of relationships that the most evident source of conflict between the professional and the organization can be found. The drive for autonomy on the part of a professional may come into direct and strong conflict with organizationally based job requirements. At the same time, the organization, as such, may be threatened by strong professional drives for autonomy. If the professionals act in a totally autonomous fashion, the goals of the organization might not be served. In the ideal situation, professional and organizational goals are identical, so that the professional is fully autonomous and, at the same time, accomplishes the purposes of the organization. Since even the autonomous professional organization contains elements antithetical to some professional attitudes, this ideal state is not achieved in reality.

The preceding discussion suggests that the professional in an organization does not and cannot operate in a totally autonomous fashion and that the organization does set limits of varying degrees of stringency on him. The most obvious question at this point is, What factors contribute to the varying levels of bureaucratization and thus to greater or lesser levels of autonomy for the professional? Part of the answer may lie in the nature of the particular profession itself. When the occupations included in my study are grouped into Wilensky's established, process, and doubtful categories, some rather definitive patterns emerge as Table 4.4 indicates.

The most evident finding is that the more professionalized groups are found in the least bureaucratized settings, which suggests that the more professionalized groups probably do not need the kinds of organizational controls required by less professionalized groups. If an occupation is self-regulating and its members can act autonomously, the organization does not need to provide an extensive control system. If, on the other hand, the occupation does not provide its members with sufficient controls in the form of self-regulation, and if the members do not or cannot act autonomously because of deficiencies in the knowledge base of the occupation, then organizational controls must be provided in the absence of alternatives. This suggests that an equilibrium can be achieved between professional and organizational control systems. The equilibrium comes about when organizational controls are present in those areas where the professional, for whatever reason, lacks the prerequisites for autonomous performance.

Table 4.4.   Average Ranks and One Way Analysis of Variance H on Degree of Bureaucratization of the Work Settings of Three Types of Professionals

	Established (Average Rank)	Process (Average Rank)	Doubtful (Average Rank)	H Value (2 df)
Hierarchy of authority	9.5	18.9	14.1	6.14[1]
Division of labor	9.2	17.8	15.7	5.57
Rules	7.9	19.1	15.9	9.65[2]
Procedures	7.3	18.5	17.3	10.96[2]
Impersonality	11.2	16.2	15.1	1.65
Technical competence	16.5	14.7	10.2	2.02

[1] $= p < .05$
[2] $= p < .001$

Just as the potential for equilibrium is present, this relationship between professional and organizational control systems is an important source of conflict. As soon as the equilibrium is upset, either the organization or the professionals will react. An example of this would be the case of an occupation that attempts to professionalize and does achieve a greater degree of authority for its professional organization. The members then believe that they should have a stronger role in determining who should be employed by the organization (the technical competence dimension of bureaucracy). If they press for their demands at all, conflict is likely. Another situation which disturbs the equilibrium is organizationally based as when an organization attempts to establish new procedures regarding the procurement of office supplies for all departments, including the professional departments. If the latter departments' members' needs are not as well met by the new procedures, conflict would again result. These examples suggest that changes in the professional groups or the organizations can destroy an existing equilibrium. Since levels of professionalization and bureaucratization are not static, the potential for conflict is great.

An additional source of tension between professionals and organizations is the situation in which there are not *enough* organizational rules for the professionals, leading to a state of *anomie*. This situation could arise when the organization does not provide sufficient structuring for the professionals. This assumes, of course, that the professionals involved do not have the equipment for the structuring of their own work. This type of condition would probably occur most often among the process or doubtful types of professions. This discussion has assumed that individual contributions to the structuring of work situations, above and beyond those of the profession or the organization, are important but also randomly distributed in the population involved so that their effect is not central.

The discussion thus far has been focused on two alternative sources for the structuring of the work of the professional—the profession and the organizational setting. It has been suggested that the organizational setting can have a powerful influence on the work of professionals, as can the degree of professionalization of the group itself. It has also been noted that little can be gained from an a priori assumption that professional departments differ from autonomous professional organizations, which are, in turn, inherently different from heteronomous organizations in terms of organizational structure. The professional and organizational bases of control are powerful, and the relative strength of each probably depends on the factors discussed above. The professional is subject to two additional control sources: the informal structure, common to almost every work situation, and client control, unique to only a few professions.

That a person is affected by his daily interactions with peers, superiors, and subordinates is obvious.[84] Industrial sociologists have long recognized the importance of such interactions in their analyses of informal structures or work-group behavior. These analyses suggest that the actual behavior of workers deviates from the officially prescribed patterns, a finding that is not surprising and that has been incorporated into most contemporary management theories. Some sociologists view this structuring of behavior as distinct from that which derives from official organizational policies. While the source of the structuring is distinct, the results on the basis of interpersonal relationships are no different from those from other sources—behavior is structured.

Miller and Form have defined this informal organization as "that network of personal and social relations which [is] not defined or prescribed by formal organization."[85] For the professional, his orientation to his profession is also extraorganizational. If he is found within an organization, he is subject to influences from his profession, the organization, and those with whom he interacts. The important elements of this informal organization, according to Miller and Form, are:

1. Congeniality groups, such as gangs, friendships, and cliques.
2. An organization and structure which defines the relations between these groups, in terms of rights, obligations, prestige, and influence.
3. Codes of conduct for group members, including customs and norms. These may be arbitrarily divided into two sections:
    a. *Internal* codes, which regulate activities within the informal social organization.
    b. *External* codes, which regulate activities toward formal organization (management and union) and other formally or informally organized out-groups.
4. Scheme of ideas, beliefs, and values which underlie and support the code of conduct and group

[84]For an extensive elaboration of this point, see George C. Homans, *The Human Group* (New York: Harcourt, Brace and World, Inc., 1950).
[85]*Industrial Sociology*, p. 224.

activities, such as "folk" knowledge, prejudices, stereotypes, myths, and ideologies which give meaning to occurrences.

5. Informal group activities, related to or independent of formal work behavior. Ceremonies, rites, gambling, recreation, swearing, and joking are examples.

6. Communication systems which inform members of ideas, sentiments, and occurrences vital to group solidarity and action.[86]

The most frequent application of the idea of the informal organization has been in analyses of production and office workers. Melville Dalton's examination of the clique structure among executives suggests the obvious—that such structuring will occur wherever there is interaction among people on or off the job.[87] This analysis of structuring among executives can be generalized to include professionals. Professionals in organizational settings do interact with one another and with nonprofessionals. This interaction will affect their performance, and the direction of the impact will depend upon the manner in which the informal structure is formed.

Professionals in individual practice are also affected by these interpersonal relationships. Johnstone and Hopson state:

> In addition to groupings of lawyers in clearly delineated formal organizations such as law firms and legal departments, regular cooperative relationships sometimes develop among particular lawyers in different formal organizations and these become so close that in effect they evolve into informal work units of the lawyers concerned. This can happen between inside corporate lawyers and the outside counsel they consistently use, between private firm lawyers in one city and those in their correspondent firm in another, or between a highly specialized practitioner and those lawyers in other firms who frequently draw on his services.[88]

A similar point is made by Oswald Hall in his analysis of the informal structuring of medical practices. Hall notes that factors such as race, religion, and ethnic background play a role in acceptance into the "inner fraternity" of physicians who dominate the medical profession in the community he examined. Hall stresses that

[86]*Industrial Sociology*, pp. 224–25.
[87]*Men Who Manage* (New York: John Wiley & Sons, Inc., 1959), pp. 52–65.
[88]*Lawyers and Their Work*, p. 33.

competence is vital to acceptance, but so is the proper personality. Nonacceptance can lead to a situation in which the possibilities for financial and professional advancement become blocked.[89] Here again, the work of the professional is structured, in this case by social factors.

The effects of this form of social structuring may have little to do with the performance of the professional in his work, or they may enhance or detract from his performance. If the peer group expects consistently high performance levels, then the consequences will be positive for both the professional and his clients or employing organization. On the other hand, if the expectation level is low, as Johnstone and Hopson suggest that it is for some corporate counsels, or if potentially well-qualified practitioners are excluded from memberships in inner circles, law firms, or other professional organizations because of racial or religious factors, the effects will be negative. Relatively little effect would be predicted in situations in which the peer group is composed of persons of equal competence whose expectations do not exceed their ability. Clearly, the impact of differing peer group types is an area requiring additional investigation.

A further, and perhaps obvious, point about the impact of peer structuring should be noted. Those professionals who are for one reason or another excluded from an informal group that is significant to them, as in the case of a physician who is not admitted to practice in a prestigious hospital or a teacher who is placed in the position of an isolate in the sociometric structure of a school, will probably still react to the group from which he is excluded. The form of the reaction could range from bitterness to attempts to behave in ways so that he would be accepted. Whatever the form of the reaction, the group still has an impact on his behavior.

client structuring

The role of the client in relationship to the nature of professions has been only briefly discussed. The solo practitioner and the professional in the autonomous professional organization are in reality the only types of professional who have individual clients. For the worker in a heteronomous organization, clients come before

[89]Oswald Hall, "The Informal Organization of the Medical Profession," *Canadian Journal of Economics and Political Science*, XXII, 11 (February, 1946), 30–44 and "Stages of a Medical Career," *American Journal of Sociology*, LIII, 5 (March, 1948), 327–36.

him in the case of social welfare cases, students, or library patrons; however, the professional and the client have little or no choice about each other, since each is typically assigned to the other on the basis of availability, school grade, etc. For the professional employed in a larger organization, the problem of determining who is the client can be a source of intrapersonal conflict. The discussion of client structuring will therefore be limited to those professionals found in individual practice or in autonomous organizations.

The professional-client relationship is often thought to be at the heart of the role of the professional. Moore suggests that the client comes to the professional in a spirit of *credat emptor*—let the buyer (client) trust.[90] The client is in a position where he needs the services of the professional, or at least believes that he does, since he is unable to supply the answers to his own problems. The professional is expected to deal with the client to the best of his ability, using his judgment for the client's benefit. The professional is also expected to be loyal to his client, not betraying the trust the client has demonstrated by coming to him. The client contributes to the one-to-one relationship by paying a fee directly to the professional for his services. In this form of relationship, both the client and the professional are characterized by high levels of individual freedom. This is the idealized description of the client-professional relationship in popular and some professional literature.

There is growing evidence that this image does not correspond to reality in many cases. Although complete evidence is not available, it is probable that this idealized image is realized in some proportion of professional practice. In many cases, however, the client relationship becomes a limiting or structuring factor for the professional. Hughes, in discussing Carlin's study of individual lawyers in Chicago, states:

As a matter of fact, there are some indications in recent studies of a great paradox. Part of the cherished freedom of a professional worker is not merely to do his work according to his own best judgment and conscience, but also to choose his own style of work and economy of effort. Lawyers who practice alone—at least in a sample of them taken in Chicago—are utterly captives and choreboys of their clients. They have no freedom to choose a branch of law and make themselves expert or learned in it. Most of them, in time, do find their practice nar-

[90]Wilbert E. Moore, "Economic and Professional Institutions," in *Sociology: An Introduction*, ed. Neil J. Smelser (New York: John Wiley & Sons, Inc., 1967), p. 322.

rowed to a special line of chores: they have become specialists by default.[91]

Oswald Hall's analysis of medical careers supplies additional evidence that the client is in many ways a structuring agent. He notes that the doctor must adopt the appropriate strategy to attract and keep clients. Since the attraction of clients takes place in a competitive environment, "intelligent enterprise may be more important than medical knowledge and skill."[92] Hall suggests that the attraction of clients, particularly for specialists because of the referral system, requires relationships with other medical practitioners, thus linking the doctor to another social structure. This attraction and maintenance of clients requires the doctor to conform to his clients' expectations as well as to those of his colleagues.

The importance of clients was stressed in Smigel's examination of the Wall Street lawyers. The initial selection of the lawyers was based to some extent on their probable abilities in client relationships. As the beginning associates sought to advance into partnership positions, they were assessed on the basis of their ability to interact with, and later attract, clients. The partners in the firms suggested that relationships with clients occupied more of their time in many instances than the practice of law. In the case of these lawyers and the doctors discussed by Hall, the ability to relate to clients was not held to be more important than the professional competence but rather an additional factor to be considered in analyzing professional work. Again, the exact amount that relationships to clients contribute to a structured work situation for the professional, as opposed to the factors already discussed, cannot be determined without additional evidence.

The discussion thus far has centered around the way in which relationships to clients affect the daily work of the professional. The evidence suggests that neither the client nor the professional is totally free in this relationship and that both must conform to the other's expectation. There is another, and somewhat neglected, sense in which the professional, who is dependent upon clients, is limited by his clients. It is extremely difficult for such a professional to be geographically mobile. Jack R. Ladinsky found, on the basis of his analysis of census data, that *"Professions that demand costly equipment purchases and close cultivation of clienteles block migra-*

[91]Everett C. Hughes, "The Professions in Society," *The Canadian Journal of Economics and Political Science*, XXVI, 1 (February, 1960), pp. 60–61.
[92]Hall, "Stages of a Medical Career," p. 322.

tion."[93] Ladinsky also found that salaried professionals (those with a direct client group) were more likely to move within and between states. The self-employed, client-oriented professional is essentially locked into a location, unless he wants to risk building a clientele again.

Hughes' words succinctly summarize the points made in this section:

> And here we are at a paradox of modern professional freedom. The effective freedom to choose one's special line of work, to have access to the appropriate clients and equipment, to engage in that converse with eager and competent colleagues which will sharpen one's knowledge and skill, to organize one's time and effort so as to gain that end, and even freedom from pressure to conform to the clients' individual or collective customs and opinions seems, in many lines of work, to be much greater for those professionals who have employers and work inside complicated and even bureaucratic organizations than for those who, according to the traditional concept, are in independent practice.[94]

a deviant case: minority groups

In much of the preceding discussion, the idea that rationality and competence are a dominant aspect of the professional world has been stressed. Most professionals attempt to work to the best of their ability and expect their colleagues to do likewise, although, of course, there are wide variations in performance. Rationality is not always dominant when minority groups are considered. Minority group status is ascribed on the basis of race, religion, ethnicity, and sex.

Admission to graduate training is often based on irrational criteria. Discrimination is particularly prevalent in choosing students for graduate training for the established professions. Until very recently most law or medical schools, for example, had quotas for Negroes or Jews admitted to each class, limiting enrollment to a fixed percentage of the class regardless of the qualifications. Dis-

[93]"Occupational Determinants of Geographic Mobility Among Professional Workers," *American Sociological Review*, XXXII, 2, (April, 1967), 257, italics in original.

[94]Everett C. Hughes, "The Professions in Society," p. 61.

crimination against women apparently still persists, even in graduate departments in sociology. The recent civil-rights movement has lessened the discrimination, but remnants of the system still provide obstacles, imagined or real, for potentially qualified practitioners.

Women and Negroes who do go to graduate or professional schools are found predominantly in areas such as social work or teaching, where the clientele is likely to be members of a minority group. The role is already somewhat ascribed, as in the case of the woman teacher, and there is a personnel shortage. Jews are also overrepresented in some fields and underrepresented in others. A rough relationship appears to exist between the strength of the professional associations and the amount of discrimination in admission policies of graduate schools. Some changes in these patterns are occurring, as most professions are attempting to attract qualified minority group members, with the possible exception of women, to their ranks. Some evidence of this is seen in James A. Davis' data, which suggests that Negroes of similar background characteristics were *"more likely to anticipate immediate advanced study than disadvantaged whites and just about as likely as whites in general."*[95] This is despite the fact that the majority of the Negroes studied came from disadvantaged backgrounds. A strong positive relationship exists between socio-economic status and plans for advanced study, that, while probably not based on discriminatory factors, is irrational from the standpoint of the professions which, theoretically, desire the most competent practitioners.

The second area in which ir- or perhaps nonrational factors operate is entrance into the profession, as illustrated by the previously cited studies of Carlin, Ladinsky, Smigel, and Hall. The individual lawyers studied by Carlin and Ladinsky tended to be members of minority groups. A common reason given for their status was their minority group position. Other factors were, of course, operative. Smigel found that the members of Wall Street law firms tended to be predominantly white, Anglo-Saxon, and Protestant, and minority lawyers were placed in positions without client contact. Hall found that ethnicity and religion were likely to keep a person out of the inner fraternity. Here again, performance potential is less important than minority group background.

The final area to be discussed is that of the work of minority group members once they are in the profession. Hughes notes:

> The woman lawyer may become a lawyer to women
> clients, or she may specialize in some kind of legal service

[95]*Great Aspirations* (Chicago: Aldine Publishing Co., 1964), p. 104, italics in original.

in keeping with woman's role as guardian of the home and of morals. Women physicians may find a place in those specialties of which only women and children have need. A female electrical engineer was urged by the dean of the school from which she had just been graduated to accept a job whose function was to give the "woman's angle" to design of household electrical appliances. The Negro professional man finds his clients among Negroes. The Negro sociologist generally studies race relations and teaches in a Negro college. [Women sociologists are often similarly expected to study the family.] A new figure on the American scene is the Negro personnel man in industries which have started employing Negro workers.[96]

Here the lack of rationality lies in the fact that, while the minority group member may in fact be ideally suited for the kind of work that he is doing, it is irrational to assume that he necessarily is so suited. The fact that the minority group professional typically works with his fellow minority group members almost forces him to work for the maintenance of segregated patterns; for he might lose his clientele if they had access to nonminority group professionals. A study by David M. Howard suggests that Negro professionals are somewhat reluctant to engage in open competition with whites, which suggests a fear of losing clientele.[97] The situation is further compounded by the fact that many minority group members do not have, or feel that they do not have, access to professionals outside their group. This, of course, limits their freedom of choice and can in some instances force them to less qualified practitioners.

For the minority professional status inconsistency is an obvious condition. He ranks low on the ascribed characteristics of race, religion, ethnicity, or sex and high on the achieved characteristics of education and occupation. Gerhard E. Lenski and Elton F. Jackson's findings suggest such a person should experience some psychological disturbance because of the inconsistency. The response pattern to this disturbance, when the inconsistency is in this direction, tends to be one of political liberalism—trying to change the system.[98] The common sense examples of the ardent feminist

[96]*Men and Their Work*, pp. 113–14.
[97]"An Exploratory Study of Attitudes of Negro Professionals toward Competition with Whites," *Social Forces*, XLV, 1 (September, 1966), 20–27.
[98]See Gerhard E. Lenski, *Power and Privilege* (New York: McGraw-Hill Book Company, 1966), pp. 26–31 and Elton F. Jackson, "Status Consistency and Symptoms of Stress," *American Sociological Review*, XXVII, 4 (August, 1962), 469–80 for a discussion of these patterns.

professional or the liberal Jew in academia support this suggestion. The recent history of the Negro civil rights movement, however, suggests that Negro professionals have not been at the vanguard of this movement and in fact have been criticized for their desire to maintain the status quo for selfish reasons. Rather clearly in this latter case, status inconsistency does not lead to the expected liberal pattern. Exactly what the reaction would be in this is not yet clear.

summary and conclusions

This chapter began with the statement that the professions are probably the most easily identified occupational type. Most of the discussion, which followed, attempted to demonstrate that the professions, while perhaps an identifiable type, are not a homogeneous lot. The variability among and within the professional occupations was examined through the use of the professional model. This model, composed of both structural and attitudinal characteristics, is an ideal type, which is not achieved in reality. Nevertheless, it does serve a useful analytical function for inter- and intraoccupational analysis. The professional model also serves a function for those occupations in the midst of the professionalization process. Since it is a model about which a good deal of consensus exists, occupations that are self-consciously trying to professionalize have a relatively clear goal for their efforts. As was suggested, however, public acceptance of an occupation as a profession may be of equal or greater importance than compliance with the professional model. In addition to their importance as an occupational type, the examination of the professions points to a major aspect of the contemporary social structure. Professions are important because of their growth in proportion to the labor force. As knowledge in most phases of human endeavor increases and specialization within the over-all occupational structure does likewise, more occupations will become professionalized. These new or emergent professions have and will come from a wide spectrum of bases. Business, educational, governmental, and service occupations are or will be a part of this professionalization movement. The nature of, and the problems confronting the professions will thus be of growing importance in social structural analyses.

The settings of professional work were analyzed for three purposes. In the first place, the setting was viewed as a contributor to intra- and interoccupational variations in the professionalization process, with the conclusion drawn that individual practice or employment in a heteronomous professional organization, for example, can inhibit the professionalization of individuals or groups in such practice. A second conclusion, which can be drawn from the analysis, is that *any* setting for professional work contains elements that pose potential conflicts for individuals or for the occupation as a whole. There is no one type of setting that maximizes professional performance above all others. Particular professions may be best adapted to a particular type of setting, but in no case was a setting found in which the ideal-type professional model could be attained. The final conclusion drawn from the analysis of the settings is that each type of setting serves as a source of external control for the professional. While the professional model strongly implies independence on the part of the professional, the setting in fact provides a strong structuring influence. In addition to the structuring or control effect of the setting of professional work, the professional is also controlled in varying degrees by his peers and clients.

In a very real sense, those occupations that are attempting to professionalize will not find themselves in a bed of roses if they are successful. At the same time the process itself appears to be inevitable for many occupations as the trends discussed earlier continue. Those occupations already recognized as professions are themselves in processes of change as the move toward more organizational work, increased internal specialization, and changing patterns of societal control affect their work environments. The concept and the reality of the professions, while at first glance both simple and static, upon closer examination become complex and dynamic.

chapter 5

managers,
proprietors,
and officials

The discussion of the professions proceeded from the relatively simple professional model to the conclusion that neither professions as a whole nor the individual professions are homogeneous. The discussion of managers, proprietors, and officials will begin with the same conclusion. The very name of the category suggests the heterogeneity of this group of occupations. Perhaps the only truly common characteristic within this category is the relatively high socio-economic status the members of the category enjoy. Another characteristic, but one which is not unique to this or most of the other categories, is that the members of the category occupy positions in organizations. The term "manager" refers to business executives, itself a very broad category. Proprietors are owners of businesses, and in the majority of the cases, proprietors are also managers, performing the same kinds of functions and occupying the same positions as top executives. They also perform a wide variety of other nonmanagerial roles. Officials are in many ways identical to managers, the major difference being the fact that officials are employed in nonprofit organizations, such as governmental agencies, school systems, hospitals, business and professional associations, etc.

They are administrators in nonbusiness organizations. The simplest description of this category is that managers, proprietors, and officials occupy *middle to high positions in organizations of all types.*

It is important to note at the outset that there is no model, such as the professional model, by which the occupations can be analyzed. In some cases, the professional model itself can be a useful analytical tool in examining similarities and differences between this set of occupations and the professions. Since both occupational categories occupy roughly equivalent positions in the social-stratification system, such an analysis is of some use. Inevitably, however, it leads to the relatively useless conclusion that these occupations are not as professional as the professions in terms of the components of the professional model. Application of the professional model in this way is inappropriate because of the implication that those occupations that do not approximate it are somehow inferior to those that do. Despite the sometimes fevered strivings of some occupations to achieve correspondence with this model, for most there is little in the way of inherent goodliness or Godliness in corresponding with the model. This is not to suggest that there is a paucity of models for executives. Writers from Frederick W. Taylor and the scientific management school to Rensis Likert and Douglas McGregor and the human relations school have provided models of how to be better executives.[1] However interesting, although inconclusive, the debate between these schools of thought has been, such approaches are of little use in understanding the nature of the occupations being examined.

One further point in the same vein should be added. The negative tone of the preceding paragraph is, to a degree, indicative of the state of knowledge about this category on the part of sociologists. It seems as though sociology has been content to accept descriptions of executives developed by such journalistically oriented writers as William H. Whyte, Jr. or, of all people, Vance Packard.[2] Whether the seeming acceptance of these generally critical approaches to these occupations is based on a bias against

[1]See Frederick W. Taylor, *Scientific Management* (New York: Harper & Row, Publishers, 1911). See also Rensis Likert, *New Patterns of Management* (New York: McGraw-Hill Book Company, 1962) and Douglas McGregor, *The Human Side of Enterprise* (New York: McGraw-Hill Book Company, 1960). For a review and critique of both of these management models, see Amitai Etzioni, *Modern Organizations* (Englewood Cliffs, N.J.: Prentice-Hall, Inc., 1964), pp. 20–49.

[2]See William H. Whyte, Jr., *The Organization Man* (New York: Doubleday & Company, Inc., 1957) and Vance Packard, *The Pyramid Climbers* (New York: McGraw-Hill Book Company, 1962). Packard's works are not highly regarded by most sociologists, but it appears that these same sociologists utilize his ideas.

business in general or a nonbiased lack of interest is irrelevant. The fact remains that sociology has contributed little to our understanding of this group. My impression is that bias does enter some analyses, when the scientists in their white jackets are pitted against executives in their grey-flannel suits. An examination of the sources of such bias would be interesting but beyond the purposes of this book. The conclusion, which should be evident at this time, is that what is known about this category comes largely from outside sociology, a fact that does not make the knowledge suspect but that does introduce difficulties into the analysis. Qualitatively and quantitatively, less is known about characteristics, work environments, and interaction patterns of members of this category than the other categories to be discussed.

With these caveats in mind the analysis of this category can proceed. To allow a more meaningful discussion, the category will be subdivided into its component subcategories.

executives

Many writers suggest that an important difference exists between managers and executives. Executives are those near or at the top of their organizations, while managers occupy lower positions in the hierarchy. This distinction will be maintained in this analysis, although it is useful only in the limited way. The ranks of executives are filled by those moving up from management so that the characteristics of the two groups cannot be totally different, except insofar as those who do move into executive positions may have measurably different characteristics from those who do not move up. Whether they do or not has been the subject of a rather large quantity of writing but is still unresolved. While executives are those higher in the organization, the characteristics of the work performed and the performers themselves will generally be viewed as similar except for the status difference.

An important statement on the functions of the executive was provided by Chester I. Barnard, a former president of the New Jersey Bell Telephone Company in his book *The Functions of the Executive*. A major contribution to organizational theory, the book views the organization as a decision-making system and also provides an overview of the work of executives. According to Barnard, executives perform three major functions. The first is the maintenance of communications within the organization, which involves the establishment of positions in the organization to form a communications system and the filling of these positions with personnel who are capable of performing the required communications functions.[3] According to Barnard, those filling these positions should be loyal to and dominated by the organization. This loyalty and domination is brought about by creating the proper incentives for the incumbents, such as interest and pride in the work, prestige, and material rewards. The last of which is the least important in this regard.[4] Barnard suggests that those lower in the hierarchy need more specific abilities than their superiors. The latter, the generalists, acquire their abilities through experience, while the former can be given specific training in their specialties. The effective organization matches the abilities of the executive with the communications requirements of the position to be filled.

The second major function of the executive is the securing of essential services from individuals which involves bringing people into cooperative relationships with the organization by promotional techniques and propaganda and eliciting the required services from the individuals once they are willing to cooperate. The services are elicited by maintaining morale and inducements, developing norms and sanctions, supervision, and socialization into the jobs.[5]

The third executive function is the formulation and definition of the purposes, objectives, or goals of the organization. More than simply stating that the goal is profit, service, or whatever, this involves the translation of the organizational goals into specific activities that are carried out all the way down the hierarchy, with the activities becoming more specific as the hierarchy is descended.[6] Barnard states that these functions are "merely elements in an organic whole. It is their combination in a working system that makes an organization."[7]

A more contemporary, but quite similar, view of executive functions is provided by the editors of *Fortune* magazine. From a compilation of definitions provided by executives, the following composite self-portrait emerged:

An American executive is a person paid for a full-time job in which he: (1) directly helps to set his company's

[3]Barnard, *The Functions of the Executive* (Cambridge, Mass.: Harvard University Press, 1947), pp. 217–18.
[4]Barnard, *The Functions of the Executive*, pp. 220–22.
[5]Barnard, *The Functions of the Executive*, pp. 227–31.
[6]Barnard, *The Functions of the Executive*, pp. 231–32.
[7]*The Functions of the Executive*, p. 233.

objectives and over-all policies; (2) is required to make or approve decisions that significantly affect profits and future plans; (3) coordinates several major corporate functions, or those of a major division or department; (4) maintains and develops an organization of trained subordinates to achieve the company's objectives; *and* (5) delegates responsibility and authority to the organization, and controls performance and results through at least one level of supervision.[8]

This last point is the simplest means of differentiating between executives and managers. The executive has a wider span of control, both in terms of personnel and policy. While many managers perform some of the functions, the true executive performs them all. In addition, the authors suggest that executives are only found in relatively large organizations of 1,000 employees or more. While the size is certainly arbitrary, the differentiation itself is not. The manager performs narrower and more specific functions, with relatively little impact on policy formulation, while the executive has a broader impact.

Before proceeding to an analysis of the ways in which men become executives, a subject of great interest to scholars, novelists, journalists, and playwrights, some consideration should be given to the characteristics of those who are executives at a given point in time. The *Fortune* study of the top three executives in the 250 largest corporations in the United States (the study was made in 1952, but the general results are probably still relevant) reveals some interesting common characteristics among these industrial leaders. These men are very well paid. The median income (before taxes) was between 70,000 and 80,000 dollars a year, and some earned more than 350,000 dollars per year. Whether or not these men are worth this much money is a relevant question, which will be touched upon in a later section. These top executives are not young men; the overwhelming majority were in their fifties and sixties. In general they had worked for the same or only one other company during their careers, and almost 60 per cent had been hired by their company while they were in their twenties.

These executives were well-educated; 81 per cent had attended college, and 22 per cent had done postgraduate study. Among the younger executives (under 50), the educational background was even more evident with only 5 per cent not having attended college and an increased proportion (over 33 per cent) having postgraduate

[8]The editors of *Fortune, The Executive Life* (New York: Doubleday & Company, Inc., 1956), pp. 17–18.

study. The older executives tended to have majored in engineering and the sciences; while the younger group was concentrated in business and economics.[9] In this sense, the educational backgrounds of executives and professionals is not too dissimilar. The professional has a more specialized and limited area of training than the executive, but the executive probably has quantitatively as much education as most professionals. Unlike professionals, however, the executive's training is often unrelated to his career in the corporation. As the authors note:

> There are . . . bizzare contrasts. Nearly half of all executives have concentrated on engineering and science, but only a third of them rose to their present eminence through these or related fields of work. Only one executive out of twelve makes use of law in his company, but one out of seven studied it. Interest in the liberal arts was scant among men who are now leaders of that highly complex social organization, the large corporation.[10]

The editors suggest that the major factor in this lack of correspondence between training and its use in the corporation as a man rises to the top is the tradition in the industry. Some industries apparently expect their top executives to come from legal or engineering backgrounds, moving potential top men into general management at a relatively early age.

Since these men are well trained, but do not necessarily use their specific training, the question of whether or not they can in any way be considered professionals is relevant. As early as 1925, Louis D. Brandeis argued that business management was in fact a profession.[11] Parsons notes that business shares with the professions the value of rationality, functional specificity, and universalism. He also suggests that businessmen are probably no less altruistic than professionals, seeking the same end of self-fulfillment and goal realization. At the same time, he notes that differences such as advertising among businessmen as opposed to the professional ethic against advertising do exist.[12] In an earlier paper, Robert M. MacIver argued that business management could not be considered a profession because of differences in ethical orientations. He did not mean that executives were inherently less

[9]The editors of *Fortune, The Executive Life*, pp. 27–43.
[10]The editors of *Fortune, The Executive Life*, p. 7.
[11]See Brandeis, *Business–A Profession* (Boston: Small, Maynard and Company, 1925).
[12]See Parsons "The Professions and Social Structure," *Social Forces*, XVII, 4 (May, 1939), 457–67.

ethical but that there is not a community that can serve as an enforcer of ethical codes.[13] In a recent paper, Evan argued that stockbrokers, a group that was considered in the section on professions but that also could be considered in the executive category, since they are in a marginal position, cannot be considered as full-fledged professionals because of their solely fiduciary relation when dealing with clients.[14] They may have an interest in selling bonds or securities, even if it is to the client's disadvantage. Many stockbrokers, of course, quite appropriately claim that this is unethical and that the majority of their members do not engage in such practices. The most obvious reason why managers and executives cannot be considered true professionals, in terms of the professional model, is the fact that there are no formal criteria in terms of education or licensure for entering the occupation; however, a college education has become necessary for entrance into the managerial ranks. While a relatively small proportion of the older executives in the *Fortune* study did not attend college, a *very* small proportion (5 per cent) of the younger executives did not. This fact, plus the growth of graduate schools of business, suggests that an informal educational criterion does exist and that coming up through the ranks from the worker level to management or office boy to president is no longer a meaningful model. In regard to business management as a profession, therefore, the conclusion of Vollmer and Mills that "business management appears to be professionalized in some respects, but not in others"[15] is the best way to summarize this discussion. Among some management occupations, such as personnel work or accounting, the interest in professionalization is growing. Among others the interest has not yet been verbalized so that the very issue is of only analytical importance.

Before turning to some of the characteristics of managers and executives a further note on the backgrounds of this category is in order. In a 1952 study of 8,000 business leaders in the United States, W. Lloyd Warner and James Abegglen developed two distinct career patterns from background data on these executives. One pattern was that of the *mobile elite*. This pattern, as the name suggests, characterizes those who have moved into the executive stratum from a lower socio-economic status. The family background of these men typically includes a dominant mother, who early in life instilled the values of discipline and striving in her son, and a weak

[13]See MacIver "The Social Significance of Professional Ethics," *The Annals of the American Academy of Political and Social Science,* CI (May, 1922), 5–11. Both the Parsons and MacIver papers are reprinted in Vollmer and Mills, *Professionalization.*

[14]Evan, *op. cit.,* pp. 80–82.

[15]Vollmer and Mills, *Professionalization,* p. 56.

father disliked by the son. The mobile-elite executive experienced some early successes in athletics, music, school politics, or some other endeavor and thus learned that he could be successful. As he began his career, this type of executive started a pattern of leaving old friends and behavior patterns behind. He left his family and friends as well as his mannerisms and attitudes as he climbed the corporate ladder, which is, of course, vital if a person is to be mobile. At the same time, this pattern allows the person to be mobile without regrets, since close ties are not established. These men often attached themselves to a successful man in their corporation, a father figure in Warner and Abegglen's terms, and moved up the hierarchy with him. He provided training and encouragement along the way. The mobile elite is characterized by a single-mindedness oriented toward the goal of getting ahead.[16] Clearly, not all who begin this way will achieve their goal of top positions, but the pattern is true for those who have been mobile.

In a somewhat similar vein, David E. Berlew and Douglas T. Hall report that challenges in an executive's first year of employment and success in meeting difficult assignments leads to continued success, both intrinsically and extrinsically, for the individual.[17] Thus a history of success contributes strongly to continued movement in corporate hierarchies.

The second basic pattern was that of the *birth elite*. These are the sons of successful fathers. While born with the proverbial silver spoon, they have to maintain their positions. In this case the father is the dominant figure, and the socialization process is designed to allow him to follow in his father's footsteps. The education of the birth elite is typically in Ivy League type schools and emphasizes development of the appropriate social graces. As the person moves into the corporate hierarchy, he is likely to begin a systematic affiliation with civic and philanthropic activities and social clubs that will assist him in achieving his desired goal. A potential source of strain for this type is that he might not want to follow in his father's footsteps, even though this is what his family and training demand. The birth elite is more likely to be found in smaller firms and the mobile elite in larger organizations.[18] Since the trend is toward larger organizations, the projection would seem to be that if the educational channels are kept open, the mobile-elite type will emerge as the more dominant type of executive.

---

[16]Warner and Abegglen, *Big Business Leaders in America* (New York: Harper & Row, Publishers, 1955), p. 82.

[17]"The Socialization of Managers," *Administrative Science Quarterly*, XI, 2 (September, 1966), 207–23.

[18]Warner and Abegglen, *Big Business Leaders in America*, p. 176.

Thus far the executive has been portrayed as a well-educated, status-striving (whether to achieve or maintain his status) person. Since the executive by definition has achieved or maintained a high status, the next question is, how does he do it? Two distinct and generally contradictory answers have been given. The first centers around the idea of a kind of conformity, while the second is based on the idea of innovativeness and taking risks.

The best known expression of the first approach is *The Organization Man* by William H. Whyte, Jr. The organization man adheres to the "Social Ethic," which is based on belief in the group as a source of creativity, belief in the rightness of belonging, and belief in the applicability of science to human affairs. According to Whyte, the organization man is not so much a conformer as one who totally accepts what the organization can do for him and society; he does not question the system. The organization man is geared to compromise and being part of the group and does not rock the boat. The education of the organization man is oriented toward orthodoxy and being well-rounded. Even the pattern of his home life in suburbia is one of conforming to neighborhood norms regarding visiting patterns and recreational activities. He engages in "inconspicuous consumption," not buying cars or appliances inappropriate to his position in the corporation. Whyte suggests that this is not conformity for conformity's sake but rather is a *moral imperative*.[19] The organization man believes in and does not question the system. Whyte's concern is with the effect that this has on the individual and society. At the individual level, the person is not allowed to reach (or fall to) his full potential. At the societal level mediocrity is a probable consequence. Whether Whyte's analysis is correct is not the central issue here, what is important is his description of the manner in which a person becomes an executive.

Robert Presthus' work reinforces this description. As discussed in Chap. 3, Presthus identifies three basic responses to the organization, the upward-mobile, the indifferent, and the ambivalent. Our interest is in the upward-mobile. According to Presthus, he has the following characteristics:

1. He accepts the organizational goals.
2. He submits to and accepts the collective values of the organization, involving power, survival, and growth.

[19]*The Organization Man*, p. 438.

3. He is obedient, accepting authority as proper and legitimate.

4. He attaches himself personally to his superiors but remains detached and impersonal toward his subordinates.

5. The organizational norms become his personal norms.

6. He exhibits high morale and job satisfaction and does not question the system and if and when failure comes, it is a personal failure not one of the system itself.

7. He is highly involved in the organization, which contributes to organizational effectiveness.

8. He is action oriented and tends to ignore conflicting alternatives and ambiguities.

9. When hostility and resentment arise, they are not voiced. He does not show anger at his superior. He tries to be "other-directed," playing the role required for success.

10. When he feels anxiety, it is not admitted. Presthus notes that a high ulcer and hypertension rate is a consequence of this.

11. He is a local rather than a cosmopolitan.

12. He shies away from controversial causes and dissent.

13. He suffers a great deal of status anxiety and is very aware of status symbols. For this reason, organizations attempt to insure that the office furnishings for executives of equal rank are identical, so that unintended distinctions are not imagined.

14. Status achievement becomes an end in itself rather than the result of significant achievement.

15. He is a joiner in community activities.

16. The rewards for the upward-mobile individual are not found in the intrinsic value of the work being performed but rather in the effect that the work will have for his position in the organization.[20]

Despite the status anxiety and the sublimation of hostility, this type of person remains optimistic and cheerful. He believes that

[20]Presthus, *The Organizational Society*, pp. 164–204.

he has the system by which he can achieve his desired mobility. Both
Whyte and Presthus suggest that the route to the executive wash-
room is paved with conformity. The system is both accepted and
embraced. These writers seem to be saying that the individual's true
personality cannot be expressed when this role is played. This is, at
best, an extremely difficult position to demonstrate empirically.
While a rather high incidence of such physical symptoms as ulcers
and hypertension are found among this group, less severe mental
and emotional malfunctioning is also found.[21] A more serious, but
equally difficult to demonstrate, problem, which these authors pose,
is the degree of acceptance by the upward-mobile individual of the
organization as normatively and morally correct in its actions. Few
would argue with the point that at various times and in various ways
organizations are neither. This, of course, is not limited to business
organizations, since governmental, educational, and religious organizations can share equally in such an indictment.

These, as well as other more polemically critical, approaches to
the nature of the modern executive and the modern organization do
not comprise the only assessments of this aspect of the occupational
world. A strikingly different picture of the modern executive is
offered by Walter Guzzardi, Jr., also with *Fortune* magazine, in his
analysis of young executives. Guzzardi's subjects were upper-level
executives in their thirties and forties. While not top executives,
they were clearly climbing the ladder of corporate success. As would
be expected, 85 per cent of these men were college graduates; 40 per
cent held advanced degrees. Interestingly, some 80 per cent of these
men had worked part time during their educational years.[22] Some
worked from necessity, while others did not have to work but did so
for a variety of personal reasons. All worked in large corporations
after graduation. It should be pointed out that the Whyte, Presthus,
and Guzzardi studies do not claim to be scientific in that their
samples are not necessarily representative of the universe under
discussion. Relatively unstructured data gathering devices were
used, and the discussions are based upon impressions rather than
statistically significant findings. Nevertheless, each does appear to
catch the essence of the group under discussion. Whether or not the
groups are the same or are representative of the class called
executives becomes the real question, to be dealt with at a later
point.

[21]A. B. Hollingshead and F. C. Redlich, *Social Class and Mental Illness* (New York: John Wiley & Sons, Inc., 1958).
[22]Guzzardi, *The Young Executives* (New York: New American Library, Inc., 1964), p. 21. Courtesy of Fortune Magazine; © 1965 Time Inc.

Guzzardi suggests that these young executives are far from conformists; instead, their "greatest psychic satisfaction comes when [they] succeed in making a change in the company's or industry's business methods."[23] They *dissent* from established practice, thrive on making decisions, and are confident in their own decision-making power. According to Guzzardi, they have self-imposed professional standards of excellence.[24] These standards, unlike those of the professionals previously discussed, do not arise from a collective response to the work situation but rather are individual standards developed from a pragmatic philosophy. Good decisions are those that show results. They rebel against their establishment if they feel their own approach is more sound. A dominant characteristic of these executives is avid reading; which tends to be highly specialized in areas useful in their work. The arts and humanities are "part of another world."[25] Although their intellectual life tends to be narrow, it is very highly developed. Instead of feeling constrained by the large corporation, they feel that there is more freedom to operate in that context. They are less influenced by their superiors, since there are multiple and non-traditional authority lines. They do not fear the advent of the computer. Instead they welcome it because of their approach to life which is based on facts, since the more facts that are available, the better the decisions. Thus far, the picture is one of a hard-driving, confident, and success-oriented man. It is probably an accurate picture as far as it goes.

While these characteristics seem to dominate the discussion, some other points in the analysis suggest that these young executives, while not "organization men" or "upward-mobiles," do in fact operate within a constraining system. They are concerned with the timing of their innovativeness, realizing that an inappropriately timed move might be personally disastrous. They believe that the corporate system is fair and that the system as a whole operates to the benefit of the total society—What is good for business is good for the nation.[26] They have little concern with the social impact of business, an outlook which is at least partially shaped by their limited intellectual range. These kinds of constraints and outlooks again are not limited to the business world.

Strikingly different approaches to the organization and to a career are evident in the two paths to executive positions which have

[23]Guzzardi, *The Young Executives*, p. 9.
[24]*The Young Executives*, p. 124.
[25]Guzzardi, *The Young Executives*, p. 42.
[26]Guzzardi, *The Young Executives*, p. 52.

been discussed. These are apparently very real differences that coexist in the corporate world and raise a number of questions, the most obvious of which is why? Guzzardi suggests that the innovative executive can only be successful in organizations open to innovation.[27] This openness can be caused by a variety of factors. In the first place, custom and tradition play a role. Some industries, such as railroading, appear to be quite bound by tradition, while others, such as office equipment, are more freewheeling and innovative. A second factor is probably the nature of the product or service being performed. Hypothetically, organizations that rely upon the innovative process itself, in the form of research and development and similar kinds of programs, should be much more open to innovativeness on the part of their personnel in areas other than specific research departments and those with less interest and investment in such endeavors less open to such innovativeness on the part of their executives. If this hypothesis is correct, then an important corollary is that such innovativeness will increase in importance as research and development increase in importance. The trends noted in Chap. 2 suggest that the innovative executive will be the "wave of the future" if this line of reasoning is correct. At the present time there is no evidence available to determine the proportion of executives who are innovators or organization men or what changes are occurring in the proportions. One further, subjective, note is in order. Whyte's *The Organization Man* was widely read and discussed in the business community as well as in academia. It would seem there was a reaction to the picture of conformity the book portrayed and that organizations became introspective in this regard, trying to move away from the kinds of pathologies which Whyte so vividly described. If this is the case, then Guzzardi's findings in regard to the innovators are not surprising, since the organizations themselves may have begun to demand this type of response.

A second, and again unanswerable, question about these two types of executives is, What is the impact of either type on the organization and on the person himself? Whyte suggests that the organization man is organizationally, as well as personally, pathological.[28] He notes that large corporations are themselves headed by men who have been hard-driving innovators. If a generation of organization men rises to the top positions in organizations, the

[27]Guzzardi, *The Young Executives*, p. 69.
[28]An extended discussion of this type of pathology is contained in Victor A. Thompson, *Modern Organization* (New York: Alfred A. Knopf, Inc., 1961). See particularly Chap. 8.

organizations themselves may assume some of the conformist, negative characteristics of their leaders. Presthus noted that the organization-man type tended to sublimate his anxieties and frustrations, leading to psychosomatic disorders and other behavioral problems. On the other hand, Guzzardi's innovators often are quite ruthless in their approach to corporate problems, laying workers and executives off and altering corporate structures. If their ideas work, all is well and good (except for those laid off or demoted, of course). If they happen to make a mistake, then the repercussions are similarly quite drastic. Although Guzzardi suggests that those he interviewed have been successful, it seems quite likely that some innovators whom he did not interview, because they did not make it to executive positions, would have actually harmed their organizations. For the innovator, accomplishment and success are highly rewarding. Since corporate hierarchies are pyramidal in shape, accomplishment could continue indefinitely, while success in terms of movement up the hierarchy might not. As soon as a career blockage occurs, the effects on the individual are clearly negative. At the same time, the hard-driving innovator may find himself in a situation wherein his personal life is not the most pleasant in the world. He may not be well liked by his cohorts in the organization, especially if their toes have been stepped on. There is some evidence that his relations with his family and children may suffer because of his intense devotion to his work. The degree to which this might affect him would probably vary widely.

The issues under discussion require intensive research if they are to be resolved. There is some empirical evidence suggesting that, while the values and orientations of executives vary widely in terms of conformity and general approaches to life, the variations themselves are not dissimilar from those found among other occupational groups. John B. Miner, for example, found that executives and professors exhibited essentially identical patterns on a test of conformity. Among both groups conformity decreased with age, and both groups exhibited wide ranges of conformity and deviance at the various age levels. Miner also suggests that demands for conformity or innovation may vary with the type of industry and with the orientation of the academic discipline.[29] In the same vein, Renato Tagiuri found little difference in the ordering of values among groups of scientists, executives, and research managers. Using the Allport-Vernon-Lindsey value questionnaire, which measures interest in theoretical, economic, aesthetic, social, political, and religious

[29]"Conformity Among Professors and Executives," *Administrative Science Quarterly*, VII, 1 (June, 1962), 96–109.

pursuits, Tagiuri found essentially the same ordering of these values; theoretical (discovery of truth), political, and economic values ranked highest for all. He suggests that some of the professional-organizational (scientist-executive) conflicts, which have been discussed, may be based on misperceptions of other groups' orientations.[30] In this case it is the research manager, as a middle man, who must mediate between the groups, hopefully allowing each group to be seen in its true light. In terms of the present discussion, the fact that values are shared between these groups and Miner's findings suggest either that executives are not the organization men they have been portrayed to be or that these other occupations are equally composed of organization men. Stated more positively, samples of executives indicate that their values and orientations toward their work and life are essentially similar to those of other highly trained members of the occupational world.

a note on decision making

Whether conformist or deviant, the executive is expected to make decisions. Much of contemporary decision-making theory is organized around mathematically based models. These assume that the knowledge of the origins of the situation about which the decision is to be made, its current status, and the probable outcomes of alternative choices is quite complete. The advent of computers and other data-processing devices has contributed to the development of this approach, which assumes rationality on the part of the participants as well as complete knowledge. There is, however, some evidence that decision-making models ignore important components of reality.

James G. March and Herbert A. Simon, whose theory of organizations is based on decision making, point out:

> Most human decision making, whether individual or organizational, is concerned with the discovery and selection of satisfactory alternatives; only in exceptional cases is it concerned with the discovery and selection of optimal alternatives.[31]

[30]Tagiuri, "Value Orientations and the Relationship of Managers and Scientists," *Administrative Science Quarterly*, X, 1 (June, 1965), 39–51.
[31]*Organizations* (New York: John Wiley and Sons, Inc., 1958), pp. 140–41. For a comprehensive overview of the limitations of the assumption of pure rationality on the part of organizations and their participants see James G. Thompson, *Organizations in Action* (New York: McGraw-Hill Book Company, 1967).

These *satisficing* decisions are based on criteria that describe minimally satisfactory alternatives and that rely on less than perfect knowledge. Optimal decisions must be based on criteria that allow all alternatives to be compared, thus being dependent on perfect knowledge of the antecedents, current status, and expected outcomes of a particular case in the decision-making process, a set of conditions unlikely to occur in reality.

In the same vein, David Braybrooke has suggested that executives do act on the basis of nonrational decisions. The successful executive has a repertoire of responses to situations, unpremeditated in their application and not fully recognized by the executive himself. The response strategies are based upon resources such as the amount of energy and its application, the air and style of leadership, skill in bargaining, and universal connections (access to sources of information and assistance) a particular person possesses. These resources are transferable from situation to situation or organization to organization. Relatively nontransferable are such resources as mannerisms appropriate to a particular setting (the differences in approach of the stereotyped public-relations man as opposed to that of the conservative banker), local connections within an organization and with its affiliates, and knowledge of, and judgment about, the men with whom the executive interacts. The executive also has information from a variety of sources at his disposal. Braybrooke suggests that these elements are combined into stratagems which are employed in the decision-making process. Some stratagems become habitual, part of a particular executive's style. In some cases new or novel stratagems are employed, based upon some new mixture of the resources available. Whether habitual or new, the stratagems are not recognized as such by the individuals involved and are not necessarily based upon rational criteria. Any strategy employed, if it is used at all consistently, while predictable will not be, at times, rational.[32]

Braybrooke states:

> A perfect organization would leave the executive paradoxically little to do; an imperfect organization, in an imperfect world, creates so many difficulties for him that even sober observers are liable to credit his successes to intuitive wizardry.[33]

Instead of such intuitive wizardry, Braybrooke believes that

[32]David Braybrooke, "The Mystery of Executive Success Re-examined," *Administrative Science Quarterly*, VIII, 4 (March, 1964), 533–60.
[33]"The Mystery of Executive Success Re-examined," p. 560.

executives combine resources into the stratagems discussed above, which allow him to proceed, but in a less than totally rational way.

executive pay

While it is not the intent of this book to examine intensively the morality of the rates of compensation for the various occupational groups examined, a brief look at executive compensation is enlightening for a number of reasons. The point that modern corporations and their executives do not operate in the most rational manner will be reaffirmed. In addition, it is apparent that the exact worth of executives is uncertain. Finally, the point made in the chapter on professions that organizational structure is an important determinant of behavior will be indirectly strengthened by the fact that executives in different segments of the economy and in different organizations within the same segment perform the same services for widely different rates of pay. Thus behavior, as expressed by the willingness to perform with the knowledge of the differences, is shaped by organizational as well as individual expectations.

The *Fortune* study of executives points out that executives performing the same functions within an industry and between industries receive widely varied salaries, ranging in their estimates from $20,000 to $100,000 for the same job. Part of the variation can be explained by the traditions surrounding compensation rates for top management. According to this report:

> Generally speaking, a president will receive in salary about a third more than his No. 2 man, about twice what his No. 3 man gets, and some three times the salaries paid to those on the fourth rung of management. Thus, if the president's salary is $100,000, the ceiling on middle management pay scales is likely to be set at around $30,000.[34]

Differing rates of pay for the top executive therefore have repercussions all the way down the hierarchy. In addition to salary, of course, a major part of executive compensation comes from non-salary items, such as bonuses, stock options, annuities, deferred pay, and fringe benefits, such as insurance, use of company cars and planes, expense accounts, etc.

In a large corporation, according to the *Fortune* analysis, this kind of system creates difficulties for the middle range executives

[34]The Editors of *Fortune*, "The Executive Life," p. 100.

and managers. Recruitment patterns are such that new college graduates must be offered higher and higher salaries as inducements to join the organization. Unless the top executives are willing either to raise their own salaries, thus raising the ceiling for the middle range, or lessen the differential between their own compensation and that of their subordinates, the middle management range is faced with the uncomfortable situation of new personnel earning almost as much as they do. Another difficulty at the middle management level is that some specialists who are in short supply earn much more than people in comparable positions in the hierarchy who are plentiful in the job market. When the upper reaches of the corporate hierarchy are analyzed, it becomes difficult to determine the relative importance of each job; thus even more nonrationality is incorporated into the compensation system. The problems of compensation are compounded by the fact that compensation per se is only one part of the over-all motivation the organizations must recognize. Security, recognition, performance, and gratifying social interaction, for example, also must be considered. As has often been demonstrated for blue-collar and clerical workers, sheer financial compensation is not the only source of motivation for effective performance. Since executives share many characteristics with other members of the higher strata in the occupational hierarchy, it could be predicted that they too would have a concern with such nonfinancial inducements. As noted previously, however, the financial rewards of a position do serve as major symbols for some of the other forms of inducements and compensation therefore remains important.

A different perspective on executive salaries is taken by Wilbert Moore, who notes strong organizational influence in this area. He states:

> There is a notable correlation between the size of corporations and the salaries of their chief officers. This appears immediately sensible, on the assumption that managing a large concern requires more talent than managing a small one. Yet for this assumption there is scant evidence. It is possible that the 20,000 dollar-a-year president of a small concern doing two million dollars of annual business has a more difficult and demanding job than the president of the corporation so large and luxurious that specialized staffs take on many functions that the lesser executive must do for himself.

Part of the explanations of high executive salaries scarcely constitute justifications. The first explanation is organizational. In a large organization there are many steps from the bottom to the top, and the idea prevails that each step should entail a net increment in income over the one below it, often around 15 per cent. If there were no income taxes, or if they were assessed at a flat rate, this would still not result in very high salaries at the top. In a 15 layer organization with a 4,000 dollar base wage and a 15 per cent increment by rank, the top salary would be only slightly over 28,000 dollars or around a ratio of 7 to 1. Although some of the differentials are substantially steeper than 15 per cent, a principal factor in the high executive salaries is the graduated income tax, which makes the preservation of net differentials an increasingly costly affair. The result in terms of gross pay may be a differential of 100 to 1, although the net ratio is much narrower.

The other explanation is less impersonal, less "circumstantial." Executive salaries are determined by the boards of directors, and executive officers are also members of the board. Good manners may prevent their voting on their own salaries, but the independence of boards and executives from external supervision or control does, I suggest, encourage all of the spurious rationalizations for what may amount to plunder or legal embezzlement.[35]

This critical approach to executive salaries and the role of the graduated income tax is extended by Gerhard E. Lenski. He points out that while incomes at the higher levels are taxed more heavily, regressive taxes, such as the sales tax, and nonprogressive taxes, such as property or gasoline taxes, make the difference in tax rates between top executives and those working for the basic wage (in a fifteen-layer organization) only about ten per cent. Lenski further suggests that executives in industries subject to public scrutiny through government regulatory agencies, such as public utilities and railroads, do not pay exceptionally high executive salaries. Much of the high pay in private industry can be attributed to the power positions of the executives in the organization, according to this analysis.[36]

This examination of executive compensation, while designed to demonstrate some of the nonrational factors that are part of this occupational group, also suggests that the executive group itself is

[35]*The Conduct of the Corporation* (New York: Random House, Inc., 1962), pp. 14–15.
[36]Lenski, *Power and Privilege* (New York: McGraw-Hill Book Company, 1966), pp. 354–56.

quite heterogeneous. While it is the successful climber, the man with the six-figure salary, or the conforming organization man who catches the eye, reality would suggest that the executive group is composed of a spectrum of individuals, performing widely varied functions and with widely varying abilities, personalities, motivations, and rewards. At the outset of this chapter it was suggested that our knowledge about executives is actually quite limited, a point which should be now evident from the often laudatory, often critical studies utilized in this examination.

managers

The discussion thus far has been focused on top executives. These personnel are the visible group within the over-all managerial hierarchy of the corporate world. Top executives are drawn from the broad group of management roles that are above first-line supervision in organizations (first-line supervisors will be considered in the section on foremen). Managers share most of the characteristics of the executives already discussed, such as education, varying aspirations, functions performed, etc. Since their positions are lower in the hierarchy, their work is more specialized and involves less responsibility and authority. Examples of such roles are production managers, sales representatives, industrial relations or personnel managers, public relations officials, accountants, maintenance superintendents, and data analysts at various levels in the hierarchy. Some of the managerial roles involve professional or professionalizing occupations, such as engineers, accountants, and public relations officials. Others are more traditional managerial roles. A major factor in the behavior of managers is that they are *specialists*, occupying well defined positions. Their training and the nature of their work limit the scope of their activities. Their positions in organizations define their interaction patterns on the job. The functions they perform are similar to those of executives, but on a smaller scale. They make decisions on policy, but only insofar as it affects their limited sphere of endeavor and within the framework of over-all corporate policy. Their performance is subject to more direct scrutiny, since they themselves are supervised. The possibility for innovation or experimentation depends on the amount of autonomy given to them.

While the managerial role is limited in terms of the organization, this does not mean that the manager is free from ambiguity or conflict. Segments of organizations have their own goals and purposes, which are part of the over-all structure, and the goals of a department may at times be in conflict with the goals of other departments. Similarly, demands from superiors may be incompatible with those from peers or subordinates. These conflicts for the manager are neatly illustrated in Delbert C. Miller and William H. Form's analysis of the role of the plant manager. The role of the plant manager, while concerned with the line production function, would be analogous to that of the personnel manager, sales manager, or other middle management positions in terms of conflicting demands. The first source of such conflict comes from top management itself, which wants production quotas met. Miller and Form point out that top management often comes from areas other than production and thus may not be sympathetic to the production manager's problems. At the same time, top management views the production manager's problem as only a part of the total picture. Thus, while his problems are only slightly significant to the top echelon, they are of overriding importance to the person himself.[37]

A second source of conflict is relations with staff departments. For example, finance departments are obviously concerned about costs. Units such as production are also concerned about their performance, using past performances as standards for comparison. A duplicate cost system can thus develop wherein people in production keep their own records on an informal basis in order to insure that their record looks good. In addition to this, the following kind of situation can develop:

> The plant manager is affected by the financial preoccupation of his underlings in an indirect way. For example, a poor record in Assembly may be due to slipshod work in Manufacturing, failure of Supply to provide requisite materials, the fact that Maintenance fell down on its job of repairing machinery, high absenteeism rates, or other factors. Since the accounting reports do not reflect these extenuating circumstances, the head of Assembly is called on the carpet. He naturally feels resentment against other department heads who may be responsible for his poor record. Recriminations against other department heads are brought to the plant manager.[38]

He in turn feels resentment against Finance for contributing to this state of affairs.

In a similar fashion, inspection departments can exert pressure

[37]Miller and Form, *Industrial Sociology*, pp. 192–93.
[38]Miller and Form, *Industrial Sociology*, p. 194.

on production by varying their inspection criteria. This may again create a situation wherein production establishes a parallel organization for protection against the inspection department. Engineering departments, because they are oriented toward change and improved technology, may constantly seek the introduction of change into the production process to justify their own existence. The introduction of change, of course, creates disruptions in production providing another source of tension for the plant manager and his subordinates. In a similar fashion, personnel and industrial relations departments may base their operations on criteria different from those which production views as optimal.

Further insights into these problems are provided by Melville Dalton's analysis of staff-line conflicts. He suggests that there are three broad conflict areas that are built into industrial organizations. In the first place, staff personnel have different backgrounds and orientations from those of the line officers. The staff personnel are younger and better educated than the line officers. They are also highly oriented toward mobility, leading to high turnover rates due to high inter- and intraorganizational mobility. The age differences lead to antagonisms on the part of the older line managers, who dislike being told what to do by the younger staff. They often do not accept or utilize the suggestions made. This leads to frustrations for the staff. They may then either attempt social manipulation to achieve their goals or look for another job where their ideas will be better accepted. Social differences in speech patterns, dress, recreational patterns, and concern for personal appearance also contributed to the distance between the groups.[39]

The second basic source of the conflict lies in the staff personnel's need to prove its worth. The staff person views himself as an agent of top management committed to new and useful ideas. Because of his level of education and close knowledge of new theories of production and supervision, he is likely to view middle and lower line officials with some degree of condescension, which in itself contributes to strained relationships. The staff person is thus in the dilemma of trying to prove his worth by his new ideas, but in so doing creating a situation which operates against acceptance of himself or his ideas.

The final source of conflict derived from the formal structure of the three plants Dalton used in his analysis. The top line officers held the highest positions in the plants; thus their approval was important for the advancement of staff members. This led to a strong

[39]Dalton, "Conflict between Staff and Line Managerial Officers," *American Sociological Review*, XV, 3 (June, 1950), 342–51.

concern on the part of the staff with the proper presentation of ideas rather than with the ideas themselves. At the same time, line officers feared being shown to be behind the times and might sabotage the ideas of the staff. When this happened, the staff person looked bad. In this situation both line and staff are subject to pressures indigenous to the situation.

These conflicts are not limited to production organizations. Whatever the line function happens to be, sales, administration of public policy, or research and development, line and administrative officials will at times be in conflict. Even in the most rational and efficient organization, where the members are committed to the achievement of the organization's goal, the translation of the goal into specific departmental activities creates situations wherein the specific operating principles of a department conflict with those of other divisions in the organization. In a case known to the author, a rapidly expanding company that depended upon and was devoted to technological developments was faced with constant conflicts between the sales, research and development, and production departments. Background differences were not an important factor in this instance, since all three were headed by and staffed by young scientists and engineers. In this case the sales personnel would study a customer's need and would promise that their equipment could alleviate the problem. Unfortunately, the equipment was not yet on the drawing boards. The salesmen knew that the equipment could be developed, but their techniques put great pressure on research and development, which had its own projects, and subsequently on production which was in the same position.

Miller and Form discuss an additional source of conflict for the plant manager, as well as for supervisory personnel in any capacity. Subordinates must be dealt with on the basis of the subordinate's own aspirations, motivations, and reactions to the work situation. Those subordinates who themselves are supervisors at a lower level must account for their unit productivity. The supervisor can thus become an enemy of sorts, making demands that appear to be unattainable. The supervisor himself is put in the position of being accountable for work for which he is not directly responsible. Since the supervisor's financial, technical, and personnel resources are themselves limited by competing demands from other organizational sectors, he cannot always provide what his own subordinates need.[40]

The discussion thus far has concentrated on the conflicts confronting the manager. Some balance to this presentation can be

[40]Miller and Form, *Industrial Sociology*, p. 200.

achieved by noting that, as discussed earlier, this stratum in the occupational hierarchy exhibited the highest levels of job satisfaction in national and cross-national surveys. While the stresses and conflicts may be severe, so are the positive rewards from the job. A study by Charles M. Bonjean suggests that managers have strong, favorable self-images and believe that their occupational roles permit "relatively full expression of their individual potential as well as opportunities to expand this potential."[41] Contrary to some expectations, Bonjean also found that the managers in his study did not feel powerless in their large organizations and were in general less alienated than samples of small businessmen and workers included in the study.

A major factor in this positive orientation toward their life and work may be that managers are in the main stream of contemporary society. As will be discussed below, it is the small business owner and others who are most adversely affected by the trends toward large corporations and large organizations in general. Another, and more negative, view of the middle manager is provided by C. Wright Mills. He suggests that, while middle management contains technically specialized personnel, the major concern of this group is the management of people rather than the utilization of technical skills.[42] This is the same point made by Dalton and Miller and Form in their analyses. The person must be accepted before his ideas can be put into practice. If the manager includes the management of people as part of his repertoire of skills, then he will feel that he can achieve his potential in the large organization. Contrary to Mills' implication, it is difficult to demonstrate that the management of people is in any way less self-realizing or moral than the utilization of material, technical skills. It certainly can be, but there is little evidence to suggest that management of people has consistently negative results for those managed or for the manager himself.

Before proprietors are analyzed, an additional point about both managers and executives should be made. The evidence presented thus far has shown that this group is oriented toward upward mobility, regardless of the technique used. It is obvious that there are limits to such mobility, given the nature of organizations. Nevertheless, the occupational group being examined is characterized by the fact that the vast majority of its members are at least somewhat mobile in their careers. Unlike the world of nature, in the

[41]"Mass, Class, and the Industrial Community," *American Journal of Sociology*, LXXII, 2 (Sept., 1966), 154.

[42]*White Collar* (New York: Oxford University Press, 1956), p. 86.

organizational world what goes up generally stays up. Demotions do occur, however, with ramifications for the individual and the organization. Organizations must at times eliminate incompetent incumbents by demotion or discharge. According to Fred H. Goldner, this forces the organization to legitimize at least a significant proportion of this failure so that deviant acts and withdrawal on the part of the participants do not ensue.[43] The participants in the system should not become alienated or have their motivation destroyed. For the individual, problems of redefinition of the self-concept become paramount.

Goldner's analysis of the demotion patterns in one organization exemplifies the issues in the demotion process. The organization examined was a diversified industrial firm with widely dispersed sales, research, and production facilities. The organization has expanded rapidly and great upward mobility resulted from its policy of promoting from within. The organization has adopted the policy of rewarding excellence by promotions that, at the same time, creates an atmosphere wherein merely adequate or inadequate performances are organizationally nonrational. In this firm, the general policy has been to retain those who are performing at the adequate level which in turn creates security for the employees at the expense of having positions filled by the most qualified personnel. In this organization, the motivation for advancement on the part of those interested in and able to be upwardly mobile is maintained, while those who are no longer performing above the adequate level are retained in the organization by demotion. The majority of the executives and managers interviewed believed that there was a good chance of their being demoted, since a belief had developed in the organization that demotion is a "normal phenomenon."[44] Those who believe that they may be demoted also believe that they may be promoted. This paradox is explained by the fluidity in the organizational structure and the manner in which the organization handles the demotion process. A major part of the demotion system is that it is obscure. Demotions are relatively invisible because of the high rate of lateral movement in the organization. A person can be transferred to another location without others knowing that he has been demoted. According to Goldner, some executives who are demoted do not realize that this has happened. Additional ambiguity is introduced by similar positions being filled by those on the way up and on the way down. Training sessions outside the company are

[43]"Demotion in Industrial Management," *American Sociological Review*, XXX, 5 (October, 1965), 714–24.
[44]Fred H. Goldner, "Demotion in Industrial Management," p. 718.

used for those who are being advanced and to help the adjustment of those being demoted. Another pattern is zig-zag mobility, where a person is changed to a lower status job and then changed again to a position of equal or higher status than his original job. This increases the ambiguity in that neither the person himself nor others can be sure whether his move is an actual demotion.

These arrangements allow the organization to maintain the norm that excellence is rewarded and at the same time provide a source of personal redefinition for those who are demoted. Since it is anticipated, demotion is not so personally damaging as it might be. Similarly, the pressures and long hours of higher positions serve as a "sour grapes " rationale for those not promoted. The organization, with its pattern of geographically shifting demoted personnel, provides additional techniques of redefinition. The individual is not forced to face friends and subordinates who knew him "when." He can turn his energies to nonwork activities in a new location, compensating for his lack of interest in his work. This particular organization attempts to protect its employees and itself by this demotional system. Although Goldner does not suggest this, it is logical that not all accept demotion gracefully and with a solid personal redefinition, nor is it probable that high motivation levels are maintained for all of those who have not yet been demoted. The organization itself, while altruistic in these patterns, also gains by not losing trained and experienced men. While they are demoted, these men still are useful in many corporate positions.

The analysis of demotion, while interesting in its own right, also illustrates a major concern of this section. The world of the executive and manager is *not* filled with one type of person with one career pattern. The analyses of the innovator versus the organization man and of demotion process illustrate this. Similarly, pictures of this group as either constantly making decisions without regard for the interests of other people or as an unhappy cog in a large corporate machine are inaccurate. In short, except in terms of factors such as educational level and relative affluence, managers and executives are a heterogeneous lot. The most important common feature of this group, perhaps, is the fact that they do work in organizations and thus must adapt to the particular organizational requirements. They do face conflicts in their position, are subject to pressures from above and below, and are demoted and fired. They also accept the purposes of their employer and are motivated to achieve within the organizational framework. It is a group which also has received relatively little systematic attention from social scientists.

The category of proprietors (owners of businesses) has undergone significant changes during the twentieth century. With very few exceptions, proprietorship today is limited to small businesses. The owners of large businesses are the diffuse stockholders, and the separation of ownership from management has been almost total. Although the owners in some cases may participate in the management of their businesses and indeed may comprise much of the top echelon of the executive hierarchy, in the large organization such a person would have the characteristics of an executive. The proprietor today is self-employed, gains at least half of his income in the form of profit or fees, and works in an organization having two, or fewer, levels of supervision.[45] Examples of such proprietorships are watch repair shops, beauty shops, delicatessens, hardware stores, and small manufacturing firms. For the most part, proprietors are found in retail and service businesses, since the opportunity in production organizations is limited by the economics of large scale production.

Walter L. Slocum suggests that most proprietorships have the characteristics of a family farm in that most of the necessary work is done by the proprietor and members of his family.[46] In addition, the proprietor performs multiple occupational roles, such as bookkeeping, cleaning, inventorying, buying, and most importantly, selling. Slocum maintains that the most important facet of the proprietor role is the maintenance of good customer relationships, since most small businesses cannot meet the prices or variety of products of chain or department stores.[47] The successful proprietor usually works long hours at a relatively low rate of pay. An additional feature of at least some forms of proprietorship is that the owner is not truly independent. Caplow, for example, points out that the veterans' legislation after World War II was directed toward the establishment of small businesses, such as filling stations, groceries, and dry-cleaning shops.[48] The products distributed to these operations are controlled by the producers and wholesalers. In many cases the prices charged for merchandise and services are set for the proprietor, so that he is not in fact an independent businessman.

[45]Bonjean, "Mass, Class, and the Industrial Community," p. 152.
[46]*Occupational Careers* (Chicago: Aldine Publishing Co., 1966), p. 58.
[47]*Occupational Careers*, p. 58.
[48]*The Sociology of Work*, p. 46.

In many proprietorships, the individual is forced by contract to purchase his materials from one source, further reducing his independence. Caplow suggests that the unit managers of the larger organizations that supply the small businesses are more adequately rewarded than those who function as owners. The owner typically must depend on corporate advertising to get the public's attention. According to Smelser, advertising has become a functional equivalent for personal contact between buyer and seller. While the small businessman does rely upon good customer relations to maintain a regular flow of business, the products purchased or used are standardized. The standard for trustworthiness, Smelser notes, has become standard prices, guarantees, brand names, and so on.[49] The only real entrepreneurship the proprietor can exercise is in the area of customer relations, since the rest of his business is in reality out of his control.

Another similarity between business proprietorship and contemporary farming is that there is a high rate of occupational inheritance. Most farmers are sons of farmers. The easiest means of entering small business is also through the family, either by blood or marriage. Small businesses require a substantial capital investment, in most cases, making it difficult, if not impossible, for potential proprietors to enter this occupation given the difficulties in amassing capital. In those instances where a small business is franchised as part of a larger organization, the lessee becomes a relatively poorly paid manager, subject to the policies of the franchising organization. As in the case of farming, the opportunities for the children of proprietors are limited, contributing to the movement away from this occupation on the part of the children.

The description thus far has suggested that proprietorship is in many ways a marginal occupation. This conclusion is strengthened when evidence regarding some personality and attitudinal characteristics of small businessmen is examined. In Bonjean's study of a Texas community, it was found that the independent businessmen, unlike the managers discussed above, exhibited relatively high degrees of alienation in terms of feeling powerless, normless, isolated from society, and low self-esteem. The businessmen also tended to rank higher on scales measuring social isolation, which involves membership in organized groups, visiting neighbors and relatives, attending religious services, and general social participation. Part of this can, of course, be explained by the long work hours that do not allow time for such social participation. On most

[49]*The Sociology of Economic Life*, p. 92.

166 of the variables included in the study, the businessmen ranked very

of the variables included in the study, the businessmen ranked very close to a sample of blue-collar workers. Bonjean attributes the reactions of the businessmen to the fact that their position in the Texas community had slipped with the arrival of industry after 1950. According to Bonjean, these are reactions to the "mass society" of which the businessmen do not feel a part.[50]

Martin Trow and later Norbert Wiley suggest additional factors that lead to the alienation of the proprietor from society. Trow notes that small businessmen in a New England community are hostile toward both big business and labor unions, two of the legitimate power sources in society.[51] Wiley interprets the small businessman as one with inconsistent class attributes.[52] Utilizing Weber's distinctions of three attributes of the social-class system, the labor market (employer-employee), the credit or money market (debtor-creditor), and the commodity market (buyer-seller), Wiley notes that two consistent sets of class attributes can be identified. The proprietor is the employer-creditor-seller, while the nonproprietor is the employee-debtor-buyer. Small businessmen and farmers comprise

> classic mixed types, for while both make their living by selling, they also do capital buying from powerful sellers, and their incomes are often affected as much by buying as selling. In addition, they are often heavily in debt and may be employers of labor, at least sporadically. Both groups, consequently, are affected with economic cross-pressure and cannot identify their interests with either big business or labor unions.[53]

Both Trow and Wiley support their conclusions by the fact that small businessmen and farmers alike have shown strong support for extreme right-wing political groups. Unable to identify with the major power blocs, identification with these extremist groups is a means of attacking the threatening forces of big business and big labor. Since, on the basis of census data, the proportion of the labor force in these occupations has declined, it would be expected that their political and social impact would do likewise.

[50]Bonjean, "Mass, Class, and the Industrial Community," p. 155.

[51]"Small Businessmen, Political Tolerance, and Support for McCarthy," *American Journal of Sociology*, LXIV, 3 (November, 1958), 270–81.

[52]Wiley, "America's Unique Class Politics: The Interplay of Labor, Credit and Commodity Markets," *American Sociological Review*, XXXII, 4 (August, 1967), 529–41.

[53]"America's Unique Class Politics: The Interplay of Labor, Credit and Commodity Markets," p. 536.

The analysis of the proprietor has focused on the marginal character of his occupation. A number of exceptions to the points made above can be found. In farming, for example, large farms now supply the majority of food. Whether in dairying, wheat, or produce, the large profitable farm resembles the modern organization more than the traditional family farm. Slocum notes that the farm manager is now typically a college graduate who performs many of the functions of managers in nonagricultural industries.[54] Similarly other occupational roles, such as equipment maintainers and agronomic or horticultural specialists, involve a much sharper division of labor than traditional farm occupations. They also involve an important change in the manner in which the occupation is entered. While the majority of agricultural experts, whether farm managers or some type of agricultural specialist, usually have a farming family, their skills are acquired through the educational system, rather than through family socialization. On the basis of these characteristics, there is little differentiation between farming occupations and those of the professionals and managers already discussed.

Another exception to the points made above is that there are a number of extremely lucrative small businesses. In the fashion and advertising industries, for example, there are many cases of startling successes for very small enterprises. (There are probably many times more cases of startling failure in this type of endeavor, but these do not receive as much notice.) Once such success is achieved, however, there is an overwhelming tendency for the enterprise to enlarge or be absorbed into a larger organization, so that the instances of small businesses staying small and highly profitable are very few.

While self-employment or proprietorship is of limited importance in the over-all occupational structure, it is also part of the American Dream. Chinoy found that the major preoccupation of the automobile workers he studied was starting their own small business.[55] While an unrealistic dream, it remains part of the culture. As was the case with the professional, however, the reality of contemporary occupations is that they are found in the organizational setting. As Caplow notes, "for the majority of the labor force, and in most modern occupations, self-employment is not a plausible alternative."[56] For those people who continue to enter the ranks of proprietors, however, the question is not really one of alternatives, since the majority of those who enter this type of occupation do so

[54]*Occupational Careers*, p. 57.
[55]Chinoy, *Automobile Workers and the American Dream*, p. 82.
[56]Caplow, *The Sociology of Work*, p. 83.

from the family setting, where the formal and informal socialization processes may limit the perception of alternatives. As has been mentioned, many children of proprietors do not follow in their father's footsteps, but those that do learn the occupation in a situation where the consideration of possible alternatives is limited by family pressures to engage in this line of work. Since there is often only room for one offspring in such an endeavor, siblings are to a great extent forced out of this occupation. For the balance of the labor force and those about to enter, Caplow's point is correct, given the problem of capitalization and the nature of the socialization process.

officials

Like the occupational types which have already been discussed in this chapter, officials are a heterogeneous grouping containing a wide variety of specific occupations. City managers, federal, state, and local administrators, hospital administrators, school superintendents, and administrators of fund-raising organizations or religious groups are part of this category. More than in the case of the business executive or manager, the official category is comprised of occupations which are sometimes considered or consider themselves professionals. Since their work tasks are almost identical with the executive functions, it is appropriate to place hospital administrators, city managers, school superintendents, etc. in the category of officials.

In general, the functions, orientations, aspirations, and conflicts of the executives and managers are applicable to the officials. They work at various levels in organizations of varying sizes. The distinctions made between executives and managers hold for the officials, also, since the areas of responsibility and authority vary similarly. Like the executive or manager, they may work in specialties where their training is particularly relevant. Academic training in administrative science (or behavior) is designed for potential practitioners in and out of the business sector. In sociology, courses in complex or formal organizations have developed from an earlier interest in industrial sociology, based on the realization that organizations have important common characteristics, regardless of their particular goal or sponsorship. In sum, the work that officials perform is almost identical to that of the executives and managers.

Despite these strong similarities, the category of officials remains as something distinct. Mills suggests that the government official suffers from a lack of income and prestige when compared with the business executive.[57] This would be true for almost all members of the category. Without considering for the moment whether or not officials are worth as much as business executives, the important implication is that such officials are given a lower position in the social-stratification system, with correspondingly less power and privilege. The major factor which accounts for this situation is that officials are at least one step removed from the income-generating source within a capitalistic system. Whether in a public organization, such as a governmental unit, or a private organization, such as a religious organization, hospital, or professional association, the official and his organization are dependent upon secondary sources of income in the form of taxes, contributions, or dues. While the potential for high organizational and individual incomes exists in such situations, this potential is seldom realized, since the taxpayers, contributors, or dues-payers have at least some control over the amount they give to the organization. Cases of government or labor-union officials who become inordinately rich at the expense of their constituents are rare. When they do occur, the fact that they are labeled deviant behavior and lead to a public outcry is indirect evidence of the belief on the part of the public or affected constituents that such behavior is inappropriate. The normal or nondeviant case is for the official to receive a modest to good income but not to be in a position to earn more than the basic salary for the position. Since constituents are not likely to part with more of their money than is absolutely necessary, it is unlikely that they will allow such salaries to get too high. This is exemplified by the salary standards of the federal civil service, one of the more prestigious areas in which officials are found. As Table 5.1 suggests, while the minimum salary levels are by and large competitive with those outside of government employment, the top salaries are far distant from those at the top of private industry.

Moore's point that corporate executives have power in determining their salaries is particularly pertinent here. If the idea of financial reward as a major motivator is correct and the minimum increments suggested by Moore (15 per cent) are reasonable, then the top salaries for federal government service are indeed too low. The Brookings Institution analysis of the federal civil service found that there was general agreement in a sample of the total population

[57]Mills, *White Collar*, p. 83.

170   managers, proprietors, and officials

Table 5.1.   Ratio of the Top Salary to the Bottom Salary in the Federal
Civil Service, 1924-1964[1]

Year	Top Salary	Bottom Salary	Ratio of Top Salary to Bottom Salary
1924	$ 7,500	$ 900	8.3
1928	9,000	1,020	8.8
1942	9,000	1,200	7.5
1945	9,800	1,440	6.8
1946	10,000	1,690	5.9
1948	10,330	2,020	5.1
1949	14,000	2,120	6.6
1951	14,800	2,420	6.1
1955	14,800	2,600	5.7
1956	16,000	2,690	6.0
1958	17,500	2,960	5.9
1960	18,500	3,185	5.8
1962	20,000	3,245	6.2
1964	20,000	3,305	6.1

[1] Sources: For 1924-1956, U.S. Civil Service Commission, Federal Employment Statistics Office, *Pay Structure of the Federal Civil Service* (June 30, 1960); for 1958-1964, relevant reports of the House Committee on Post Office and Civil Service

SOURCE: Franklin P. Kilpatrick, Milton C. Cummings, Jr., and M. Kent Jennings, *The Image of the Federal Service* (Washington, D.C.: The Brookings Institution, 1964), p. 44.

that such salaries should be higher.[58] Those in the federal service also agreed. The same study suggests that where the need is the greatest, at the highest levels, the salary scales are the least attractive, making it difficult to fill such positions.

Federal government employees are in many ways the elite of officialdom. The great growth in state and local government, discussed in Chap. 2, has been a major source for the growth in numbers in the officials category. In comparison with federal employees, these local officials are generally poorly paid. If financial rewards are important motivators, then this segment of society does not contain adequate motivational devices. If this is correct, legitimate questions concerning the quality of persons attracted to this

[58]Franklin P. Kilpatrick, Milton C. Cummings, Jr., and M. Kent Jennings, *The Image of the Federal Service* (Washington, D.C.: The Brookings Institution, 1964), pp. 181-85.

type of officialdom could be raised. In nongovernmental official positions the picture is somewhat more complex. While the officials concerned are dependent on support from members or contributors, the level of support varies according to the affluence of the supporters and to the value attached to the positions supported. A professional association, for example, might be willing and able to pay its administrators handsomely, if their functions are viewed as important to the constituency. Another official in a less financially secure organization, performing the same functions, might have a significantly lower salary. In general, officials are paid less than their counterparts in business.

Since man does not live by bread alone, however, other motivational factors and rewards must be considered. A study of upper-level federal executives conducted by W. Lloyd Warner et al. suggests that these executives emphasize intelligence, general intellectual values, culture, restraint, respect from others, and respect from themselves.[59] The Kilpatrick, Cummings, and Jennings' study found essentially the same concerns among their sample; involvement in their work, devotion to duty, and the need for challenge characterized the sample in that study. Both studies emphasize that the upper-level personnel in federal service believe in what they are doing, and this belief serves as an important motivator.[60] It is probable that officials in other areas have rather strong beliefs in their organization and its purposes, especially those near the top of the hierarchy. As was the case for certain of the professions, for these people dedication to a purpose or cause may, in some ways, compensate for lower levels of financial rewards.

The discussion thus far has centered around the financial and motivational characteristics of officials. An important additional component of the status of officials is the prestige they are accorded. As Mills notes, government employees are generally given less prestige than those in business, and this is true for other officials according to national surveys of occupational prestige. Government officials have been the subject of more intensive examination than other members of this category and will serve as the basis for the discussion of prestige. The Kilpatrick, Cummings, and Jennings' study found that high-status persons outside of federal employment viewed the civil servant as "security conscious, lacking in ambition, adaptable to a routine, a poor worker, and noncreative and dull."[61]

[59]The American Federal Executive (New Haven: Yale University Press, 1963), p. 235.
[60]The Image of the Federal Service, pp. 56–85.
[61]The Image of the Federal Service, p. 240.

The federal employees themselves stress the importance of security as a positive factor in their employment. The general public sees the civil servant as honest and devoted to his duty. The general picture seems to be one of a person locked into an organization that does not allow creativity and that permits performance at a minimal level. The term "public servant" seems to express part of the image of many officials, since the idea of the servant is one of low status, serving the needs and desires of masters. Nongovernment officials are in a similar position, serving the needs of their constituents. While they may have power in their own organizations, officials are in the position of being subservient to an external power group that, at least theoretically, can recall the official when it so desires. While business executives are in the same position in relation to stockholders, they are given more autonomy in their operations. The official is more subject to the pressures of being in the public's eye and suffers in prestige because of his servant position.

While the rewards and prestige of the official are generally less than those of the executive in business, on other characteristics he is much like his counterpart in business. The Warner, *et al.* examination of federal executives, for example, found that on almost every background characteristic the government officials were very similar to the big business leaders studied by Warner and Abegglen. An interesting difference was that the federal executives were more educated than their business counterparts.[62] Since the officials category is comprised of many professionalizing occupations for which the educational requirements are becoming increasingly stringent, the same is probably true for most of the particular occupations in this category. There are strong indications that businesses are facing increasing difficulties in the recruitment of trainees from colleges, and it would seem that the officials category is recruiting personnel who are not easily differentiated from those going into the business world. Of course, competition for well-trained personnel is intense in all areas, including the professions, which compete among themselves for potential members. The point is that officials probably cannot be differentiated from business executives and managers in terms of training and ability. More empirical evidence is necessary before the image of the official as being noncreative and lacking in ambition can be demonstrated. Like most stereotypes, that of the official is probably incorrect.

While strong similarities exist between officials and executives, except for the pay and prestige factors, for some officials an additional component of the work situation provides an important source

---

[62]Warner *et al.*, *The American Federal Executive*, pp. 400–7.

of strain above and beyond that faced by most members of this category. Occupations such as the school superintendent, city manager, or hospital administrator are confronted with demands from the environment from which other members of the category are largely insulated. The business executive and the government official must be cognizant of the environment, but in most cases they are separated from it by personnel whose specific function is to deal with outside demands. To be sure, top executives in business must make decisions in the face of environmental pressures. The goals of business, however, are generally quite explicit, and decisions can be made, at least partially, on the basis of a clear conception of the goals.[63] For the type of official under discussion, however, the situation is less clear-cut. Gladys M. Kammerer, in a discussion of the role of the city manager, points out that the role is not played in a vacuum but must take into consideration the institutional-structural arrangements of the community, the style of politics, the local economy, and demographic characteristics.[64] As was seen in the discussion of officials' pay, their position in this case is subject to direct pressures from constituents. While the organization he is heading may itself have quite specific goals, the environmental pressures are such that decisions based on the goals may conflict with the interests of significant groups in a community. The official in this case must mediate between conflicting interests in the relevant environment as well as within his own organization. If he makes decisions that are rational on the basis of his assessment of the situation, he risks offending significant groups in the community, thus jeopardizing effective implementation of the decision and, at the extreme, his own position. If he is too cognizant of the conflicting demands, he may not act at all or act so indecisively that the organization becomes ineffective. This type of position thus becomes one of balancing between alternative pressures, pressures which may be very diffuse in their range but intense in their force.

[63]Most analyses of organizations suggest that environmental pressures are ubiquitous. For the kinds of organizations under discussion and their officials, however, environmental pressures would be directly felt. Moreover, decisions are generally not based on pure rationality in any organization. Where the goals are less specific and, at times, in conflict with each other, the decision-making process becomes even more difficult. For a discussion of the nature of decision making based on goals (rational model) and the effects of the environment on the decision-making process, see Alvin Gouldner, "Organizational Analysis," in Sociology Today, eds. Robert K. Merton, Leonard Broom, and Leonard S. Cottrell, Jr. (New York: Basic Books, Inc., Publishers, 1959) and James D. Thompson, Organizations in Action (New York: McGraw-Hill Book Company, 1967).

[64]"Role Diversity of City Managers," Administrative Science Quarterly, VIII, 4 (March, 1964), 423.

summary and conclusions

The managers, proprietors, and officials are obviously a heterogeneous lot in terms of the organizations in which they are found, the auspices under which they work, their level in the various hierarchies, and the tasks performed. At the same time, with the exception of proprietors, they share high socio-economic status, educational backgrounds, and the constraints of organizational life. While proprietorship may be an element of the American Dream, the contemporary American and Western image is probably best portrayed by managers and officials. For college graduates this kind of organizational work is the only viable alternative, with the exception of the professions. Members of the latter group often become executives or officials as they move into supervisory positions in their employing organizations. For the less well educated, organizational life is probably the only alternative in most cases.

While central to the contemporary occupational world, the many facets of this category do not allow crystallization into a coherent model as with the professions. The conformist-innovator and the dedicated-opportunistic axes of the descriptions of this group suggest both the relative paucity of information available and varieties of behavior exhibited. The array of literary and scholarly descriptions of this category are probably accurate in that they lead to the conclusion that the category itself is multidimensional. As a broad grouping of people with relatively similar socio-economic characteristics, the category is useful; as a distinctive group of occupations, it is not. The most important common denominator of the category, again with the exception of the proprietors, is that these are organizationally based occupations. This means that the members of the category are filling positions that contain built-in obligations, rewards, and relationships. The contents as well as the incumbents of particular positions are determined by the organization. The question of the criteria upon which the positions are filled, whether by innovators or conformists or by dedicated or opportunistic actors has not yet been answered. Undoubtedly a wide range of behavior is both permitted and rewarded; yet what is permitted and rewarded in one setting may lead to dismissal, demotion, or lack of advancement in another. It is thus the organization that determines the kinds of, and routes to, success or failure for its members. The role of the individual is vital but only within the limits set by the organization.

chapter 6

white-collar workers

The settings for white-collar work are the same as those for the managers and officials just discussed, the organization. For many white-collar workers, much of the interaction is with the managerial hierarchy. Despite the similarity in work environment, a major difference in the occupations is evident. The difference involves not only the work performed but also the total role of the people involved, and the basis for it is what Caplow calls the "status schism" inherent in almost all organizations.[1] This status schism is between the decision makers and the decision followers, between the big people and the little people in Kahl's terms.[2] Components of the difference include wide variations in the reward structure, limits on the amount and kind of fraternization allowed between members of the categories, power differences, and, most importantly, significant differences in the social backgrounds and the orientations toward work of the individuals and in the work performed itself.

[1]Caplow, *Principles of Organization* (New York: Harcourt, Brace & World, Inc., 1964), p. 60.
[2]See Joseph A. Kahl, *The American Class Structure.*

Specific groups included in this category are secretaries, stenographers, typists, telephone operators, receptionists, and airline stewardesses, predominantly women's occupations. More sexually mixed groups in this category are bookkeepers and cashiers, shipping and receiving clerks, office machine operators, and mail carriers. The latter are called clerical and kindred workers in the census. Another major group in the white-collar category is the retail sales worker. The sales worker operates at the individual customer level rather than at the corporate sales level as do sales executives. The white-collar worker, almost by definition, is an organizational employee, and individual work, either as a solo practitioner or as a proprietor, does not exist for this group.

The white-collar category has grown steadily in size in recent decades. According to the 1960 U.S. Census, the number of white-collar workers exceeded the number of manual workers for the first time. The census definition included professionals, managers, proprietors, and officials, but the direction of the trend is significant for a number of reasons. The proportion of the labor force in the category of managers, proprietors, and officials actually decreased in the decade from 1950 to 1960, while both professionals and white-collar workers increased. In an overview of some trends in the labor force, Everett M. Kassalow states:

> Yet, one must note that while the percentage of white-collar workers in the labor force has increased steadily for decades, the nature or source of this increase has changed in the past ten years. Until 1950, gains in the white-collar sector reflected declines in extractive employment, such as agriculture and mining; other manual percentages were still advancing slightly or holding even. Between 1900 and 1930, for example, the farm-work force declined from 37.5 per cent to 21.2 per cent as a percentage of the total civilian labor force. Correspondingly, white-collar workers advanced from 17.6 per cent to 29.4 per cent of the total; manual workers also increased moderately as a relative share of the labor force, rising from 35.8 per cent to 39.6 per cent. Between 1930 and 1950, the share of manual workers in total employment continued to rise slightly, and the percentage of farm workers fell once more. The number of white-collar employees once again increased on a relative as well as an absolute basis.
>
> The trend in the 1950/1960 decade, however, was of a different nature. Farm employment continued to decline, but so did manual or blue-collar employment. The upsurge of white-collar workers in the 1950's was a result of a relative decline in the number of both farm and

manual workers. Employment in the service industries also showed an important relative increase in the 1950/1960 period.[3]

Kassalow attributes much of the increase to the shift in consumer demands. While the level of commodities sought probably has actually increased, commodity consumption has declined relative to the consumption of services. Kassalow correctly notes that the service industries, which include governmental agencies at all levels, tend to employ a higher proportion of nonmanual workers than do industries producing goods.[4] If the trends projected in Chap. 2 regarding the human-resources era are correct, white-collar employment should continue actual and relative growth with regard to the labor force. An additional factor is the growth of organizations. Some evidence indicates that as organizations grow in size and complexity the number of personnel in administrative work (white-collar work) grows disproportionately to the number engaged in production work.[5] If this is the case, further growth from this source should remain important over the long run. Changes in the production process itself, such as the introduction of automation, are having an impact on the labor force, although the importance of computers and other equipment designed for speeding the administrative process will probably substantially alter white-collar employment in the long run. The impact of technological changes on the production and administrative process will probably continue to increase the relative size of the white-collar category, but the composition of the category will change as fewer persons are engaged in routine information-handling chores, such as simple clerical tasks (filing and preparing customers' bills, for example), and as more personnel are needed for the equipment that takes these tasks over and for direct interaction with organizational customers and clients in a service capacity.

In addition, white-collar occupations are the first occupational category discussed where women form a significant segment of the labor force. In 1960, women comprised over 50 per cent of white-collar employees.[6] With the exception of teaching, nursing, social work,

---

[3]Kassalow, "United States," in *White Collar Trade Unions*, ed. Adolph Sturmthal (Urbana: University of Illinois Press, 1966), p. 306.

[4]Kassalow, "United States," p. 308.

[5]See William A. Rushing, "The Effects of Industry Size and Division of Labor on Administration," *Administrative Science Quarterly*, XXII, 2 (September, 1967), 273–95. After reviewing the literature and his own data, Rushing concludes that increased complexity (greater division of labor) is the major factor in the growth of clerical personnel. Growth in size without increased complexity appears to have the opposite effect.

[6]Kassalow, "United States," p. 309.

etc. in the professional category, white-collar work is the domain of women in the labor force. As will be seen, this has an impact on the white-collar workers as a whole.

Most analyses of white-collar workers suggest that they are a group in which "middle-class values and the faith in upward mobility are likely to be strongest."[7] This characteristic aligns them with the groups already discussed and, at the same time, contributes to the antipathy that sometimes exists between production workers and office workers. It also contributes to the relatively limited impact of unionization on white-collar occupations. As will be discussed, the conditions under which these workers are employed are increasingly like those of the production process, and the opportunities for mobility are really quite limited. Nevertheless, the orientation lingers on. Part of the reason for this is the history of office work and the background of white-collar workers.

background

A perceptive analysis of the history of white-collar work and its impact on contemporary practices and images is offered by C. Wright Mills. Early offices were small, as were the businesses they serviced. A dominant figure in the nineteenth- and twentieth-century office was the bookkeeper, essentially the hub around which the owner and other workers revolved. According to Mills, he was an

> old-young man, slightly stoop shouldered, with a sallow complexion, usually dyspeptic-looking, with black sleeves and a green eye-shade. . . . Regardless of the kind of business, regardless of their ages, they all looked alike. . . . He seemed tired and he was never quite happy, because . . . his face betrayed the strain of working toward that climax of his month's labors. He was usually a neat penman, but his real pride was in his ability to add a column of figures rapidly and accurately. In spite of this accomplishment, however, he seldom, if ever, left his ledger for a more promising position. His mind was atrophied by that destroying, hopeless influence of drudgery and routine work. He was little more than a figuring machine with an endless number of figure combinations learned by heart. His feat was a feat of memory.[8]

[7]Edward Gross, *Work and Society*, p. 65.
[8]Mills, *White Collar*, p. 191.

While the work of the office worker has changed drastically, the probability of advancement out of this position has not. In many ways, the tasks performed, while changed in content, seem to have the same kinds of effects.

Major changes in white-collar work occurred concurrently with changes in technology and in organizational forms, as the processes of growth and bureaucratization continued. As organizations became larger, administrative demands became more compelling, leading to increases in the size of office staffs. Large offices departmentalized and rationalized emerged. The growth of banking, financial, and insurance industries created "office industries," according to Mills.[9] The growth of government as an employer had a similar impact. The development of office machinery, from typewriters, through duplicators, collators, and comptometers, to computers, has subdivided the work performed, so that specialization and work flow patterns make the office work increasingly like factory production processes. A major factor in the changing nature of office work is the trend toward centralization. While much of the production process and the provision of organizational services can be decentralized, administrative processes are increasingly more centralized, a trend greatly facilitated by information-handling machines, such as the computer. This further increases the size of offices and the potential for standardization of office work. Mills suggests that standardization is facilitated by decreasing the number of private offices and opening up the office setting into almost floor-wide work units.[10]

These changes have had a drastic effect on the nature of office work. Where a distinct hierarchy of prestige, if not pay, once existed, standardization has minimized status differences. Once the private secretary was the pinnacle of success for the office girl. She "takes care of his appointments, his daily schedule, his check book— is, in short, justifiably called his office wife. If her boss's office warrants it, she may even have stenographers and typists working for her."[11] Next in the hierarchy was the stenographer who can take dictation as well as type. The typist, who works only with the machine, copying matter where speed and accuracy are the most important skills, has a position higher than that of simple clerks. Remnants of this hierarchy remain, of course, but the pooling of typists and the advent of dictating machines has flattened the skill

[9] *White Collar*, p. 192.
[10] *White Collar*, p. 197.
[11] Mills, *White Collar*, p. 207.

differentials and the corresponding status differences. For the male white-collar worker a similar flattening process has occurred.

Not all white-collar workers are found in the office. Mail carriers, sales workers, and shipping and receiving clerks, for example, are neither predominantly feminine nor office occupations. At the same time, they are affected by the processes discussed above. Mechanization and routinization have shrunk the range of skills required (the sales clerk does not bargain, nor does he have control over the amounts or the prices of the goods for sale). Status differentials have similarly become flattened in these occupations.

The objective conditions of white-collar work have changed markedly; yet, to a large extent the workers themselves have not. Mills notes that in American folklore the white-collar girl is usually born of small-town, lower-middle-class parents. After graduation from high school or a year or so at a business college, she goes to the big city. She views her job as a move up in the status hierarchy.[12] While the majority of white-collar workers today come from an area contiguous to the urban area, the idea of mobility remains an important component of the occupation.[13]

Nancy G. Morse's study of white-collar workers and their reactions to their jobs exemplifies the contemporary nature of, and reactions to, white-collar employment. While an analysis of one organization cannot be taken as representative of the total picture, the description of the workers and their reactions does seem typical of much white-collar employment. It was suggested above that white-collar work is becoming increasingly standardized. From the evidence presented by Morse, it appears that white-collar workers are also quite standardized. She states:

> The population studied is homogeneous in many ways. The demographic statistics indicate some of the characteristics of this predominantly female group (84 per cent). Usually American-born themselves (96 per cent), many of them have fathers (55 per cent) and mothers (60 per cent) who were also born in this country. Many (79 per cent) were born in or very near the city in which they work. After finishing their education [usually gradu-

[12]Mills, *White Collar*, p. 202.

[13]In contrast, Michael Crozier notes that in a French governmental clerical agency, he studied, the majority of the women employees came from the provinces because the agency could not compete for local (Parisian) girls. Since the employment opportunities are limited in the rural areas, the positions are accepted despite the relatively low pay. The idea of mobility appears to hold even there. Crozier, *The Bureaucratic Phenomenon* (Chicago: University of Chicago Press, 1964), p. 16.

ating from high school (79 per cent)], many of them came to work in this company as their first job (68 per cent). Most of them are unmarried (76 per cent) and the majority are under twenty-five (53 per cent). They often live at home with their families (66 per cent) and in only one out of three of these is the head of the household in a professional or white-collar job. All of the employees interviewed, on the other hand, are in white-collar jobs, although many of them (62 per cent) are doing routine clerical work.[14]

This standardization or homogenization of background is accompanied by rather common outlooks toward the work itself. Morse further states:

> First of all, they seem to like their community and its facilities. The employees are generally satisfied with their housing (77 per cent) and the community in which they live (75 per cent), and find it quite easy to get to work (85 per cent).
> Their attitudes toward the company are predominantly favorable. During the interview the majority of them expressed no desire at all to leave the organization (65 per cent) and would advise a friend to work in the organization (64 per cent). They feel that the company has shorter hours than other organizations of its kind in the area (66 per cent), express strong approval for the shorter hours (57 per cent) and like the company's providing lunches (63 per cent). While many of them never take part in the company recreational and athletic activities (64 per cent) and never have submitted a suggestion to the company suggestion system (59 per cent), nearly all of them read every issue of the company magazine (90 per cent). Many of them mentioned spontaneously that the company takes good care of its employees, and provides them with many benefits, and they like this particular aspect of the organization (57 per cent). Nearly all of them report that their families approve of their working in the company (85 per cent). While the younger generation, as represented by their friends, are not so overwhelmingly approving, many of them (60 per cent) report their friends as also approving of their working in the company.
> In the job area also, there are some commonalities of attitude and perception. The majority of employees feel

[14]*Satisfactions in the White-Collar Job* (Ann Arbor: Survey Research Center, University of Michigan, 1953), p. 8.

that their job is above average in importance (54 per cent), while some (17 per cent) feel that it is very important. Many (57 per cent) report that they make decisions on their jobs, but a larger proportion (70 per cent) would like to make more decisions. The descriptions of how their jobs tie in with the rest of the company indicate that many of them (58 per cent) had little or no understanding of its relation to the total operation of the company. Involved in only a small segment of [the] total operation of the company, it is not surprising that they failed to see the connection between their work and the overall purpose of the organization. In contrast to their lack of information on the tie-in of their job to the total company operations was their knowledge of immediately relevant information. The majority (54 per cent) knew the maximum salary which could be achieved for their jobs. In view of the type of jobs they are in, it is also not surprising that a large percentage of them (82 per cent) have not taken any course related to their work since they have been working in the company.[15]

Despite the homogeneity of the work situation and the workers themselves, employees do not react to the situation in terms of alienation. Morse found

Most of the employees do not think in terms of autonomy and individuality or the lack of it in describing the work situation (64 per cent), nor do they talk about equality or inequality in describing the social situation in the office (87 per cent). They do not think of the organization in any terms which bear a close relationship to "democratic" or "authoritarian." Such a continuum did not appear to be a salient one for them.[16]

These findings reinforce the point made earlier that the meaning of work to the individual is a function of the interaction of his own expectations about the work with his perceptions of the conditions of the work situation. The objective situation is one of routine and largely repetitive work. The workers, while they would like to make more decisions, are generally satisfied and do not indicate feelings that reflect alienation. The social analyst might well view such work as stultifying and, in the long run, damaging for the

[15]*Satisfactions in the White-Collar Job*, p. 8–9.
[16]*Satisfactions in the White-Collar Job*, p. 10.

individual and for society as a whole. At the present time, however, the impression is one of relatively satisfied workers employed in a setting that generally satisfies their expectations.

If expectation levels change, less satisfaction is felt. In a further analysis of the bases of satisfaction among these workers, Morse found that the need for variety and the opportunity to use one's skills and abilities was generally rather important among the workers. Those who were in the more varied and skilled jobs reported more satisfaction than those in the more routine, unskilled jobs. Job content is therefore a component of satisfaction, although not all employees had similar needs. Those with lower levels of aspirations are less satisfied with a challenging job and those with high aspiration levels less satisfied with a more routine job. An additional factor in the satisfaction-dissatisfaction syndrome is, of course, the surrounding context, which includes such things as supervision patterns, general satisfaction with the company, pay, and relations with fellow workers.[17] Employee needs should be matched with job content, if the contextual factors remain constant. On a broader level, changing patterns in education, technology, and training could create a situation in which employee needs are such that routine jobs become increasingly less satisfying for greater proportions of the population. The reverse is also conceivable. For our purposes, however, the important consideration is that the exact nature of a job can lead to satisfaction or dissatisfaction, depending on the employees' background and aspirations and the contextual factors. The fact that a position is routine does not allow the conclusion that the incumbent by definition feels frustrated and bored. Similarly, the fact that a position demands decision making and a wide variety of activities does not lead necessarily to satisfaction and intrinsic enjoyment of the work. The standardization of white-collar work is an objective fact, but the impact of this on the worker apparently varies in terms of his expectations. If there is a general raising of such expectations, then routine work will lead to increasing discontent. Increasing unionization of white-collar workers suggests that the standardization may be becoming frustrating to workers with the expectation level remaining constant or that the expectation levels are in fact rising. Other factors are, of course, associated with increased unionization, a topic to be discussed below.

The organizational basis of white-collar work also has an impact on workers' reactions to their occupations. Parsons has

[17]Morse, *Satisfactions in the White-Collar Job*, pp. 66–67.

suggested that the American occupational system is in general universalistic and achievement oriented.[18] "Universalistic" in this sense means that responses to individuals and situations are based upon impersonal, utilitarian, and organizationally based norms in contrast to "particularistic," which means based on responses to the individual or situation as a unique and personalized event. A study by Louis A. Zurcher, Jr., Arnold Meadows, and Susan Lee Zurcher suggests that individuals who have universalistic orientations toward their work, in an organizational setting, are less likely to be alienated from their work than those who have particularistic orientations. This particular study was carried out in banks in southwestern United States and northern Mexico. Workers of Mexican origin were found to be more particularistically oriented than their American counterparts. The authors attribute this to the cultural climate of Mexico, which values personal relations more than the impersonal universalistic standards that prevail in the United States and modern organizations. Bank employees of Mexican origin employed in Mexican banks exhibited more alienation than Mexican-Americans or Anglo-Americans employed in American banks. The Mexican-Americans in this case apparently changed their reference group to the Anglo-American white-collar world with the result that the work situation did not prove to be a source for alienative responses.[19]

The findings of this study suggest that small-town girls coming to the big city, while today only a minor contributor to the ranks of white-collar workers, may be subject to more alienation and less satisfaction than is generally found. Since rural areas and small towns tend to have particularistic values, migrants from these areas would adjust poorly to the modern organization. Morse's findings in regard to the geographical origins of the white-collar workers in her study partially explain the generally high level of satisfaction she found among the workers. The urban background and education in urban schools appear to be the appropriate preparation for persons entering this kind of work. Although urban background may contribute to acceptance and even liking of routine and universalistically oriented white-collar occupations, the question of what are the long-run implications of such orientations for the individual remains unanswered.

[18]Parsons, *Essays in Sociological Theory* (New York, The Free Press of Glencoe, 1949), p. 79.

[19]Zurcher, Meadows, and Zurcher, "Value Orientation, Role Conflict, and Alienation from Work: A Cross Cultural Study," *American Sociological Review*, XXX, 4 (August, 1965), 539–48.

the nature of white-collar work

The standardization and routinization of much white-collar work is evident. So also is the fact that it is carried out in the organizational setting. Less apparent is the fact that white-collar workers occupy two different positions within the organizational framework. Some, like the salesclerk, receptionist, or mail carrier, are at the boundary of the organization and have contact with customers or clients. The other type of position is within the organization where the contacts are only with others performing essentially the same function. Clerks and typists are typical of this group. The most obvious difference between the groups is that the former deals with unstandardized humans in the form of customers or clients, and the latter group does not.

Those in boundary positions are at times the first, often the last, and sometimes the only contact outsiders have with an organization. For organizations that must rely upon good public relations, it becomes imperative that persons in these positions present a good image. Thus attractiveness in looks and personality become important prerequisites for positions such as the receptionist or airline stewardess. While such occupations do deal with a heterogeneous client or customer group, their interaction patterns are in reality very standardized. The bureaucratic norm of impersonality is extremely evident in these occupations. While the smile and welcome to an office or airline might well be genuine, it is the same for all who enter. Universalistic standards thus prevail in this boundary position. The same is true for the mail carrier, who has quite different physical and personality prerequisites. The mail carrier obviously is not expected to show any favoritism in his work. While there is not the same kind of expectation for the carrier as there is for the receptionist, the carrier has an image (through rain, sleet, and snow . . .) he is expected to portray.

These boundary positions are quite different from the boundary position of the sales person. Contemporary economic conditions are such that the person who interacts with the salesclerk comes to the clerk with a predisposition to purchase at a price that is already fixed. An exception to this would be the case of the major appliance or the automobile, where some bargaining does occur but within limits set by the selling organization. Even here, the customer comes with the desire to purchase. The fact that those with whom the sales person has contact come to him allows a wider range of behavior than is allowed the receptionist or stewardess. The customer's needs can only be met by dealing with the sales person. The customer has the option of choosing among several organizations selling the same commodity or service, but he cannot control the type of sales person with whom he deals. It is obvious, of course, that if a sales person drove potential customers away, he would not earn a living, if he is paid on a commission basis, or would not be retained by the organization, if he were paid a straight salary.

Analyses of the behavior of sales personnel have been relatively limited. The work that has been done suggests that the general motivational framework used in previous discussions is relevant here. Many types of sales personnel are on a direct or partial commission basis, which emphasizes economic motivations. The commission serves as a motivator but not in a direct way and not in the same way for all sales personnel. Judson B. Pearson, Gordon H. Barker, and Rodney D. Elliott, for example, found that the direct commission served as an incentive only for the most successful salesmen. These salesmen, engaged in direct sales from truck routes, were ranked according to their sales performance. For those with very high performance records, the incentive system was a source of satisfaction; for the balance of the salesmen, the commission incentive did not affect satisfaction. The authors infer that the system also did not provide a strong source of motivation for the balance of the personnel.[20]

In a related study, Nicholas Babchuck and William J. Goode found that a sales group that had been highly competitive changed to a cooperative work organization. Production (sales) levels remained high. At the same time, hostility within the group decreased and morale increased.[21] Here again motivations other than strictly economic ones play a role in the over-all motivational system.

The conclusions for these white-collar jobs are, of course, congruent with the findings from studies of the production process, which have systematically found quota restrictions in effect when incentive (piecework) systems are in effect. Thus the findings in regard to sales workers are not surprising in light of the general knowledge available about work. What is important is that this group of white-collar workers, probably typical of the class that espouses middle-class values and mobility aspirations, does not respond to the incentives that are thought to be central in the

[20]"Sales Success and Job Satisfaction," *American Sociological Review*, XXII, 4 (August, 1957), 424–27.

[21]"Work Incentives in a Self-Determined Group," *American Sociological Review*, XVI, 5, (October, 1951), 679–87.

upper-middle-class world. Values other than the purely economic ones intrude in the motivational framework at this level. The question these findings raise is, To what degree are the kinds of responses found among these sales personnel typical of the occupational structure in general? Since there is evidence that blue-collar workers respond in much the same way, the focus of the analysis should be on those higher in the occupational hierarchy. It could be hypothesized that since white-collar workers in general and probably sales workers in particular do reflect the general value orientations of the American middle-and upper-middle classes, the members of higher status occupations would engage in similar kinds of practices. That is, executives, officials, and professionals respond to more than the economic motivation and therefore do not always work to maximize this particular reward. Thus the members of these occupations could well engage in "quota restrictions" when other values are of greater importance. However, this type of analysis has not been attempted.

Since sales work involves a direct presentation of self before a customer, the reactions to this component of the work should be examined. According to Stephen J. Miller, the salesman attempts to control the customer to protect his self-concept as well as to facilitate the sales process. Using automobile salesmen as the basis for analysis, Miller found that the salesmen prefer having customers that they have recruited, because such customers give the salesman the advantage of knowing what the customer wants in the situation. The potential customer who drops in off the street is threatening to the salesman, since he is in an unstructured situation. The salesman does not know if the person is merely trying to get warmed up, is browsing around for a car, or is actually a real prospect. The salesman also knows nothing about such a customer and thus has no leads by which the situation can be controlled. Miller points out that the salesman has economic and noneconomic interests in the transaction. In addition to his self-concept, his status as a salesman is affected by the outcomes of the various transactions in which he is engaged. Regardless of the outcome, he wants to be known as a good salesman.[22]

The nature of the sales process is such that not every customer is a purchaser. This is a fact of life to which the salesman must adjust. F. William Howton and Bernard Rosenberg suggest that the salesman adjusts to this situation by defining rebuffs in their work in terms of accepting humiliation as part of the work, but they do

[22]Miller, "The Social Bases of Sales Behavior," *Social Problems*, XII, 1 (Summer, 1964), 15–24.

not define the occupation itself as humiliating.[23] Rebuffs thus become part of the day's work, not especially enjoyable but still acceptable. Since rebuffs are given this social meaning, it would follow that success in the form of sales are also given a social meaning.

A related, but more critical, view of the sales person is taken by Mills in his analysis of salesgirls in department stores. He points out that a wide status discrepancy exists between the salesgirl and her customers on most occasions. The contact between customer and salesgirl is usually so brief that meaningful interaction is impossible. While surrounded by attractive goods the customers can afford, the salesgirl is limited in her own purchasing power, which makes deprivation even more evident.[24] At the same time, the relationship between customer and salesgirl is one in which the salesgirl is put in the position of "waiting on" the customer, which in and of itself has negative status consequences.

Mills suggests that the role of salesgirl can be performed in a variety of fashions. The "wolf," for example, pounces on customers as they appear in her area. More aggressive is the "elbower" who pushes through her sales colleagues in an attempt to monopolize as many customers as possible. The "charmer" relies upon her personal attraction to lure potential customers, with the goods being sold of lesser importance. The "ingénue" is self-effacing and looks for support from colleagues and customers. While not as effective in the sales process, she receives socio-emotional support. The "collegiate," as the name implies, is a part-time worker who makes up in eagerness what she might lack in other skills. The "drifter" moves around gossiping with colleagues. She is highly concerned with social interaction at the expense of sales volume. The "social pretender" attempts to create an image of herself as coming from a high socio-economic status background. This can be an effective approach for certain kinds of customers. The "old-timer" has made a career out of this occupation. She has her own approach to customers, a routine developed through years of practice. This type approaches all customers in the same way, and does not rely on the gimmicks of the other types.[25]

While this categorization of the salesgirl cannot be taken as an exhaustive typology, it does illustrate the fact that a variety of behaviors are possible in the sales process. Mills tends to assume

[23]"The Salesman: Ideology and Self-Imagery in a Prototypic Occupation," *Social Research*, XXXII, 3 (Autumn, 1965), 277–98.
[24]Mills, *White Collar*, p. 174.
[25]Mills, *White Collar*, pp. 174–75.

that economic motivations are dominant for the sales person. An examination of the types such as the drifter or the charmer suggests that the economic factor may be less important than social responses for some engaged in sales work.

The sales roles discussed by Mills reinforce the idea presented earlier that these boundary positions in organizations are important for the organizations involved. For this reason, sales personnel, like the receptionist discussed above, do act according to regularized patterns. They may act friendly, appealingly, or even hostilely toward potential customers. Whichever pattern is followed, the fact that it is followed is further evidence of the impersonality built into the contemporary sales process. Mills quotes from an observation of a salesclerk in a department store:

> I have been watching her for three days now. She wears a fixed smile on her made-up face, and it never varies, no matter to whom she speaks. I never heard her laugh spontaneously or naturally. Either she is frowning or her face is devoid of any expression. When a customer approaches, she immediately assumes her hard, forced smile. It amazes me because, although I know that the smiles of most salesgirls are unreal, I've never seen such calculation given to the timing of a smile. I tried myself to copy such an expression, but I am unable to keep such a smile on my face if it is not sincerely and genuinely motivated.[26]

The implication here, of course, is that the sales person is alienated from himself. While there is the evident impersonality Mills discusses, caution must be exercised in assuming that the sales person is self-alienated. It is very conceivable that he may not feel self-alienation, a serious condition in and of itself, or that if he does feel it, it is confined to the work situation, with other outlets provided for self-expression off the job. A complete analysis of the situation would require data that would describe the varying amounts of alienation felt, the sources of such alienation, and consequences of alienation for the individuals involved. The approach taken by the Morse study is relevant here. If the sales person, or any other person for that matter, takes expectations of meaningful social interaction into the job and such expectations are not met, alienation and dissatisfaction are likely to ensue. On the other hand, the absence of such expectations would have different consequences when the same situation is confronted. As is so often

[26]Mills, *White Collar*, p. 184.

the case, the impact of the mass society on the individual has been widely, and often polemically, discussed but has been inadequately researched.

The white-collar worker on the organizational boundary is confronted with an additional job component that affects his behavior. He is the contact between the outside world and the organization. As such, he receives pressures, which can be incompatible, from both sources. Whyte's analysis of waitresses in the restaurant industry vividly shows the kinds of problems this can create. Waitresses are generally considered semiskilled service workers rather than white-collar workers, but the situations they face are analogous to those being discussed. The restaurant industry itself is somewhat unique in that it is both a production and service organization confronted with a largely unpredictable market. The waitress is under pressures from customers who want food and service to their individual demands. At the same time, the waitress depends upon the customer for tips, which in this case serve the same function as commissions. She must also interact with the rest of the organization, the pantry, kitchen, and bar workers. They have power over her in the sense that their lack of cooperation can make it very difficult for the waitress. The waitress can be put into the position of demanding things from the rest of the organization that cannot easily be delivered, such as changed or special orders or volume of demand too large for the facilities. The real problem for the waitress, however, appears to be her relationship to the customer. If she can control the situation by holding the initiative in the customer-waitress relationship, she can reduce the amount of pressure on herself by providing the customer's order at her own pace. If, on the other hand, the customer gets control of the situation or the relationship is ambiguous, the waitress is under more pressure, leading to maladaptive practices such as anger toward the customer or other personnel in the restaurant, poor relationships with supervisors, or nervous reactions such as crying or getting the shakes.[27] Whyte suggests that since control of the situation at all times is impossible to achieve, a component of the occupation is unresolvable pressures from the environment in the forms of customers and from other segments of the organization. The same general condition confronts white-collar workers in boundary positions. Thus, while the impersonal component can serve as a control mechanism, situations are still diverse enough to bring about pressures and pleasures in the occupation.

[27]Whyte, "When Workers and Customers Meet," in *Industry and Society*, ed. William F. Whyte (New York: McGraw-Hill Book Company, 1946), pp. 123–47.

For white-collar workers not in boundary positions the component of customer or client is missing. The central parts of the occupation are the work itself; the organizational structure, which defines the work process, prescribes the directions of social interaction, and outlines the nature of the expected social interaction and the work group. Before examining these components, it is necessary to point out that the organizational structure is a given in the occupation. While cliques, work quotas, and social interaction are important in the analysis of this form of white-collar work, the work itself is carried out within a structure set down by the employing organization. The assignment of a new employee to a position in effect defines the work performed, the individuals with whom it is possible to interact, and the probable directions of the interaction. This same process operates for others in organizations, but for the white-collar worker in this setting and for many blue-collar workers the fact of the organizational structure is the basic framework for analysis. The other components of the white-collar position are variations from the theme set by the organization. This is not to imply that such variations do not take forms widely divergent from the official organizational structure but that the structure is the point of origin for such variations.

With this in mind, a description of the nature of these internal white-collar occupations can begin. Technological changes in the form of automation or computerization of the office are having a tremendous impact on these occupations. In order to understand the nature of the impact, a series of studies dealing with nonautomated white-collar work will be examined.

Crozier's analysis of a French governmental clerical agency, which is perhaps atypical in its factorylike atmosphere, illustrates the fact that white-collar work is not inherently dissimilar from factory work, despite the status difference ascribed to it. The particular agency studied employed about 4,500 workers, divided into four main work sections for administrative purposes. The work was largely repetitive and self-supervising. The workers were expected to accomplish all of the work that came in on a given day, and the load was such that the workers were forced to keep busy or fall behind, reducing the need for close supervision. Thus the majority of the workers were at the same level and performed the same duties. "The technology of the Agency's work is simple, and it has remained basically unchanged for 35 years. The employees, all female, work in production units on heavy cross tabulating accounting machines (with six or two tabulators)."[28] The organization reflects the nature of the technology in its simplicity.

[28]Crozier, *The Bureaucratic Phenomena*, p. 14.

The basic units of work organization are the four-girl work teams. These teams, to which more than 60 per cent of the employees belong, are in charge of the direct productive function of the Agency—ie., the carrying out and accounting of the customers' orders . . . The Agency as a whole . . . remains a rather rare example of a large modern organization in which everything still revolves around a large set of autonomous and parallel productive units, working independently of one another. . . . Work therefore, does not depend on supervisory decisions and group relationships, but on the impersonal pressure of the public at large. . . . Within the work team . . . there are division of work and a great deal of interdependence. Two girls work at the tabulating machines and two at checking. The work process begins with a check of the customer's credentials, then the girl at the first (six-tabulator) machine types, at one time, all documents necessary for carrying out the order. The figures are then checked by the third employee; and they are finally tabulated again, for balancing the accounts, by the fourth.[29]

This same process is repeated throughout the day and day after day.

A very similar picture is drawn by George C. Homans in his description of "cash-posting" in an American organization. He states:

The cash-posting job was essentially as follows: Bundles of bill stubs, representing paid bills, came from the cashier's office to the desk of the poster's supervisor. A cash poster took one of these bundles, went to the right "ledger" [file] and pulled out the cards whose numbers corresponded to those on the stubs. . . . When a cash poster had finished one bundle she started on the next one, while the "pulled" cards were sent to another room to be tabulated against one another. . . . The supervisors expected each poster to "pull" an average of at least 300 cards per hour, and each one did. This was the "quota." But aside from this there was no group norm of output and no incentive pay, and individual posters varied from just over 300 to almost 500 cards per hour.[30]

In this case the cash posters were not in the majority of the clerical workers of the organization. Others performed duties which re-

[29]Crozier, *The Bureaucratic Phenomena*, pp. 17–18.
[30]Homans, "Status Among Clerical Workers," *Human Organization*, XII, 1 (Spring, 1953), 6–7.

quired more discretion and involved less repetition. For these the process still involved handling a large volume of work in a systematic way.

An analysis of telephone operators provides much the same picture of white-collar work. The operators sit in front of switchboards in rows, completing calls and writing out tickets in accordance with company policies. The work requires discipline and is performed under conditions of close supervision unusual for white-collar employment. The operator cannot normally leave her switchboard without being replaced, nor can she talk with her fellow workers. The work of the operator is clean and of the white-collar variety, but the supervision is as close and discipline as exacting as one can find in a factory.[31]

The discussion thus far has concentrated on the more repetitive of the internal white-collar occupations. The work of key-punch operators or typists in typing pools shares many of the characteristics discussed above. There are other internal occupations that do provide more variety and freedom from close supervision. The secretary, whether private or shared among a number of executives, enjoys a higher status and a greater diversity in the work performed. Shipping and inventory clerks are more closely linked to changes in organizational demands and generally have more freedom of movement and interaction. It would appear, however, that the majority of these internal white-collar workers are engaged in repetitive and stationary work. This, at first glance, seems incompatible with the findings reported earlier that such workers are generally satisfied in their work.

The incompatibility can be resolved when a number of factors are examined. In the first place, white-collar workers do tend to believe that they are part of the management process and are thus important for the functioning of the organization. This belief apparently carries over into the general assessment of the job to the extent that their own importance is imagined, even though it is not real in terms of individual contributions to the system. A second factor is that the work is clean and in the office area of an organization, a positive attribute in the assessment of an occupation.[32] A third factor is that this type of office work has traditionally permitted meaningful social relationships which apparently tend to overcome some of the objective components of the

[31]See Joel Seidman et al., The Worker Views His Union (Chicago: University of Chicago Press, 1958).

[32]For a discussion of this point, see Caplow, The Sociology of Work, pp. 46–47.

situation. Homans, for example, notes that the work of the cash posters did allow for social interaction and much of the meaning of work for these girls is derived from such interaction.[33]

An extended analysis by Gross suggests that "cliques" or interaction patterns in the office perform three major functions for its members. First, cliques provide a source of information for their members. This is especially true when they cross specific work group lines, allowing different perspectives to be brought into discussions. In this sense they provide the worker with information about what the larger organization is doing. Although there is no guarantee that the information shared in cliques is always correct, it does tend to integrate the individual into the larger whole. The second function of cliques is simply providing a source for congenial social interaction, which as can be seen from the discussions above is not present within the formal structure. The final function is perhaps the most important. Gross suggests that work in an office has less meaning to the worker than does work in a factory. The cliques provide personal response and satisfaction for the worker. He is responded to as a person by other workers who also provide him with a basis for seeing the relationship between his work and the whole.[34]

The nature of this internal white-collar work is such that social interaction may provide the *only* source of positive satisfaction for the individuals beyond the minimum provided by the money earned and the idea of keeping busy. If this is actually the case, or if social interaction is even a moderate contributor to work satisfaction, then the limitation of possibilities for interaction should reduce satisfaction levels. Crozier's evidence supports this interpretation in that a generally low level of satisfaction was found. The workers were restricted to the four-member work team. The pressures for productivity were very strong and the organization of work was such that there was little interdependence between the units. Crozier found that in such situations the "amount of interaction will be rather low and solid supportive cliques will be rare."[35]

In a related study, Bernard Karsh and Jack Siegman found that a group of keypunch operators, confronted with more rigid standards and closer supervision, because of the installation of a computer in their office, reacted negatively to the change. Their reactions were that management no longer trusted them to do a good job and that their work was useless and their positions inferior. The

[33]"Status Among Clerical Workers," p. 7.
[34]Gross, "Characteristics of Cliques in Office Organizations," *Research Studies of the State College of Washington*, XIX (1951), 131–36.
[35]*The Bureaucratic Phenomena*, p. 37.

closer supervision and raised standards were required because errors were more costly in the installation of a computer.[36] The impact on the operators reflects the social meaning attached to the work. There apparently was an absence of supportive cliques in this situation. In addition the heightened standards required closer attention to the work and hence less opportunity for social interaction.

White-collar workers in the organization are faced with an official structure that demands impersonality in the sense that people of equal ranks and in equivalent positions are to be treated equally. This official structure serves as a point from which social interaction develops. Social interaction has been shown to be an important component for satisfaction and a sense of meaning in the work situation. If the official structure changes so that less social interaction is possible, then the result is less satisfaction. The official structure is changing as automation makes rapid inroads into the administrative process.

automation of the office

Most of the discussion of the impact of changing technology on white-collar workers will be deferred until the section on technology and occupations. Some of the issues raised above, however, are directly related to technological change and should be examined at this time. As has been seen, the work structure for white-collar personnel has already been drastically affected by the introduction of business machines, routinized work flow, pooled typists and clerks, standardization of products sold, and over-all rationalization of office work. Contemporary changes and those projected for the future will have an equal or greater impact, especially in the areas which at the present time are major sources for positive reactions to these occupations types.

There are some problems in terminology in discussing technological change in this area. The term automation itself is somewhat inappropriate here in that it is usually applied to the production process, involving controlled input, production processes, and output linked together by continuous operations and feedback mechanisms, which allow simultaneous adjustments to variations in any component of the process. White-collar work is most directly affected by

[36]Karsh and Siegman, "Functions of Ignorance in Introducing Automation," *Social Problems*, XII, 2 (Fall, 1964), 141–50.

computers and other electronic data-processing equipment. This "hardware" is part of the general process called "cybernetics," which implies that information centers high on information but possessing little energy control other activities that contain less information but more energy.[37] The cybernetic process is basic to the technological changes under discussion, but this term itself implies a wider range of phenomena than those central to this discussion. Total organizations are affected by cybernetics, but the impact of technological change on the white-collar worker seems to be more limited. Despite the fact that automation has been normally utilized as a concept for the production process, in many ways it appears to be a reasonable term for use here. The impact on the workers involved is one of tighter control of input, process, and output. The process itself is more continuous and less spasmodic. Feedback in terms of accountability for errors is heightened in the process. Thus, the term automation will be used, although the usage is not exact.

Ida R. Hoos has suggested that those displaced by automation (the number displaced and the nature of the displacement will not be discussed at this time) are the "accounting, bookkeeping, filing, and ledger clerks, often called the 'backbone of the clerical force' and their superiors."[38] These occupations, of course, correspond almost identically to those described by Crozier and Homans. The displacement takes the form of replacement of these positions by key-punch operators and operators and programmers for the new equipment. While some former white-collar workers may move up into programming and similar positions, the complexity of these tasks and the growing sophistication of the equipment involved precludes a high rate of such movement. Key punching is a quite different form of white-collar work and has important consequences for the social patterns of white-collar work. It is a

> dead-end occupation, with no promotional opportunities. The work is simple, monotonous, and repetitive, but requires a high degree of accuracy and speed. The pressure for great speed, coupled with the demand for precision, creates much tension, especially since practically all organizations maintain an objective count of production. Although measurement of clerical output is not a new

[37]This definition of cybernetics is from Talcott Parsons, *Societies: Evolutionary and Comparative Perspectives* (Englewood Cliffs, N.J.: Prentice-Hall, Inc., 1966), p. 9.

[38]"When the Computer Takes Over the Office," *Harvard Business Review*, XXXVIII, 4 (July–August, 1960), 103.

practice, the simplification and routinization of office
tasks which accompany EDP (electronic data processing)
have provided further incentive for applying production
room thinking to office operation.[39]

Hoos further notes that the "former occupations involved a certain
amount of moving about the office and contact with other employees
or customers. The workers now complain of 'being chained to the
machine.' "[40]

If this is in fact the case, the sources of satisfaction in office
work discussed above are in real jeopardy. The automated office
will be more like that described by Crozier, even though the work
process in the French clerical agency itself appears very simply
automated, than those described by Gross and Homans. The opportunity for social interaction and the resultant satisfactions deriving
therefrom are severely limited in such a situation. Since social interaction has been shown to be perhaps the major source of satisfaction
in this form of white-collar work, a lessening or leveling of satisfaction levels in the office could be predicted.

Another impact of automation on the office is that the office will
probably increasingly operate on more than a one-shift basis. The
original investment in equipment, whether purchased or rented, is
such that "down time," time when the equipment is not in use, is
extremely uneconomical. There is a strong tendency to utilize the
equipment on at least a two-shift basis. This, plus the changed
nature of the work itself, will minimize the differences between the
office and the production units in many organizations. In the non-
production organization white-collar work will change in a similar
direction, although the comparative basis will be absent. In a sense,
white-collar work becomes machine tending, rather than machine
operating or being based on manual and mental dexterity. This
growing similarity with factory work may contribute to increasing
unionization of this segment of the white-collar population.

White-collar employees in contact with the public have been
and probably will be less affected by this form of technological
change. While certain low-skill contact jobs can be replaced by
machines, as in the case of automatic food-vending machines, the
majority of such occupations will not be affected. As the emphasis
on service grows, these occupations will probably increase in proportion to the labor force. The skills involved here, however, differ from
those of the internal white-collar worker, which suggests that

[39]Hoos, "When the Computer Takes Over the Office," p. 105.
[40]"When the Computer Takes Over the Office," p. 105.

a simple transfer to contact white-collar positions is not a ready alternative for people displaced by automation or potential office employees.

white-collar workers and unions

The trends discussed above suggest that a good part of white-collar work is becoming more like manual work, with pressures for production, linkage to machine technology, shift work, and the diminishing opportunities for social interaction. In addition, with the growth of larger and larger organizations, white-collar workers can be found in increasing numbers in sizable units, rather than scattered throughout an organization or community. Despite these trends, white-collar unionism remains relatively weak. Kassalow estimates that only 11 per cent of white-collar workers are organized (using essentially the same definition of white-collar worker that has been utilized here) while 50 to 60 per cent of manual and service workers are organized.[41]

There are a number of factors operating against unionization of white-collar workers, even though union history in the United States contains a number of old and strong white-collar unions, such as those of the retail clerks, postal employees, and railway clerks. According to Dick Bruner, a union organizer, white-collar workers are simply "different." He feels that they think in terms of their skills which can be taken from employer to employer if the conditions in one situation are not desirable. Bruner also suggests that white-collar workers have a greater allegiance to their employers and turn whatever grievances they have toward their supervisors rather than the organization itself. Bruner's observations about mobility aspirations among white-collar workers coincide with the discussions above in that the workers believe that promotions will come with hard work and diligence on the job. They identify with management and professional persons. Unions themselves are viewed negatively, according to Bruner. The idea of striking and the image of union workers as accepting the rare corruption within some unions also is a negative factor.[42]

Kassalow suggests that other factors also operate against the unionization of white-collar workers. An important consideration is that the majority of such workers are women. "Women workers are

[41]"United States," p. 338.
[42]Dick Bruner, "Why White Collar Workers Can't Be Organized," *Harpers Magazine*, CCXV, 1287 (August, 1957), 44–50.

frequently much less oriented to their jobs in a career sense and often look upon their work status as 'temporary.' "[43] In this sense their emotional and temporal investment in their job is minimized, leading to less involvement in work related activities in general and unions in particular. Another factor is that the white-collar workers whose fathers or mothers worked at blue-collar occupations may not view their jobs as being onerous and may view them as a form of upward mobility. These people may have favorable orientations toward unions from their family background but feel that they have escaped from an occupational status that retains certain negative connotations. Those white-collar workers who come from a higher socio-economic status are likely to bring with them sentiments that are not prounion.

In the important area of wages and fringe benefits, white-collar workers have fared reasonably well. Many employers attempt to match or better union contracts for manual workers for their white-collar workers. Form and Miller suggest that on some benefits, such as severance pay and discounts for purchasing company products, white-collar workers fare better.[44] Whether the pattern of equaling or bettering union settlements is done in the sense of paternalism or in an attempt to forestall unionization of white-collar workers, the effect has been to make unions appear less desirable because there are no evident benefits from union membership.

Despite these handicaps, white-collar unionization has made modest gains in recent years. Retail clerks, railway clerks, telephone workers, and office workers have unions that have grown in proportion to employment in these occupations. Many industrial unions have made strides in organizing white-collar workers in industries such as autos and steel. Rapid growth has occurred among federal, state, and local governmental employees.[45]

Recent militancy among professional groups, such as teachers and nurses, may hasten unionization of white-collar workers if these professional groups serve as any sort of model for the white-collar employee. Unionization is obviously not a panacea for the problems faced by these occupations. The changes, however, are of a nature which would lead to a prediction of greater likelihood of unionization. An additional factor, which may contribute to this trend, is the decreasing opportunity for advancement for the white-collar worker. The previously described educational prerequisites, the

[43]Kassalow, "United States," p. 356.
[44]William H. Form and Delbert C. Miller, *Industry, Labor and Community* (New York: Harper & Row, Publishers, 1960), pp. 402–404.
[45]Kassalow, "United States," 339–49.

growing complexity of technological developments, and the increasing standardization of work (at a relatively low skill level) would tend to preclude advancement beyond a minimal degree. The traditional attachment of white-collar workers to management, based to some extent on the image of the secretary and her relationship to her superior, will probably be affected by this limitation on advancement possibilities. Even within the secretarial and typing segments of white-collar work, technological changes have occurred and are projected which may drastically alter the traditional relationships. New techniques of reproduction of printed materials and the potential for equipment which will transcribe directly from the recorded voice to the typed page without human interpretation have important implications for a large segment of this population, their work relationships, their position in the labor force, and the over-all image of white-collar work.

Another factor important to unionization among white-collar workers is the degree to which they identify and work closely with other unionized employees. Railway clerks and airline stewardesses, for example, are much more likely to be unionized than receptionists for lawyers because of their general work environment and their contacts with other unionized employees, even though their work may actually be less routine and structured. Unionization and antagonism toward unions are thus a result of a series of factors. If the changes described above continue, it seems that the factors in favor of unionization should begin to outweigh those that operate against it.

summary and conclusions

In a number of ways white-collar work is similar to the occupations which have been discussed under the headings of professionals and managers, proprietors, and officials. Similarities exist in the occupational setting, organizations and offices; in the fact that the work is generally clean and carried out in pleasant surroundings; and in common orientations, white collar workers identifying with management and believing in the possibility of upward mobility. These similarities have important consequences for the worker himself as he reacts to his job and its setting.

At the same time, white-collar occupations have significantly less power within the employing organizations than those occupations previously discussed. White-collar workers *work for* the members of the higher ranked groups. They do not participate in the decision-making process, even though they are an important part of it in terms of their role as information transcribers and handlers. The white-collar worker is rather easily replaced, since the skills involved are available in a wide segment of the population. The most important difference, perhaps, is that the white-collar worker carries out activities within the organization which are determined for him. He can exercise little discretion in what, when, or how he carries out his functions. The same is true for many lower level managers and some professionals, but for these occupations the realistic expectation exists that the individual will, or will have the opportunity to, move to positions that will give him more discretion. The white-collar worker, on the other hand, is in the position of not being able to make this transition into the decision making strata. Given the technological trends affecting white-collar work, the white-collar worker is liable in time to be put in a position where even less discretion is available, while the manager moves in the opposite direction. Despite this trend, members of this category still tend to be oriented toward the managerial ranks.

This orientation is apparently based on a number of factors. White-collar work was an avenue by which many men moved up into managerial positions. The woman could become a private secretary or assume supervisory positions within the office. Since these higher positions are increasingly being filled by persons brought in from outside the work force, college graduates who did not come up from the ranks, the potential mobility is increasingly a memory, but one which lingers on. A good deal of white-collar work, especially the internal variety, is carried on in an office setting, where members of the higher ranked occupations are visible and present. The work performed is utilized by the executives or professionals in the organization, even though the particular work of a white-collar worker may be only a small part of the whole. Another historical consideration is that white-collar work has traditionally been viewed as superior to manual work. These factors combine to yield the still prevalent upward orientation, which proves to be a source of positive satisfaction for many workers. When white-collar workers compare themselves with blue-collar workers, these factors combine to produce a sense of pride in the work and satisfaction in the status. The reality of the situation becomes less relevant than the definition of the situation. At the same time, this orientation can serve as a source of dissatisfaction, when the fact of blocked mobility becomes apparent or when the scope of the position is decreased through technological change.

An important characteristic of the white-collar category is that it is composed largely of occupations in which women play an important role. The implications for unionization have been noted above. Equally important, perhaps, is the fact that women tend to exhibit less stable work patterns. Since it can be predicted that a certain proportion of women will leave their positions in any given time period, employing organizations are likely to attempt to find ways in which their investment in training and related expenses are minimized. This contributes to further standardization and routinization. The fact that women often intend to leave the occupation, not planning long careers even though an increasing number of women are in the labor force for extended periods, tends to minimize some of the negative aspects of white-collar work. The impersonality and routinization may well be more tolerable if the job is viewed as only temporary.

White-collar workers in boundary or contact positions are placed between two conflicting parties, their employing organizations and the public with which they have contact. While this can be a source of frustration, as in the case of the waitresses, it also allows more individual freedom in terms of the techniques selected to handle the situation. While each customer may be treated in the same way, the worker still has a range of possible techniques to choose from in his approach to the public outside the organization. Whether or not the individual becomes alienated from himself because of a constant image projection that may be at variance with his own feelings toward the public is still an unanswered question. The suggestions from the analyses of sales behavior lead to the conclusion that boundary personnel have a strong personal investment in their work. If this is the case, then the alienation may not be as severe as Mills' analysis suggests.

An important component of white-collar work is social interaction. The boundary position is based around such interaction, and feelings of success or failure are based upon the manner in which it is handled. The internal white-collar position does not require such interaction and, in fact, may discourage it in terms of official expectations. It has been shown, however, that this is perhaps the most important component in reactions to the job. Since work is given a social definition, even the view of a particular job as being good or bad is shaped in this interactional framework. More importantly, social interaction per se is vital in the general orientation to the work. While such interaction is not intrinsic in the job, it becomes part of the basis for the over-all reaction to the job. Clique formation and the possibilities for social interchange become an important source of job satisfaction. When this aspect is threatened, as in the case of technological change or where supervisory patterns become more strict, satisfaction is likely to decrease. At the same time, the relationship between supervision and productivity is such that for the organization concern with satisfaction may not be central. For the individual, however, satisfaction is of paramount concern.

As the production process becomes relatively less important as a basis for occupations and as service industries grow in importance, white-collar work will probably become an even larger occupational grouping. The growth will occur in the boundary positions, since service involves relatively unstandardized components and relationships with those being served. The internal white-collar occupations will probably decrease in importance as many tasks can be automated and/or eliminated. The older skills that characterized the internal position, such as typing or shorthand, will decrease as marketable commodities and the internal positions themselves will undoubtedly become more factory-like. As will be seen, factories are changing in the direction of becoming more like offices, so that the differentiations that existed may become meaningless.

chapter 7

craftsmen
and foremen

The analyses of professionals; managers, proprietors, and officials; and white-collar workers have suggested a descending order of occupations based on their general socio-economic status. In a simple classification, all of the occupations thus far discussed have been white-collar. At this point blue-collar occupations enter the discussion for the first time. Despite the socio-economic ranking implied in the order of presentation, craftsmen and foremen are often viewed as occupying equal or higher strata than the white-collar workers just discussed. Even though blue-collar work implies manual, rather than mental, work and dirty, as opposed to clean, working conditions, craftsmen and foremen rank higher than white-collar workers on many relevant socio-economic criteria. With regard to income and power within the organization, craftsmen and foremen rank ahead of the lower-level white-collar occupations. At the same time, the prestige accorded these blue-collar workers is somewhat lower than that accorded the white-collar worker.[1]

[1]For a comprehensive discussion of the components of occupational prestige and general socio-economic status, see Albert J. Reiss, Jr., *Occupations and Social Status* (New York: The Free Press of Glencoe, Inc., 1961).

Regardless of their position in the over-all stratification system, craftsmen and foremen are the elite of manual, or blue-collar, workers. The reasons are quite simple. The craftsman has skills, which are marketable and relatively scarce, while the foreman is in a position of some power within the work organization. At the same time, the foreman is expected to utilize interpersonal skills in his work, a component not necessarily required from those being supervised. Both the craftsman and the foreman generally receiver higher incomes than the balance of manual workers.

The combination of craftsmen and foremen into the same category by the census and other occupational analyses reflects the relative homogeneity of their socio-economic status. At the same time, the natures of the two basic occupation types included in this category are distinctly different in terms of the type of work performed, the manner in which membership in the occupation is achieved, and usually the setting of the work. The two types will therefore be analyzed separately.

craftsmen

The position of the crafts in the labor force has remained relatively constant, in spite of changing technologies and variations in societal demands for goods and services. Within the craft or skilled-worker category changes have occurred as some occupations, such as those of the blacksmith or wheelwright, faced obsolescence and others, such as those of the automobile mechanic or television repairman, came into prominence. Table 7.1 indicates both the stability of this category and the changes which are occurring within it. The most obvious shift is toward the service crafts and away from the production activities, which have diminished as a proportion of the labor force. This trend should continue as more goods become available to wider segments of the population and thus require servicing. The increased demands for service in general should also contribute to continued growth within this category.

The position of the crafts within the occupational structure can be attributed largely to their possession of scarce skills. This is, of course, the position of professionals and executives, and in many ways, the crafts share other characteristics with the professions. Caplow has provided an insightful analysis of these similarities. His focus is on building craftsmen, such as carpenters, masons, steam-fitters, or electricians, but can probably be extended to certain other

Table 7.1.   Craftsmen, Foremen, and Kindred Workers in Labor Force, by Decade (As Per Cent of All Employed Males)

	1960	1950	1940
Foremen	2.5	1.9	1.4
Mechanics and repairmen	5.1	4.2	2.4
Metal craftsmen, except mechanics	2.5	2.7	2.8
Construction craftsmen	5.5	5.8	8.3
Other craftsmen, not elsewhere classified	3.9	4.0	
Total: craftsmen, foremen, and kindred workers	19.5	18.6	14.9

SOURCE: U.S. Department of Commerce, *General Social and Economic Characteristics: Final Report PC (I) IC* (Washington, D.C.: U.S. Government Printing Office, 1960), p. 1-219, Table 89.

craftsmen, such as the printers or railroad engineers. The similarities are less true of many of the newer, service-oriented crafts.

The first similarity is in the manner of recruitment to the occupation. Caplow states:

> As in the case of professions, the rights and duties of candidates are specified with precision at each stage of their advancement, and the power of the state is often invoked to prevent outsiders from practicing the occupation. The most important differences are that the ultimate judges of competence are members of "higher" occupations, such as engineering, and that governmental authority cannot be overtly exercised by the occupational association. The control of recruiting is seldom complete—apprenticeship has partly given way to trade schooling organized by outsiders; effective occupational monopoly is usually limited to a local community and ceases abruptly at the urban limits; and the penalties for violation are nominal, unless they are reinforced by personal violence or by agreements with employers or suppliers.[2]

This recruitment pattern serves a number of purposes. It allows the occupation to establish a monopoly of the skills involved. By limiting the number of practitioners, it insures greater rewards for those in

[2]*The Sociology of Work*, pp. 102–3.

the field, if there is a demand for the product or service. Some people argue that this type of monopolization of skills is based entirely on the desire to restrict or eliminate competition and thus optimize the earning power of the members of the occupation. Another explanation is that the recruitment pattern serves to protect the occupation from incompetent practitioners and thus raise the quality of the performance of duties. Both factors are probably operative for the professions and the crafts. The fact that the crafts have a more limited control system in recruitment than the professions should not obscure the fact that the system is *occupationally* controlled, a factor not present in the majority of nonprofessional occupations.

An additional common characteristic of professions and crafts is the lifelong involvement in the occupation. Once in the occupation, it is extremely unlikely that an individual will change jobs. Seniority provisions in craft unions strengthen the position of the older worker and insure insofar as possible, that the individual has security in his field once he is accepted. Caplow suggests that the involvement of the craftsman is not as strong as that of the professional, since the craftsman is faced with seasonal fluctuations and occasional opportunities or desires to go into business for himself or to assume supervisory positions.[3] The identification with the specific occupation does, however, tend to remain. The involvement is strengthened by the fact that the craftsman passes through a series of stages in training and apprenticeship to reach his position. Once he is a full-fledged member of the craft, his income is maximized; however, there is little improvement in status or income after occupational membership is achieved. The potential income of the craftsman is achieved earlier in his career than the case of the professional, but the likelihood of changing occupations is equally slight for both groups.

Another similarity, which exists in principle for both professions and crafts, is the occupation's control over evaluation of merit and performance. As was the case with the professions, the reality of the situation is such that evaluation is difficult, if not impossible. Moreoever, an additional evaluatory agent is almost always present in the form of the employing organization and its engineering staff. In the crafts there is the general assumption that journeymen are in a position to judge apprentices and that masters are in a position to judge both journeymen and apprentices. As this traditional relation breaks down in the face of trade-school education and technological development, evaluation becomes more difficult for members

[3] *The Sociology of Work*, pp. 107–198.

of the craft and is increasingly in the hands of the employing organization.[4] Caplow points out that a strong craft union can retain a good deal of control in the face of these developments. If the traditional apprentice-journeyman-master distinctions are retained and the union has been able to standardize production rates, materials, and techniques, the employing organization is unable to distinguish between the different categories within the craft in terms of performance, since it is standardized by level, which allows the union to retain control. Such practices are given the negative connotation of featherbedding or stalling, but from the union's point of view they are necessary for continued power of self-control.[5] This form of standardization creates a situation in which members of the craft at the various levels are viewed as being interchangeable and retains the power of work assignment for the union.

In addition to the power of evaluation of merit and performance, some craft unions have succeeded in obtaining contracts covering all employers in an urban area. These contracts are designed to allow craft control over a wide variety of activities of concern to both its members and the employing organizations. In some ways these contracts contain elements analogous to the codes of ethics of the professions; these include provisions to protect outsiders from incompetence and unqualified practitioners and provisions designed to "safeguard the socio-economic position of insiders."[6] These provisions include, in addition such things as specifications of standard hourly wages together with provisions for overtime and other special conditions; rules of eligibility and ineligibility; which include the number of apprentices allowed per job and hiring and seniority standards; specifications of safety rules and acceptable tools and methods; and clauses pertaining to the union's right to a monopoly over certain activities. This allows occupational self-control to the extent that outside influence from employing organizations is unlikely to intrude except during contract negotiations. As is true of the professions, the actual extent of such self-control is likely to be rather limited.

Caplow's analysis is primarily concerned with, and relevant to, the building trades, which have been affected by technological changes to the extent that standardization of techniques and output is an evident component of the work. Other occupations included in the crafts have been or will be so affected. At the same time, the crafts contain elements that allow the worker to view his individual

[4]Gross, *Work and Society*, p. 57.
[5]Caplow, *The Sociology of Work*, pp. 111–112.
[6]Caplow, *The Sociology of Work*, p. 113.

contribution to the whole. He can see what he has done, making his contribution somewhat unique and providing the opportunity for intrinsic satisfaction because of this ability to identify with a completed product or service. This again is similar to the work of the professional. Blauner's analysis of the printing craft is instructive in this regard.

Printing involves an unstandardized product, the printed page, with which the individual can identify, since each member of the craft can see what his individual contribution is. In addition, this type of craft involves

> the freedom to determine techniques of work, to choose one's tools, and to vary the sequence of operations . . . Because each job is somewhat different from previous jobs, problems continuously arise which require a craftsman to make decisions. Traditional skills thus involve the frequent use of judgment and initiative, aspects of a job which give the worker a feeling of control over his environment.[7]

Blauner's analysis of alienation suggests that this feeling of control contributes to the lack of feeling of powerlessness among the printers. In this sense, the craftsman, like the professional, has control over his work and its environment even with the standardization noted above. There is freedom to vary the rate of performance and its sequence. The judgment factor enters the picture in terms of decisions regarding appropriate tools and techniques.

Another important consideration, suggested by Blauner, is that printers form an occupational community in that they identify strongly with the occupation.[8] He notes:

> Craft identification, a product of socialization, sometimes begins early in life, since there is a strong tendency for sons to follow fathers into the same skilled trade. The long apprenticeship period is the formal process through which a craftsman learns occupational norms as well as proficiency in work. Craft identification and loyalty is further reinforced through membership in craft unions.[9]

This is very similar to the "use of the professional organization as a major reference" as discussed in the section on professions.

[7]Blauner, *Alienation and Freedom*, p. 43.
[8]For an extensive analysis of the printing craft and the relationship between it and union structure, see Seymour M. Lipset, Morten A. Trow, and James S. Coleman, *Union Democracy* (New York: The Free Press of Glencoe, Inc., 1956).
[9]Blauner, *Alienation and Freedom*, p. 47.

The salience of this occupational community can be seen in William F. Whyte's analysis of a group of glassworkers. The glass factory studied made fine crystal, which requires largely hand technology. Aside from changes in the composition of the basic materials and methods for handling it, the over-all technology has changed little over time. A hierarchy of skills exists within the work group, and tradition and union provisions require that a person work his way up through the hierarchy. At one time only workers of Swedish extraction reached the top position, because of the communal belief that the Swedes were the only group that had the requisite skills and artistic sense for the job. This pattern created an even stronger occupational community. The Swedish dominance declined when the sons of the older workers did not continue in the glass industry because of continued education. The unionization of the total plant and the entire glass industry in the urban area also had an impact, since seniority provisions replaced ethnic ties as the major factor in advancement.

Despite these changes, the sense of community remained, which was evident in the traditions and lore surrounding the work situation. The most skilled of the workers were constantly being compared to famous old-timers. In the case of non-Swedes, the comparisons were usually negative, at least from the perspective of the older workers. The composition of the work groups helped retain the sense of community, since a strong tendency existed for workers to belong to the same work groups for a length of time. This strengthened the social ties within the group, leading to some competition between groups and also to a more general identification with the occupation. Whyte notes that the movement of younger workers into top positions did create friction between the younger and older workers. The older workers believed that the young men in top positions did not have the all-round skills characteristic of top men in the past. The fact that there was friction reinforces the idea that the occupation is a central focus for these workers. Rather than being apathetic, they appear to feel strong emotional involvement in the work. Whyte's analysis also suggests that these craftsmen were also highly involved in their personal performance on the job; pride in craftsmanship was an important component of the job. All of these factors contribute to the high level of identification with the occupation.[10]

It would be useful to have data comparing levels of involvement in the occupation among a variety of crafts in a variety of

[10]Whyte, *Men at Work* (Homewood, Ill.: Richard D. Irwin, Inc., 1961), pp. 149–78.

setting, as was the case for some of the professions. This is unfortunately not available. It would seem that the sense of community or involvement would be greater in those cases where workers systematically interact, as in the case of the glassworkers or printers and less in some building trades where the work group composition would change with particular projects. Another factor tending to affect this variable is technological change. Change of this sort probably has a dual impact. The threat of technological change, with the possibility of lost jobs, changed working relationships, weakened craft unions, and lowered skill requirements, may increase the level of involvement and create heightened solidarity. Once changes are instituted, the level of involvement would probably decline over a period of time, as skill requirements became less rigorous, remaining vestiges of the apprentice-master system disappeared, and the work contained fewer elements allowing individual discretion.[11] If this is the case, the long term trend for the crafts would appear to be a decline in the occupational community, since technological changes, while often resisted, are largely inevitable in the crafts.

Further inroads into the sense of the community may develop as restrictions on recruitment into the crafts are eased. In the case of the glassworkers, for example, the union represented all of the workers in the particular glass factory. This weakened the grip of the Swedes on the top positions and allowed non-Swedes access to these positions. When unions are organized along strictly craft lines, as is the case in most of the building trades, ethnic solidarity remains but is threatened by demands for equal employment opportunities for all eligible applicants. As these threats become reality, the ethnic base of a good deal of the solidarity is weakened and this, coupled with changing technology, probably diminishes the level of involvement.

The crafts, however, do have a stronger sense of occupational identification than other manual and many white-collar occupations. Richard R. Myers' study of the building industry suggests that personal ties together with ethnic, religious, and racial considerations play an important role in the hiring process. The actual work groups tend to be composed of craftsmen who know and like each other.[12] Within any work situation, cohesive work groups are likely to be based on common background characteristics, such as race, religion, or ethnicity, as well as on such factors as sex, age, or educational level. The important finding in the Myers' study is that

[11]Gross notes this change in *Work and Society*, p. 57.
[12]Myers, "Interpersonal Relations in the Building Industry," *Human Organization*, V, 2 (Spring, 1946), 1–7.

the initial composition of the groups is almost totally based upon such factors. Personal acquaintance is the key to the hiring process, creating a situation in which the solidarity is likely to be heightened and outsiders effectively excluded.

A recent study by Harold L. Sheppard and A. Harvey Belitsky, concerned with the nature of job seeking in Erie, Pennsylvania, substantiates the importance of the craft as a major reference point. The community and its metropolitan area were faced with a declining economy which was further depressed by the departure of a major employer. A comparison of skilled, semiskilled and unskilled workers was undertaken to determine the techniques utilized in finding employment by the workers who had been laid off. Skilled workers generally had a higher rate of re-employment in their old jobs as economic conditions improved. An exception to this was older workers, a group that generally faces more difficulties in finding employment. There were no skilled workers under 38 still unemployed at the time of the study. Since there is a tendency for skilled workers to be older, their chances in the labor market are adversely affected by this factor, but are enhanced by their skills.

The actual techniques used in seeking new jobs for those workers not rehired by their original employer varied by skill level. The union was an important source of information about new jobs for skilled workers but not for other groups. The union was also an effective means of locating new positions for the skilled group. The other groups had more success from information from friends and relatives or by applying directly to companies that were hiring at a particular time. At the same time, skilled workers who applied directly to companies had good success; their skills were a marketable commodity.[13]

The skilled worker has a distinct advantage in the labor market as compared with blue-collar workers of lesser skill levels. The importance of skills is not, of course, limited to the blue-collar world. What is important for the discussion is that the union is an important factor in the labor market for the skilled worker, even in times of high unemployment rates. The craftsman, however, looks to his colleagues as a resource. Here again the orientation may not be as strong as among some professions, but it is an important source of differentiation from other occupational categories in both blue-collar and white-collar occupations.

The importance of the union for the craftsman is further shown in Caplow's discussion of the total labor market for the crafts. To

[13]Sheppard and Belitsky, *The Job Hunt* (Baltimore, Md.: Johns Hopkins Press, 1966), pp. 31–100.

some extent the supply of craftsmen is fixed by the recruitment patterns into the occupation, which tend to limit the number of persons in a particular craft within a geographical area. The control of the labor supply is not absolute, however, since noncraftsmen can attempt many of the jobs normally performed by craftsmen. Caplow points out that there is a rather constant supply of amateur or marginal painters, ready, willing, and, to varying degrees, able to undertake painting projects of differing magnitudes.[14] The same is probably true for many other craft skills, such as plumbing, electrical work, or roofing, despite the personal and financial risks involved in such do-it-yourself projects.

> The union, on its side, has recourse to a number of familiar devices to preserve its monopoly. Employers who hire nonunion labor for craft work may be permanently boycotted by all the crafts. Personal violence against these competitors is not unheard of. The most effective controls are embodied in local ordinances and agreements [Note the close similarity of this practice with the professions' control over licensing and certification procedures], so that in many cities building permits, permits to operate machinery, and other necessary licenses will be revoked if inspection discloses the use of nonunion labor. While this control often ceases at the city limits, it is sufficiently effective in most communities to restrict the use of nonunion labor on craft work to small projects of no economic importance. There are, of course, some conspicuous exceptions in either direction: entire villages have been built by large scale contractors with nonunion labor; while in other places, private householders have been effectively prevented from doing plumbing or wiring on their own premises.[15]

The supply of labor can thus be controlled to some extent; the demand, on the other hand, is often highly variable. In the building and construction trades, climactic changes have an important effect. In addition, in the building trades and many other crafts the employers are likely to be small and relatively insecure, lending further instability to the demand factor. These conditions create real problems for the craft unions in that they must somehow provide for their members during slack periods and face the situation of not having a fixed entity with which to bargain. The most effective technique, which the unions have developed, is the es-

[14]*The Sociology of Work*, p. 165.
[15]Caplow, *The Sociology of Work*, p. 165.

tablishment of a fixed or just price for the work performed, high enough to allow earnings during full-employment periods to cover those periods when seasonal or industry declines occur. At the same time, the unions seek to become the only source for hiring, so that potential employers must come to the union for their workers. This gives the union power over the employers and its own members. Caplow points out that the unions are most successful in these practices during times of full employment. During periods of low employment their control over potential employers and their own members is lessened as the individual members use their own resources in trying to find work.[16] Except in times of low employment, the union is a powerful force for the craftsman and his employer. This power would tend to strengthen the union's position as a major reference for its members.

The discussion thus far has suggested that crafts and professions share a number of characteristics. To use the approach taken in the section on the professions, on both structural and attitudinal characteristics, the crafts in many ways approximate the professional model. Major differences exist between the groups, however, which prevent the two occupational types from being viewed as one. The basic difference is that the professions stress mental prowess, while the crafts stress manual dexterity. Some professions, such as surgery and some forms of engineering, require dexterity; nevertheless, the basis for the work is the exercise of mental skills. The simple mental-manual differentiation is based upon a more fundamental difference. The professions are built around a body of theoretical knowledge that can be applied in specific situations. Professionals contribute to the knowledge base and apply that knowledge, which is available. In practice, the professional may not always refer back to the theoretical underpinnings of a case. He may simply prescribe, decide, or advise, in a mechanical way, on the basis of the simple facts presented to him; when a particular symptom appears, a standard remedy is suggested. At this level, his actions are little different from the craftsman. The differentiation is based on the assumption that the professional can back up his decision with the theoretical considerations on which the simple mechanical decisions were based. Whether or not every practicing professional can do this is subject to investigation, but professional training is designed to allow the person to do so.

The craftsman, on the other hand, is trained in techniques without the theoretical background. He may, in many instances,

---

[16]Caplow, *The Sociology of Work*, p. 168.

apply principles from theoretical sciences. The tool and die maker, for example, utilizes principles from trigonometry and analytical geometry in his work, but he does so without realizing it. Theoretical knowledge allows operation in situations that have not previously been experienced, but for the craftsman such knowledge is unavailable. This is not to suggest that the craftsman is unable to adjust to new problems and situations. He does so on the basis of this experience and by trial and error.

Another difference between professionals and craftsmen is the colleague group. As Caplow notes, craft unions are locally based, and community boundaries are usually the limit of jurisdiction. Professional associations, on the other hand, are organized on a local, state, regional, and national basis, and some professionals utilize the national group as their reference. More important the regulative power of the associations is much more broadly based than the local community.

Training for skilled work takes three basic forms. The traditional apprenticeship is still the most visible technique, but the number of apprentices has declined in recent years. Trade schools also provide training for the crafts. Trade schools and vocational training in the secondary schools have suffered the stigma of lower status when compared to college training or college preparatory curricula in the secondary schools. In the case of trade schools, the financial deprivation involved during the training period is such that the schools are underutilized. Vocational curricula in secondary schools often do not fit the demands of the labor market, because they emphasize skills that are in low demand and do not adjust to changes in technology.[17] At times trade or vocational school graduates do not find employment in the crafts because of lack of recognition by the union of the training programs. A third method for learning a craft is on the job. In this case the worker picks up the skills while assisting a skilled worker or on his free time. Here again union contract provisions may prevent this if it contains clear specifications of who is to do what kind of work. Governmental and private programs have been developed to increase the number of skilled workers and to upgrade the skills of members of the labor force. The success of such programs depends on union and employer cooperation as well as the willingness of a segment of the labor force to undergo additional training. Preparation for the crafts, while longer and more intensive than for many white-collar occupations

[17]Grant Venn, "Man, Education, and Work," in *The Manpower Revolution*, ed. Garth L. Mangum (New York: Doubleday & Company, Inc., 1966), pp. 406–7.

and for most other blue-collar occupations, is not comparable to professional training. The diversity of the programs and their relationship to unions suggest a less coordinated approach to training for crafts.

The discussion thus far has suggested that the craftsmen are the elite of the manual workers and that they share a number of characteristics with the other elite, the professionals. The position of the craftsmen results in part from their traditional role in the labor force and also from their ability to demand and receive rewards, in the form of income, recognition, and autonomy, that are higher than those received by other workers in both the blue- and white-collar groups. The orientation of the craftsman, however, tends to be toward the other blue-collar workers, rather than toward those of equal or higher status in the white-collar category.

Richard F. Hamilton's recent examination of the behavior and values of skilled workers provides some important insights into this relationship. Using data from a national survey that grouped craftsmen with foremen, a combination which is common but unfortunate for our purposes, he found that craftsmen's membership in voluntary associations was more like that of semiskilled workers than of white-collar workers (clerical and sales personnel). The craftsman and the semiskilled worker both belong to fewer such organizations than the white-collar workers. Similarly, the skilled workers' reading patterns were closer to the semiskilled than to the white-collar group. An important exception is that the skilled workers did read more trade magazines than either of the other groups. Hamilton suggests that this is further evidence of the independence of the crafts. At the same time the other reading patterns are closer to the other blue-collar patterns.[18]

In other areas, the relationship is maintained. The similarity of political and educational beliefs and attitudes on foreign policy and domestic issues reflect the proximity of the craftsmen to other blue-collar workers. An interesting finding in regard to the life style of the craftsmen is that they are more likely to own their own homes than the white-collar workers. Hamilton suggests that skilled workers actually comprise a semiautonomous status group, closer to the balance of the blue-collar category than to the white-collar group. They are not "interstitial" in the sense of standing between the other status groups but instead lean toward the rest of the blue-collar group while retaining independence in certain areas.[19]

[18]Hamilton, "The Behavior and Values of Skilled Workers" in *Blue Collar World*, eds. Arthur B. Shostak and William Gomberg (Englewood Cliffs, N.J.: Prentice-Hall, Inc., 1964), p. 49.
[19]Hamilton, "The Behavior and Values of Skilled Workers," pp. 55–56.

Hamilton attributes the autonomy of the skilled workers partially to the high rate of occupational inheritance within the group. There is some mobility into the crafts from the lesser skilled categories, but this is largely among workers who are already of the appropriate background, since the crafts can control entrance. At the same time, those who are downwardly mobile from the white-collar group tend to bypass the crafts, entering the labor force at the semiskilled level and not bringing their values into the crafts.

Most of the discussion thus far has been oriented around the traditional crafts. The growth of the craftsman category is based on the emergent service crafts, such as television or automobile repairing, and the behavioral and attitudinal characteristics discussed may not be relevant for the newer craft occupations. Similarly, the discussion of the professionlike nature of the building and printing crafts may be inapplicable. Certainly the new crafts do not have the common ethnic, racial, and religious backgrounds of the older groups. Other traditions are also probably absent. Whether they model themselves on the older tradition of craft occupations would have to be determined by research, but seems somewhat unlikely, since the social origins of the new craftsmen are not in the old crafts (the rate of occupational inheritance is such that the sons of the old-style craftsmen would either go into the same craft or attain higher educational levels and leave the craft system). Part of the reason Hamilton found relatively close identification of craftsmen with semiskilled workers may be that the newer crafts recruit from the semiskilled worker level. If this is the case, there would tend to be some carry-over of attitudes and behavior into the new occupation. This again is a topic for additional research.

The new crafts are similar to the new professions in their partial conformity to the traditional conceptualization of what a craft or profession is. While the crafts have not been investigated as intensively as the professions, some factors in the differences are evident. The new crafts do not have the long tradition of apprenticeship. Skills are acquired in vocational or training schools or on the job. Entrance is thus less structured, and there are fewer controls on the number entering the field and the nature of the prerequisites for entry. This could lead to a diminished emphasis on racial or ethnic considerations. At the same time, the differentiation between crafts and noncrafts becomes more difficult because training periods are less formalized and comprehensive. It is difficult to determine, for example, exactly which auto mechanics are skilled workers and which are semiskilled; no clear criteria exist. The simplest differentiation would probably be whether or not the individual can sell his skills on the labor market. If he can be hired as a mechanic, rather than as an employee, he would be considered skilled. Such a differentiation may be oversimplified, but it does represent much of the essence of the crafts. As was the case with the professions, however, the line between members and nonmembers of the occupational category cannot be drawn with certainty.

foremen

Foremen, although a relatively small proportion of the total labor force and of this occupational category (see Table 7.1), have been the subject of intensive analyses because of their pivotal positions in organizations. The foreman is at the bottom of the managerial hierarchy and at the top of the blue-collar segment of the organization. He can be called foreman, first-line supervisor, chief, or group leader. The position is one filled from below, and people are promoted out of the ranks to the position. Miller and Form describe the position as follows:

> . . . an office that requires supervision of the actual production or service as a full-time job. The person filling this office must have official contacts with both supervisory officials and the operators or clerks on the job. He must spend most of his time on the plant floor supervising personally, or supervising people who are part-time supervisors and part-time workers. Paper work must not occupy so much of his time that he has to have a secretary. He does not spend more than one-third of his day on it. In fact, paper work irritates him and keeps him off the floor. Further, he does not participate in policy-making. In short, his orientation is downward toward the workers and their problems. He must have enough authority so that workers obey his technical commands.[20]

The foreman's position is ubiquitous. At some point in most organizations (extremely small organizations in which members perform highly specialized functions would be the most obvious exception), such supervision is vital to the work process. Joan Woodward has noted that the ratio of supervisors to supervisees varies according to the technology of an industry, but even in those industries where human supervision is minimized, foremen

[20]Miller and Form, *Industrial Sociology*, p. 206.

are still present and have a wide span of control.[21] Charles R.
Walker, Robert H. Guest, and Arthur N. Turner suggest:

> In a sense, the *foreman* is one species in a very large
> genus of human beings. The genus may be said to include
> all who directly supervise men and women, such as the
> lower ranks of officers and noncommissioned officers in
> the armed services, head nurses in hospitals, senior clerks
> in banks and law offices, and many others.[22]

The foreman's position is thus one of coordination of workers'
efforts to accomplish the goals of the organization. Such a position is
obviously vital. It is also subject to a variety of conflicting pressures
and to the impact of change.

A basic source of conflict for the foreman is that he is caught
between his superiors' demands that he identify with them and
embody organizational authority to his men and the workers' demands that he assist them in evading the rules and maintaining work
group solidarity. Caplow notes that the resulting marginality or
ambivalence is inherent in the position and is a major reason for the
fact that foremen have been the principal targets for "supervisory
training, conference systems, performance appraisals, and so
on . . ."[23] Caught between these conflicting demands, the foreman
has four alternative identification patterns which he can assume,
according to Miller and Form.

He can identify with his superiors and adopt the management
ideology.[24] Miller and Form believe that pattern is especially likely
when the foreman is brought in from outside the work group and
expects that the position of foreman is a prelude to advancement
into higher management positions. Since there appears to be a
tendency to hire college trained junior-executive types for the
foreman's position, this type of identification should become more
dominant.[25] The obvious problem with this form of identification is
the social distance that develops between the foreman and his
workers. "The latter will not confide in him or have much to do with
him outside of work. On the contrary, they will withhold information, restrict their work, and use the union to make his life

[21]Joan Woodward, *Industrial Organization: Theory and Practice* (London: Oxford University Press, 1965), pp. 55–56.
[22]*The Foreman on the Assembly Line* (Cambridge, Mass.: Harvard University Press, 1956), p. 3.
[23]"Principles of Organization," p. 247.
[24]Miller and Form, *Industrial Sociology*, pp. 215–16.
[25]This tendency will be discussed in more detail below. For a general
discussion of this trend, see Whyte, *Men at Work*, pp. 382–89.

uncomfortable."[26] Such relatively dire consequences undoubtedly occur, but if the pattern of "imported" foremen continues, it would seem that such management orientation would come to be expected. The social distance need not necessarily lead to organizationally dysfunctional behavior. Miller and Form's point about social distance is relevant, however, to the extent that such distance affects the relationship between worker and foreman. In some cases, however, greater social distance could be organizationally useful and personally satisfying to both parties.

A second form of identification for the foreman is with the workers. This is particularly likely when the foreman has risen from the ranks and is viewed as still "one of the boys." This identification tends to lead a foreman to "cover up for his men, resist changes imposed from above, understand the union's demands, and modify his orders to fit the local situation."[27] He is also likely to have friendly relations with the workers on and off the job. As the upwardly oriented foreman suffers in his relationship with his men, this type suffers in his relationship to superiors. Rather obviously, this type of orientation, like that of the upwardly oriented, can have functional or dysfunctional consequences for both workers and the organization. The employee-oriented foreman can maintain a system wherein the workers have few grievances and maintain production schedules. At the same time, such an orientation can obstruct the organization in times of innovation or of crisis. For the worker such a situation could lead to lessened earnings, if the basis for solidarity is restriction of output. This could be individually dysfunctional over a period of time if other bases for cohesion are not developed.

The other two forms of identification are less common. The foreman can try to straddle the barrier between management and labor and maintain a dual loyalty. Miller and Form suggest that this is reasonably likely to occur among those who have recently been appointed foreman from the ranks. Sympathy for, and allegiance to, the workers' points of view are retained. At the same time the fact of promotion leads to the orientation toward management. Foremen can retain this dual orientation until a crisis occurs, at which time a position must be taken. Miller and Form believe that the choice will be with management. Once this move is made, the identification is likely to be maintained. The fourth form of identification is with other foremen through foremen's unions or associations. This is a result of realization by the foreman of his marginal status and an

---

[26] Miller and Form, *Industrial Sociology*, p. 215.
[27] Miller and Form, *Industrial Sociology*, p. 216.

attempt to strengthen his position through common actions. While unions lead to solidarity, the chances for development of real power are minimal.[28]

The marginal position of the foreman leads to the alternative identification system. Since he is at the bottom of the management hierarchy, he must accomplish the difficult job of supervision by translating organizational policies and purposes into coordinated action by his workers. At the same time, his direct contact with the workers, regardless of his orientation, make him susceptible to their reactions to the work and his supervision. Since he is responsible for work output, he is dependent upon the workers. Too great a dependence, however, diminishes the little power he has. He is caught between two systems that contain contrasting and occasionally conflicting orientations toward work.

The position of the foreman contains an additional element that leads to further power reduction. Many functions, once performed by the foreman or at least part of his responsibility, have been taken over by other personnel within the organization. In theory, at least, the foreman should know

> . . . not only (1) the company's policies, rules, and regulations and (2) the company's cost system, payment system, manufacturing methods, and inspection regulations, in particular, but also frequently (3) control, and time and motion study in general. He also has to know (4) the labor laws of the United States, (5) the labor laws of the state in which the company operates, and (6) the specific labor contract which exists between his company and the local union. He has to know (7) how to induct, instruct, and train new workers; (8) how to handle, and where possible, prevent grievances; (9) how to improve conditions of safety; (10) how to correct workers and maintain discipline; (11) how never to lose his temper and always be "fair"; (12) how to get and obtain cooperation from the wide assortment of people with the shop steward. And in some companies he is supposed to know (13) how to do the jobs he supervises better than the employees themselves. Indeed, as some foreman training programs seem to conceive the foreman's job, he has to be a manager, a cost accountant, an engineer, a lawyer, a teacher, a leader, an inspector, a disciplinarian, a counselor, a friend, and above all, an example.[29]

[28]Miller and Form, *Industrial Sociology*, pp. 218–19.

[29]Fritz J. Roethlisberger, "The Foreman: Master and Victim of Double Talk," *Harvard Business Review*, XXIII, 3 (Spring, 1945), 283.

A person possessing all of these skills and the related knowledge would be a rare individual indeed. Rather obviously, many of these functions are the responsibility of staff departments within the organization. The foreman's position is further weakened if the staff is more expert than he in these areas. The staff departments responsible for these areas transmit their ideas of appropriate actions, and the foreman must carry them out, even if he disagrees with the plans. He is lower in the organizational hierarchy than the staff officials and may lack the specialized knowledge necessary for instituting his own ideas. He is surrounded by experts with power who make decisions regarding the work which he supervises. He is put in the position of carrying out policies and procedures he has had no role in forming. Fig. 7.1 indicates the nature of the erosion of the foreman's position.

This analysis suggests that the principal role of the foreman is supervision. In some ways the removal of other responsibilities and the concentration on direct supervision would seem to make the position less difficult. The foreman, however, is in the position of attempting to supervise with few resources in terms of ideas or power. The supervisory function itself contains a strong potential

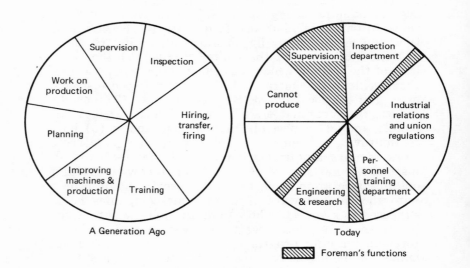

A Generation Ago   Today

▨▨▨ Foreman's functions

Fig. 7.1. The Foreman's Functions: A Generation Ago and Today.

SOURCE: Delbert C. Miller and William H. Form, *Industrial Sociology* (New York: Harper and Row, Publishers, 1964), p. 211.

for ambiguity, as Etzioni's analysis suggests. Following the work of Talcott Parsons, Robert F. Bales, and others, Etzioni notes that supervision contains two elements.[30] The *instrumental* aspect is the "need to acquire resources, or means, and to allocate them among the various role clusters in the system," while the *expressive* function involves the "need to maintain the integration of various parts of the system with each other as well as with its normative system."[31] The instrumental leader is task oriented, while the expressive leader is concerned with the social and emotional stability of the group.

Research evidence consistently indicates that the two functions are separated in practice. Where they are combined, as in the case of a few great men, the problems to be discussed are minimized. Etzioni suggests a division of workers into those who are alienated and those who are committed to their work and to the employing organization. The alienative response is more likely among blue-collar workers. For this type of worker, the foreman is able to play only an instrumental role and this to a limited degree. He can enforce compliance only to the limits of the contractual relationship. The work groups develop their own expressive leadership. Even in the instrumental area, some of the foreman's prerogatives are removed by control of production rates and allocation of work within the work groups. In this kind of situation, the foreman has minimal controls in either area. The worker-oriented foreman may hold a slightly stronger position than the management-oriented person, but according to this analysis, is still effectively barred from the exercise of too much power.[32] The earlier analyses of alienation suggest that this phenomenon is most likely to occur in the more routinized production systems.

An exception to this would perhaps be in work on assembly lines. In this case the highly routinized work requires very little instrumental control. This gives the foreman the opportunity to engage in expressive activities. If another informal leader is present in the work group, however, the foreman is likely to lose in the competition. In such a situation the foreman's over-all power is quite low.

Workers who are more committed to their work and organization, such as skilled or white-collar workers, relate to their foreman

[30]*A Comparative Analysis of Complex Organizations*, pp. 113–25.
[31]These definitions appear in a later work by Etzioni, "Dual Leadership in Complex Organizations," *American Sociological Review*, XXX, 5 (October, 1965), 689.
[32]Etzioni, *A Comparative Analysis of Complex Organizations*, pp. 113–15.

in a slightly different fashion. Even in these cases, however, the foreman can seldom play more than an instrumental role, according to Etzioni's analysis. For the committed workers, however, a useful distinction is introduced. Some foremen, principally in low-productivity units, rely upon the *official* power of their position. Those in high-productivity units have some degree of personal influence over the workers in instrumental matters. Etzioni calls the former "foreman-officials" and the latter "foreman-leaders."[33] The point here is basically that the foreman-official relies solely upon his position in the organization, while the foreman-leader utilizes personal relations with the workers in realizing the instrumental goals. In a sense, therefore, the foreman-leader does utilize an aspect of the expressive relationship. This is only the case in instrumental activities. He can appeal to the workers through personal ties in the area of work itself. The foreman-official does not have this resource.

This distinction makes a difference in the foreman's actual operations on the job. The foreman-official spends less time in actual supervision than the foreman-leader. Etzioni suggests that the foreman-official is likely to attempt to increase productivity by engaging in production himself. The foreman-official also tends to supervise closely, when he engages in supervision, while the foreman-leader utilizes a more general supervisory style. The foreman-leader also engages in more teaching activities than the foreman-official. The foreman-leader is more likely to be found among the more committed workers.

While stressing the point that the foreman-leader utilizes personal influence in his supervision, Etzioni also suggests that this type cannot become an expressive leader for his work group. This leads to the conclusion that programs designed to develop the foreman's expressive leadership abilities (human relations training) may be doomed to failure. "Psychological and social tensions in the work situation will increase rather than diminish [as a result of this kind of training] because the average foreman is encouraged to attempt what is for him the impossible: to wear two hats at the same time.[34] In order to gain in terms of his expressive position, the foreman often must resort to activities that weaken his position as an instrumental leader, such as overlooking tardiness or ignoring deviations from official norms in terms of quantity or quality of the work. The suggestion here is that the two forms of activity are incompatible. Etzioni states:

[33]*A Comparative Analysis of Complex Organizations*, p. 116.
[34]Etzioni, *A Comparative Analysis of Complex Organizations*, p. 119.

The foreman, expected to please two masters, or rather his masters and his "servants," is caught in the conflicting role-prescriptions. He cannot perform either of the two effectively. His level of dissatisfaction and personal strain increases, as does that of most persons who are in role-conflict. His relationship with the workers becomes strained because he cannot be consistently expressive and because he tends to threaten the informal leader of the group (to the degree that one exists) by his endeavors to build up his own expressive leadership. Relations with higher levels of management become strained as the foreman becomes less effective instrumentally. In short, we suggest that it is quite likely that this form of leadership training leads to results opposite to those expected by its advocates.[35]

The fact that most foremen are relatively dissatisfied with their position and undergo a considerable amount of psychological and social strain is taken as evidence for the validity of this position. Etzioni concludes that foremen who have had human relations training are more likely to suffer these negative consequences. If this is the case, then the orientation of the foreman to management or to the workers, as discussed previously, will be differentially affected by such training. The worker oriented foreman, who already may have some expressive relationships with his workers, will be drawn further away from management, inducing more strain in that direction. The management oriented foreman, on the other hand, will probably find that his efforts in an expressive direction are rebuffed, again leading to stress and strain.

The analysis thus far has suggested that the foreman's role is demanding and inherently conflict laden. The actual job requirements and the alternative orientations available present the foreman with conflicts not easily resolved. These difficulties are evident to the analyst as well as to the potential foremen in the ranks of workers. Chinoy's findings in his study of automobile workers illustrate this point. Less than 10 per cent of the workers interviewed expressed a desire to become foremen. Half of the men had not given any thought to the possibility of moving up to the foreman's position, one-sixth had given up hopes of becoming foremen, and almost a quarter of the men interviewed claimed that they *would not want to take such a position.*[36] These findings are particularly striking in light of Chinoy's conclusion that such a move is probably the "only

[35]*A Comparative Analysis of Complex Organizations*, p. 120.
[36]Chinoy, *Automobile Workers and The American Dream*, p. 49.

way up for factory workers."[37] Movement into skilled or white-collar work or into a position out of the factory is very unlikely, thus foremanship is the most reasonable means of upward mobility.

The workers' own definition of the situation was that a foreman's position was unlikely and undesirable, in many ways an objectively correct view of the situation. There were relatively few openings for foremen. Those who held these positions were likely to keep them for some time. Opportunities were greater for skilled workers, since the work groups tended to be smaller, which lead to a higher ratio of foremen to workers. Another factor affecting outlooks of these workers was that the means of achieving foremanship was unclearly defined. Management, in this case, claimed that performance and ability were the major criteria for the positions but at the same time utilized education and training as the chief factor in promotions. This led to a preference for younger men who possessed a high-school diploma and additional training. Older men who did not have these prerequisites thus felt that the situation was hopeless.

Many of the workers in this study believed that the promotion process was filled with uncertainty and favoritism. Merit and ability were not seen as the real paths to advancement. This outlook was compounded by the difficulties in demonstrating the kinds of merit and ability needed for the foreman's position. There was little opportunity to demonstrate "initiative, leadership, resourcefulness, and cooperativeness."[38] The workers also believed that pull and connections were major factors in the promotion process and that the person who did move up was someone who had gained the personal interest and support of his foreman. Membership in the right religious and fraternal organizations was also felt to contribute to advancement. These social ties, if they were important in the promotions process, were themselves viewed negatively by most of the workers. Those who actively sought such ties were given clearly negative appellations, such as brownnose or bootlicker. Chinoy notes that this form of reaction may be only rationalizations of failure to gain advancement or expressions of lack of interest in the position. At the same time they also serve as mechanisms which "inhibit interest and stifle hope."[39]

The objective lack of opportunity and the subjective reactions to the situation serve as impediments to advancement into foremanship. At the same time the rewards of the position were sufficient to

[37]*Automobile Workers and The American Dream*, p. 46.
[38]Chinoy, *Automobile Workers and The American Dream*, p. 54.
[39]Chinoy, *Automobile Workers and The American Dream*, p. 57.

make it a desirable one for the workers. Greater pay and freedom were available to the foremen. This kind of attractiveness was counterbalanced by the negative components of the position, which have been discussed. The workers viewed the position as one filled with grief. They recognized the pressures coming down from management and staff experts. The uncertainty and difficulty of the position made it one that was not attractive to many of the men. At the same time, the responsibility of the position was viewed by many as undesirable or beyond their competence. Chinoy notes that the modern mass-production factory gives little opportunity to learn how to handle responsibility, making positions which demand it threatening to the workers.[40]

A contrasting view of the possibilities of becoming a foreman and the reactions of foremen to their position is offered by Walker, Guest and Turner.[41] These studies, also carried out in an automobile factory, suggest that a greater proportion of the workers desire to become foremen and see the advantages in the position. The majority of the foremen studied liked their jobs and viewed the rewards they received and the challenges on the job as positive reinforcements. The stresses and strains discussed above were present but were outweighed by the advantages. The differences between these findings and those of Chinoy are largely attributable to differences in the organizations studied. The Walker, Guest, and Turner studies were carried out in a new plant and opportunities for advancement were much greater than in the older, more stabilized plant Chinoy studied. The former plant also attempted to upgrade workers whenever possible, so that the workers learned new skills and the orientation toward advancement on the job. There was also an attempt to give the foreman as much authority as possible in personal relationships. He had a voice in personnel, in training, and in disciplinary matters.

It would be useful to know the extent to which the foreman's position in other kinds of organizations approximates that in the two auto plants studied. Both analyses suggest, however, that the position is ambiguous and difficult. The position is difficult to fill. From the standpoint of the organization, its crucial nature demands that it be occupied by the most qualified persons. From the standpoint of the workers, it may represent an undesirable move, since a man can lose the security of seniority and gain the headaches

[40]*Automobile Workers and The American Dream*, p. 59.
[41]See Walker, Guest and Turner, *The Foreman on the Assembly Line* and Walker and Guest, *The Man on the Assembly Line* (Cambridge, Mass.: Harvard University Press, 1952).

described, even in organizations such as that described by Walker, Guest, and Turner.

The problems and the changes confronting the foremen have contributed to a growing tendency toward redefinition of the place of the foreman in the organization. The foreman has traditionally been viewed as being on the bottom of the management hierarchy and at the top of the worker level. The position has been traditionally filled by people moving up from the ranks of workers. The emerging view of the foreman, however, appears to be one which emphasizes the management aspect. The trend is to bring college graduates in from the outside to be foremen. These foremen are at the start of their careers in the organization rather than at the end, as is the case with foremen who have been promoted from the ranks. The foreman's position is part of the on-the-job training.

George Strauss has suggested that the growing interdependence of work processes and more complicated technologies are specific contributors to this trend.[42] Comprehension of the total situation is thought to require more education than that possessed by the old-style foreman. Walter S. Wikstrom found essentially the same factors operative in his analysis of the foremanship patterns in four organizations. Organizations that produced special-order single-unit items and small organizations tended to utilize the older pattern. Organizations based on mass production and continuous flow technology were found to have the newer, managerially oriented foremen.[43] Melville Dalton found foremen possessing engineering degrees in a study of an electronics firm.[44] Here the production process itself required highly trained supervision.

Analyses of the change in the foreman's position have been limited to production organizations. The same conclusions are probably applicable in service organizations and in the administration of all organizations as technological sophistication becomes more widespread. Evidence is unfortunately not available in regard to the extent of this transition. The impact of the change will probably be that the foreman will play an even more instrumental role, if Etzioni's analysis is correct. Foremen who come from outside the ranks of workers will further minimize opportunities to utilize

---

[42]"The Changing Role of the Working Supervisor," *The Journal of Business*, XXX, 3 (July, 1957), 204.

[43]Wikstrom, *Managing at The Foreman's Level*, p. 205 (New York: National Industrial Conference Board, 1967).

[44]"Changing Staff-Line Relationships," *Personnel Administration*, XXIX, 2 (March–April, 1966), 3–5.

expressive relationships in the position. It is conceivable that the expressive or informal leader will play a more important role as an officially or unofficially defined "straw boss" in these cases. The rather vast amount of data regarding supervisory practices does suggest that the supervisor, in this case the foreman in the position of a potential higher level manager, should utilize expressive leadership in his attempts to achieve the organization's goals. Since he has not been and cannot be one of the workers, this role cannot be played by the foreman. At the same time the structure that develops in work situations cannot be ignored and requires that the foreman utilize the resources available to him. Strauss concludes that the supervisory powers of the straw boss (working supervisor in Strauss' terms) have diminished with the advent of the new style foreman.[45] It is likely, however, that his informal position has not been affected, which presents the foreman with an existing social structure he must take into account.

summary and conclusions

Foremen and craftsmen comprise the elite of manual workers. Their status derives from their hierarchical position and use of mental and interpersonal skills in the case of foremen and the possession of highly developed and scarce skills in the case of craftsmen. Both groups continue to be affected by technological changes, and the effects appear to be adverse for the traditional foreman and some of the traditional crafts. New crafts have emerged in response to technological and social changes, which accounts for the relative stability of this group within the labor force.

Both foremen and craftsmen are strongly affected by the social environment. Foremen must utilize the existing social structure of those they supervise in their work. Craftsmen gain entrance to their trades and specific jobs through the structure surrounding their craft. The craftsman is generally supported by his peers, while the foreman may be threatened by his former peers. Recruitment into both groups is similarly affected by these kinds of social considerations. The craftsman traditionally had to be a member of the correct racial or ethnic group. Potential foremen may decline the opportunity for advancement because of the definition of the posi-

[45]"The Changing Role of the Working Supervisor," p. 206.

tion by their work group. At the same time, the presence of the work group, whatever its degree of cohesiveness, has an impact on the foreman's work.

Despite changes in the nature of the work and altered relationships surrounding these occupations, they will probably remain in their position among blue-collar workers. The need for scarce skills and the fact that first-line supervision must be performed should guarantee the continued viability of these occupations.

chapter 8

semiskilled and
unskilled workers

This is the final chapter based on types of occupations, and its position suggests an important characteristic of the occupations involved. They are at the bottom of the occupational hierarchy, and of course, the semiskilled are ranked higher than the unskilled. While these are the last occupations to be formally discussed in this section, they are not unfamiliar in the light of previous discussions. Chapter 3, on work and the individual, largely focused on the reactions of the semiskilled worker to his job in terms of his level of alienation or job satisfaction.

A difficulty in dealing with these occupational types is that much of the literature about them has been rather ideologically based and has attempted to demonstrate either the plight or the progress of the worker, which leads to something less than analytical accuracy. At the same time, a large amount of other research and writing about this segment of the labor force has focused on the participation of these workers in work groups. Here also a polarization of outlooks can be seen. These work groups are viewed as a means by which workers goldbrick on the job, as a potential

231

management resource if utilized by trained supervisors, or as the basis of fulfillment for the individual worker, the only source of meaningfulness for him on the job. The approach taken in these cases seems to have a strong impact on the findings. While neutrality in research is not always a virtue, it is unfortunate that this category of the labor force has been studied as it has, since it is often difficult to distinguish perspective from persuasive findings.

These complications illustrate an important characteristic of the occupations being discussed; they are not a homogeneous lot. The groupings of the semiskilled and unskilled into a single chapter is primarily in the interest of space and simplicity, since there are some important differences between the two occupational types. Within either group significant (not necessarily statistical) differences also exist. The purpose of the present chapter is to describe the occupations involved and analyze their relationships with the wider social structure. The material covered in earlier chapters will not be reviewed here.

Table 8.1.   Semiskilled and Unskilled Workers in Labor Force, by Decade (As Per Cent of All Employed Males)

	1960	1950	1940
Semiskilled Workers			
Operatives (durable and nondurable goods manufacturing and nonmanufacturing industries)	14.7	15.4	13.5
Service workers, except private household	6.0	5.8	5.8
Drivers and deliverymen	5.2	4.7	4.4
Subtotal	25.9	25.9	23.7
Unskilled Workers			
Private household workers	0.1	0.2	0.3
Farm laborers and farm foremen	2.8	4.9	8.3
Laborers, except farm and mine	6.9	8.1	9.0
Subtotal	9.8	13.2	17.6
Total	35.7	39.1	41.3

DERIVED FROM: U.S. Department of Commerce, *General Social and Economic Characteristics: Final Report PC (1) — IC* (Washington, D.C.: U.S. Government Printing Office, 1960), p. 1-219, Table 89.

Table 8.2.   Semiskilled and Unskilled Workers in Labor Force, by Decade (As Per Cent of All Employed Females)

	1960	1950	1940
Semiskilled Workers			
Operatives (durable and nondurable goods manufacturing and nonmanufacturing industries)	15.4	19.2	18.1
Service workers, except private household	13.4	12.2	11.0
Subtotal	28.8	31.4	29.1
Unskilled			
Private household	7.9	8.5	17.7
Farm laborers and farm foremen	1.1	2.9	2.9
Laborers, except farm and mine	0.5	0.7	1.0
Subtotal	9.5	12.1	21.6
Total	38.3	43.5	50.7

DERIVED FROM: U.S. Department of Commerce, *General Social and Economic Characteristics: Final Report PC (I) — IC* (Washington, D.C.: U.S. Government Printing Office, 1960), p. 1-219, Table 89.

One important aspect of the relationship with the social structure is illustrated by the employment patterns within these groups. Tables 8.1 and 8.2 indicate the changing distribution of personnel within these categories for both men and women. The most obvious change is the growth of service work and the decline of direct production among these workers. This reflects the impact of automation *and* the growth of demand for services. The table also suggests that the unskilled group is declining rather rapidly as a proportion of the labor force in both rural and urban occupations.

the semiskilled

The term "semiskilled" implies one of the important characteristics of this segment of the labor force. These workers do not possess the skills of the craftsman. Their skills are more easily learned in shorter periods of time. Caplow states that for semiskilled workers

Their common characteristic is that no lengthy experience is required to perform the work, and that movement from one occupation to another is easy and frequent. Indeed, the mark of a semiskilled occupation is its vagueness . . . Lifetime involvement in a job is rare. Men and women perform comparable work under comparable conditions. Job titles do not correspond to organized social groupings; and each occupation merges into many others.[1]

This vagueness implies an important component of semiskilled work; the worker performs a job defined for him by the employing organization. His title often reflects the particular machine with which he is working or the part of the production process in which he participates. Job titles thus vary from industry to industry. He may be working with no one with the same specific title, but all will be semiskilled workers. The titles themselves do not carry the symbolic meanings attached to many other occupations.

While there is vagueness, there is also variety. Blauner's discussion is indicative of this variety. He states:

Even within the manufacturing sector (a declining component of the total economy in contrast to the growing and highly differentiated service industries) modern factories vary considerably in technology, in division of labor, in economic structure, and in organizational character. These differences produce sociotechnical systems in which the objective conditions and the inner life of the employees are strikingly variant. In some industrial environments the alienating tendencies that Marx emphasized are present to a high degree. In others they are relatively undeveloped and have been countered by new technical, economic, and social forces.[2]

A series of studies that have dealt with the semiskilled worker illustrate the variety of work performed within the semiskilled category. Many of the studies to be discussed were designed to demonstrate the importance of work groups, the presence of nonofficial patterns of performance, or the potential for alienative responses to the work situation. For the moment, they will be used simply as descriptions.

The automobile worker has been studied more intensively than

[1] *The Sociology of Work*, pp. 84–85.
[2] *Alienation and Freedom*, p. 5.

other semiskilled workers, despite the fact that the nature of his work is not typical of semiskilled work. Nevertheless, he does exemplify work on an assembly line. On the automobile assembly line, the

> major operations are performed by the workers them-selves rather than by machinery. Though the work is carried out by hand with the aid of small power tools, such as electric drills and ratchet screwdrivers, it is not craft work, since the highly rationalized organization of work assignments and work flow standardizes the basic manual operations.[3]

Technology divides the production process into small units. Each worker performs one or only a few of the basic tasks. The average task requires one minute for completion. The worker performs his task on parts of a car moving down the line. When he is finished he moves back to the next car and performs the same task. The process is continued throughout the work shift.

Within the automobile factory a great variety of specific tasks are performed. In the factory studied by Chinoy, about 25 per cent of the workers were directly on the assembly line. Here a variety of functions was performed, corresponding to the components of the automobile itself.

> Most line workers were engaged in the assembly of a major component, such as the motor or axle, of the fin-ished product on the final assembly line, although other operations such as painting and finishing fenders and hoods were also performed by men who remained sta-tioned in one place, doing their repetitive tasks while the materials moved past on an endless conveyor belt.[4]

Another 30 per cent of the workers operated automatic or semiauto-matic machines, such as grinders, drill presses, or boring machines. These are essentially repetitive tasks, in that the worker simply inserted the pieces on which the operation was to be performed, started the machine, and removed the parts when the operation was completed. Another 15 per cent of the workers were engaged in production jobs, such as welding, riveting, or repair work. These last two jobs did not require traditional skills and could be learned in a short period of time. Twenty-five per cent of the workers were in

---

[3]Blauner, *Alienation and Freedom*, p. 95.
[4]Chinoy, *The Automobile Worker and The American Dream*, p. 35.

"off-production jobs." Some of this off-production work involved inspection, which according to Chinoy, was also semiskilled. Inspection in this case involved the use of automatic or semiautomatic machines or visual or tactile examination. Others in off-production work had a variety of functions, such as stock pickers, stock loaders, trim shop attendants, conveyor attendants, power truck operators, stock chasers, and hand truckers. The off-production jobs were generally more highly regarded by the workers and had higher pay scales. The work was less repetitive and paced. The remaining 5 per cent of the workers were craftsmen in skilled maintenance or in areas such as tool makers or jig builders.[5]

Even though 95 per cent of the work in this factory can be labelled semiskilled, the wide variety of specific tasks performed exemplifies the difficulties in identifying a characteristic component of semiskilled work. Even on the assembly line itself, the complexity of the modern automobile requires great variation among the specific tasks performed. The variety of work is due to the extreme rationalization of the work process itself. The planning of each small contribution to the whole allows the intense division of labor. A specific individual is thus not central to the total process. He is rather easily replaced, since the jobs do not require a long learning process, and his contribution to the whole, while vital, is minimal in terms of the importance of the single individual. This, of course, contributes to the alienation felt by the automobile worker.

A quite different form of assembly line work is described by Whyte. In this case the product was steel barrels.

> This line began where men known as rollers took sheets of steel and put them on a machine that shaped them in a circular form. The shells then rolled to the welders who welded the two sides together. Then the testers checked the welds for leaks. Next came the beader men, who put the shells on a machine that put the beads (protruding ribs) into them. The shells then rolled into a spray booth, where their insides were sprayed with paint or lacquer. The double seamer operators attached both ends of the barrel. The barrel might then go on to another spray booth where an outside coat of paint or lacquer would be applied. Some orders called for a baked enamel finish, and the barrels were carried through bake ovens on conveyors for that purpose.[6]

The significant difference between the barrel assemblers and the auto workers is that the former can control the speed of

[5]Chinoy, *The Automobile Worker and The American Dream*, p. 36.
[6]Whyte, *Men at Work*, p. 137.

production. The workers worked in pairs on either side of the line and could pace their own work. Whether or not this necessarily led to any less alienation or greater satisfaction is impossible to determine. The work itself apparently required little difference in skill from that required of the auto worker.

A still different kind of semiskilled work is that of the worker in continuous flow production. Blauner's description of the work of men in a chemical refinery exemplifies this. In this case,

> Practically all physical production and materials-handling is done by automatic processes, regulated by automatic controls. The work of the chemical operator is to monitor these automatic processes: his tasks include observing dials and gauges; taking readings of temperatures, pressures, and rates of flow; and writing down these readings in log data sheets. Such work is clearly of a nonmanual nature.[7]

In addition to the different activities performed, a greater potential for self-pacing and widened scope of the work also exists for the chemical worker. The process operators' work cycle extends over a 2 hour period, rather than the 1 minute for the auto worker. In taking his readings, the operator may check on fifty different instruments located throughout his area of jurisdiction. For workers not involved in actual production, a similar variety and diversity exists. Maintenance workers, for example, who comprise 40 per cent of the work force, react to emergent situations. There is no prescheduled program for maintenance needs. There is even variety for workers who load and unload trucks or railroad cars or work in pumping operations. As in the previous examples, the nature of the work is clearly affected by the technology involved.

Another case studied by Blauner is the textile worker. Here again the emphasis is on the impact of the technological component of the work situation.

> The job of the typical worker is to mind or tend a large number of spinning frames, looms, or similar machines. He may feed yarn to, and remove yarn from, the machines when necessary and watch out for and repair breaks in the yarn when they occur. He does not operate an individual machine, as is characteristic in the garment and shoe industries. Instead he minds or tends dozens of identical machines lined up in rows in the carding, spinning, weaving, and other rooms of the textile mill.[8]

[7]*Alienation and Freedom*, 132–33.
[8]Blauner, *Alienation and Freedom*, p. 59.

This work requires little training and a minimal amount of physical exertion. The jobs in a textile mill, other than skilled maintenance work, require little more than alertness and some dexterity and can be learned in a relatively short period of time. Here again the emphasis is on the impact of technology on the work process and the workers.

The variations in the semiskilled worker have thus far been viewed as a consequence of variations in the technological demands of the job. While technology plays an unquestionably important role, the employing organization also plays a vital role in the way it arranges the work to be performed. Friedmann describes the changes which affected semiskilled workers in an office equipment manufacturing firm. This organization decided to embark on a program of job enlargement. The product itself did not change, but the work process did. Before job enlargement,

> A part was lifted by the worker and placed in the machine. The machine was started; a cutting tool or drill did the job on the part. The machinery was stopped by the operator and the part removed. All preparatory work, including the setting up of the machine, had previously been done by the specialists.

The process of job enlargement included

> tool sharpening, the setting up of the machine for each new series of blueprints, a knowledge of calibration, of how deviations from tolerances will affect the part subsequently, and, what was no doubt the most important addition of all, the complete checking of the finished part, which meant using testplate, height gauge, and comparator.[9]

Friedmann concludes that this program had benefits for both the organization and the workers. For the organization production costs were lowered slightly and production quality was raised. The workers were more satisfied, which also benefited the organization. The workers themselves earned more pay and gained in personal job satisfaction.[10] For our purposes the important thing is that the work was altered within the context of a constant technological system. The employing organization can thus vary the work environment and affect the nature of semiskilled work. Whether or not this is possible in all semiskilled work is, of course, questionable, as is whether or not such a program will continue to yield such benefits

[9]Friedmann, *The Anatomy of Work*, pp. 45–46.
[10]Friedmann, *The Anatomy of Work*, p. 47.

over a period of time. Nevertheless, the organizational structure itself can be taken as an important determinant of the work environment for the individual.

A final example of semiskilled work is that of the cabdriver. This is a service occupation, which involves direct interaction with the public. It is also an occupation that is much less structured in terms of work patterns and social relationships. The cabdriver is dependent upon finding fares. Although there are some locations where fares are more likely to be found, such as at airports, hotels, railroad stations, near downtown shopping areas and entertainment and so on, there is little predictability where the fares wish to be taken or if new fares will be found in the area. The nature of the work is such that there are almost no steady customers with whom established relationships allow some certainty of either income or social relationships. The cabdriver also suffers from the fact that his skills are rather difficult to distinguish from those of his customers. Most people can drive cars and many know exactly how to get to their destination. The cabdriver thus is a convenience but usually not a necessity.[11]

Another interesting component of the cabdriver's job is the manner in which he relates to his fares. Davis mentions

the man and wife who, managing to suppress their anger while on the street, launch into a bitter quarrel the moment they are inside the cab; or the well-groomed young couple who after a few minutes roll over on the back seat to begin petting; or the businessman who loudly discusses details of a questionable business deal. Here the driver is expected to, and usually does, act as if he were merely an extension of the automobile he operates. In actuality, of course, he is acutely aware of what goes on in his cab, and although his being treated as a nonperson implies a degraded status, it also affords him a splendid vantage point from which to witness a rich variety of human schemes and entanglements.[12]

At the same time, other fares will pour out their problems and life histories to the driver, placing him in a position similar to some bartenders. Bartending, of course, is another semiskilled service occupation.

Another interesting facet of this type of work is the depend-

[11]This discussion is based on Fred Davis, "The Cabdriver and his Fare: Facets of a Fleeting Relationship," *American Journal of Sociology*, LXV, 2 (September, 1959), 158–65.

[12]"The Cabdriver and his Fare: Facets of a Fleeting Relationship," p. 160.

ence upon tips as a major part of the income. Davis found that cabdrivers had a well developed vocabulary which described the various types of tippers. The typology of fares, which develops, allows the driver to order his universe to some degree. The driver also can attempt to manipulate the situation by using techniques he has found effective in improving the amount of tips he receives. The power of such manipulation is generally slight, however.

While the majority of the cabdriver's social relationships are with his fares, the relationships themselves are not the most rewarding to the driver. At the same time, he is not in a position to establish other relationships while he is working. When idle, he can talk with other drivers, but he is not earning money while doing so. His work thus is largely solitary and does not contain the potential for supportive relationships on the job. The possibility of developing meaningful relationships with fares is constrained by the nature of the relationship. Here the nature of the work itself is the important determinant of the occupational subculture.

The discussion and examples thus far suggest the great diversity of occupations included in the semiskilled category. The exact number of specific occupations that could be included in this category is probably limited only by the number of job titles used by the employing organizations. A more important conclusion to be drawn is that the *semiskilled worker has his work defined for him.* The structure of the labor market is such that the potential worker presents himself to the employer for a position but not for a specific job. Since semiskilled work assumes that the skills can be learned in a relatively short period of time, the potential employee essentially sells his ability to learn the techniques needed for the particular job in the particular organization. If he changes organizations, he generally learns new skills for a new job. This is not to say that he may not become highly skilled in and attached to his work. It does imply, however, that semiskilled work is highly structured and that the structuring is largely out of the hands of the worker himself.

Three factors have been presented as contributors to this structuring. First was the nature of the technology utilized in the industry as in the case of Blauner's discussion of the chemical, textile, and auto workers. Here the work process itself provides limits on what the semiskilled person does. A second factor is the employing organization. As was illustrated by the office equipment manufacturing firm, the technological level can remain constant, but the work itself can change drastically. This is not meant to imply that the organization can overcome the limitations set by the technological system in all cases. While an automobile firm could obviously engage in some job enlargement, limits seem to be built in in terms of the complexity of the automobile itself and the economics of the production process. Automation in the auto industry does increase the scope of a particular worker's activities, but on the traditional assembly line the size of the product together with its complexity preclude extensive enlargement. The third factor which structures the semiskilled workers' occupation is the nature of the work itself. Service occupations differ from production work. Social relationships as well as the specific functions performed are affected in this way. For all three reasons the semiskilled worker's occupation is predefined for him. In terms of his specific job related activities, he can exercise relatively little discretion.

The discussion thus far has been centered around the "formal" aspects of the semiskilled worker's occupation. This is obviously not the total picture. Extensive and intensive studies of the informal work group have clearly demonstrated that much more happens on the job than simply the officially prescribed activities in the officially prescribed ways. The influence of peers, as discussed in the chapter on professions, is relevant here, as it is for all of the occupations discussed. These work groups provide a source of meaning for the worker on the job and provide a major part of his definition of his work situation. They develop norms, which may deviate in a number of directions from those which are officially prescribed. They provide a context in which meaningful social interactions can take place. All of these functions have been well documented in studies by industrial sociologists and psychologists.

Before examining some of the specific contributions made by these unofficial work groups, one point should be stressed. Walker and Guest and others have pointed out that the specific membership of such groups is in a large measure determined by the organization itself.[13] The organization cannot define who will like whom and who will be included in or excluded from participation. It does define, however, where the workers are placed in the organization. Since such groups must be formed through social interaction and such interaction can only take place among workers in contact with each other, the organization thus determines who will interact with whom. The factor of spatial contiguity is also vital, since it is difficult if not impossible for such groups to form across distances. The shift a person works determines with whom he has the opportunity to interact. Other factors such as the noise level and the amount of attention demanded by the job will affect interaction

[13]Walker and Guest, *Man on the Assembly Line*, pp. 67–72.

patterns. In some jobs there simply is no opportunity for such patterns to develop, as for the cabdriver.

While these unofficial social relationships are strongly affected by official considerations, the informal work group does have an existence apart from official prescriptions. As new employees enter the situation, they are introduced to the unofficial norms, which persist over time and personnel changes. Miller and Form state:

> The new employee must learn many things about the social behavior in his work situation. He must learn *who's who* (the informal status pattern or pecking order), *what's what* (the "ropes" or how things are done), and *what's up* (the current situation in his work area). But most important of all he must learn how he fits in. He must learn to play an acceptable role and no formal organization chart or manual will help him very much. He must know how role boundaries are established by his associates.[14]

The impact of these work groups and their norms and values has been intensively examined, and the studies suggest that the behavior of work group members deviates from the officially prescribed patterns. From the organization's perspective, this deviation is generally in a negative rather than positive direction. From the point of view of the individual worker, such deviations give him some control over the work situation, allow him to protect his earnings potential, and allow him to have some control of the rate of and quality of his output.

The actual operation of these unofficial patterns is graphically illustrated in Joseph Bensman and Israel Gerver's analysis of "crime and punishment in the factory."[15] The study was carried out in an airplane factory. The specific instance examined was the use of a device called a "tap." The tap is a hard steel tool designed to redrill holes in nuts so that a bolt can be inserted and tightened.

> In wing assembly work bolts or screws must be inserted in recessed nuts which are anchored to the wing in earlier processes of assembly. The bolt or screw must pass through a wing plate before reaching the nut. In the nature of the mass production process alignments between nuts and plate openings become distorted. Original

[14]*Industrial Sociology*, p. 231.

[15]Joseph Bensman and Israel Gerver, "Crime and Punishment in the Factory: The Function of Deviancy in Maintaining the Social System," *American Sociological Review*, XXV, 4 (August, 1963), 588–98.

allowable tolerances become magnified in later stages of assembly as the number of alignments which must be coordinated with each other increase with the increasing complexity of the assemblage. When the nut is not aligned with the hole, the tap can be used to cut, at a new angle, new threads in the nut for the purpose of bringing the nut and bolt into a new but not true alignment. If the tap is not used and the bolt is forced, the wing plate itself may be bent. Such new alignments, however, deviate from the specifications of the blueprint which is based upon true alignments at every stage of the assembly process. On the basis of engineering standards true alignments are necessary at every stage in order to achieve maximum strength and a proper equilibrium of strains and stresses.[16]

Since bolts and screws on aircraft are designed to prevent their backing out of the nuts due to vibration in flight and the use of the tap removes the holding power of the nut, tap usage is defined as a criminal offense. The mere possession of a tap is grounds for dismissal. Use of the tap also covers up structural defects in the plane in the form of deviations from standards. Despite the severity of the penalties and the seriousness of the offense itself, one-half of the workers in a position to use a tap own at least one.

The worker coming into this factory is gradually introduced to the use of the tap under the supervision of an older worker. He is instructed under what circumstances its use is justified and the conditions in which it is safe to use it. The foremen in this situation recognize the necessity of the tap and use it themselves when they believe the situation so demands. Another element of this unofficial practice is that indiscriminate use of the tap is frowned upon. The expectation is that the tap is to be used with good judgment and the proper etiquette.

Etiquette is vital in the relationship between workers and inspectors. The inspectors are in many ways dependent upon the workers. Inspectors realize that they must depend upon the workers to do a good job on parts that are inaccessible so that an inordinate amount of time is not spent on simple inspections. The inspectors also fraternize with the workers when they are waiting for work. The etiquette is that the inspector turns his back or walks away when the tap is to be used. When the inspectors get pressure from the Air Force, the purchaser of the planes, the workers respond by limiting their use of the tap. This results in a slowdown of the work

[16]Bensman and Gerver, "Crime and Punishment in the Factory: The Function of Deviancy in Maintaining the Social System," p. 590.

until the pressure on the inspectors is reduced. When Air Force inspectors themselves are nearby, the word is passed down the line to cease the use of the tap. Relations with the foremen are similarly governed by such norms of appropriate behavior.

Aside from the fact that such deviations from the official norms are an important component of all work groups at every level in the occupational hierarchy, this case suggests two additional conclusions. The first point, while obvious, is often overlooked in analyses of unofficial behavior. The deviations discussed are based upon the *official* norms. These norms serve as the starting point from which deviation may or may not occur. The official structure thus sets the stage for the deviation by prescribing the amount of work to be expected, the technologies to be employed in achieving the qualitative and quantitative goals, and the sanctions for norm enforcement. If the parts of the wing to be assembled did not themselves vary from the allowable tolerances, there would be no need to use the tap. If there were not production quotas to be met, parts could be returned or scrapped if alignments were not perfect. If the sanctions for using a tap were not so stringent, there would be little need for the involved system of etiquette surrounding its use. The deviations observed thus have their origins in and are judged by the official structure.[17]

The second conclusion which can be reached on the basis of this study is that not all instances of unofficial behavior are oriented toward quota or output restriction. In this case the deviations occurred in an attempt to meet the quota set by the organization and thus to contribute to the total system. A basic motivation here undoubtedly was to maximize individual earnings, rather than a belief in the appropriateness of the quota for its own sake, but the actions taken were in the direction of higher production rather than lower. Other studies have found restrictions placed on production by such work groups.[18] Such groups can thus either impede or contribute to the amount of work turned out in a specific work situation. The factors which influence the direction of the work group's own norms in relation to the official output expectations appear to be such things as the ease with which the quota is met; the likelihood, as perceived by the workers, of having the rate of pay reduced if the quota is systematically met or exceeded; and the perception of the appropriateness of the quota. Semiskilled workers, like all other

[17]Walker and Guest in *Man on the Assembly Line*, pp. 68–69, make this same point.
[18]See Donald F. Roy, "Quota Restriction and Goldbricking in a Machine Shop," *American Journal of Sociology*, LVII, 5 (March, 1952), 427–42.

workers, develop sets of behaviors and expectations surrounding their work. The starting point for these behaviors and expectations is the work itself in interaction with the social situation of the occupation.

While our concern is not primarily with the individual, the extensive and varied literature surrounding the impact of semiskilled work on the individual should be briefly mentioned. As was demonstrated in Blauner's analysis of alienation among semiskilled workers, the reactions of the individual to his work situation are not constant. Since the work itself is very heterogeneous, so are the reactions. Even within one industry such variety exists as demonstrated by Walker and Guest's conclusion that

> There are many jobs in modern industry, including jobs on moving belts, which the worker can perform automatically or "without thinking." On such jobs he may turn inward to his own thoughts or carry on connected conversations with his fellow workers. Such jobs are less fatiguing than those which, though without special skill, require a high and continuous degree of mental attention without accompanying absorption. Our own observation is that a majority of automobile assembly jobs fall, with variations as to degree, into the latter category.[19]

The conditions of the job have an impact on the responses of the workers to their total life situation. S. M. Miller and Frank Reisman in a review of the literature on the life-style and values of the semiskilled note that a strong emphasis on stability and security is evident among this group.[20] The possibility of layoff and unemployment is operative here. In a similar vein, Paul E. Mott et al. found that shift work and work over the normal weekend period affect social participation and family life.[21] The conditions of semiskilled work, as is the case with the other types of occupations, have an impact above and beyond the work situation itself. From the middle class perspective, that of most of the analysts, the impact of semiskilled work is such that the individual is adversely affected by his occupational conditions. He is more subject to the conditions of his job than most of the occupations discussed.

An important consideration in analyzing the semiskilled worker is automation and technological change. The details of this

[19]*Man on the Assembly Line*, pp. 8–9.
[20]"The Working-Class Subculture: A New View," *Social Problems*, IX, 1 (Summer, 1961), 86–97.
[21]*Shift Work* (Ann Arbor: University of Michigan Press, 1965), pp. 288–89.

development will be covered in the chapter on technological change, since the majority of studies concerning the impact of automation on the worker have dealt with the semiskilled. It should be noted here that the fact that the semiskilled have been the major subjects of study in this area indicates their relative powerlessness in determining the conditions of their occupational life. They generally are subject to, rather than participants in, this change process. In this regard they are similar to the lower level white-collar workers, although the change itself seems to be in the opposite direction in that the semiskilled occupations so affected are becoming more like traditional white-collar positions.

the unskilled

This final occupational type is at the bottom of the occupational hierarchy. Like the semiskilled, the unskilled are being affected by technological change but in a very different way. The nature of the work of the unskilled has not changed very much but the number of jobs available to this category has been drastically affected. Table 8.1 indicates the sharp drop in this form of employment for both men and women, a trend which will apparently continue. A related change is that in the educational composition of the population as a whole and the educational requirements for positions in the occupational structure. As the general level of education has increased, so have the educational requirements for entry into the system. Those persons with minimal educational backgrounds are at an obvious disadvantage in the labor market. At the same time, there are fewer persons with such a minimal background. The unskilled worker category has thus decreased as persons with sufficient education move into more highly ranked occupations and, concomitantly, the number of jobs available at this occupational level decrease.

It is rather difficult to pinpoint exactly who the unskilled are. The most obvious characteristic is that the unskilled worker sells his personal labor to his employer and utilizes little in the way of technology or machinery in his work. Caplow notes:

> Although most occupational categories include a category of the unskilled, it is difficult to attach any precise meaning to the term. It is only careless usage which regards freight-handlers and farmhands in regular employment as less qualified than punch-press operators, and it is sheer snobbery that leads certain of the occupational classifiers to group all household servants as unskilled.[22]

[22]Caplow, *The Sociology of Work*, p. 172.

Caplow suggests that a more accurate criterion for determining the unskilled is to use the regularity of employment. Those who are regularly employed in the same job would be classified as semiskilled according to this criterion.

Despite Caplow's imputation of carelessness and even snobbery, most classifications do include the farmhand, freight-handler, and household servant in the unskilled category. A more relevant criterion than Caplow's idea of regular employment would be the amount of training required for a job. The semiskilled do learn their jobs in a short period of time. The unskilled, on the other hand, are simply told to go to work, with the assumption that the skills required are in the possession of the total population and do not necessitate any training. Caplow himself states: "Industry, retail commerce, and even the private household maintain a continuous demand for 'hands,' hired on a day-to-day basis for clean-up jobs, moving, heavy construction, snow removal, digging, carrying, hewing of wood, and drawing of water."[23] While these jobs may be irregular, they also involve sheer physical labor together with almost no on-the-job learning. A person is hired simply because he is available, with little anticipation of permanence and few assumptions about ability to learn.

Some private household and general maintenance workers are undoubtedly an exception to these conclusions, but not on the basis of lack of snobbery. Some maids or other household servants, for example, occupy positions of real permanence and perform highly skilled activities in the form of cooking and child rearing. The majority, however, probably engage in simple cleaning chores. Maintenance or janitorial work is becoming increasingly complex as the composition of floors and walls varies widely and must be cleaned with only the appropriate agent. Reading and understanding the type, amount, and frequency of use of cleaning agents requires at least skills in reading. Here again, however, the majority of such work is probably limited to such chores as sweeping, dusting, and window washing. Job titles at this level may thus be misleading. In general, the occupations included in Table 8.1 and 8.2 as unskilled appear to fit most criteria of such work.

The composition of the unskilled category is quite varied. Caplow suggests that it is composed of

the partly retired, the pensioners, and the partly unemployable, the drifters and drunks, the physically and mentally handicapped . . . those who normally belong to

[23]*The Sociology of Work*, pp. 172–73.

higher occupational categories but have been temporarily laid off or are waiting out a strike or an off-season, together with the migratory farm workers, and stranded travelers, the part-time students, the part-time criminals, and many others.[24]

This mixture of people has been approached from another perspective by S. M. Miller. Miller's concern is with poverty, but the typology he develops in dealing with the poor is useful for clarifying the composition of the unskilled. Miller utilizes two criteria in categorizing the American lower class. The economic factor is treated in terms of the amount and stability of the income, yielding categories of "high (security) and low (insecurity)."[25] The second factor is the general style of life of the groups involved. The basic component here is family stability or instability as an indicator of the manner in which the family copes with its problems. While our concern here is not with the family, it is an important indicator of the general style of life. Using the criteria of economic and family status, Miller derives the following fourfold table (Table 8.3).

Cell 1 is the *stable poor*. They are characterized by regular but low skill employment. According to Miller, they are predominantly farm, rural nonfarm, and small town persons, from white rural Southern populations. The category also includes a good number of older people and urban Negroes who have obtained steady employment. Given these conditions, either of location or minority group status, it is unlikely that these persons will move out of the unskilled category, although Miller suggests that there is a good likelihood that their offspring may.[26]

The second cell, the *strained*, is composed of low-wage unskilled workers. Their instability may result from "wildness" on the part of younger workers or alcoholism on the part of older persons. Members of this group are likely to have "skidded" into their positions as a result of the extra-occupational activities. These same activities are also likely to lead to decreased economic and job security over time.[27]

The third cell, the *copers*, "manifest economic insecurity and familial stability—families and individuals having a rough time economically but managing to keep themselves relatively intact."[28]

[24]*The Sociology of Work*, p. 173.
[25]S. M. Miller, "The American Lower Classes: A Typological Approach," *Social Research*, XLVIII, 3 (April, 1964), 13.
[26]"The American Lower Classes: A Typological Approach," pp. 14–15.
[27]"The American Lower Classes: A Typological Approach," p. 15.
[28]Miller, "The American Lower Classes: A Typological Approach," p. 16.

Table 8.3.   Types of Economic Security and Familial Stability

Economic	Familial	
	Stability: +	Instability: −
Security: +	++(1)	+−(2)
Insecurity: −	−+(3)	−−(4)

SOURCE: S.M. Miller, "The American Lower Classes: A Typological Approach," *Social Research,* XLVIII, 3 (April, 1964).

This group's size increases during times of layoff or economic recession. It is composed of a large number of urban Negro families and probably also many Southern white migrants to urban areas. The skill level and patterns of discrimination are such that there is little likelihood of the parents moving out of the unskilled group, although here again the offspring might.

The fourth cell, the *unstable poor*, are obviously beset by economic and family problems. "Partially urbanized Negroes new to the North and to cities, remaining slum residents of ethnic groups which have largely moved out of the slums, long-term (inter-generational) poor white families, and the *déclassé* of Marx" comprise this group.[29] They are unskilled and irregular workers. They are likely to suffer long term unemployment and are the least able to find work when it is available.

Miller's analysis is useful in that it points out the variety found among the unskilled as well as suggesting the interplay between occupational and other social factors. The unskilled vary not only in terms of the nature and frequency of their work but also in their orientations toward it. Some take the position of the semiskilled and other more highly ranked categories that work is essential for security and that life should be at least partially oriented around one's occupation. Others become almost unemployable because of their skill levels and orientations toward work. It is not clear at this time what factors contribute to these varying orientations.

The discussion thus far has suggested that the unskilled range from those with steady employment in manual or service work to the

[29]Miller, "The American Lower Classes: A Typological Approach," p. 16.

most marginal members of the labor force. The unskilled are also characterized by the high proportion of persons suffering personal or social handicaps. These factors contribute to the conclusions that many components included in the analyses of the other occupational types are somewhat irrelevant in this case. For example, the possibility of upward mobility, remote as it is for many white-collar and semiskilled workers, is almost out of the question for the unskilled, at least within the individual's own generation. Lack of skill coupled with frequent discrimination remove mobility from their realm of the possible. As Miller's analysis suggests, it may be possible for some offspring to be mobile, but only within certain settings.

In the occupational setting itself clear differences between the unskilled occupations and the other types are evident. For the manual unskilled worker, there appears to be a greatly lessened potential for structured social relationships. This is the case particularly for those who are hired on a day-to-day basis for work crews with constantly changing compositions. For those in a stable situation, the likelihood of such relationships developing is as high as in other occupations. The stable unskilled worker is, however, much more subject to layoffs than workers with higher skill levels, which would tend to make any such work group relationship much more tenuous.

For the unskilled in service occupations, a different picture can be seen. In the case of workers in larger social structures, such as the busboy or dishwasher in a restaurant or the orderly or attendant in a hospital, the location at the bottom of the social structure generally precludes much interaction with those with higher status. At the same time, the possibilities for meaningful interaction with others with the same status is limited in small organizations where there may be few possible associates. In the larger organization the same possibilities exist as for other occupations.

The domestic servant also faces problems in his interaction system. As the proportion of live-in servants decreases, the opportunity for meaningful interactions with family members decreases. Chaplin points out that labor saving devices for the home and the presence of packaged home services has diminished the demand for even full-time domestic help, forcing those in the occupation to serve a number of masters, as in the case of the cleaning lady who comes once a week to each of her mistresses, and further minimizing the opportunity for meaningful relationships.[30] The fact that many

[30]David Chaplin, "Domestic Service and The Negro" in *Blue Collar World*, eds. Arthur B. Shostak and William Gomberg (Englewood Cliffs, N.J.: Prentice-Hall, Inc., 1964), pp. 527–38.

domestic servants are members of minority groups adds an additional complication to the picture. Vilhelm Aubert, in an analysis of the housemaid, has suggested that the nature of the contemporary servant-mistress relationship makes it difficult or impossible for the servant even to evaluate her work, since the mistress sets the standards and there are no objective criteria.[31] When there are multiple mistresses, the problem is enlarged even further. The domestic servant faces the additional difficulty of working in isolation. Aubert points out that there are no informal emotional contacts with colleagues at the place of work. "She cannot satisfy her craving for companionship in this way, and she does not have a role in a work group as a possible substitute for direct work satisfaction."[32]

Like the cabdriver discussed above, these servants can engage in some manipulation of the situation, but the opportunities are limited in most cases. The permanent servant, on the other hand, can do much more in structuring his social relationships but is still faced with his low status, as Ray Gold's analysis of apartment house janitors suggests. The janitor in this case may not actually fall within the unskilled category, in terms of his skills and his income, but he generally is given a very low status by the tenants. In this sense there is real incongruence between his status and his income. The unionization of janitors has led to a relatively secure economic position. In the case of the janitors Gold studied, they also were provided with an apartment in the basement of the buildings serviced, giving them additional security. At the same time, factors such as the frequent minority group status, generally dirty clothes as a "uniform," garbage removal as a duty, and living in the basement as a symbol of his position, all contribute to the low status. Gold states: "In the public's view it seems that the janitor merely is a very low-class person doing menial work for the tenants."[34] The performance of such personal services is generally stigmatizing in terms of status.[35]

Gold found that the janitors were treated on the basis of their status, as defined by the tenants, rather than on the basis of their income. Those tenants with incomes below or at the same level as the janitor resented the fact that the lowly janitor could afford personal

[31]"The Housemaid—An Occupational Role in Crisis," *Acta Sociologica*, I, 3 (1956), 149–58.

[32]Aubert, "The Housemaid—An Occupational Role in Crisis," p. 198.

[34]Gold, "Janitors Versus Tenants: A Status-Income Dilemma," *American Journal of Sociology*, LVII, 5 (March, 1952), 487.

[35]Caplow notes in *The Sociology of Work* that this form of personal service is almost always thought to be degrading. See pp. 48–49.

possessions, such as a new car or television set. The higher status tenants tended to treat the janitors as family employees or servants. The janitors themselves preferred having rich tenants, since they did not engage in attempts to demonstrate their own higher status. Lower status tenants constantly were trying to demonstrate their superiority to the janitor by demanding additional services or by verbal comments. The janitors, unlike the housemaids, had a union whereby they could discuss their common problems and develop an occupational identity. Nevertheless, the status ascribed to them precluded meaningful relationships on the job.

The discussion thus far has indicated that in addition to the low status implicit in unskilled work, members of this category work in situations that do not provide the same kind of social rewards found in other occupations. This is consistent with Kornhauser's finding that mental health varies consistently with the level of job held—the lower the skill level, the poorer the mental health.[36] Although the exact processes leading to this relationship are not clear, social isolation in many of the jobs and lack of security in many areas are probably operative here. Urban unrest, as exemplified by rioting and looting, is undoubtedly partially a consequence of the marginal position of the unskilled within the labor force and their general lack of integration into the social system.

In a sense, the unskilled, while part of the occupational structure in terms of their performing work and receiving rewards, are outside the structure in terms of the analytical considerations utilized for the balance of the occupational types. There is little, if any, potential for mobility, either individually or collectively. The impact of fellow workers in the same work organization or as colleagues is minimized. The unskilled worker does, of course, work within the social context of his background and current living conditions, which in the case of limited education and minority group status serve as occupational impediments. The utilization of knowledges or skills on the job is also minimized, particularly in the case of workers hired on a day to day basis.

summary and conclusions

This chapter has dealt with two types of occupations, defined almost exclusively by the amount of skill required for their performance. The occupational titles themselves suggest that a major crite-

[36]Kornhauser, *Mental Health of the Industrial Worker*, pp. 76, 261.

rion here is the amount of skill brought to the job. Once the person has taken a position, his specific job title is defined by the machine with which he works or his specific function within an organization. For both the semiskilled and the unskilled, the assumption is that no particular skills are brought to the job. The significant difference between the types is in the amount of training received after a position is obtained. Both types of occupations allow little discretion on the part of the individual in terms of the functions he performs while on the job, although deviation from the officially prescribed standards does occur. The semiskilled and the unskilled share the general orientation that their work is a means to an end, rather than an end in itself.[37] Intrinsic satisfactions in life are generally found off the job or in nonjob related activities, in the case of those workers who derive real satisfaction from the comraderie of the work group.

It has been shown that the actual work performed, the reactions to the occupation and its setting, and the social relationships surrounding the occupations vary widely. Neither the semiskilled nor the unskilled are a homogeneous group. At the same time, they are quite distinct from the other occupations discussed. One exception is the service occupations in which the line between white-collar service occupations and semiskilled service occupations must be arbitrary. If a waitress is a white-collar worker at an exclusive restaurant, her occupation at the local greasy spoon is not that different, even though her status is. The distinction between the unskilled and the semiskilled is itself unclear, although the criteria used above do seem relevant.

A major change occurring among the semiskilled is the shift toward service based work, as the production process is increasingly affected by technological change. While this change is probably not extensively affecting individuals, in the sense that relatively few persons move from production positions into service positions, the occupational opportunities are increasingly in the service area. The movement into the service occupations is probably across generations. The major change occuring among the unskilled is the sheer

[37]Robert Dubin in, "Industrial Workers' Worlds: A Study of 'Central Life Interests' of Industrial Workers," *Social Problems*, III, 2 (Fall, 1956), 131–42 found that 85 per cent of a sample of industrial workers derived their major satisfactions in life off the job. This is in contrast to Louis Orzack's finding that two-thirds of a sample of nurses found their major personal satisfactions *on* the job. See Orzack, "Work as a 'Central Life Interest' of Professionals," *Social Problems*, VII, 2 (Fall 1959), 125–32. For a more general discussion of this phenomenon, see Joseph A. Kahl, *The American Class Structure*, pp. 205–15.

decline of unskilled work. As will be discussed later, the majority of persons who might have entered unskilled work are apparently receiving sufficient training to allow them to enter the labor force at a higher level. Increasing educational requirements for almost all positions will probably continue to diminish the number of unskilled jobs available. Whether this will create a situation of full employment with the formerly unskilled upgraded or a situation in which there is a permanent cadre of unemployed and unemployable persons is still an open question.

PART III

OCCUPATIONS
AND THE
SOCIAL STRUCTURE

This final section will further develop the central theme of the book—occupations and the occupational structure are systematically related to the wider social structure. Examples of this relationship, which have already been discussed, are the formal licensing of some professions, the high rate of occupational inheritance among craftsmen and proprietors, and the impact of automation on white-collar workers. In this section the focus will be shifted to the relationships between occupations and broad segments or institutions within the total social structure, and the implied relationship between occupations and social stratification will be examined in detail. The impact of, and relationships between, the familial and educational systems and the occupational structure will be similarly examined. Aspects of the relationships between technological change and occupations that have not previously been discussed will also be covered in this section. The final chapter deals with the relationships between occupations and politics. The emphasis here will be on the local and national political system, but some attention will be paid to the role of political relationships within occupations themselves.

Two such relationships not examined, for quite different reasons, are those between occupations and the economy and religion. In the case of the economy, the relationship is perhaps overly obvious. Occupations are the major link between the individual and the economy. Those not in the occupational system, such as minors or the aged, are vitally affected by the system, minors by their parents' occupations and the retired by their previous occupation which determines their present economic situation. For those who are unemployed, their very status indicates the direct relationship between occupations and the economy. At the same time, the close relationship between occupations and social stratification reflects the link between occupations and the economy. Economic factors alone do not determine an individual's position in the stratification system. They do, however, play an important role. The importance of economic incentives also indicates the close relationship between occupations and the economy. The occupational system is not the same as the economic system; however, the relationship is clear enough that it does not require a separate analysis.

Religion is a quite different matter. The relationships between religion and occupations are much less clear. Lenski has suggested that the religious factor does play an important role in the development of occupational behavior as evidenced by attitudes toward work and leisure.[1] Weber, of course, suggested the importance of

[1] See Lenski, *The Religious Factor*, pp. 82–128, 213–55.

the Protestant ethic in the development of capitalistic, industrialized societies and the interplay between religion and other social phenomena.[2] The problem for this analysis is that it is very difficult to separate religious from other phenomena, such as socio-economic status or the impact of the family on the individual. This difficulty plus the real absence of information on the subject leads to the omission of an extensive discussion of religion.

One additional point to be made before the analysis begins is that the concern with the relationships between occupations and the social structure in no way assumes that the relationship is one of total equilibrium or harmony. While in some cases there are clear compatibilities, such as the separation of work from the family, which allows the head of the household to follow occupational norms while at work and family norms while at home, or the close relationship between the occupational system and the stratification system, there are also some evident incompatibilities. For example, the role of women in the occupational structure is not clearly defined. The growing concern about the place of educated women in the occupational and familial systems is evidence of this. Similarly, the fact that technological changes can totally disrupt some individuals' occupations demonstrates the incompatibility between these components of the social structure. The analysis will thus focus on both the compatibilities and conflicts which exist.

[2]See *The Protestant Ethic and the Spirit of Capitalism.*

chapter 9

social stratification, mobility, and career patterns

The analysis thus far has been partially based on the fact that occupations have varying statuses within the social system. In this chapter the relationship between occupations and social stratification will be examined in detail. The examination will consist of an analysis of reasons for the close relationship between occupational rankings and the over-all stratification system, an overview of some attempts to describe the relationship, and a discussion of approaches to the explanation of the existence of stratification within the total social system. The important issue of mobility will then be discussed, particularly the movement within and between generations as it is related to the occupational and wider social systems. Career patterns, as a component of intragenerational mobility, will then be considered.

occupations and the stratification system

The most untrained observer recognizes the close relationship between occupations and social status. When meeting someone for the first time, one of the most common questions asked is: "What do you do?" Knowledge of what a person does provides a handy indicator of where a person fits vis à vis one's self. The rather common and unfortunate phrase, "I'm just a housewife" indicates both the status ascribed to that occupation and the importance of occupational identification and the resultant placement within the social system. This does not mean that the resultant placement is always consistent or accurate at this level. The author has been in situations in meeting people for the first time when the response, "I'm a college professor" called forth reactions varying from "That's too bad" to "My, it must be nice." Also imputed to the occupation and thus to the individual are such characteristics as extremely high intelligence, radical political and social beliefs, impracticality, love of students, love of writing, disdain for material goods, etc.; none of which is necessarily correct. The important point is that occupations are used in common social interaction as a major means of locating the individual within the social system.

Approached more analytically, a number of factors act in the close relationship between occupations and social status. Peter M. Blau and Otis Dudley Duncan note: "In the absence of hereditary castes or feudal estates, class differences come to rest primarily on occupational positions and the economic advantages and powers associated with them."[1] Approaching the issue from a different perspective, Albert J. Reiss Jr. states:

> Both individual income and educational attainment, which are used as measures of socio-economic status, are known to be correlated with occupational ranks; and both can be seen as aspects of occupational status, since education is a basis for entry into many occupations, and for most people income is derived from occupation.[2]

Caplow notes that occupational identification has displaced other status-fixing attributes such as ancestry, religious office, political affiliation, or personal character.[3] These authors are saying that the occupation has become the most meaningful indicator for placement in the stratification system *and* that occupation is indicative of and closely related to other indicators, such as education or income, which might be used. For research purposes, occupation has the

---

[1] *The American Occupational Structure* (New York: John Wiley & Sons, Inc., 1967), p. vii.
[2] *Occupations and Social Status* (New York: The Free Press of Glencoe, Inc., 1961), pp. 83–84.
[3] *The Sociology of Work*, p. 30.

great advantage of simplicity. In nonindustrialized societies, of course, occupation is generally less important than considerations of ancestry or caste.

In interpreting the reasons for this convergence upon occupation as the major indicator of social status and for the close relationship between occupational position and position within the stratification system, Caplow has suggested three factors as central for industrialized societies. *Aggregation*, or the sheer increase in size in social groupings, has led to the substitution of formal organizations for informal groupings. The large work organization is characterized by greater anonymity and impersonality than the smaller family unit. A person's position is thus usually responded to more than the individual himself. The term "job description" indicates that duties are ascribed to an office or position rather than to the individual. At the same time the growth of urban communities diminishes the extent to which social interaction based upon an individual's complete knowledge of others is possible. Caplow notes this when he states:

> The urban dweller tends to define his own relationship to his fellows in functional terms, since other means of identification with the community are attenuated. Then too, the separation of home from workplace and the necessity for casual interaction with many unrelated people require various shorthand methods for recognizing others, of which occupational designations are the most convenient, after sex, age, and race.[4]

A second factor is *differentiation*, or occupational specialization. As this occurs, the scope of each individual's activities are lessened and at the same time become more hidden from people in other occupations. According to Caplow, the requirements of each occupation, its responsibilities, and the evaluation of performance become more and more esoteric and removed from the area of judgment of the layman. The response is thus to the occupational title and not to the qualities of the individual in the occupation. Differentiation has also led to more highly developed authority systems within organizations, as additional specialties require their own hierarchies and each hierarchy requires coordination with the whole. Higher status is given to those occupations higher in the hierarchy, and again the response is to an individual's title rather than personal characteristics or performance.[5]

[4]*The Sociology of Work*, p. 30.
[5]Caplow, *The Sociology of Work*, p. 31.

This is related to the third factor, *rationalization*. Rationalization refers to the substitution of formal controls of behavior for informal, personal, and spontaneous controls. This leads to the assumption that the occupational position of an individual has been decided by "scientific," "appropriate," and "efficient" techniques.[6] Caplow suggests that the modern reliance upon occupational position assumes that the occupation is indicative of a person's intelligence, ability, character, and personal acceptability. If a person is promoted to a better position, it is assumed that he has worked diligently and well, not that he is the son of the corporation president. If a person is not promoted, it is also generally assumed that he does not have what it takes. The process of rationalization thus leads to the important assumption that a person's occupation is an effective indicator of the kinds of attributes that would be brought into an assessment of his status if complete knowledge of these other attributes were available. The assumption is that the formal controls are themselves rational.

In particular cases there are undoubtedly variations from the primacy of occupation as the major status determinant. At the local community level, particularly in smaller communities, ancestry still plays a role. Factors, such as sex or race, can override occupation in many cases. Nevertheless, occupation stands out as the major status determinant in industrialized societies. The next question to be considered then is, What are the characteristics of occupations that contribute to the various rankings given the spectrum of occupations?

An important determinant of the status of a particular occupation is the specific nature of the work being performed.[7] A simple differentiation here is whether the occupation involves the manipulation of physical objects, symbols, or other people. In general, the manipulation of physical objects gives the least status, while the manipulation of symbols gives the most. There is some evidence to suggest, however, that social manipulation, as in the case of some executives, also gives high status. Those individuals engaged solely in symbol manipulation, such as artists or scientists, generally have lower status than those whose occupations involve both symbolic and social factors. The relationship between the physical and the symbolic-social forms of work is not perfect. Some craftsmen, for example, have higher status than lower level white-collar workers. At the same time, as Caplow points out, the manipulation of phys-

[6]Caplow, *The Sociology of Work*, p. 31.
[7]This discussion follows the suggestion of Reiss, *Occupations and Social Status*, pp. 10–11.

ical objects is a prized skill in many leisure activities, such as sports and many hobbies.[8] It could be hypothesized that the greater involvement in symbolic-social manipulation in the occupation, the greater the concern with physical manipulation during leisure time. This relationship is affected, of course, by the greater access members of the more rewarded occupations have to such physical settings as sports facilities, gardens, or home shops. In terms of the status of occupations, the physical-symbolic-social differentiation does remain important, regardless of the relationship in non-occupational activities.

Another factor affecting the status of an occupation is the prerequisites for entry; the amount of education or training required, the presence of certification or licensing procedures, and the experience needed. In general, the more stringent the entrance requirements, the higher the status of the occupation. This accounts for the high status of the professions in the general white-collar category and that of craftsmen among blue-collar workers. There are some exceptions, as in the case of some professions, which have not achieved public acceptance, but the relationship holds in most cases.

According to Reiss, an additional determinant of the status of an occupation is whether the task is performed on an individual or group basis. Although he does not specify which type of social organization has the higher status yield, it appears that work carried out on an individual basis gives an occupation higher status, since individual work implies that the individual is capable of accomplishing the total project on his own. This is also reflected in the traditionally high status of the individual practitioner in the professions. As this image changes the importance of this component of status determination may be lessened.

The place of an occupation within the interpersonal-relationship structure on the job also affects its status. Occupations involving supervision have higher status than those which are supervised. The position of an occupation in an organizational hierarchy has a similar status relationship. The important thing is the formal position of an occupation. Related to this are the demands made on an occupation by the work structure. The amount and type of responsibility are crucial. The more the responsibility, the higher the status in most cases. As was the case in terms of the specific task performed, responsibility for social or symbolic activities yields a higher status than that for physical objects.

[8]Caplow, *The Sociology of Work*, p. 44.

In addition to the characteristics of the work performed, Reiss suggests that the work situation plays a role in determining occupational status. One factor here would be the institutional setting of the work. A factory has a lower status than an office, and a research laboratory has a higher status than a machine shop. The work situation also determines the kinds of rewards earned from particular occupations, such as income, recognition, tenure, retirement programs, etc. It is obvious that work situations vary in terms of the kinds of rewards they offer. Persons with the same title and responsibilities can receive highly varied rewards, as was demonstrated in the section on executives. Related to this is the fact that, within a community, various employing organizations occupy different statuses. Workers in automated factories usually enjoy a higher status than their counterparts in nonautomated situations. A secretary may derive higher status from working at a university than at an automobile dealership. Industries themselves vary in the amount of status accorded them. At the present time, for example, the electronics industry appears to yield more status than the railroad industry, although these patterns change in time. A final consideration in the work situation is the nature of the employment itself, whether it is public, private, or self-employment. The last type of employment has traditionally been given high status. In general, private employment has higher status than public, except among elected public officials in high positions such as governors of states or congressmen.

The configuration of these work and work situation attributes determines the status given an occupation. The work related attributes tend to be more universal, in that the characteristics involved extend across a variety of work situations. The situational considerations operate most obviously at the local level, where knowledge of the differences between the work settings is most evident. The combination of the work and situational aspects is the basis for the evaluation of occupational status. The fact that there is this local variation is part of the difficulty in determining status in an objective manner. Every occupation, however, does possess characteristics which can be evaluated according to the criteria discussed above. Whether all of these factors are taken into consideration in the assignment of occupational status in concrete situations is another question.

The discussion thus far has centered around the reasons why occupation has become the major determinant of status and some of the factors which contribute to the differential status of occupations. Before delving further into the explanations that have been developed to explain why the stratification system takes the form that it does, some of the techniques used to measure the status of various occupations will be analyzed. These techniques are designed to demonstrate the existence of a system of ranking and to serve as research tools for further analyses of the relationships between social status and other conditions.

One of the most commonly used measurement devices, which was also the general basis for the previous discussion on types of occupations, is that used by the U.S. Census Bureau, sometimes called the Edwards Scale after its developer, Alba Edwards. The scale ranks occupations in the following manner:

1. **Unskilled workers**
   1-a Farm laborers
   1-b,c Laborers, except farm
   1-d Servant classes
2. **Semiskilled workers**
3. **Skilled workers and foremen**
4. **Clerks and kindred workers**
5. **Proprietors, managers, and officials**
   5-a Farmers (owners and tenants)
   5-b Wholesale and retail dealers
   5-c Other proprietors, managers, and officials
6. **Professional persons**

Edwards suggests that these occupational groupings encompass some major components of stratification and states:

> It is evident that each of these groups represents not only a major segment of the Nation's labor force, but, also, a large population group with a somewhat distinct standard of life, economically, and to a considerable extent, intellectually and socially. In some measures, also, each group has characteristic interests and convictions as to numerous public questions—social, economic, and political. Each of them is thus a really distinct and highly significant social-economic group.[9]

Most analysts would not go as far as Edwards in attributing such clear distinctions to and between these occupational groupings. Nevertheless, the scale, if considered as a rather gross form of measurement, is useful as an analytical and research device. The scale provides an ordering of occupations without permitting the

---

[9]Alba M. Edwards, *Comparative Occupational Statistics for the United States, 1870–1940* (Washington D.C.: U.S. Government Printing Office, 1943), p. 179.

assumption to be made that the intervals between the various positions on the scale are in any way equal.

This type of scale according to Caplow contains some important assumptions. The first is that white-collar work is superior to manual work. In most cases, this is a fact of social life as indicated by occupational preferences. At the same time, the situation of many craftsmen (long training and high incomes) would give them higher status than many white-collar workers according to the other status criteria. The position of a craftsman who is also a proprietor is also unclear from this perspective, as are the variations in skill among manual workers who are not craftsmen. Many semiskilled or operatives enjoy incomes and other status-yielding attributes above those in some white-collar occupations.[10]

Another assumption of this form of ranking is that self-employment is superior to employment by others. As Caplow suggests, much of this orientation is a carry-over from an earlier era, but the idea lingers on. As was discussed in the section on proprietors, the supposed advantages of this type of occupation are limited to a small proportion of the category. Another assumption, based on historical factors, is that clean occupations are preferable to dirty ones. Thus junk dealers and coal miners suffer in status in relationship to their incomes and other status determinants. There is a strong tendency for the elimination of dirty occupations through mechanization. Also, the professionalization of occupations such as morticians and sanitary engineers has removed some of the stigma attached to their work.[11]

Another assumption of this type of scale is that the size of the employing organization is positively related to occupational status, since large organizations tend to have more prestige than smaller ones. Nevertheless, extremely high incomes can be earned in smaller businesses that do not have the controls established by stockholders or boards of directors found in larger organizations. At the interpersonal level, supervisors in smaller organizations are better known and thus often accorded higher status than their counterparts in large organizations. The relationship is confused even further by the fact that the functions performed in smaller organizations often do not correspond to those in larger organizations. Caplow cites the example of the editor of the small town newspaper who has no counterpart in a metropolitan paper. A similar example is that of the college professor who also serves as dean of students

[10]Caplow, *The Sociology of Work*, pp. 43–45.
[11]Caplow, *The Sociology of Work*, pp. 45–47.

on a small college campus, in contrast to the large university with full-time student personnel administrative apparatus.[12] These difficulties contribute to the grossness of the measurement.

A final assumption is that personal service is degrading. The low status given household servants by the scale is probably accurate in that there is a real absence of personal freedom in such work. The problem with this assumption is with the nondomestic service occupations, such as taxi driver or janitor, which have been discussed, or the barber, bartender, or beautician. These are personal service occupations but occupy often contradictory statuses. Caplow notes that a small-town barber is often one of the leading citizens of the community. Similarly, barbers and bartenders can be on a first-name basis with top executives and professionals, a relationship not available to many who interact with these people on their jobs. Personal service is thus degrading only in the case of domestic service, even though some other service occupations are accorded rather low status by these scaling devices.[13]

The census classification is designed to allow placement of occupations into relatively homogeneous categories in terms of socio-economic characteristics. Difficulties in placement of some occupations, lack of real homogeneity, and the overlapping of socio-economic characteristics make such a scale less than perfect. It can, however, serve as a gross indicator of the differential ranking of occupations. A quite different approach has been taken by those interested in occupational prestige. The prestige dimension of social stratification deals directly with the status accorded occupations, since prestige is only something attributed to something else. Occupations do not have prestige, rather they are given it by the public. Since the public acts on the basis of its interpretation of an occupation, or any other social phenomenon for that matter, prestige is an important component in the ranking of occupations.

Of the various attempts to measure occupational prestige, the best known and most widely used approach is the North-Hatt or National Opinion Research Center (NORC) survey conducted in 1947 and since expanded and refined. This study was designed to "secure a national rating of the *relative prestige* of a wide range of occupations," to determine the standards of judgment people use in evaluating occupational status, and to investigate the standards used in determining the relative desirability of various occupations.[14] The study also was concerned with attitudes about the appropriate

[12]Caplow, *The Sociology of Work*, pp. 47–48.
[13]Caplow, *The Sociology of Work*, pp. 48–49.
[14]Reiss, *Occupations and Social Status*, p. 4.

amount of education needed to get along in the world and with occupational mobility. In addition to being a study of occupational prestige, the findings from the NORC survey have become a major *scale* of occupational prestige. The original findings have been extrapolated to include many more than the 90 occupations analyzed in the original study, and the rankings obtained have been used to measure the prestige of occupations in a whole series of studies.

The data for the original study were obtained from a national sample of 2,920 respondents. A major problem encountered in the study was the varying amount of knowledge the respondents had about the occupations being rated. While over 99 per cent of the respondents could rank occupations such as school teacher, garage mechanic, or truck driver, less than half were able to rank nuclear physicists. Other occupations were also difficult to rank. This presented a real problem in that the occupations included in the study were rather well-known and did not include many with esoteric titles. The more education a respondent had, the more likely he was to know about the occupations being ranked. Differences in the ability to rank also were related to the type of community of the respondent and his own socio-economic status. An additional problem encountered was that different criteria were used by respondents in their evaluations of the occupations.[15] The basic question asked was:

> For each job mentioned, please pick out the statement that best gives *your own personal opinion* of the *general standing* that such a job has.
>
> 1. *Excellent* standing
> 2. *Good* standing
> 3. *Average* standing
> 4. *Somewhat below average* standing
> 5. *Poor* standing
> X. I don't know where to place that one[16]

Each of the ninety occupations was then ranked by the respondent on the five point scale. The final rankings were obtained by a scoring system that gave an occupation that received 100 per cent *excellent* a score of 100 and those which were unanimously rated as poor a score of 20. None achieved unanimity, of course. The occupations ranked, the final scores, and the proportion of the respondents giving each response are shown in Table 9.1.

[15]Reiss, *Occupations and Social Status*, pp. 6–18.
[16]Reiss, *Occupations and Social Status*, p. 19.

The respondents were then asked to name the "one main thing" about the jobs rated *excellent* that gave them this standing. The results of this question are shown in Table 9.2 with variations in the respondents' community type, age, education, general socio-economic standing, and geographical region held constant. While the potential rewards from a job are the most frequently mentioned criteria, the expected variations by education and occupation stand out as a partial verification of the point that more intrinsic rewards are more central to those higher in the occupational hierarchy. As Reiss points out, it is those lowest in financial status who are most likely to mention financial rewards as central to an occupation's standing. These responses also reflect the central values of Americans in regard to their work.[17]

The NORC survey has become a benchmark in analyses of occupational status, despite the methodological and conceptual difficulties involved. The findings can only be considered as an ordering of occupations, since the intervals between the scores cannot be demonstrated to be equal. The original scores and extrapolations from them to occupations not included in the original study have been utilized as indicators of the relative status of occupations in a large number of studies and as indicators of the general social status of members of the occupations involved. There is some evidence that this is not an unwarranted procedure. Reiss, for example, reports that such "hard" indicators of socio-economic status as income and educational level are highly associated with the NORC scores. Using the median income and educational levels of the civilian labor force of the occupations in the NORC study, he found rank order correlation coefficients (Kendall's *tau*) of +.85 between income and NORC score and +.83 for educational attainment and NORC score.[18] Prestige is thus rather strongly related to other indices of socio-economic status.

While the NORC findings do show a general ordinal ranking of occupations, Reiss suggests that a unidimensional scale for all occupations cannot be derived from such an approach.[19] While income and education are strongly associated with occupational prestige, they do not always agree with each other. At the same time, since prestige scales rely upon the perception of the respondents and since such perception usually involves some distortion of reality, the prestige scales themselves cannot be taken as totally

[17]*Occupations and Social Status*, p. 35.
[18]Reiss, *Occupations and Social Status*, p. 84.
[19]See Reiss, *Occupations and Social Status*, Chaps. 2 and 3.

Table 9.1. Per Cent Distribution by Respondent Rating, Average Score and Rank for 90 Rated Occupations: NORC, March, 1947

Occupation	Excellent	Good	Average	Somewhat below Average	Poor	Don't Know	Score	Rank
U.S. Supreme Court justice	83%	15%	2%	%	% = 100	3%	96	1
Physician	67	30	3			1	93	2
State governor	71	25	4			1	93	2
Cabinet member in the federal government	66	28	5	1		6	92	4
Diplomat in the U.S. Foreign Service	70	24	4	1	1	9	92	4
Mayor of a large city	57	36	6	1		1	90	6
College professor	53	40	7			1	89	7
Scientist	53	38	8	1		7	89	7
United States representative in Congress	57	35	6	1	1	4	89	7
Banker	49	43	8			1	88	10
Government scientist	51	41	7	1		6	88	10
County judge	47	43	9	1		1	87	12
Head of a department in a state government	47	44	8		1	3	87	12
Minister	52	35	11	1	1	1	87	12
Architect	42	48	9	1		6	86	15
Chemist	42	48	9	1		7	86	15
Dentist	42	48	9	1			86	15
Lawyer	44	45	9	1	1	1	86	15
Member of board of directors of large corporation	42	47	10	1		5	86	15
Nuclear physicist	48	39	11	1	1	51	86	15
Priest	51	34	11	2	2	6	86	15
Psychologist	38	49	12	1		15	85	22
Civil engineer	33	55	11	1		5	84	23
Airline pilot	35	48	15	1	1	3	83	24
Artist who paints pictures that are exhibited in galleries	40	40	15	3	2	6	83	24
Owner of factory that employs about 100 people	30	51	17	1	1	2	82	26
Sociologist	31	51	16	1	1	23	82	26
Accountant for large business	25	57	17	1		3	81	28
Biologist	29	51	18	1	1	16	81	28
Musician in a symphony orchestra	31	46	19	3	1	5	81	28

Table 9.1.   (continued)

Occupation	Excellent	Good	Average	Somewhat below Average	Poor	Don't Know	Score	Rank
Author of novels	32	44	19	3	2	9	80	31
Captain in the regular army	28	49	19	2	2	2	80	31
Building contractor	21	55	23	1		1	79	33
Economist	25	48	24	2	1	22	79	33
Instructor in public schools	28	45	24	2	1	1	79	33
Public-school teacher	26	45	24	3	2		78	36
County agricultural agent	17	53	28	2		5	77	37
Railroad engineer	22	45	30	3		1	77	37
Farm-owner and operator	19	46	31	3	1	1	76	39
Official of an international labor union	26	42	20	5	7	11	75	40
Radio announcer	17	45	35	3		2	75	40
Newspaper columnist	13	51	32	3	1	5	74	42
Owner-operator of a printing shop	13	48	36	3		2	74	42
Electrician	15	38	43	4		1	73	44
Trained machinist	14	43	38	5		2	73	44
Welfare worker for a city government	16	43	35	4	2	4	73	44
Undertaker	14	43	36	5	2	2	72	44
Reporter on daily newspaper	9	43	43	4	1	2	71	48
Manager of small store in a city	5	40	50	4	1	1	69	49
Bookkeeper	8	31	55	6		1	68	50
Insurance agent	7	34	53	4	2	2	68	50
Tenant farmer—one who owns livestock and machinery and manages the farm	10	37	40	11	2	1	68	50
Traveling salesman for a wholesale concern	6	35	53	5	1	2	68	50
Playground director	7	33	48	10	2	4	67	54
Policeman	11	30	46	11	2	1	67	54
Railroad conductor	8	30	52	9	1	1	67	54
Mail-carrier	8	26	54	10	2		66	57
Carpenter	5	28	56	10	1		65	58
Automobile repairman	5	21	58	14	2		63	59

Table 9.1.   (continued)

Occupation	Excel- lent	Good	Aver- age	Some- what below Aver- age	Poor	Don't Know	Score	Rank
Plumber	5	24	55	14	2	1	63	59
Garage mechanic	4	21	57	17	1		62	61
Local official of labor union	7	29	41	14	9	11	62	61
Owner-operator of lunch stand	4	24	55	14	3	1	62	61
Corporal in the regular army	5	21	48	20	6	3	60	64
Machine operator in factory	4	20	53	20	3	2	60	64
Barber	3	17	56	20	4	1	59	66
Clerk in a store	2	14	61	20	3		58	67
Fisherman who owns own boat	3	20	48	21	8	7	58	67
Streetcar motorman	3	16	55	21	5	2	58	67
Milk-route man	2	10	52	29	7	1	54	70
Restaurant cook	3	13	44	29	11	1	54	70
Truck-driver	2	11	49	29	9		54	70
Lumberjack	2	11	48	29	10	8	53	73
Filling-station attendant	1	9	48	34	8	1	52	74
Singer in a night club	3	13	43	23	18	6	52	74
Farm hand	3	12	35	31	19	1	50	76
Coal miner	4	11	33	31	21	2	49	77
Taxi-driver	2	8	38	35	17	1	49	77
Railroad section hand	2	9	35	33	21	3	48	79
Restaurant waiter	2	8	37	36	17	1	48	79
Dockworker	2	7	34	37	20	8	47	81
Night watchman	3	8	33	35	21	1	47	81
Clothes-presser in a laundry	2	6	35	36	21	2	46	83
Soda-fountain clerk	1	5	34	40	20	2	45	84
Bartender	1	6	32	32	29	4	44	85
Janitor	1	7	30	37	25	1	44	85
Share-cropper—one who owns no live- stock or equipment and does not manage farm	1	6	24	28	41	3	40	87
Garbage collector	1	4	16	26	53	2	35	88
Street-sweeper	1	3	14	29	53	1	34	89
Shoe-shiner	1	2	13	28	56	2	33	90
Average	21.6	30.9	29.5	11.4	6.6	4.0	69.8	

SOURCE: Albert J. Reiss, *Occupations and Social Status* (New York: The Free Press of Glencoe, Inc., 1961), pp. 54-57.

Table 9.2. Criterion Respondents Gave as the One Main Thing That Gives a Job Excellent Standing, by Selected Social Categories

Category	Pays Well	Social Prestige	Good Future; Field Not Crowded	Security, Steady Work, Money	Education, Hard Work, Money	Morality, Honesty, Responsibility	Intelligence, Ability	Service to Humanity, Essential	Pleasant, Safe, Easy	Chance for Initiative, Freedom	Miscellaneous; Don't Know
All Respondents	18	14	3	5	14	9	9	16	2	*	10
Region											
Northeast	19	17	3	5	13	8	10	14	2	1	8
Midwest	15	15	4	5	14	11	8	16	2	*	10
South	21	12	4	3	14	8	8	15	1	*	13
West	14	11	2	4	17	9	11	22	1	1	8
Size of Place											
Metro. district											
1,000,000 and over	17	17	4	6	14	9	9	15	2	*	7
50,000-1,000,000	16	13	3	4	14	11	9	18	2	1	9
Urban places and towns	17	12	3	4	15	9	10	18	2	*	10
Rural farm	23	12	4	5	13	7	5	14	2	*	15
Age (years)											
14-20	21	15	4	3	13	5	8	17	3	*	11
21-39	16	16	4	6	15	6	9	16	2	1	9
40 and over	17	12	3	4	14	13	9	16	1	1	10
Sex											
Male	19	14	4	5	14	9	9	14	2	1	9
Female	16	14	3	4	14	9	9	18	2	1	10

Occupation Group											
Prof. and semiprof.	10	20	*	3	13	6	15	26	1	1	5
Mgrs., prop., and off.	14	16	3	4	19	9	10	16	1	1	7
Sales, clerical, and kindred	14	18	5	5	15	13	9	13	1	*	7
Crafts, fore., and kindred	16	13	5	5	14	10	8	19	2	†	8
Operatives and kind.	21	11	5	8	13	6	8	13	2	1	12
Pvt. household and service	22	14	*	4	13	9	7	12	3	†	16
All farm	24	11	4	4	12	8	6	14	2	*	15
Nonfarm labor	26	8	3	4	14	6	8	14	2	†	15
Yrs. of Schl. Comp.											
Some college	7	21	2	4	13	9	13	24	3	*	6
Some high school	17	14	4	5	13	9	9	16	*	1	88
8th grade or less	24	9	3	5	16	11	7	11	2	*	15
In school	18	19	4	3	13	5	8	19	3	*	8
Economic Level											
Prosperous	15	19	3	3	14	11	8	20	1	1	5
Middle class	15	15	3	5	15	9	10	16	2	1	9
Poor	23	10	4	5	13	9	6	13	2	*	15

* Less than one-half of 1 per cent.
† No responses.

SOURCE: Albert J. Reiss, *Occupations and Social Status* (New York: The Free Press of Glencoe, Inc., 1961), pp. 32-33.

accurate appraisals of the stratification system. Distortions enter the picture from the tendency of people to underrate occupations lower than their own and overrate their own occupational positions. This problem is compounded when it is remembered that the level of education affects an individual's ability to rank positions in the first place. High status occupations are thus ranked high by people with greater knowledge, although those in lower status occupations, while ranking their own occupations rather high, lack the ability to rank much of the rest of the occupational system. Relying upon either high or low status occupations for ranking purposes introduces real distortions. Surveys such as the NORC study, which attempt to get a representative sample of the population, while minimizing the distortions introduced by reliance upon particular segments of the population, include in their composite scores the distortions from every population group. These distortions are apparently not eliminated by the inclusion of representative groups from the total population, since the kinds of distortions from each group do not counterbalance each other. Despite these problems, the North-Hatt scale has been a widely used research device.

In an attempt to provide a more meaningful method for measuring and describing occupational status, Duncan combined measures of education and income. He correctly notes that occupation is "the intervening activity linking income to education."[20] Education prepares a person for an occupation from which he derives his income. While each can be taken separately as an indicator of social status, the combination of these two factors yields what is essentially a multidimensional scaling of occupations. Duncan calls this a "socioeconomic index," containing variables reflecting both the social and economic components of the stratification system.

Using sophisticated indicators of the education and income variables, Duncan's socioeconomic index can be used to predict scores on the NORC scale.[21] Table 9.3 indicates the scores on the socio-economic index and their transformations to NORC scores for occupations in the detailed occupational classification of the U.S. Census Bureau, 1950. The socio-economic index cannot be taken as an exact representation of the status of individuals in each occupation or as an exact representation of the stratification system of the society. There are also, undoubtedly, community and regional variations in the relative socio-economic positions of the occupa-

[20]Reiss, *Occupations and Social Status*, p. 117.
[21]The details of the development of this scale is contained in Reiss, *Occupations and Social Status*, Chap. 6.

Table 9.3. Socio-Economic Index for Occupations in the Detailed Classification of the Bureau of the Census: 1950

Occupations, by Major Occupation Group	Socio-Economic Index	Transform to NORC Scale	Population Decile Scale	Notes[1]
Professional, Technical, and Kindred Workers				
Accountants and auditors	78	80	10	a
Actors and actresses	60	74	9	—
Airplane pilots and navigators	79	81	10	a
Architects	90	86	10	a
Artists and art teachers	67	76	10	b
Athletes	52	71	9	—
Authors	76	80	10	a
Chemists	79	81	10	a
Chiropractors	75	79	10	—
Clergymen	52	71	9	a
College presidents, professors, and instructors(n.e.c.)	84	83	10	a
Dancers and dancing teachers	45	69	8	—
Dentists	96	93	10	a
Designers	73	79	10	—
Dieticians and nutritionists	39	67	7	d
Draftsmen	67	76	10	—
Editors and reporters	82	82	10	a
Engineers, technical	85	83	10	c
Aeronautical	87	85	10	—
Chemical	90	87	10	—
Civil	84	83	10	a
Electrical	84	83	10	—
Industrial	86	84	10	—
Mechanical	82	83	10	—
Metallurgical, and metallurgists	82	83	10	—
Mining	85	83	10	—
Not elsewhere classified	87	85	10	—
Entertainers (n.e.c.)	31	64	6	—
Farm- and home-management advisors	83	83	10	b
Foresters and conservationists	48	70	8	—

[1]See end of table for explanation of "Notes."

275

Table 9.3.   (continued)

Occupations, by Major Occupation Group	Socio-Economic Index	Transform to NORC Scale	Population Decile Scale	Notes
Funeral directors and embalmers	59	74	9	a
Lawyers and judges	93	89	10	a
Librarians	60	74	9	—
Musicians and music teachers	52	71	9	b
Natural scientists (n.e.c.)	80	81	10	b
Nurses, professional	46	70	8	—
Nurses, student professional	51	71	9	d
Optometrists	79	81	10	—
Osteopaths	96	93	10	—
Personnel and labor-relations workers	84	83	10	—
Pharmacists	82	82	10	—
Photographers	50	71	9	—
Physicians and surgeons	92	89	10	a
Radio operators	69	77	10	—
Recreation and group workers	67	76	10	b
Religious workers	56	72	9	—
Social and welfare workers, except group	64	75	9	a
Social scientists	81	82	10	b
Sports instructors and officials	64	75	9	—
Surveyors	48	70	8	—
Teachers (n.e.c.)	72	78	10	a
Technicians, medical and dental	48	70	8	—
Technicians, testing	53	72	9	—
Technicians (n.e.c.)	62	74	9	—
Therapists and healers (n.e.c.)	58	73	9	—
Veterinarians	78	81	10	—
Professional, technical, and kindred workers (n.e.c.)	65	75	9	—
Farmers and Farm Managers				
Farmers (owners and tenants)	14	53	3	b
Farm managers	36	66	7	—
Managers, Officials, and Proprietors, except Farm				
Buyers and department heads, store	72	78	10	—

Table 9.3 (continued)

Occupations, by Major Occupation Group	Socio-Economic Index	Transform to NORC Scale	Population Decile Scale	Notes
Buyers and shippers, farm products	33	65	7	—
Conductors, railroad	58	73	9	a
Credit men	74	79	10	—
Floormen and floor managers, store	50	71	9	—
Inspectors, public administration	63	75	9	c
Federal public administration and postal service	72	78	10	—
State public administration	54	72	9	—
Local public administration	56	72	9	—
Managers and superintendents, building	32	65	7	—
Officers, pilots, pursers, and engineers, ship	54	72	9	—
Officials and administrators (n.e.c.), public administration	66	76	10	c
Federal public administration and postal service	84	83	10	—
State public administration	66	76	10	—
Local public administration	54	72	9	—
Officials, lodge, society, union, etc.	58	73	9	b
Postmasters	60	74	9	—
Purchasing agents and buyers (n.e.c.)	77	80	10	—
Managers, officials, and proprietors (n.e.c.)—salaried	68	77	10	c
Construction	60	74	9	—
Manufacturing	79	81	10	—
Transportation	71	78	10	—
Telecommunications, and utilities and sanitary services	76	80	10	—
Wholesale trade	70	77	10	—
Retail trade	56	72	9	c

Table 9.3. (continued)

Occupations, by Major Occupation Group	Socio-Economic Index	Transform to NORC Scale	Population Decile Scale	Notes
Food- and dairy-products stores, and milk retailing	50	70	8	—
General merchandise and five- and ten-cent stores	68	77	10	—
Apparel and accessories stores	69	77	10	—
Furniture, home furnishings, and equipment stores	68	77	10	—
Motor vehicles and accessories retailing	65	75	9	—
Gasoline service stations	31	65	7	—
Eating and drinking places	39	68	8	—
Hardware, farm implement, and building material, retail	64	75	9	—
Other retail trade	59	74	9	—
Banking and other finance	85	84	10	—
Insurance and real estate	84	83	10	—
Business services	80	81	10	—
Automobile repair services and garages	47	70	8	—
Miscellaneous repair services	53	71	9	—
Personal services	50	71	9	—
All other industries (incl. not reported)	62	74	9	—
Managers, officials, and proprietors (n.e.c.)—self-employed	48	70	8	c
Construction	51	71	9	a
Manufacturing	61	74	9	a
Transportation	43	69	8	—
Telecommunications and utilities and sanitary services	44	69	8	—
Wholesale trade	59	74	9	—

Table 9.3. (continued)

Occupations, by Major Occupation Group	Socio-Economic Index	Transform to NORC Scale	Population Decile Scale	Notes
Retail trade	43	69	8	a, c
Food- and dairy-products stores, and milk retailing	33	65	7	—
General merchandise and five- and-ten-cent stores	47	70	8	—
Apparel and accessories stores	65	75	9	—
Furniture, home furnishings, and equipment stores	59	73	9	—
Motor vehicles and accessories retailing	70	77	10	—
Gasoline service stations	33	65	7	—
Eating and drinking places	37	67	7	b
Hardware, farm implement, and building material, retail	61	74	9	—
Other retail trade	49	70	8	—
Banking and other finance	85	84	10	a
Insurance and real estate	76	80	10	—
Business services	67	76	10	—
Automobile repair services and garages	36	66	7	—
Miscellaneous repair services	34	65	7	—
Personal services	41	68	8	—
All other industries (incl. not reported)	49	70	8	—
Clerical and Kindred Workers				
Agents (n.e.c.)	68	77	10	—
Attendants and assistants, library	44	69	8	d
Attendants, physician's and dentist's office	38	67	7	d
Baggagemen, transportation	25	61	6	—
Bank tellers	52	71	9	—
Bookkeepers	51	71	9	a
Cashiers	44	69	8	—

Table 9.3. (continued)

Occupations, by Major Occupation Group	Socio-Economic Index	Transform to NORC Scale	Population Decile Scale	Notes
Collectors, bill and account	39	68	8	—
Dispatchers and starters, vehicle	40	68	8	—
Express messengers and railway mail clerks	67	76	10	—
Mail-carriers	53	71	9	a
Messengers and office boys	28	63	6	—
Office-machine operators	45	69	8	—
Shipping and receiving clerks	22	60	6	—
Stenographers, typists, and secretaries	61	74	9	—
Telegraph messengers	22	59	6	—
Telegraph operators	47	70	8	—
Telephone operators	45	69	8	—
Ticket, station, and express agents	60	74	9	—
Clerical and kindred workers (n.e.c.)	44	69	8	—
Sales Workers				
Advertising agents and sales-men	66	76	10	—
Auctioneers	40	68	8	—
Demonstrators	35	66	7	—
Hucksters and peddlers	8	46	2	—
Insurance agents and brokers	66	76	10	a
Newsboys	27	63	6	—
Real-estate agents and brokers	62	74	9	—
Stock and bond salesmen	73	79	10	—
Salesmen and sales clerks (n.e.c.)	47	70	8	c
Manufacturing	65	75	9	—
Wholesale trade	61	74	9	b
Retail trade	39	67	7	a
Other industries (incl. not reported)	50	71	9	—
Craftsmen, Foremen, and Kindred Workers				
Bakers	22	60	6	—
Blacksmiths	16	55	4	—
Boilermakers	33	65	7	—

Table 9.3. **(continued)**

Occupations, by Major Occupation Group	Socio-Economic Index	Transform to NORC Scale	Population Decile Scale	Notes
Bookbinders	39	67	7	—
Brickmasons, stonemasons, and tile-setters	27	62	6	—
Cabinetmakers	23	60	6	—
Carpenters	19	58	5	a
Cement and concrete finishers	19	58	5	—
Compositors and typesetters	52	71	9	—
Cranemen, derrickmen, and hoistmen	21	59	5	—
Decorators and window-dressers	40	68	8	—
Electricians	44	69	8	a
Electrotypers and stereotypers	55	72	9	—
Engravers, except photo-engravers	47	70	8	—
Excavating, grading, and road-machinery operators	24	61	6	—
Foremen (n.e.c.)	49	70	8	c
Construction	40	68	8	—
Manufacturing	53	71	9	c
Metal industries	54	72	9	—
Machinery, including electrical	60	74	9	—
Transportation equipment	66	76	10	—
Other durable goods	41	68	8	—
Textiles, textile products, and apparel	39	68	8	—
Other nondurable goods (incl. not specified mfg.)	53	72	9	—
Railroads and railway express service	36	66	7	—
Transportation, except railroad	45	69	8	—
Telecommunications, and utilities and sanitary services	56	73	9	—
Other industries (incl. not reported)	44	69	8	—
Forgemen and hammermen	23	60	6	—

Table 9.3. (continued)

Occupations, by Major Occupation Group	Socio-Economic Index	Transform to NORC Scale	Population Decile Scale	Notes
Furriers	39	67	7	—
Glaziers	26	62	6	—
Heat treaters, annealers, and temperers	22	60	6	—
Inspectors, scalers, and graders, log and lumber	23	60	6	—
Inspectors (n.e.c.)	41	68	8	c
Construction	46	70	8	—
Railroads and railway express service	41	68	8	—
Transport, exc. r.r., communication, and other public util.	45	69	8	—
Other industries (incl. not reported)	38	67	7	—
Jewelers, watchmakers, goldsmiths, and silversmiths	36	66	7	—
Job-setters, metal	28	63	6	—
Linemen and servicemen, telegraph, telephone, and power	49	70	8	—
Locomotive engineers	58	73	9	a
Locomotive firemen	45	69	8	—
Loom fixers	10	49	2	—
Machinists	33	65	7	a
Mechanics and repairmen	25	61	6	c
Airplane	48	70	8	—
Automobile	19	58	5	a
Office machine	36	66	7	—
Radio and television	36	66	7	—
Railroad and car shop	23	60	6	—
Not elsewhere classified	27	62	6	—
Millers, grain, flour, feed, etc.	19	58	5	—
Millwrights	31	65	7	—
Molders, metal	12	51	2	—
Motion-picture projectionists	43	69	8	—
Opticians, and lens grinders and polishers	39	67	7	—
Painters, construction and maintenance	16	56	4	—

Table 9.3. (continued)

Occupations, by Major Occupation Group	Socio-Economic Index	Transform to NORC Scale	Population Decile Scale	Notes
Paperhangers	10	48	2	—
Pattern- and model-makers, except paper	44	69	8	—
Photoengravers and lithographers	64	75	9	—
Piano and organ tuners and repairmen	38	67	7	—
Plasterers	25	61	6	—
Plumbers and steam-fitters	34	66	7	a
Pressmen and plate printers, printing	49	70	8	—
Rollers and roll hands, metal	22	60	6	—
Roofers and slaters	15	54	4	—
Shoemakers and repairers, except factory	12	51	2	—
Stationary engineers	47	70	8	—
Stone-cutters and stone-carvers	25	61	6	—
Structural-metal workers	34	66	7	—
Tailors and tailoresses	23	60	6	—
Tinsmiths, coppersmiths, and sheet-metal workers	33	65	7	—
Toolmakers, and die-makers and setters	50	71	9	—
Upholsterers	22	60	6	—
Craftsmen and kindred workers (n.e.c.)	32	65	7	—
Members of the armed forces	18	56	4	e
Operatives and Kindred Workers				
Apprentices	35	66	7	c
Auto mechanics	25	61	6	—
Bricklayers and masons	32	65	7	—
Carpenters	31	64	6	—
Electricians	37	67	7	—
Machinists and toolmakers	41	68	8	—
Mechanics, except auto	34	66	7	—
Plumbers and pipe-fitters	33	65	7	—
Building trades (n.e.c.)	29	63	6	—

Table 9.3. (continued)

Occupations, by Major Occupation Group	Socio-Economic Index	Transform to NORC Scale	Population Decile Scale	Notes
Metalworking trades (n.e.c.)	33	65	7	—
Printing trades	40	68	8	—
Other specified trades	31	64	6	—
Trade not specified	39	67	7	—
Asbestos and insulation workers	32	65	7	—
Attendants, auto service and parking	19	58	5	a
Blasters and powdermen	11	50	2	—
Boatmen, canalmen, and lock-keepers	24	61	6	—
Brakemen, railroad	42	69	8	—
Bus-drivers	24	61	6	—
Chainmen, rodmen, and ax-men, surveying	25	61	6	—
Conductors, bus and street railway	30	64	6	—
Deliverymen and routemen	32	65	7	—
Dressmakers and seam-stresses, except factory	23	60	6	—
Dyers	12	51	2	—
Filers, grinders, and polishers, metal	22	59	6	—
Fruit, nut, and vegetable graders and packers, exc. factory	10	48	2	—
Furnacemen, smeltermen, and pourers	18	57	4	—
Heaters, metal	29	64	6	—
Laundry and dry-cleaning operatives	15	54	4	b
Meat-cutters, except slaughter and packing house	29	63	6	—
Milliners	46	70	8	d
Mine operatives and laborers (n.e.c.)	10	49	2	c
Coal mining	2	25	1	a
Crude petroleum and natural gas extraction	38	67	7	—

Table 9.3. (continued)

Occupations, by Major Occupation Group	Socio-Economic Index	Transform to NORC Scale	Population Decile Scale	Notes
Mining and quarrying, except fuel	12	51	2	—
Motormen, mine, factory, logging camp, etc.	3	28	1	—
Motormen, street, subway, and elevated railway	34	65	7	a
Oilers and greasers, except auto	15	54	4	—
Painters, except construction and maintenance	18	57	5	—
Photographic-process workers	42	68	8	—
Power-station operators	50	71	9	—
Sailors and deck hands	16	55	4	—
Sawyers	5	39	1	—
Spinners, textile	5	39	1	—
Stationary firemen	17	56	4	—
Switchmen, railroad	44	69	8	—
Taxicab-drivers and chauffeurs	10	49	2	a
Truck- and tractor-drivers	15	54	4	a
Weavers, textile	6	42	1	—
Welders and flame-cutters	24	61	6	—
Operatives and Kindred Workers (n.e.c.)	18	57	4	c
Manufacturing	17	56	4	a, c
Durable goods				
Sawmills, planing mills, and misc. wood products.	7	44	2	c
Sawmills, planing mills and mill work	7	44	2	—
Miscellaneous wood products	9	46	2	—
Furniture and fixtures	9	48	2	—
Stone, clay and glass products	17	56	4	c
Glass and glass products	23	60	6	—
Cement; and plaster gypsum; and plaster products	10	48	2	—
Structural clay products	10	48	2	—

Table 9.3. (continued)

Occupations, by Major Occupation Group	Socio-Economic Index	Transform to NORC Scale	Population Decile Scale	Notes
Pottery and related products	21	59	5	—
Misc. nonmetallic mineral and stone products	15	54	4	—
Metal industries	16	55	4	c
Primary metal industries	15	54	4	c
Blast furnaces, steel works, and rolling mills	17	56	4	—
Other primary iron and steel industries	12	51	2	—
Primary nonferrous industries	15	54	4	—
Fabricated metal ind. (incl. not spec. metal)	16	55	4	c
Fabricated steel products	16	55	4	—
Fabricated nonferrous metal products	15	54	4	—
Not specified metal industries	14	53	3	d
Machinery, except electrical	22	60	6	c
Agricultural machinery and tractors	21	59	5	—
Office and store machines and devices	31	64	6	—
Miscellaneous machinery	22	59	6	—
Electrical machinery, equipment, and supplies	26	62	6	—
Transportation equipment	23	60	6	c
Motor vehicles and motor vehicle equipment	21	59	5	—

Table 9.3. (continued)

Occupations, by Major Occupation Group	Socio-Economic Index	Transform to NORC Scale	Population Decile Scale	Notes
Aircraft and parts	34	65	7	—
Ship and boat building and repairing	16	55	4	—
Railroad and misc. transportation equipment	23	60	6	—
Professional and photographic equipment and watches	29	63	6	c
Professional equipment and supplies	23	60	6	—
Photographic equipment and supplies	40	68	8	—
Watches, clocks, and clock-work-operated devices	28	63	6	—
Miscellaneous manufacturing industries	16	55	4	—
Nondurable goods				
Food and kindred products	16	55	4	c
Meat products	16	55	4	—
Dairy products	22	59	6	—
Canning and preserving fruits, vegetables, and sea foods	9	47	2	—
Grain-mill products	14	53	4	—
Bakery products	15	54	4	—
Confectionery and related products	12	51	2	—
Beverage industries	19	58	5	—
Misc. food preparations and kindred products	11	50	2	—
Not specified food industries	19	57	5	—
Tobacco manufactures	2	26	1	—
Textile mill products	6	42	1	c
Knitting mills	21	59	5	—
Dyeing and finishing textiles, exc. knit goods	8	45	2	—
Carpets, rugs, and other floor coverings	14	53	4	—
Yarn, thread, and fabric mills	2	26	1	—

Table 9.3. (continued)

Occupations, by Major Occupation Group	Socio-Economic Index	Transform to NORC Scale	Population Decile Scale	Notes
Miscellaneous textile mill products	10	49	2	—
Apparel and other fabricated textile products	21	59	6	c
Apparel and accessories	22	60	6	—
Miscellaneous fabricated textile products	17	56	4	—
Paper and allied products	19	57	5	c
Pulp, paper, and paperboard mills	19	58	5	—
Paperboard containers and boxes	17	56	4	—
Miscellaneous paper and pulp products	19	58	5	—
Printing, publishing, and allied industries	31	64	6	—
Chemicals and allied products	20	59	5	c
Synthetic fibers	9	47	2	—
Drugs and medicines	26	62	6	—
Paints, varnishes, and related products	15	54	4	—
Miscellaneous chemicals and allied products	23	60	6	—
Petroleum and coal products	51	71	9	c
Petroleum refining	56	72	9	—
Miscellaneous petroleum and coal products	14	53	3	—
Rubber products	22	60	6	—
Leather and leather products	16	55	4	c
Leather: tanned, curried, and finished	10	49	2	—
Footwear, except rubber	9	47	2	—
Leather products, except footwear	14	53	3	—
Not specified manufacturing industries	16	55	4	—

Table 9.3. (continued)

Occupations, by Major Occupation Group	Socio-Economic Index	Transform to NORC Scale	Population Decile Scale	Notes
Nonmanufacturing industries				
(incl. not reported)	18	57	4	c
Construction	18	57	5	—
Railroads and railway				
express service	15	54	4	—
Transportation, except				
railroad	23	60	6	—
Telecommunications, and				
utilities and sanitary				
services	21	59	5	—
Wholesale and retail trade	17	56	4	—
Business and repair services	19	57	5	—
Personal services	11	50	2	—
Public administration	17	56	4	—
All other industries (incl.				
not reported)	20	59	5	—
Private-Household Workers				
Housekeepers, private house-				
hold	19	58	5	c
Living in	10	49	2	d
Living out	21	59	5	—
Laundresses, private household	12	51	2	d
Living in	—	—	—	d
Living out	12	51	2	d
Private-household workers				
(n.e.c.)	7	44	2	c
Living in	12	51	2	—
Living out	6	42	1	—
Service Workers, except				
Private Household				
Attendants, hospital and other				
institution	13	52	2	—
Attendants, professional and				
personal service (n.e.c.)	26	62	6	—
Attendants, recreation and				
amusement	19	58	5	—
Barbers, beauticians, and				
manicurists	17	56	4	a
Bartenders	19	58	5	a

Table 9.3. (continued)

Occupations, by Major Occupation Group	Socio- Economic Index	Transform to NORC Scale	Population Decile Scale	Notes
Boarding- and lodging-house keepers	30	64	6	—
Bootblacks	8	46	2	a
Charwomen and cleaners	10	48	2	—
Cooks, except private household	15	54	4	a
Counter and fountain workers	17	56	4	a
Elevator operators	10	48	2	—
Firemen, fire protection	37	67	7	—
Guards, watchmen, and door-keepers	18	57	5	a
Housekeepers and stewards, except private household	31	65	7	—
Janitors and sextons	9	47	2	a
Marshals and constables	21	59	6	—
Midwives	37	67	7	d
Policemen and detectives	39	68	8	c
Government	40	68	8	a
Private	36	66	7	—
Porters	4	36	1	—
Practical nurses	22	59	6	—
Sheriffs and bailiffs	34	66	7	—
Ushers, recreation and amusement	25	61	6	—
Waiters and waitresses	16	55	4	a
Watchmen (crossing) and bridge-tenders	17	56	4	—
Service workers, except private household (n.e.c.)	11	50	2	—
Farm Laborers and Foremen				
Farm foremen	20	59	5	—
Farm laborers, wage workers	6	42	1	b
Farm laborers, unpaid family workers	17	56	4	—
Farm-service laborers, self-employed	22	60	6	—
Laborers, except Farm and Mine				
Fishermen and oystermen	10	49	2	b

Table 9.3. (continued)

Occupations, by Major Occupation Group	Socio-Economic Index	Transform to NORC Scale	Population Decile Scale	Notes
Garage laborers, and car-washers and greasers	8	46	2	—
Gardeners, except farm, and groundskeepers	11	50	2	—
Longshoremen and stevedores	11	50	2	b
Lumbermen, raftsmen, and wood-choppers	4	36	1	b
Teamsters	8	46	2	—
Laborers (n.e.c.)				
Manufacturing	8	45	2	c
Durable goods				
Sawmills, planing mills, and misc. wood products	3	33	1	c
Sawmills, planing mills, and mill work	3	34	1	—
Miscellaneous wood products	2	23	1	—
Furniture and fixtures	5	40	1	—
Stone, clay, and glass products	7	43	2	c
Glass and glass products	14	53	3	—
Cement; and concrete, gypsum, and plaster prod.	5	39	1	—
Structural clay products	5	39	1	—
Pottery and related products	7	44	2	—
Misc. nonmetallic mineral and stone products	5	38	1	—
Metal industries	7	44	2	c
Primary metal industries	7	44	2	c
Blast furnaces, steel works, and rolling mills	9	46	2	—

Table 9.3. (continued)

Occupations, by Major Occupation Group	Socio-Economic Index	Transform to NORC Scale	Population Decile Scale	Notes
Other primary iron and steel industries	4	37	1	—
Primary nonferrous industries	6	42	1	—
Fabricated metal ind. (incl. not spec. metal)	7	44	2	c
Fabricated steel products	7	44	2	—
Fabricated non-ferrous metal products	10	49	2	—
Not specified metal industries	9	46	2	d
Machinery, except electrical	11	50	2	c
Agricultural machinery and tractors	14	53	3	—
Office and store machines and devices	17	56	4	d
Miscellaneous machinery	10	48	2	—
Electrical machinery, equipment, and supplies	14	53	3	—
Transportation equipment	11	49	2	c
Motor vehicles and motor vehicle equipment	13	52	2	—
Aircraft and parts	15	54	4	—
Ship and boat building and repairing	2	28	1	—
Railroad and misc. transportation equipment	8	45	2	—
Professional and photographic equipment and watches	11	50	2	—
Professional equipment and supplies	10	49	2	d
Photographic equipment and supplies	16	55	4	d

Table 9.3. (continued)

Occupations, by Major Occupation Group	Socio-Economic Index	Transform to NORC Scale	Population Decile Scale	Notes
Watches, clocks, and clockwork-operated devices	—	—	—	d
Miscellaneous manufacturing industries	12	50	2	—
Nondurable goods				
Food and kindred products	9	47	2	c
Meat products	8	45	2	—
Dairy products	13	52	2	—
Canning and preserving fruits, veget., and sea foods	6	42	1	—
Grain-mill products	6	42	1	—
Bakery products	10	48	2	—
Confectionery and related products	10	48	2	—
Beverage industries	16	55	4	—
Misc. food preparations and kindred products	5	40	1	—
Not specified food industries	14	53	3	—
Tobacco manufactures	0	20	1	f
Textile mill products	3	33	1	c
Knitting mills	4	36	1	d
Dyeing and finishing textiles, ecx. knit goods	9	46	2	d
Carpets, rugs and other floor coverings	14	53	3	—
Yarn, thread, and fabric mills	1	22	1	—
Miscellaneous textile-mill products	6	41	1	d
Apparel and other fabricated textile products	9	47	2	c
Apparel and accessories	11	49	2	—
Miscellaneous fabricated textile products	6	42	1	d
Paper and allied products	7	43	2	c
Pulp, paper, and paperboard mills	6	41	1	—

Table 9.3. (continued)

Occupations, by Major Occupation Group	Socio-Economic Index	Transform to NORC Scale	Population Decile Scale	Notes
Paperboard containers and boxes	10	48	2	—
Miscellaneous paper and pulp products	8	45	2	—
Printing, publishing, and allied industries	23	60	6	—
Chemicals and allied products	8	45	2	c
Synthetic fibers	4	37	1	—
Drugs and medicines	22	60	6	d
Paints, varnishes, and related products	8	46	2	—
Miscellaneous chemicals and allied products	8	45	2	—
Petroleum and coal products	22	60	6	c
Petroleum refining	26	62	6	—
Miscellaneous petroleum and coal products	3	28	1	—
Rubber products	12	51	2	—
Leather and leather products	6	43	1	c
Leather: tanned, curried, and finished	2	28	1	—
Footwear, except rubber	10	49	2	—
Leather products, except footwear	12	51	2	d
Not specified manufacturing industries	8	45	2	—
Nonmanufacturing industries (incl. not reported)	7	44	2	b, c
Construction	7	43	2	—
Railroads and railway express service	3	34	1	—
Transportation, except railroad	9	47	2	—
Telecommunications, and utilities and sanitary services	6	43	1	—

294

Table 9.3.   (continued)

Occupations, by Major Occupation Group	Socio-Economic Index	Transform to NORC Scale	Population Decile Scale	Notes
Wholesale and retail trade	12	51	2	—
Business and repair services	9	47	2	—
Personal services	5	39	1	—
Public administration	7	43	2	—
All other industries (incl. not reported)	6	41	1	—
Occupation not Reported	19	57	5	—

a. One of 45 occupations used in deriving socio-economic index from predictors of NORC prestige ratings.

b. One of 16 occupations poorly or partially matched to NORC titles.

c. Occupation omitted from statistical analysis of 425 detailed occupations, because it is a grouping of specific titles listed below it.

d. Occupation omitted from statistical analysis of 425 detailed occupations, because census data are based on fewer than 100 sample cases (corresponding to an estimated population of fewer than 3,000 males).

e. Occupation omitted from statistical analysis. The census data do *not* pertain to current members of the armed forces, but to currently unemployed civilians whose last occupational experience was in the armed forces. The data for this occupation do *not*, therefore, describe soldiers, sailors, and related occupations.

f. The computed value of the socio-economic index for this occupation was −3. To avoid the inconvenience of having one index value with a negative sign, this index was arbitrarily changed to zero, which remains the lowest value in the table.

SOURCE: Albert J. Reiss, Jr., *Occupations and Social Status* (New York: The Free Press, 1961), pp. 263-75.

tions involved. Changes over a period of time would also affect the scores for a number of occupations. Nevertheless, the scale is a distinct advance in the description and measurement of occupational status. It is interesting to note, in passing, that the scale does demonstrate the overlap between white-collar and manual occupations, since some white-collar occupations score lower than some manual occupations.

An additional approach to the description and analysis of occupational status is to include the concept of *situs*. An occupational situs, or family, is a set of occupations whose status system may be viewed as a unit. The situs concept divides the occupational system into a series of relatively parallel status systems. Paul K.

Hatt proposes eight such situses, the political, professional, business, recreation and aesthetics, agriculture, manual work, military, and service. Each has its own status system, and mobility, when it occurs, is most likely to occur within a situs.[22] A later study by Richard T. Morris and Raymond J. Murphy utilizes a different set of situses based upon the functions performed in each situs for society.[23] These are represented in Fig. 9.1. The occupational titles in Fig. 9.1 were placed in the situses by a sample of undergraduate college students. The ambiguities in the placement of occupations on a prestige continuum can also be seen in this placement into situses. Another obvious problem posed by this approach is that some occupations perform functions in more than one situs. As Morris and Murphy suggest, the minister may be as concerned with teaching as the alleviation of distress and the milk-route man is both a salesman and a truck driver. They suggest that this is symptomatic of a changing occupational structure that is on the way to greater specialization.

Although the occupations included in the Morris-Murphy study are not meant to be inclusive, those in the study suggest that the situs concept, if it is to be used, must include the realization that some situses may have shorter or longer hierarchies than others. Using the Duncan socio-economic index, for example, we can see that the hospital attendant, the lowest ranked occupation in the health and welfare situs, is ranked higher than the lowest occupation in manufacturing. At the same time, the highest ranked occupations in the health and welfare situs are given higher scores than those in the manufacturing area. The situses themselves vary in terms of their outer status limits. Although Morris and Murphy state that situses should not be invidiously compared, there are obvious status differentials between situses.[24] The earlier discussion about the situational determinants of occupational status also supports the conclusion of differential status among situses. Reiss notes that there is a tendency for individuals to place occupations within the situs concept when occupations are being ranked, which suggests that the situses themselves are ranked.[25] The situs concept is thus a useful, but as yet undeveloped, addition to the understanding of occupational status.

[22]Paul K. Hatt, "Occupations and Social Stratification," *American Journal of Sociology*, LV, 6 (May, 1950), 533–43.

[23]Richard T. Morris and Raymond J. Murphy, "The Situs Dimension in Occupational Structure," *American Sociological Review*, XXIV, 3 (April, 1959), 231–39.

[24]"The Situs Dimension in Occupational Structure," p. 233.

[25]*Occupations and Social Status*, p. 46.

SITUSES

Prestige rank quartiles (Student Ratings)	1 Legal Authority	2 Finance & Records	3 Manufacturing	4 Transportation	5 Extraction	6 Building & Maintenance	7 Commerce	8 Aesthetics & Entertainment	9 Education & Research	10 Health & Welfare
STRATA 1	Supreme Court Justice, Lawyer	City Manager	Owner of a large factory	President of a railroad		Architect		Conductor of a symphony orchestra	College president	Physician, Minister
STRATA 2		Banker	Biologist for a pharmaceutical company	Airline pilot	Geologist in an oil company	Building contractor	Advertising executive, Commercial artist		Philosopher, County agricultural agent	Welfare worker
STRATA 3	Policeman	Book-keeper	Machinist		Farmer, Forest ranger		Manager of a hardware store	Radio announcer, Singer in a night club	Music teacher	Fireman
STRATA 4	Prison guard	Cashier in a restaurant	Restaurant cook	Mail carrier, Truck driver	Coal miner	Waiter in a restaurant, Garbage collector	Milk route man	Barber		

Fig. 9.1. Theoretical Situs Location of Selected Occupations and Empirical Location Made by Sample of Student Raters. "Arrows indicate that 25 per cent of the students placed the occupation in a situs other than that theoretically expected on the basis of situs definitions supplied. . . ."

SOURCE: Richard T. Morris and Raymond J. Murphy, "The Situs Dimension in Occupational Structure," *American Sociological Review*, XXIV, 2 (April, 1959), 237.

explanations of occupational status differences

An individual's occupation is a major determinant of his position within the stratification system. Reiss has suggested that characteristics of the work and the work situation contribute to the rankings assigned to occupations. Although prestige rankings are important indicators of the occupational status system, they represent only those characteristics of occupations as they are judged by some segment of the public involved in the prestige ranking process. The basic question to be considered is, Why do occupations occupy different positions within the stratification system itself? Why does a bank president, for example, have higher status than an airplane mechanic? In order to answer this basic question about the nature of the social order itself, two alternative explanations will be explored.

Perhaps the best known, and most often criticized, explanation for the differences in status is the "functional theory of stratification" as suggested by Talcott Parsons and fully articulated by Kingsley Davis and Wilbert Moore.[26] Davis and Moore approach stratification as a series of positions in society. Their concern is not with the specific individuals occupying those positions. A basic requirement for society is the placement and motivation of people in the social structure. The motivation must occur in two related ways. Individuals with appropriate skills must be motivated to fill the positions in which their skills can best be utilized. Once in the position, the motivation to carry out the duties of the position must be maintained.[27] The argument thus far suggests that society needs to have a variety of tasks performed for the society to exist and that individuals must be motivated to fill the positions that perform these tasks and then be motivated to perform the tasks once they are in the positions.

Any need for varying levels of reward would be eliminated if the duties associated with the various positions in society were all equally pleasant to perform, all equally important to societal maintenance, and all equally in need of the same ability and talent. Fortunately or unfortunately, this is not the case. Some positions are more pleasant than others. Some also are more important to the

---

[26]See Talcott Parsons, "An Analytical Approach to the Theory of Social Stratification," *American Journal of Sociology*, XLV, 3 (November, 1940), 841–62 and Kingsley Davis and Wilbert Moore, "Some Principles of Stratification," *American Sociological Review*, X, 2 (April, 1945), 242–49.

[27]Davis and Moore, "Some Principles of Stratification," p. 242.

society as a whole. At the same time, the amount of ability, training, and skill required in the various positions varies widely. Since
this is the case, a system of rewards must be established to act as
inducements to fill positions which hold varying amounts of intrinsic
appeal to the members of the society. A method for the differential
distribution of these rewards according to the positions must also be
developed.[28]

According to Davis and Moore, these rewards can take a
variety of forms. One type of reward is a contribution to the
individual's "sustenance and comfort." This, of course, would be
some form of material reward. A second form of reward is "contributions to humor and diversion." This would involve the intrinsic
enjoyment of the work and satisfying social relationships. A final
type of reward is "things that contribute to self-respect and ego
expansion." These rewards are the feeling of accomplishment in a
position and the sense that the position contributes to one's own and
general societal welfare. All three types of rewards are differentially
distributed according to position.[29]

The analysis thus far suggests that societal positions vary in
their importance, their demands in terms of ability, and their ease
of performance. The differences in their functional importance demand that society provide sufficient rewards to insure that the positions are filled competently. The less essential positions should not
compete with the more essential positions for personnel. If a position is easily filled, it does not have to be heavily rewarded. If a
position is hard to fill, the reward structure must be such that people are attracted to the position despite its difficulties.

Another important consideration is that there is a "differential
scarcity of personnel." The more scarce the personnel and the more
difficult and important the position, the higher the rewards must be.
The ability to fill a position can be acquired either through heredity
or training or some combination thereof. From this perspective, it
does not matter which source is operative, since it is the position
itself which must be filled and the requirements can include hereditary considerations, as well as the more democratic training requirements. The Davis-Moore "theory" thus involves considerations of
the differential importance of positions in society, variations in the
requirements of the positions, and differences in the kinds of abilities necessary to fill the positions. The positions are thus differen-

[28]Davis and Moore, "Some Principles of Stratification," p. 243.
[29]Davis and Moore, "Some Principles of Stratification," p. 243.

tially rewarded in order to insure their occupancy by competent personnel. The differential rewards lead to a stratified society.[30]

The Davis-Moore formulation has led to a continuing dialogue and debate, principally with Melvin Tumin.[31] Tumin questions the explanatory power of the functional approach and suggests that the term "functional importance" is itself ambiguous and difficult to apply. It is difficult to establish if long run or short run functional importance determines the rewards structure. Tumin notes that unskilled workers in a factory are as important as its engineers, since the workers must be present to produce the product. Davis responds to this criticism by noting that while it is difficult to determine the exact functional importance of a position, the general process occurs whenever a totalitarian nation determines where its financial and social resources should be utilized or when organizations decide which positions are important and which are not. At the same time, Davis suggests that Tumin overlooked the differential scarcity of personnel component—engineers are more difficult to replace than are unskilled workers.[32]

Tumin criticizes the Davis-Moore formulation from the standpoint that the potential for locating the best possible talent for difficult positions is minimized in a stratified society. A stratified society does not give equal access to opportunities to develop and demonstrate one's talents. Access to education, for example, depends on parent's wealth, rather than the potential of the person. Thus stratification in one generation limits the likelihood of discovering talent in the next. It also affects the motivational component of succeeding generations. In addition, according to Tumin, there is a noticeable tendency for elites to restrict access to their privileged positions.[33] To these criticisms Davis responds that it does not really matter how the valued positions are filled, so long as they are filled.[34] If a caste system decrees that positions are filled by inheritance and there is a belief in the appropriateness of the system, the fact that talent is not sought throughout all castes does not make any difference, because the higher position is valued as are the requirements for access to the position. At the same time, in another sense, it is unimportant if some potential talent is missed. If positions are filled adequately, the source does not matter. This is, of

[30]Davis and Moore, "Some Principles of Stratification," pp. 242–43.
[31]See Melvin Tumin, "Some Principles of Stratification: A Critical Analysis," *American Sociological Review*, XVIII, 4 (August, 1953), 387–94.
[32]Davis, "Reply," *American Sociological Review*, XVIII, 4 (August, 1953), 394.
[33]"Some Principles of Stratification: A Critical Analysis," pp. 388–89.
[34]Davis, "Reply," pp. 395–96.

course, contrary to democratic principles, but in terms of explaining stratification patterns, such principles are on a moral rather than analytical level. These statements do not deny some of the negative consequences of stratification but rather place them in the context of undesirable, but not inevitable, consequences of an inevitable system.

A third criticism raised by Tumin regards the nature of the training for the more highly rewarded positions. This training, according to the functional theory, involves some sacrifice on the part of the individual, a sacrifice that is later compensated for by the higher rewards of the more valued positions in society. Tumin suggests that any financial sacrifice is not usually borne by the individual undergoing the training, but by his parents, who have accumulated wealth in their own lifetime. At the same time, income not earned during the training period can be rather quickly "made-up" once the person is in the labor force. Tumin suggests that within a decade after professional school, for example, the professional will earn as much as he would have earned if he had been working during his training period and the succeeding decade. After his first decade, his earnings far outstrip those of his less well-trained cohorts.

In addition to the relatively quick process of catching up financially with those who have not undergone advanced training, Tumin also points out that:

> What tends to be completely overlooked, in addition, are the psychic and spiritual rewards which are available to the elite trainees by comparison with their age peers in the labor force. There is, first, the much higher prestige enjoyed by the college student and the professional-school student as compared with persons in shops and offices. There is, second, the extremely highly valued privilege of having greater opportunity for self-development. There is, third, all the psychic gain involved in being allowed to delay the assumption of adult responsibilities such as earning a living and supporting a family. There is, fourth, the access to leisure and freedom of a kind not likely to be experienced by the persons already in the labor force.[35]

To this criticism Davis responds that it in fact makes no difference who assumes the burden of the training period. The important point is that there is a burden. He also suggests that the criticism that the earning power of the well-trained person outstrips

[35]"Some Principles of Stratification: A Critical Analysis," p. 390.

that of the person who has not undergone the training is itself a confirmation of the functional theory. Differential rewards must be available for the more functionally important positions. At the same time, the fact that such training does involve psychic rewards reflects the fact that these psychic rewards are largely a reflection of the anticipated rewards to be obtained after the training is completed. Davis also suggests that while the status and reward system surrounding the student role might be relatively high in comparison with those not in the role, studying itself is burdensome. Many youths are unable or unwilling to undergo the difficulties of studying for the highly rewarded positions.[36]

An additional criticism of the functional theory is based on the motivation and reward system. Tumin suggests that additional motivational bases should be considered and that the rewards available are often unequally utilized. To this Davis responds that this is true, but it essentially makes no difference. Davis also notes that the original formulation includes the possibility of differing reward and motivational structures. A final criticism of Tumin's regards the inevitability and dysfunctionality of stratification.[37] Davis replies that the theory is not concerned with the indefinite or utopian future in terms of inevitability but rather with societies as they are found in the historical and contemporary world. He also notes that dysfunctions can and do exist but that in the case of Tumin's criticisms they revolve around the family rather than the differential positional rewards in terms of the inheritance of status.[38]

A later dialogue between Moore and Tumin reduces some of their areas of disagreement.[39] Tumin recognizes the general need for some differentiation of rewards; at the same time he questions the extent of the differentiation necessary. Moore more explicitly recognizes some additional components of dysfunctionality in a stratified system. The basic issue regarding the moral rightness of differential rewards remains—Tumin arguing that the possession of talent, itself an inherited condition from either the biological or sociological perspective, should not necessarily be more highly rewarded. Moore maintains that the factor of individual motivation and effort must also be considered in any reward system. This functional approach to the nature of a stratified society and the

[36]Davis, "Reply," p. 396.
[37]"Some Principles of Stratification: A Critical Analysis," pp. 391–93.
[38]Davis, "Reply," pp. 396–97.
[39]See Moore, "But Some Are More Equal Than Others," and "Rejoinder" and Melvin Tumin, "On Equality," *American Sociological Review*, XXVIII, 1 (February, 1963), 13–18, 26–28, and 19–26.

closely related occupational system thus remains an explanation of why positions must be rewarded unequally if persons are to be motivated to fill the positions. From this perspective, the inheritance or learning of the scarce talents becomes an irrelevant issue, since there is a differential distribution of such talent and those who possess greater amounts of some scarce talent must have some form of inducement to utilize the talent in ways societal values support. The form of inducement remains a point of contention. The contention on this point, however, exists far beyond the current debate.

Tumin's view is close to that of another major approach to stratification. The so-called conflict explanation of stratification, as exemplified by Marx's theory of control of wealth and of the means of production and Ralf Dahrendorf's theory of control of power, is based primarily on the assumption that those in power will try to remain in power and that the oppressed or less powerful will be in more or less continual conflict with the elite.[40] Gerhard Lenski, in a major attempt to bridge the gap between the functionalists and the conflict theorists, leans toward the conflict group.[41] His theoretical development will be used to contrast that of the functional school and at the same time will serve as the basis for an attempt to resolve the differences between the two approaches and to yield a more comprehensive view of the stratification process as it affects the occupational system.

After noting that men are obliged by nature to live with other people and that men almost always act on the basis of self-interest, Lenski notes that most desired objects are in short supply leading to competition for these objects. Like the functionalists, Lenski notes that men are unequally endowed with the attributes which lead to success in the competitive effort. Since men tend to follow habits and customs, the form of competition is likely to remain the same.[42] As societies developed, more or less coordinated efforts of the total society are directed toward common goals, even though this may harm individual members of the society. There is a general attempt to maintain political stability in more stratified societies or to maximize production in minimally stratified societies.[43]

A society will become more stratified as its survival needs are met more successfully and surpluses become available for distribution. According to this analysis, the distribution of the surplus

[40]See Dahrendorf, *Class and Class Conflict in Industrial Societies* (Stanford: Stanford University Press, 1959).
[41]See *Power and Privilege.*
[42]Lenski, *Power and Privilege*, pp. 25–32.
[43]Lenski, *Power and Privilege*, pp. 41–42.

valued items will be determined by the power structure of the society. A question not fully answered in this approach is the determination of the power structure in the first place. It would appear that power would be in the hands of those who perform valued functions for the society, such as the best hunter or fisherman or a religious leader. If this is the case, then at least a component of the functional theory would be operative at this level.

Since power determines the distribution of surpluses, it also then determines who has privileges in the society. According to Lenski, prestige is largely derived from privilege, privilege in this case being the differential opportunities available within the system. As technological advances occur, the power variable will grow in importance. In this formulation, the distribution of rewards in society (privilege and prestige) is a function of the distribution of power not of *system* needs. While functional inequality existed in "primitive" societies, the basis of the inequality shifts to the power system.[44]

In order to support this thesis, Lenski amasses an impressive array of historical data. These data indicate that the amount of inequality within a system will continue to increase, based upon the power variable, until the onset of industrialization. At this point in a society's history the trend is reversed, and the degree of inequality lessens as the middle classes emerge. Related to the general shift toward industrialization is the movement toward more constitutionalism in government. This also facilitates the development of the middle class. As further industrialization and the development of constitutional forms of government occurs, "for most members of industrial societies, *the occupational system . . .* is the chief determinant of power, privilege, and prestige."[45] This is essentially the same point noted at the outset of this chapter—the occupational system is the major determinant of status in industrialized societies. Lenski maintains that the occupational system is based upon power rather than functional importance in determining the stratification system in modern societies. In support of this position he notes the high level of many managerial salaries, which appear to be greater than that needed to insure adequate motivation.

The Lenski approach attempts to bridge the gap between the functional and conflict approaches to stratification. In this attempt both approaches are utilized in a sequential model moving from functional inequality in primitive societies to a power based system in preindustrial systems to essentially a combined system in the

[44]Lenski, *Power and Privilege*, pp. 44–63.
[45]Lenski, *Power and Privilege*, p. 346.

industrialized society. Lenski appears, however, to lean toward the power explanation rather than the functional approach in explaining societal stratification. Since the societal system is closely related to the occupational system, this approach can then be taken to indicate that the distribution of persons into occupations and the privileges and prestige derived therefrom are based largely upon their original (parent's) power within the system. The various occupations have differing amounts of power themselves leading to a maintenance of the system.

Walter Buckley's discussion of the functional theory lends credence to this interpretation. He states: "In other words, positions are determined on the whole by social inheritance, and only secondarily, *within this pattern*, by 'performance.' Although 'performance' by itself may be important, it is the *chance to perform* that is at stake here."[46] According to Buckley, the functional theory is not a theory of stratification, but a "theory of certain aspects of social differentiation and hierarchical organization. . . ."[47]

If Buckley's points are correct, a further *rapprochement* between the functional and conflict explanations is possible. Tumin and Lenski are undoubtedly correct in their assessment that parental position and power play a dominant role in educational and eventually occupational attainment. The data on intergenerational mobility, to be discussed, indicate that the majority of the labor force in modernized societies is at essentially the same level as its parents. At the same time, those who are mobile, in particular, and those who remain at the same general level are at the same time placed within the system according to the tenets of the functional theory. That is, once a person has gained entrance to an occupation, either by inheritance of the occupational level or further education than might have been expected according to his background, his movement or lack of movement within the system is based upon his performance, his contribution to the system, and the scarcity of his skills. In other words, once a person is in the labor force, many of the considerations of the functional theory are operative. This would appear to be particularly true for members of organizational hierarchies, where judgments about performance appear to be based on rational criteria. Thus the place of the individual within an organization depends upon the skills he possesses. The rewards of his position depend upon the importance of the position and the scarcity of personnel available to fill it. This assumes, of course, that he has

[46]Buckley, "Social Stratification and Social Differentiation," *American Sociological Review*, XXIII, 4 (August, 1958), 374.
[47]"Social Stratification and Social Differentiation," p. 370.

the required amount and kind of training, a function of his original placement within the social system.

These various explanations of the presence of a stratification system and the differentiation among occupations serve to illustrate the central thesis of this volume. Occupations are vitally affected by the broader social system and at the same time affect it. Further evidence to support this thesis is available in the analysis of social mobility.

mobility and occupations

Mobility is an important consideration in the nature of social systems as a whole, as in comparisons of caste and open class systems, and an important consideration for the analysis of occupations. The analysis of mobility in empirical research is increasingly and almost exclusively based on data about occupations. Mobility is usually approached from a number of dimensions.[48] One such dimension is the time phase of mobility. Here intergenerational mobility can be distinguished from intragenerational mobility, even though the two forms can exist simultaneously for individuals and collectivities. A second dimension of mobility involves its direction. Three separate but often related directional axes can be identified. The most commonly analyzed is vertical mobility, movement up or down within the stratification system. A second axis is a change in social function that does not involve a change in status, or horizontal mobility. The third axis is spatial mobility, change in the location of the occupation. While each of these axes is analytically distinct, they are frequently related in reality. Each also plays an important role in intergenerational and intragenerational mobility.

Caplow's discussion of the forms of mobility contains elements that should be considered in this analysis. A major point is that intragenerational vertical mobility can take a variety of forms. For example, a change in occupation has been a traditional means of moving up in the stratification system. At the same time, it is a relatively infrequent form inasmuch as there are limitations on the opportunities for such occupational shifts. Persons with professional or craft training are unlikely to change occupations and thus lose their educational investment. Seniority and tenure provisions also diminish the likelihood of occupational changes for many em-

[48]These distinctions follow those suggested by Caplow, *The Sociology of Work*, pp. 59–99.

ployees at all levels of large scale organizations. For lower level white-and-blue-collar workers occupational changes may be fairly common, particularly at the outset of the work career. In most cases, however, such job changes do not involve much vertical mobility.

According to Caplow, there are occupational groups that engage in occupational change to a relatively high degree and at the same time experience vertical mobility. He states:

> The careers of agents and brokers (outside large business bureaucracies), small proprietors, artists and entertainers, politicians, and salesmen are characterized by relatively frequent changes of employment and of specific occupational activity, accompanied by a tendency to move between related occupations. It is within this group that the sharpest short-run changes in income and prestige take place, and that the total range of social reward is greatest.[49]

Much of this sort of mobility involves occupations tied in one way or another to the communications system. Entertainers and athletes, for example, can demand extremely high incomes over short periods of time, after which they normally must change occupations at a financial loss to themselves. For most of the occupations subject to this form of status fluctuation publicity and personal contacts appear to be a prime force. In general, however, occupational change does not appear to be a major contributor to vertical mobility. Blau and Duncan, in a major analysis of mobility within the United States, conclude that where occupational changes do occur, the move is likely to be a short distance move rather than a long distance one. In the light of the trends discussed throughout this chapter, the place of occupational change as a component of vertical mobility will probably decline in importance in the coming years.

A second form of intragenerational mobility is promotion or demotion within an organizational hierarchy. Given the importance of organizational employment as a condition of contemporary occupations, this becomes a dominant component of the mobility process. While important, the promotional process is really meaningful only in terms of mobility within the executive-professional hierarchy of organizations. It has become extremely unlikely that a person will move from blue-collar or lower level white-collar positions into the executive-professional hierarchy, because of the educational prerequisites for the hierarchy. While the office boy to president or

---

[49]Caplow, *The Sociology of Work*, p. 63.

factory worker to plant manager image remains and many cases of this kind of promotion can still be found in the occupational system, today the system precludes such movement. Blau and Duncan note that there are two semipermeable lines that limit downward mobility between and within generations but permit upward mobility. These lines are between the blue- and white-collar occupations and between farm and manual occupations.[50] It would appear that the upward mobility in this case would almost exclusively come *between* generations. Given the rather universalistic standards of most organizations, the social origins of an individual should not be a hindrance to his mobility, if he has the prerequisites for such mobility. Within organizational hierarchies, the major such prerequisite is education. Once entrée to the hierarchy is gained at the outset of an individual's career, performance and other factors would be operative. The barrier between the organizational hierarchy and the rather undifferentiated lower level white- and blue-collar occupations is a real one within a generation. It can be crossed between generations, which opens up the possibility for mobility through promotions.

A final type of mobility within a generation, which can be identified, is that associated with a "normal" career. *Within* an occupation there is generally a normal progression that carries with it not only a higher income over a period of time but also some prestige, which accrues with the status of having seniority or tenure, being experienced, being an old-timer, and so on. Although there are limits to the extent to which advancing age is honored in Western societies, the normal career curve does carry with it some upward mobility.

The second major form of vertical mobility is that between generations. This form of mobility has been of particular interest because of the inferences that can be drawn from data on this form of mobility about the nature of the stratification system itself. High rates of intergenerational mobility are often taken as indicative of an open stratification system and a proper operation of the democratic system. In reality the relationship between the amount of intergenerational mobility and the openness of the system is not that simple. In the first place, there are some occupations which exhibit a high degree of occupational inheritance and, hence, low degree of mobility. Independent professionals, proprietors, and farmers "neither supply to other careers in the next generation or recruit from others in the last,"[51] according to Blau and Duncan. While this

[50] Blau and Duncan, *The American Occupational Structure*, pp. 58–59.
[51] *The American Occupational Structure*, p. 76.

contributes to occupational solidarity, it also diminishes the gross mobility rate. At the same time, the data of Blau and Duncan suggest that the lower level blue-collar and white-collar occupations supply a disproportionate amount of manpower to the occupational system. The occupations at the top have expanded while those at the bottom have contracted. This in and of itself is a major factor in the continued presence of upward mobility between generations in the United States.

Blau and Duncan's data on intergenerational mobility indicate that it increased in the 1952–1962 decade. Opportunities for mobility have thus increased during that decade. These data also indicate that the opportunity structure is greater for the United States than other Western countries. This is true for "distant moves," from working and manual classes into elite positions, and for the shorter move from other white-collar positions into elite.[52] While these considerations are valuable in terms of the opportunity structure and its relationship to societal values, they are less relevant for an understanding of the relationships between intergenerational mobility and the occupational system.

Blau and Duncan's research points out an important characteristic of intergenerational mobility. One usual component of the measurement of intergenerational mobility is father's occupation. The respondent is asked his own occupation and then that of his father. Differences between the socio-economic standing of each are taken to be gross indicators of mobility. Among the problems in such an approach the most severe is that the labor force itself changes in composition; some occupations decline and some grow. Farming, for example, turns out to be a dominant occupation among the fathers of adult males. As was discussed above, there has been an expansion of the labor force at the upper levels and a contraction at the lower levels, including farming. At the same time, farming undoubtedly was a higher status occupation in previous generations. Thus comparisons across generations encounter difficulties that make exacting measurement of this form of mobility difficult. A further difficulty is that at any point in time, both the respondents (sons) and their fathers are at different periods in their careers. This problem can be partially overcome in the case of the fathers by asking for the father's major occupation, but even here lack of knowledge or the real possibility that the father is still in the labor force and has not reached his major occupation make such comparisons less than perfect.

Blau and Duncan recognize the methodological problems in-

[52]Blau and Duncan, *The American Occupational Structure*, pp. 433–35.

volved in this sort of analysis. The severity of the problem is lessened in their analysis by their important shift in the conceptualization of the impact of the father's occupation. They point out that the knowledge of father's occupations of a sample of 20,000 men in the labor force in 1962 does not yield distinctive socio-economic groupings of fathers for the reasons noted above. This knowledge does, however, give good insights into the *social origins* of the sons.[53] This, after all, is really the important issue. What is important in terms of intergenerational mobility is the extent of movement from social origins on the part of the son. In this way historical changes in the occupational structure have less impact on the measurement. Rather obviously, intergenerational and intragenerational mobility are interrelated. If a person moves up or down from his social origins, he is exhibiting both kinds of mobility. An important distinction, necessary here, is the idea of the first job. An individual, through education for example, may achieve a relatively high level first job after which he exhibits little upward movement. This would be an example of intergenerational mobility without intragenerational mobility. The son of any army officer who achieves the same rank in his own lifetime would exhibit intragenerational mobility without the intergenerational form. In most cases the interrelatedness of the two forms exists.

In summarizing their findings in regard to intergenerational mobility, Blau and Duncan conclude:

> A man's social origins exert a considerable influence on his chances of occupational success, but his own training and early experience exert a more pronounced influence on his success chances. The zero-order correlations with occupational status are 0.32 for father's education, 0.40 for father's occupation, 0.60 for education, and 0.54 for first job. Inasmuch as social origins, education, and career origins are not independent, however, their influence on ultimate occupational achievements are not cumulative. Thus the entire influence of father's education on son's occupational status is mediated by father's occupation and son's education. Father's occupational status, on the other hand, not only influences son's career achievements by affecting his education and first job, but it also has a delayed effect on achievements that persists when differences in schooling and early career experience are statistically controlled. Although most of the influence of social origins on occupational achievements is mediated by education and early experience, social origins have a

continuing impact on careers that is independent of the two variables pertaining to career preparation. Education exerts the strongest direct effect on occupational achievements . . . with the level on which a man starts his career being second. . . .[54]

A major exception to the impact of education is the Negro; the better educated Negro does not achieve occupational status to the degree predicted from the model. In fact, the better educated Negro is less mobile than the poorly educated Negro. Blau and Duncan suggest that the effects of discrimination are more pronounced for the better educated Negro, since his movement would be up into occupations long dominated by whites.

Blau and Duncan's findings indicated that there is a high rate of occupational inheritance and that what movement there is tends to be into adjacent occupational status categories. Table 9.4 indicates the percentages of sons of each social origin supplied to the various occupations in 1962. Table 9.5 indicates the proportion of the men in each occupational category recruited from the various occupational origins. The categories of salaried professional and manager, for example, receive members disproportionately from the lower level white-collar groups. These occupations have expanded, with 18 per cent of the sons in these occupations and only 6.5 per cent of the fathers. In terms of recruitment, it is evident from Table 9.5 that farmers have supplied a disproportionate number of sons to the rest of the labor force and that sons of proprietors are also supplied to the more highly ranked occupations. The potential for mobility is strongly associated with changes in the over-all occupational structure.

Horizontal and spatial mobility are generally closely related to vertical mobility. As has been discussed above, job changes are an important component of the vertical mobility process. At the same time, geographical mobility is also a component of this process. Blau and Duncan found that: "immigration has in recent decades become increasingly effective as a selective mechanism by which the more able are channeled to places where their potential can be realized."[55] Spatial mobility has in many ways become a prerequisite for vertical mobility. The obvious exception is the self-employed professional, proprietor, or farmer.[56] Another exception is the rural migrant to the large city who is likely to fare more poorly than the

[54] *The American Occupational Structure*, pp. 402–3.
[55] *The American Occupational Structure*, p. 274.
[56] See Jack Ladinsky, "Occupational Determinants of Geographic Mobility Among Professional Workers."

Table 9.4. Mobility from First Job to Occupation in 1962, for Males 25-64 Years Old: Ratios of Observed Frequencies to Frequencies Expected on the Assumption of Independence

First Job	Respondent's Occupation in 1962																
	1	2	3	4	5	6	7	8	9	10	11	12	13	14	15	16	17
Professionals																	
1 Self-employed	37.3	2.5	0.2	1.5	0.4	0.2	0.0	0.2	0.1	0.0	0.1	0.0	0.0	0.0	0.6	0.0	0.4
2 Salaried	4.5	5.4	1.6	0.9	0.8	0.8	0.2	0.2	0.3	0.1	0.1	0.2	0.2	0.0	0.1	0.2	0.1
3 Managers	0.9	2.0	4.5	1.4	1.3	1.1	1.5	0.3	0.6	0.6	0.2	0.2	0.2	0.3	0.3	0.1	0.2
4 Salesmen, other	0.4	0.8	3.2	7.6	1.8	0.8	1.8	0.1	0.5	0.3	0.5	0.5	0.5	0.0	0.0	0.1	0.0
5 Proprietors	0.6	0.7	2.4	2.0	5.2	0.4	1.7	0.2	0.3	0.1	0.4	0.6	0.5	0.4	0.5	0.7	0.0
6 Clerical	1.1	1.3	2.2	2.3	0.8	2.9	1.2	0.6	0.6	0.5	0.6	0.6	0.8	0.5	0.4	0.2	0.1
7 Salesmen, retail	1.4	1.0	2.0	2.3	1.7	1.9	3.3	0.6	0.7	0.6	0.6	1.0	0.6	0.5	0.4	0.2	0.0
Crafts																	
8 Manufacturing	0.6	0.9	1.0	0.8	1.7	0.7	0.5	3.1	1.0[1]	0.9	0.9	0.5	0.7	0.4	0.9	0.4	0.0
9 Other	0.2	0.9	0.8	0.6	1.5	0.7	2.2	1.5	3.0	1.0	0.7	0.7	0.7	0.6	0.4	0.2	0.4
10 Construction	0.2	0.5	0.4	0.5	1.6	0.5	0.2	1.2	1.8	5.3	0.5	0.6	0.4	0.5	0.7	0.4	0.5
Operatives																	
11 Manufacturing	0.3	0.6	0.7	0.6	1.0	1.0[1]	1.1	1.9	0.9	0.9	1.9	1.0	0.9	1.5	0.8	0.4	0.3
12 Other	0.3	0.5	0.8	0.9	1.3	0.7	0.7	1.0[1]	1.5	1.4	1.0	2.0	1.1	0.7	1.0[1]	0.4	0.6
13 Service	0.3	0.7	0.6	0.4	0.9	0.8	0.8	0.5	0.9	1.3	1.3	1.0[1]	3.6	1.2	1.4	0.1	0.3
Laborers																	
14 Manufacturing	0.2	0.5	0.5	0.5	0.4	1.0[1]	0.8	1.5	0.7	0.8	1.8	1.2	1.3	3.8	1.5	0.3	1.0
15 Other	0.2	0.5	0.7	0.8	1.0	0.7	0.8	0.8	1.4	1.4	1.1	1.4	1.1	1.1	2.7	0.4	0.6
16 Farmers	0.2	0.2	0.3	0.6	0.5	0.5	0.8	0.6	0.8	1.1	0.8	0.7	0.9	0.7	0.8	7.0	3.0
17 Farm laborers	0.1	0.2	0.3	0.2	0.7	0.4	0.7	0.7	0.9	1.1	1.0	1.2	1.1	1.3	1.6	3.7	4.1

[1] Rounds to unity from above (other indices shown as 1.0 round to unity from below).

SOURCE: Peter M. Blau and Otis Dudley Duncan, *The American Occupational Structure* (New York: John Wiley & Sons, Inc., 1967), p. 34.

Table 9.5. Mobility from Father's Occupation to Occupation in 1962, for Males 25-64 Years Old: Inflow Percentages

Father's Occupation	Respondent's Occupation in 1962																
	1	2	3	4	5	6	7	8	9	10	11	12	13	14	15	16	17
Professionals																	
1 Self-Employed	14.5	3.9	1.5	3.8	0.8	0.8	1.1	0.3	0.3	0.6	0.3	0.3	0.4	0.2	0.6	0.5	0.6
2 Salaried	7.0	9.5	4.9	5.8	2.1	3.8	3.4	1.6	1.9	0.6	2.1	2.1	1.9	1.4	0.4	0.5	0.3
3 Managers	8.7	7.9	8.7	7.0	4.0	4.4	2.6	2.7	2.6	2.2	1.4	1.2	1.0	1.8	0.7	0.3	0.3
4 Salesmen, Other	5.6	3.4	5.2	8.1	2.6	1.7	4.4	0.8	1.5	0.8	0.5	1.0	0.6	0.0	0.4	0.4	0.3
5 Proprietors	18.5	9.6	16.5	13.2	16.3	7.1	15.2	3.5	5.2	5.7	3.7	3.4	3.7	1.6	2.0	1.5	1.6
6 Clerical	4.9	7.3	4.4	5.9	2.3	4.5	2.6	2.9	3.1	1.2	1.2	1.9	3.2	1.5	1.3	0.8	0.0
7 Salesmen, Retail	0.9	2.3	3.0	4.7	2.8	1.8	2.9	1.4	0.8	1.1	1.5	1.1	1.4	0.1	1.2	0.7	0.0
Craftsmen																	
8 Manufacturing	3.8	8.3	6.1	4.3	5.1	5.7	6.3	12.0	5.1	5.1	6.2	4.7	4.8	4.5	3.2	0.5	0.4
9 Other	4.0	7.0	7.4	7.9	6.0	8.0	6.1	6.9	11.0	5.8	5.3	7.8	5.4	3.8	4.1	1.2	1.2
10 Construction	3.0	3.2	4.4	4.1	5.8	6.2	2.6	6.9	5.5	13.7	3.6	3.9	4.6	2.6	4.9	0.8	1.8
Operatives																	
11 Manufacturing	5.2	6.4	5.1	6.5	6.1	7.5	7.1	12.9	7.7	4.9	13.7	6.9	7.1	14.5	6.3	1.2	2.8
12 Other	2.8	7.5	4.2	5.4	6.2	6.7	6.0	6.5	8.6	6.6	6.9	10.9	7.1	6.5	6.4	1.2	4.4
13 Service	2.3	3.7	4.0	4.8	3.7	6.3	5.3	4.8	3.9	4.7	5.1	4.6	8.2	5.4	3.3	0.8	0.6
Laborers																	
14 Manufacturing	0.0	1.0	1.2	0.4	0.8	1.3	0.8	2.6	1.5	1.0	3.2	2.2	3.0	5.9	2.4	0.6	0.9
15 Other	1.0	2.0	1.9	3.3	2.1	6.0	4.7	4.5	4.8	4.8	5.3	5.9	6.2	6.7	9.6	0.7	2.8
16 Farmers	11.2	10.8	13.3	10.1	24.3	18.3	17.6	20.1	24.4	30.4	26.6	29.4	22.8	29.5	32.6	82.0	59.7
17 Farm Laborers	0.3	0.5	0.9	0.5	1.5	1.5	2.1	2.3	2.4	3.1	3.4	3.7	3.6	3.9	5.6	2.9	14.5
18 Total¹	100.0	100.0	100.0	100.0	100.0	100.0	100.0	100.0	100.0	100.0	100.0	100.0	100.0	100.0	100.0	100.0	100.0

¹Columns as shown do not total 100.0, since men not reporting father's occupation are not shown separately.

SOURCE: Peter M. Blau and Otis Dudley Duncan, *The American Occupational Structure* (New York: John Wiley & Sons, Inc., 1967), p. 39.

native of the large city or his rural counterparts who do not move.[57]

The discussion thus far has centered on structural aspects of mobility. The importance of these structural factors, such as amount of education or the socio-economic origins of the individual, for mobility has been clearly demonstrated. At the same time, the motivational factor should not be overlooked. While not the central concern of this book, differing kinds and levels of motivation are undoubtedly important for almost all facets of occupational life. In terms of mobility, Lenski's work regarding the differential impact of religious beliefs has already been cited. A study by Harry J. Crockett Jr. suggests that the strength of the achievement motive is clearly related to upward mobility among sons of lower strata fathers, but not among sons of upper strata fathers. For this latter group education, a structural factor in our terms, appears to be the crucial variable.[58] At the present time it is almost impossible to determine the relative importance of motivational *vis à vis* structural considerations in terms of their impact on mobility. Certainly motivation is important for the individual in his educational attainments. It would also play a role in determining his willingness to be spatially mobile. At the same time, structural factors appear to play a major role in the formation of differential motivation.

In a study of working-class youths Krauss found that higher aspirations in regard to education were present among boys whose mothers have higher status jobs or come from higher status origins than their fathers. The peer relationships of the youths also played a role in their motivational structure. Those who had family members or friends who attended or were planning to attend college had higher educational aspirations.[59] The linkage of the individual to the social structure through the family or friendship ties thus affected the motivational level. The issue in regard to the importance of motivational versus structural determinants of mobility thus remains open. A more appropriate perspective on the issue would be to view the two factors as interdependent as is suggested by the evidence available. The present state of knowledge in this regard does not allow determination of the exact contribution of either factor to mobility or stability patterns. The emphasis on structural factors taken here does reflect, however, the author's own orientation on this matter.

[57]Blau and Duncan, *The American Occupational System*, p. 272.
[58]Harry J. Crockett, Jr., "The Achievement Motive and Differential Occupational Mobility," *American Sociological Review*, XXVII, 2 (April, 1962), 191–204.
[59]See Irving Krauss, "Educational Aspirations Among Working Class Youths."

In order to understand more fully the components of intragenerational mobility, approaches to the patterning of careers will be discussed. This will provide additional insights into the factors which promote or impede mobility. Miller and Form provide a useful description of the phases of careers.[60] The first or *preparatory* phase is the period in school and family in which the individual begins to develop the behaviors and attitudes he takes into the occupational system. The second phase is the *initial* period of part- and full-time jobs during the educational process itself. These jobs are viewed as temporary but again have relevance for the development of behaviors and attitudes important in the full-time occupation. According to Miller and Form, this period provides the individual with important expectations and orientations relevant to his career.

The third phase of the career is the *trial* period in which the person gets his first full-time job. The period continues, with rather frequent job changes, until the person secures a more or less permanent position (Miller and Form suggest that three or more years represents permanence). During this period the individual develops distinctive career orientations, ranging from ambition to resignation and defeat. The factors which lead to these differing orientations are unfortunately not specified. The point that orientations are probably set in this period does seem to be correct, however. The fourth, or *stable*, period is characterized by real job permanence in which the individual develops strong ties to his position and the related social structure. The stable period continues until death, retirement, or a change in jobs. If job change occurs, a new trial period is entered. The final *retirement* period is affected by work experiences but is also a distinct period in that new adjustments must be made.

The Miller and Form framework allows categorizations of individuals within their careers and identifies career related factors contributing to the presence or absence of mobility. The framework does not allow the determination of the factors associated with differing mobility patterns, but it is somewhat useful as a means of ordering information about careers.

A more analytical approach to the nature of careers is taken by James D. Thompson, Robert W. Avery, and Richard Carlson.[61]

[60]*Industrial Sociology*, pp. 539–604.
[61]See *Occupations, Personnel and Careers* (Pittsburgh: Administrative Science Center, University of Pittsburgh, 1962).

They note that careers are actually unfolding sequences of jobs usually related to each other. Most careers are orderly, in that the various jobs in a career utilize skills, training, and experience related to each other. Disrupted careers occur when occupations not related to each other are part of the individual's history. According to this formulation, careers have three bases. The first factor in a career is the competence of the individual. A second factor is the aspirational pattern of the individual. Aspirations are important both in terms of their direction, toward work or family for example, and their strength. The third factor in careers is the structure of opportunities as perceived by the individual. While the actual job market sets limits, the relevant factor is the belief of the individual in regard to his place within it. The competence, aspiration level, and structure of the job market factors contribute to the patterns followed by the individual in the course of his career.[62]

These factors are modified by the orientation of the individual toward his career, according to this formulation. He can adopt one of four career strategies. The "heuristic" strategy is one oriented toward advancement, without regard to organizational or occupational boundaries. The individual is oriented toward personal attainment as he defines it. A second strategy is tied to the occupation. The individual is sensitive to opportunities within his occupation and does not consider organizational boundaries to be important. The "organizational" strategy is concerned with opportunities within the employing organization, without strong ties to a particular occupation. The "stability" strategy is one in which considerations of another job are irrelevant for the individual, representing resignation or satisfaction with the present position. The authors correctly note that these strategies may shift over the course of a career. The strategies may also be consciously or unconsciously adopted.[63]

Careers are vitally affected by the source of the occupational role definition. For many occupations the role is defined by the employing organization or enterprise. It sets the job requirements and the duties and responsibilities of each position. For other occupations, of course, definition of the occupational role lies within the occupation itself, as in the case of the professions. Organizations generally adopt such occupations into their job structure, "rather

[62]Thompson, Avery and Carlson, *Occupations, Personnel and Careers*, pp. 5–6.
[63]Thompson, Avery and Carlson, *Occupations, Personnel and Careers*, pp. 12–14.

than creating them."[64] Another basic consideration in a career is the progression within an occupation. Here Thompson, Avery, and Carlson identify two forms of progression. The "early-ceiling" occupation is one in which the pinnacle or ceiling in the career is reached at an early phase in the career. The machine operator or secretary can attain the top skill and salary levels within a short time on the job and expect to stay at the same level. The "late-ceiling" occupation, on the other hand, contains possibilities for advancement in later stages of the career.[65]

On the basis of the source of the occupational role definition and the form of progression within a career, four basic career patterns can be identified. The *enterprise defined-early ceiling* career involves little advance preparation for the career and rather minimal skill and aptitude expectations. The individual going into this type of work adopts the heuristic strategy at the outset of his career as he shops around between jobs and organizations. As he attains seniority and responsibilities, this will shift to an organizational strategy and then to one of stability. The *enterprise defined-late ceiling* occupation is typified by the executive. Advanced education is generally a prerequisite. After finishing his formal education, he will generally develop the heuristic strategy as he looks for the best opportunities for his skills. After this he utilizes the organizational strategy and changes jobs within his organization until his personal ceiling is reached or his aspirations are satisfied, at which time the stability strategy is adopted.

The colleague-defined occupations are also late and early ceilinged. The *early ceiling-colleague defined* career is characterized by skills transferrable from organization to organization but also rather standardized in terms of the rewards offered. Nurses, teachers, and technicians exemplify this category in that merit is evaluated by the occupation itself and by occupations that are themselves given higher ranking (medical doctors or engineers, for example). Since the ceiling is achieved early in the career, any movement which does occur is usually based on an attempt to improve living conditions or other nonwork activities. The occupational strategy is followed at the outset of the career with a typically early shift to the stability strategy. As in the case of the early-ceiling enterprise defined group, further advancement is sought through collective

[64]Thompson, Avery and Carlson, *Occupations, Personnel and Careers*, p. 18.

[65]Thompson, Avery and Carlson, *Occupations, Personnel and Careers*, pp. 16–20.

action in the form of unions or professional associations once the stable strategy is employed. The final pattern is the *colleague defined-late ceiling* occupation, exemplified by the professions. Once the person has met the prerequisites for entrance to the occupation, the limits to his profession are few, assuming that aspirations and perceived opportunities remain high. The authors note that there really is no assurance that skill levels are maintained among this group but that once a person is a member of the occupation it is assumed that he has the required skills. This type will adopt the occupational strategy which will continue until rather late in life, when the stability strategy is adopted. An exception to this is in the case of professionals who are dependent upon clients, where the stability strategy is adopted rather early, even though the ceiling for the individual comes later in life.[66]

These orderly patterns are typical of most careers. Disrupted careers occur when these patterns are altered, as in the case of a person who moves from a colleague defined occupation to an enterprise defined position. The nurse or teacher who goes into administration exemplifies this. According to the authors, this sort of disruption is likely when the occupation has an early ceiling, when the individual lacks confidence in his ability to remain visible within his occupation, or when there is a demand for rewards that cannot be anticipated in the occupation. As might be expected, the individual can face problems in these cases if he has a strong attachment to his occupation. Another disrupted pattern is from enterprise to colleague definition. This is a rare pattern, but occupations in the process of professionalization may place their members in this situation. A final form of the disrupted career is the "late heuristic strategy." In this case the individual takes a position entirely different from those which have preceded it, as in the case of retired generals or diplomats who become college presidents, or bankers or business executives who become members of presidential cabinets. This type of disruption is very dependent upon visibility within the social system and is again rare.[67]

The identification of these forms of career patterns has served to specify some of the considerations which are part of the mobility process. It can be concluded that the social origin of the individual and his educational background have the greatest impact on his subsequent career, as was found to be the case for mobility in

[66]Thompson, Avery and Carlson, *Occupations, Personnel and Careers*, pp. 20–32.

[67]Thompson, Avery and Carlson, *Occupations, Personnel and Careers*, pp. 33–40.

general. Careers are thus tied directly to the social structure, both in terms of the factors which define the careers and those which determine the pattern that it takes.

summary and conclusions

Two themes have provided the basis for this chapter. The first is the obvious one that the occupational structure is a major determinant of the social stratification system. It has been demonstrated that occupations have become more important as status determinants than other considerations and that occupational rank is closely associated with other means of ranking, such as education or income. Occupations are central, therefore, in conceptual and methodological approaches to stratification. The second major theme is that the stratification system itself vitally affects occupations. The social origins of an individual play a major role in the determination of his eventual occupational placement. The social system and the occupational system as part of the broader system are thus in a two directional interaction process. An important consideration in this relationship is the linkage between the two systems. This linkage is largely provided by the family and educational systems, the next topics to be considered.

chapter   10

family and education

For the individual the importance of and relationships between family and educational socialization patterns for his occupational life are probably already quite clear. The centrality of the family in the general socialization process has been documented to the point where the issue is one of detail rather than substance. Similarly the importance of education as both preparation and prerequisite for occupational life is well established. The intent of this chapter is not to belabor these points but to discuss some aspects of the relationships not yet covered. The family will be treated from the perspective of change. The changing occupational system has brought about changes in the family and vice versa. In this section the place of women in the occupational context will also be discussed. This placement may offend some ardent neofeminists but seems logical given both the value system and empirical data. Education will also be viewed on the basis of its compatability or incompatability with the occupational system.

the family

The closeness of the relationship between the occupational and familial systems can be seen from the perspective of the historical changes that have occurred. The extended family has been the dominant family form throughout history. This form involves the presence of minors, their parents, and combinations of adult siblings, grandparents, aunts and uncles, and in-laws within the same effective family unit. The exact form such a family takes depends on the cultural context, which prescribes the line of descent and place of residence. The specific form is less important, however, than the fact that the extended family is well suited to societies in which agriculture or crafts dominate the occupational structure. In the agricultural setting a relatively exacting division of labor can be established wherein each family member has specified tasks to perform. These tasks are learned in the general family socialization process and are thus only analytically separable from general family roles. As the individual passes through the life cycle his specific tasks change according to the ascribed tasks to be performed by his age cohort. Sexual ascription occurs in a similar fashion. For craft technologies the family is also an effective work group. Many crafts involve idiosyncratic methods and trade-secrets effectively transmitted in the family context. The apprentice-master relationship lends itself to the family setting very easily. The same general factors are operative in the small family business or proprietorship.

This family form was almost totally compatible with nonindustrial occupations. In many cases the products of the farm or craft were consumed on the spot or in the local area. Little competition in the form of new techniques or ideas entered the picture. The advent of industrialization, either in the past as in the industrial revolution or currently for areas in the process of modernization, drastically affects the previous compatibility. As might be expected, it is typically the younger person who is at the forefront in experiencing and perhaps rebelling against the incompatibilities. He is usually the family member who is first to seek and find employment outside the home. When he does so, the opening wedge of change is brought into the family. As he earns money outside the home and is exposed to differing behaviors and values, as a consequence of contacts with a wider range of individuals, ties to the family are weakened. He may not want to turn over all of his income to the family, which is essentially what happened in the earlier system. He is also less dependent on the family. At the same time new behaviors or values he learns at work may well conflict with those of his family, which adds another source of discontent.[1]

As this pattern is repeated throughout a society, the family form itself evolves into the nuclear family, in which the unit is simply the husband and wife and minor children. Other members of the extended family are expected to maintain their own residences and affective units. Viewed from another perspective, this change appears to be inevitable, inasmuch as the extended family system contains a number of elements incompatible with the modern occupational system. In the extended family workers are almost totally selected by chance rather than by rational personnel practices. Since there is as yet no control over the genetic processes, the availability and quality of workers (children) is beyond the control of the work unit. At the same time, the inclusion of the aged and infirm in the extended family means that incapable workers may be part of the work force, despite the fact that their inclusion might provide important emotional gratifications for the individual involved. In the extended family system the workers are thus often those who are considered most marginal in the contemporary industrialized situation. The young and the old, both are a dominant part of the labor force.

In addition to personnel problems, the extended family as an occupational unit also contains some other incompatible elements when the contemporary occupational situation is considered. The span of generations and the general orientation toward tradition predisposes such a family against the introduction of technological change. Further inflexibilities are introduced by the fact that such a family can usually not be spatially mobile, an important requirement for both locating employment and maintaining it if such movement is demanded. The family system would also tend to limit the development of new skills for the occupations involved. The relatively small numbers of personnel involved make it unsuited to a highly developed division of labor.[2]

These incompatibilities were resolved largely by the growth of the nuclear family as the dominant family form concomitant with the move toward industrialization.[3] Vestiges of the extended family

[1]This discussion has generally followed the lines suggested by Caplow, *The Sociology of Work*, pp. 248–52.

[2]Caplow, *The Sociology of Work*, p. 251.

[3]Morris Zelditch, Jr. has noted a number of exceptions to this pattern in "Family, Marriage, and Kinship," in *Handbook of Modern Sociology*, ed. R. E. L. Faris (Chicago: Rand McNally & Company, 1964), pp. 724–25, but the basic relationship described appears to be the dominant pattern.

are still visible, especially among the upper classes, but the nuclear unit is clearly the dominant type. While the extended family form has largely disappeared, some of its elements remain in the face of industrialization and urbanization. For example, recent studies have shown that financial assistance and visiting patterns are still strongly tied to the extended family.[4] There is a strong expectation that the adult establish his own residence, but the expectation of maintenance of the ties remains. These ties do not interfere with the occupational system in that they are not incompatible with occupational expectations. The effective family unit remains the small nuclear group. The consequences of this for some groups in society are undoubtedly not as beneficial as they are in terms of the relationship with the occupational system. In the nuclear family system the aged, widowed, divorced, or "never married" person is largely cut off from ongoing family relationships. At the same time, these persons have more freedom of self-determination in their occupational life, whether they want it or not.

An additional component of the nuclear family, which should be noted, is its generally small size. For agricultural, craft, and some proprietorship pursuits, large numbers of children are an economic asset, since more workers are provided. In the industrialized and urbanized setting, however, large numbers of children become an economic liability. Children contribute little or nothing from their own "occupation" as students. At the same time they are an additional cost factor for the members of the occupational system. Large numbers of children also appear to limit the likelihood of spatial mobility for the parents. The nuclear family is thus in all probability the optimal arrangement for the contemporary occupational system. It could be argued that an even more compatible system would be an arrangement whereby some of the major family functions of the woman are carried out by nonfamily agencies, which would free her from the confines of the home. This assumes, of course, that the child rearing function can be satisfactorily handled in another fashion. Given the values surrounding the family and child rearing, it is unlikely that this will occur in any great proportion of families in the near future. The contemporary nuclear family is probably about as small a family unit as can be developed.[5] The patterns being discussed are particularly evident among the middle classes, especially in urbanized areas. As noted above, among some upperclass families the extended family norm

[4]Zelditch, "Family, Marriage, and Kinship," pp. 725–28.
[5]See Caplow, *The Sociology of Work*, p. 253.

remains. Rural patterns also appear to be following the older norms, although the birth rate differential between urban and rural areas is lessening. The well documented female dominance of the lower-class Negro family is also an exception. Many analyses of the latter situation point to the incongruities between this family form and the demands of the urban occupational system.

While the small nuclear family is in general compatible with the occupational system, according to Parsons' analysis, the family system as a whole still contains elements incompatible with the occupational system. He notes that the occupational system is characterized by an emphasis on technical efficiency and acceptance of rational criteria. The family system, on the other hand, relies upon customary behavior and highly emotional relationships. Similarly, the occupational system utilizes objective and impersonal standards of performance, while the family utilizes status ascription based upon age and sex.[6] From another perspective this analysis points out the problems which would be involved in attempting to carry out contemporary occupational requirements within the family setting. An individual would be placed in the position of having to decide which set of norms to follow when either set might not meet the expectations of others in his role set.

This dilemma is at least partially resolved by the dominant arrangement, which is designed to insure that only one member of the family participates on a full-time basis in the occupational system. According to Parsons this allows the man to play the occupational role separate from the husband-father role. If the wife attempts the same sort of thing, damaging competition in the occupational roles is likely to ensue. Although this analysis points toward conflict as the probable consequence of both members of the marriage being in the labor force, the evidence in this regard is scanty. Ideally, research should match couples who work in the same occupation, who work in different occupations, and who only have the male working in order to determine differing patterns of conflict and accommodation which may exist. The author does know of a number of couples who have the same occupations and in whose case the wife tends to inhibit her occupational aspirations for the sake of her husband's. In some, the wife appears to be the more qualified, which reflects the prevailing value system for better or for worse (or for richer or for poorer).

[6]See Parsons "The Social Structure of the Family," in *The Family: Its Function and Destiny*, ed. R. N. Anshen (New York: Harper & Row, Publishers, 1949), pp. 190–96 and Talcott Parsons and Robert F. Bales, *Family, Socialization and Interaction Processes* (New York: The Free Press of Glencoe, Inc., 1955), pp. 12–13.

The analysis will now turn to a consideration of women's occupations. The data available suggests that an increasing proportion of women, and notably married women, are participating in the labor force. The impact of this on the family is at present unclear. The impact of this on the women involved has been the subject of a growing amount of speculation and debate. The purpose here is not to take sides on the issue of whether women should participate fully

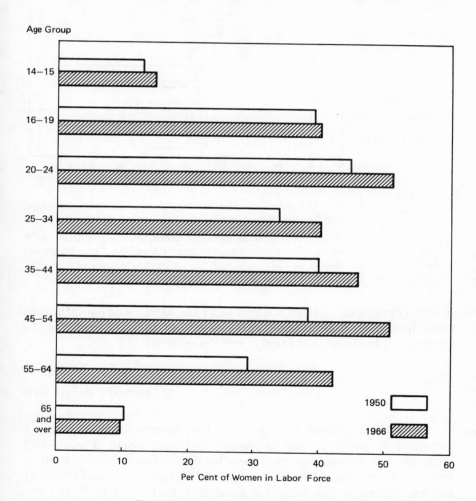

Fig. 10.1. Proportion of Mature Women Working Has Increased Sharply.

SOURCE: U.S. Department of Labor, Women's Bureau, *Utilization of Women Workers*, reprint from the *1967 Manpower Report*, p. 134.

Occupational Group

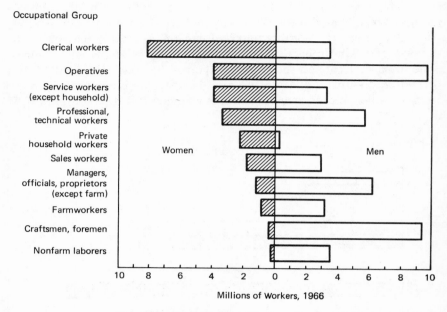

Fig. 10.2. Most Women Workers Are in Clerical, Operative, and Service Occupations.

SOURCE: U.S. Department of Labor, Women's Bureau, *Utilization of Women Workers*, reprint from the *1967 Manpower Report*, p. 136.

in the occupational system but to look at the extent and conditions of participation and to assess the evidence as to its effects on the woman, her husband, her family, and the system itself.

women's occupations

The most evident fact in regard to women is that they are increasingly participating in the occupational world. Figure 10.1 indicates the percentage increases by age category from 1950 to 1960. The largest increases in participation are clearly among mature women, which reflects a number of factors. A U. S. Department of Labor report states:

Women have moved into the work force in response, first of all, to the availability of jobs. At the same time, new appliances and services have freed women from many of their traditional chores in the home, and the rise in both living costs and the standard of living has impelled many women to seek paid jobs. Earlier marriage and lengthening of life span have extended the period when their interest in work outside the home is likely to be renewed. In addition, improved educational opportunities have raised women's qualifications as well as their aspirations for greater participation in the economic world.[7]

Before examining some of the factors associated with the greater participation, it is important to look at the nature of the participation. The most striking aspect of women's work is that it is concentrated in only a few occupations. Figure 10.2 illustrates this concentration as well as the contrasts with the dominant male occupations. The same Department of Labor report states:

> The limitations on the employment opportunities open to most women are suggested also by their occupations, which are, by and large, very different from those of men . . . Three out of every five women workers are in clerical, operative, or service jobs. About one-third of them are in just seven occupations (according to data from the 1960 census) : secretary, saleswoman, private household worker, elementary school teacher, bookkeeper, waitress, and professional nurse. Relatively few women are in professional and technical work. Fewer still are in managerial occupations, in which "only the exceptional, indeed the overqualified, woman can hope to succeed."[8]

Within some of these broad occupational categories, certain specific occupations stand out as woman's occupations. Among the professions and for college educated women, teaching, nursing, social work, and librarianship stand out as the dominant occupations which receive women. In sales work there is a definite sex segregation. Very few women sell automobiles, appliances, furniture, or sporting goods. Similarly, few men are found in toiletries or curtains and draperies. In some service occupations, such as restaurants or beauty shops, the top positions still seem to be dominated by men. Even in the same occupations women tend to receive lower wages than their male counterparts.

A major factor in the nature and conditions of women's work

---

[7] United States Department of Labor, *Manpower Report of The President* (Washington, D.C.: U.S. Government Printing Office, 1967), p. 134.
  [8] *Manpower Report of The President*, pp. 136–37.

is the family. The occupations heavily staffed by women tend to be those that can be entered and left. This relatively transitory status, particularly during the earlier phase of a potential career, is in many ways congruent with the occupations under discussion. In the professions, for example, there is in fact little opportunity for progression; the occupations are "early-ceilinged." If the individual leaves the field for marriage or childbearing, she can return to work at a later time without having lost very much in terms of progression in her field, except at the intellectual level. This fact, of course, operates against women who by choice or chance do not participate in the traditional family system. For these women the attitude is that they are part of a category that will act in a particular way. This is the rather common discriminatory pattern seen in the racial or religious spheres. The family is thus a salient factor for women themselves, their potential employers, and their colleagues at work whether in actuality or imagery.

Before continuing the analysis of the conditions of feminine employment, the nature and extent of work outside the home should be examined more intensively. Single women comprise the largest proportion of women in the labor force. Almost all women enter the labor force after they finish their education. They view their work as temporary. In a study of work patterns among a sample of English women, Viola Klein found that only 15 per cent of the single women wished to continue working permanently after marriage.[9] As Table 10.1 indicates, the distribution of persons wishing to continue on a part- or full-time basis does vary by occupational level. There is a fairly strong tendency for those in professional occupations to want to continue their employment permanently after marriage. At the same time, this group has the highest percentage of persons who wish to give up their employment at marriage, which probably indicates both the multiple work motivations involved and the heterogeneity of the category itself.

The most dramatic change in terms of women and occupation is the increase in employed married women. F. Ivan Nye and Lois W. Hoffman report that the percentage of married women in the labor force rose from 14.7 in 1940 to 30.5 in 1960. This accounts for most of the increase of women in the labor force. The increase is also seen among mothers. For those with school age children, labor force participation increased 116 per cent during these two decades. Participation of mothers of preschool children increased 108 per

[9]*Britain's Married Women Workers* (London: Routledge & Kegan Paul, Ltd., 1965), p. 50.

Table 10.1.   Plans for Continuity of Employment After Marriage, Classified by Type of Present Occupation

	Unskilled and Semiskilled	Skilled	Professional	Total
	%	%	%	%
Wishes to continue temporarily	48	60	32	50
Wishes to continue permanently	17	7	32	15
Wishes to continue in part-time job	1	5		3
Wishes to give up employment	28	24	32	28
Depends on husbands' finances	6	4	4	4
Total	100	100	100	100
Total in Numbers	54	55	22	137
			6 others	

ADAPTED FROM: Viola Klein, *Britain's Married Women Workers* (London: Routledge & Kegan Paul, Ltd., 1965), p. 51. (New York: Humanities Press, Inc.)

cent.[10] The general pattern of participation remains discontinuous, however, since the majority of women do leave the labor force for childbearing and child rearing through the preschool years.

An important factor for the married women, in addition to the vital variable of availability of work, is the attitude of their husbands. Klein's findings, summarized in Table 10.2, indicate a strong relationship between husband's approval of work and the fact of working. The family factor thus enters the occupational picture at the level of the dynamics of interaction between husband and wife. Klein's findings are interesting in terms of the distribution of approval and disapproval along social class lines. She states:

> There is a distinct class differentiation in the answers. The higher the social class, the greater the percentage of married men approving, both conditionally and unreservedly, of married women being gainfully employed. The largest percentage of expressed disapproval is to be found among [the lower classes] and among men whose

[10]Nye and Hoffman, *The Employed Mother in America* (Chicago: Rand McNally & Company, 1963), p. 8.

Table 10.2.   Men's Stated Views on Employment of Married Women (Classified by Marital Status and Type of Wives' Employment)

| Attitude to Married Women Having Jobs | Percentage of Married Men Whose Wives Have | | | | |
	Full-Time Job	Part-Time Job	No Paid Job	Total	Single Men
	%	%	%	%	%
Unconditional disapproval	14	4	45	32	28
Unconditional approval	52	42	11	23	31
Approval conditional on:					
there being no young children	19	14	18	17	15
household being in financial difficulties	5	14	8	9	7
not working too long	1	2	1	1	2
it being a part-time job		6	1	2	1
miscellaneous circumstances		7	2	3	2
Neutral: neither approves nor disapproves	2	4	4	4	3
Neutral: but specifically says it is up to wife	3	3	3	3	3
Neutral: but disapproves if there are young children	3	2	5	4	2
Don't know	1	1	2	2	5
Not stated					1
Total	100	100	100	100	100
Total in Numbers	104	118	422	644	287

SOURCE: Viola Klein, *Britain's Married Women Workers* (London: Routledge & Kegan Paul, Ltd., 1965), p. 66. (New York: Humanities Press, Inc.)

wives are not employed. The class distinction is, however, reversed among single men.[11]

The discrepancy between the responses of the married and single men, at least in the upper classes, is explained by Klein as probably resulting from the fact that the single men utilize their own mothers, who probably didn't work, as their models and have not had the interaction with women who desire to work.

[11]Klein, *Britain's Married Women Workers*, p. 67.

When the reasons for women working outside the home are analyzed, several distinct patterns can be seen. The first is that financial considerations are the major factor regardless of husbands' income or their own education. Tables 10.3 and 10.4 indicate these patterns. Table 10.3, based on the Klein study, shows that the importance of financial consideration increases as the women's socio-economic status decreases. Table 10.4, based on a sample of 1957 college graduates who were surveyed in 1964, shows the obvious relationship between marital status and working patterns. These figures also suggest the relativity of financial considerations. In this study, over half of the 1957 graduates were working in 1964. For those who were married the likelihood is that their husbands' incomes were reasonably high, since most would also be college graduates. The financial consideration in working for this group thus is not subsistence but the desire to obtain more comforts or luxuries or develop savings programs. For low income families,

Table 10.3.   Main Reasons for Employment By Social Class Of Respondent[1]

Main Reasons for Going Out to Work	Class			Total
	Upper	Middle	Low	
	%	%	%	%
Financial reasons	43	67	79	73
Need of mental stimulus (not enough to do at home, mind not occupied)	14	20	11	13
Enjoys it	21	10	4	7
Need of social stimulus (likes meeting people, company, not so lonely)	4	12	4	6
Works with husband, helps him	25	10	2	6
Independence (money of one's own)		4	2	2
Other answers (e.g., to make use of training, sense of achievement, "keeps me healthy," "keeps me young," absence of husband, own business, etc.)	18	6	9	9

[1]This table adds to more than 100 per cent because some respondents gave more than one reason.

DERIVED FROM: Viola Klein, *Britain's Married Women Workers* (London: Routledge & Kegan Paul, Ltd., 1965), p. 37. (New York: Humanities Press, Inc.)

Table 10.4. Main Reason of Graduates for Working, by Marital Status, 1964

Main Reason for Working	Total Number	Per Cent	Single	Married (Husband Present) Total	With Children Under 6 Years[1]	6-17 Years	With No Children	Widowed, Separated, Divorced
Graduates represented	42,845		12,685	27,175	13,654	2,192	11,329	2,985
Per cent		100	100	100	100	100	100	100
To support self and/or others	14,881	35	78	8	5	10	12	92
To increase family income	13,509	32	(²)	49	51	55	46	2
To have a career	5,763	13	17	13	9	21	16	3
To get actual work experience	1,694	4	1	6	7	4	5	1
Like to work	1,402	3	1	5	4	3	6	1
To do something worthwhile	742	2	2	2	2	1	2	
To use talents and keep alert	330	1	(²)	1	2	2	(²)	
To help husband establish a career	1,929	5		7	8	1	7	
To escape household routine	2,360	6		9	12	4	5	
Other reasons	235	1	(²)	1	1		1	

[1] Includes some graduates who had children 6 to 17 years of age also.
[2] Less than 0.5 percent.

SOURCE: U.S. Department of Labor, Women's Bureau, *College Women, Seven Years After Graduation, Resurvey of Women Graduates—Class of 1957* (Washington, D.C.: Government Printing Office, 1966), Bulletin 292, p. 41.

the work of the mother is much more of a necessity, and the financial factor appears to override other considerations, such as the presence of young children in the home. In extremely low income families the wives and mothers have to work.

These data suggest another important consideration in women's work. The second most commonly mentioned factor in both studies was the idea of a career or mental stimulation. Not unexpectedly, women appear to derive the same kinds of intrinsic satisfactions from their work as men. There is a general relationship between the desire to work for personal enjoyment and development and educational and socio-economic status. This again is consistent with findings from general motivational research. The implication of this data is that increased educational opportunities for women will be related to increased desires to be part of the work force.

The desire to participate and the actual participation are confronted with the realities of the situation which present a series of difficulties for women. Cynthia F. Epstein, in a paper dealing with women in the professions, notes that many occupations are "sex-typed."[12] Table 10.5 shows the unevenness of the distribution of women within a number of professions. When occupations are defined as male,

> women who seek entry in them are defined as social deviants and accordingly subjected to social sanctions. They will be less often motivated to consider professions which are defined as incompatible with women's other roles. And the women in these occupations will tend to be discouraged from seeking advancement when they thus perceive the opportunity structure within a profession as being limited for them.[13]

Sex typing of occupations results in an uncomfortable social context for either sex in the wrong occupation. Epstein also points out that some work itself is defined as masculine or feminine. The cultural basis of these definitions can be seen in comparative studies which show high participation of women in occupations which are defined as masculine in the United States. In the Soviet Union, for example, women comprise a significant part of the engineering, legal, and medical professions. Despite the cultural basis of the definition of

[12]"Woman's Place: The Salience of Sex Status in the Professional Setting," paper presented at the 62nd Annual Meeting of the American Sociological Association, San Francisco, August 1967.
[13]Epstein, "Woman's Place: The Salience of Sex Status in the Professional Setting," p. 7.

Table 10.5.   Women as Per Cent of All Workers in Selected Professional Occupations, U.S.A., (1900-1960)

Occupation	1960	1950	1940	1930	1920	1910	1900
College professors, president instruction	19.0	23.0	27.0	32.0	30.0	19.0	
Doctors	6.8	6.1	4.6	4.0	5.0	6.0	
Lawyers[1]	3.5	3.5	2.4	2.1	1.4	1.0	
Engineers	0.8	1.2	0.3				
Dentists	2.1	2.7	1.5	1.8	3.2	3.1	
Scientists	9.9	11.4					
Biologists	28.0	27.0					
Chemists	8.6	10.0					
Mathematicians	26.4	38.0					
Physicists	4.2	6.5					
Nurses	97.0	98.0	98.0	98.0	96.0	93.0	94.0
Social workers	57.0	66.0	67.0	68.0	62.0	52.0	
Librarians	85.0	89.0	89.0	91.0	88.0	79.0	
Clergy	5.8	8.5	2.2	4.3	2.6	1.0	4.4

SOURCES: U.S. Bureau of the Census, *Census of Population, 1960*, Vol. 1, Table 202, pp. 528-533. 1900-1950 statistics from *Changes in Women's Occupations, 1940-50*, Washington: U.S. Dept. of Labor, 1954, Women's Bureau Bulletin No. 253, p. 57.

some work as masculine or feminine, the definitions remain part of the social context and must be dealt with in considering occupational choice.

Women who do become members of high status professions, such as medicine or law, are typically found in the lower status specialties within these professions. In all professions the woman is handicapped by a social system that encourages sponsorship of the neophyte. Epstein notes that the acceptance of the protégé by the sponsor implies a relationship which may be resented by the wife of the sponsor and/or the husband of the protégé, which again indicates the incompatability of some occupational norms with some family norms. It is interesting to note that such questions and resentments do not arise when the sponsor and his protégé are of the same sex, a relationship that in another context would be questioned.

The same general pattern operates against women gaining entrance to the inner circles in many professions.[14]

In addition to these subtle and not so subtle blockages to women in the professions, Epstein notes that women behave in ways that are less professional than would be expected. In the academic profession they tend to publish less, although this may be a factor of their location at less prestigious institutions. They also devote fewer hours to their work, obviously reflecting performance of duties associated with marriage and the family. Participation and membership in professional associations are also less frequent for women. This lowered level of participation represents a reaction to early discriminatory patterns but, at the same time, contributes to the perpetuation of such discrimination.[15]

Despite this rather pessimistic view of women in professions, Epstein suggests that a number of changes are occurring that may further equalize opportunities. The extension of educational opportunities and the exposure of men to women who are their intellectual equals may lead to less resistance on the part of the men. More important, perhaps, is the need for specialists in a wide variety of areas. As this need increases, barriers, such as sex or race, may have to be ignored. The civil rights movement may also have an impact. The direction of changes in the recent past has been toward more equality of opportunity. If the demand for trained personnel, in or out of the professions, continues to increase, discrimination of this sort will undoubtedly decrease.[16] At the present time, however, women comprise an occupationally disadvantaged group.

The problems faced by women in their work are based on more than simple prejudice or the desire to maintain status on the part of men. Women do have higher turnover rates than men. An employing organization can predict that a high percentage of its women workers will leave each year, representing a high cost factor to the organization. At the same time, women whose families are grown have very low turnover rates. The gross turnover rates, however, can be used to demonstrate women's discontinuity in the labor force, and this tends to operate against all women. Another factor contributing to the relatively disadvantaged position of women is the fact that

[14]Epstein, "Woman's Place: The Salience of Sex Status in the Professional Setting," pp. 13–20.

[15]Epstein, "Woman's Place: The Salience of Sex Status in the Professional Setting," pp. 22–26.

[16]Epstein, "Woman's Place: The Salience of Sex Status in the Professional Setting," pp. 35–39.

they tend to be more immobile than men. The married woman is much less likely to be able to accept a transfer, since this would involve insuring that her husband also could locate work in a new area. This factor would operate particularly at the executive or professional level, where such movement is commonplace.

Women in the labor force are confronted with prejudice and discrimination. The demands of family roles set limits on the potential for participation. These facts contribute to the uniqueness of women's position in the occupational structure. The morality of the prejudice and discrimination and the necessity of some of the family obligations can be questioned from a number of perspectives. Nevertheless, the situation is different for women than for men.

the housewife

Any discussion of women and occupations is incomplete without a consideration of the housewife, the dominant feminine occupation and the most heavily populated single occupation within the total system. It also has the widest range of abilities and aptitudes of any occupation. Caplow states:

> This occupation is the only one which shows approximately the same distribution of intelligence and of all aptitudes as the general population. One of the reasons for the widespread maladjustment of housewives may be inferred from the circumstance that the same job requirements are imposed on morons and women of superior intelligence. There is no age requirement either. Girls of ten years and upwards may be able to keep house competently; and it is frequently done by women in their eighties.[17]

Caplow's analysis focuses on the particular work performed by the housewife along the same lines used in this analysis. The important affective components in child rearing and husband satisfying are ignored. Qualitative differences in the nature of, and reactions to, these affective relationships are also ignored. These appear to be central to the role of the housewife, but at the same time, these affective components are present to varying degrees in all other occupations. Despite this intentional omission, Caplow's analysis is instructive as it pinpoints some major components of the housewives' role and dilemma.

Training for the role of housewife has changed little. The

[17]*The Sociology of Work*, pp. 260–61.

socialization process is still largely informal, as it is in the case of farming and some of the crafts. The vast majority of the training occurs in interaction with the mother. Since schooling takes a great amount of the time available, the learning takes place in evenings, on weekends, and over vacations. Caplow suggests that much of the training during adolescence is specifically oriented toward courtship.[18] The results of the courtship process determine the kind of house the woman will keep as a wife. Given the relative uncertainty of this period, the girl cannot be trained for a specific housewife role. In the educational system, little attention is paid to the occupation of housewife.

> High school curriculums and even college curriculums usually include a few courses on cooking and allied matters, but these are essentially meant as symbolic gestures, and are no more likely to train housewives than the shop courses offered to boys under similar conditions are likely to produce skilled carpenters. Full-scale training in home economics or household management is limited to correctional institutions, schools for the retarded, and a few colleges of agriculture.[19]

If this analysis is correct, then the rather harsh conclusion could be reached that the role itself perhaps does not require much training, and as Caplow suggests, anyone can do it.

The range of activities included in the housewives' role is enormous and ranges from interior decorating to gardening, from diaper changing to gourmet cooking, and from mopping floors to arranging flowers. Caplow identifies three major components of the role under which the spectrum of activities can be arranged; *food preparation*, including activities from purchasing to eventual clearing of dishes; *cleaning*; and *child care*.[20] The activity that varies the most is child care, since it usually is not present at the onset of the career and ends long before the career itself does.

In tracing a typical career, Caplow notes that at marriage the work load is usually quite light, since the living quarters are small and the duties only involve two people. The husband usually helps during this phase, and the wife typically is employed outside the home. This is generally the period in which the greatest amount of learning occurs. The arrival of a child drastically alters the role. There is little formal preparation for the work of child care, since

[18]*The Sociology of Work*, p. 261.
[19]Caplow, *The Sociology of Work*, p. 262.
[20]Caplow, *The Sociology of Work*, p. 262.

the small family unit generally precludes much exposure to the processes involved and baby-sitting offers only a limited experience for only some girls. Caplow states:

> Further, for reasons too complex to explore here, the entire pattern of middle-class child raising is marked by strong anxiety feelings centered on the child. This anxiety can only be held in check if the baby is raised by the most perfected technic available. The mainstay of the housewife's special literature is the provision of timely advice to mothers. The manufacture of clothing, furniture, and miscellaneous devices for babies is a major industry, and few medical specialties are more profitable than pediatrics. The presence of this elaborate apparatus to prevent or mitigate errors in child raising technic reassures the housewife, but at the same time strengthens the basis of her anxiety and strengthens the elements of compulsive ritual which are already present. Moreover, the whole complex—like any dynamic culture complex—tends to expand by continually accepting innovations, and each of the activities involved in child care has a tendency to grow increasingly complicated. It is not unusual for the feeding of a very small baby to require more time, effort, and equipment than the feeding of the rest of the household.[21]

This intense phase is, by definition, limited since the child will grow and enter the outside world through the educational system. As nursery and prenursery schools become more prevalent, the age for leaving the family for at least a portion of the day diminishes. There are undoubtedly limits on the extension of formal child care systems outside the home, but the intense period is lessening in its span. As the child gets into the regular school system and can begin self-discipline, with its related reduction of the work load for the family, the role requirements of child care are correspondingly lessened. The presence of more than one child will extend this period, but at most the intense child care period comprises only a small proportion of the over-all career. Caplow notes that the intense period of child care usually alters the manner in which the other role requirements are met. The husband may help the wife with some of her activities during this period or provide assistance in the form of labor-saving devices or help from outside the home.[22]

The decline of the role requirements continues as the child or

[21]*The Sociology of Work*, p. 263.
[22]Caplow, *The Sociology of Work*, p. 264.

children approach adolescence, and the work load is drastically reduced. It also appears to be a period of crisis for the woman. While her husband is typically at the period of greatest involvement in his own occupation, particularly in middle-class families, the wife is almost without an occupation. The range of alternatives open to the wife during this period include involvement in community activities, self-entertainment in clubs and social groups, self-improvement through varied forms of education, or returning to the labor force. The last alternative is difficult since the woman has been out of the labor force for some time and also faces the problems discussed above. Recognizing this dilemma, a number of colleges, universities, and other educational organizations are beginning to provide retraining facilities specifically oriented toward this group.[23] There appears to be a growing awareness of the problems involved by potential employers. Nevertheless, the period is one of crisis and potentially may leave the woman in partial idleness for over half of her life. Caplow states that the housewife at fifty comprises the "most conspicuously maladjusted segment of the population."[24]

This quite pessimistic appraisal of the housewife's career is compounded by two additional points. The motivation and reward system is generally reversed from that of any other occupation. Hard work is rewarded minimally, while idleness is highly rewarded. High family status is associated with less work to do. Similarly, the highly efficient housewife has more time on her hands and thus the potential for greater frustration than her less efficient counterpart who is always behind in her labors. An additional anomaly is the fact that the substitute for the housewife, the domestic servant, occupies the lowest status in the occupational hierarchy. Added to this, the woman who utilizes domestic help so that she herself can be employed is more likely to be criticized than the woman who has help so that she can be idle.[25]

The discussion thus far has focused on the distribution and intensity of the components of the occupation of housewife. It has ignored such qualitative factors such as the intelligence and creativity associated with the child rearing function. This particular phase of the occupation has obviously vital consequences for the child. It can also be a source of real satisfaction for the housewife. The time

[23] See U.S. Department of Labor, Women's Bureau, Pamphlet 10, *Continuing Education Programs for Women* (Washington, D.C.: U.S. Government Printing Office, 1966).
[24] *The Sociology of Work*, p. 266.
[25] Caplow, *The Sociology of Work*, pp. 266–69.

span of real activity in this area is limited, however, to a short
period in the over-all occupational career. Another aspect of the role
that can have a positive intrinsic yield is in the area of affectional
relationships. This component is also present in the role of husband,
so that it cannot really be considered unique to the housewife's
occupation. For middle-class wives in particular, an additional part
of the role can be facilitation of the husband's career.[26] Although
the exact extent to which the wife contributes is not known, it is
reasonably clear that she can have an impact in this regard.

The nature of the occupation of housewife in particular and
women's occupations in general suggests that while the nuclear
family is in general compatible with the contemporary occupational
system, there is maladjustment on the feminine side of the family
equation. The separation of work and home works well for the man.
For the woman technological and social changes have not led to this
neat accommodation. The role of the housewife and the obstacles
faced by women in the occupational system suggest that additional
changes are necessary if the woman is to enjoy the kind of relationship to the wider social system that the man now does. If changes in
this area do occur, the rather delicate balance between the family
and occupational systems will be further altered, if not upset.

**some additional relationships between
family and occupation**

An important and obvious relationship between the occupational and familial systems is that a man's occupation is in essence
the status determinant for his entire family. The whole style of life
of the family is thus affected by participation in the occupational
system. The woman's participation in occupations outside the home
apparently does not make as much difference. If the woman is the
sole supporter, this is generally associated with relatively low status. If she is single or married and her husband is in the labor force,
her own work has relatively little status impact. In some ways the
single woman worker is actually not part of the stratification
system, since there is usually the anticipation that she will get
married and assume her husband's status. Since the overwhelming
majority of women are married at some point in their lives, their
status is basically that of their husbands.

The occupation of the husband has an additional impact on the

[26]See Whyte, *The Organization Man*, pp. 287–91.

family in that his position in the occupational system is apparently related to his position in family relationships. Research on unemployment suggests that when a man is unemployed his power within the family diminishes. Joan Aldous reports that among lower-class families the income of the husband is directly related to his participation in the family. The more he earns, the greater his power and involvement.[27] While there is thus a general relationship between occupational status and status within the family system, the relationship can become curvilinear in that deep involvement in an occupation can lead to withdrawal from the family. Such involvement is particularly likely among high status occupations, although it can also occur among lower status occupations. It is therefore at the middle of the occupational system where the husband is most likely to have power and be intensively involved in the family.

An additional aspect of some high status occupations affecting relationships is that the man may move ahead of his wife in terms of his educational or social accomplishments; the wife may perform her housewife and mother role very adequately but not keep in phase with her husband who operates in a changing intellectual and social system. Occupations that demand a great deal of time away from home, such as truck or bus drivers or some salesmen, or that have hours incompatible with normal family relationships also have an impact on family relationships in that the man is simply not available for participation.[28]

Occupations, as links to the wider social structure, thus have a significant impact on marital relationships. There also appear to be some occupationally linked differences in the performance of the parental role, according to Aldous' analysis. Professionals and executives, for example, have rather clear ideas of the kinds of sons they want to have. They attempt to instill in their sons the behaviors and mannerisms appropriate to their own status. Less concern about their daughters is expressed, under the assumption that they will not be as involved in occupations outside the home.[29]

The general importance of the family in the socialization process has been well documented. It is the first link a child has with the occupational system. His father's occupation becomes known to him, although usually in a somewhat inaccurate perspective. He is

[27]Aldous, "Parental and Marital Function as Related to Occupational Status," (Unpublished paper, University of Minnesota, 1967), pp. 3–4.

[28]Aldous, "Parental and Marital Function as Related to Occupational Status," pp. 6–7.

[29]Aldous, "Parental and Marital Function as Related to Occupational Status," p. 12.

taught behaviors he will carry into his occupational life. His aspirations and expectations are at least partially formed in the family setting. The socialization impact of the family is carried over into, and expanded by, the educational system.

occupations and education

The basic relationship between the educational and occupational systems is obvious. Particular amounts, and in many cases particular kinds, of education are prerequisites for entrance into the occupational system. In discussing this Burton R. Clark states: "Men become part of the potential labor force by qualifying for the work required, and increasingly, capability is defined by formal schooling. Advanced education offers competence; little schooling defines occupational incompetence. Thus occupational achievement is prefigured by education."[30] Implicit, but vital, in this relationship is the fact that the educational system has become the basis for the distribution of individuals within the total social system. Since occupations are the link for the individual and his family to the stratification system and all that that implies and also are simply a major portion of the life of the adult, the educational system can be viewed as a major factor in placement of people within the total social system.

The distributional aspect and the close relationship of education and occupations is a very recent phenomenon. The advent of industrialization was linked to a general growth of the educational system. Universal education became a fact and literacy became a general expectation. At the same time, however, formal educational requirements for most occupations were minimal until very recently. Most professions, for example, did not establish training schools until the 19th century. The practice of "reading" law or medicine at the feet of an established practitioner has only recently disappeared. Many major corporations were developed by real Horatio Alger types. While there are many executives at all levels who have not had a college education, almost no one today enters this organizational level without a college education. Within a generation the proportion of executives without such training will undoubtedly shrink to insignificance.

The same general trend is evident within all types of occupa-

[30]"Sociology of Education," in *Handbook of Modern Sociology*, ed. Robert E. L. Faris, p. 737.

tions. The untrained and unskilled individual has essentially lost his place in the labor market. There is a strong inverse relationship between unemployment rates and level of education. Clark notes that the high school dropout is in reality a problem because of his position in the labor force.[31] At one time he could sell his unskilled labor, but now he no longer can, since it is often less costly to mechanize work than utilize unskilled workers. Education in the form of retraining has become a major consideration for all occupational levels. Most professions engage in continuing educational programs for their members. "Engineers need to go back to the classroom to maintain competence; with the growth in new knowledge, the engineer of 10 years experience who has not engaged in substantial re-education may have less value than a new engineering graduate."[32] Retraining of workers displaced by automation has become a major societal concern. Most corporations have embraced the concept of "executive development" or continuing education.

The point made at the outset of this book that society is moving from an industrial to a services and human resources era is related to the changing educational requirements. Research and development are dominant concerns of all sectors of the society. Clark states that "Brain workers of an ever-higher calibre are *the* economic need of societies in advanced stages of industrialism."[33] As this trend continues, even more emphasis and pressure will be put on the educational system.

Before examining the contemporary situation in more detail, a brief look at the role of education in developing nations is instructive. These nations are attempting to industrialize as a means of economic development. Industrialization is viewed as being largely dependent upon educational development within the populace. Anderson has noted that: "The importance of schooling for growth in the short run may be quite minor; yet, in the long run, schooling may be decisive by virtue of its role in sustaining the broader milieu that favors change."[34] This point is strengthened by Passin's examination of the Meiji and their emergence from a preindustrial stage. He concludes:

At the very least, literacy made it possible for people to be aware of things outside of their own immediate experi-

[31]"Sociology of Education," p. 738.
[32]Clark, "Sociology of Education," p. 738.
[33]"Sociology of Education," p. 738.
[34]C. Arnold Anderson, "The Impact of the Educational System on Technological Change and Modernization," in *Industrialization and Society*, eds. Bert F. Hoselitz and Wilbert E. Moore (Mouton: UNESCO, 1966), p. 261.

ence. It also made it possible for them to conceive of arrangements that differed from those with which they were familiar. They were therefore much more accessible to new ideas and new techniques than they otherwise would have been.[35]

Education and the literacy resulting therefrom are thus viewed as necessary conditions for economic development and industrialization and technological change. From the perspective of this book, education is thus a prerequisite for occupations in the industrialized and technologically changing setting.

While education is clearly such a prerequisite, there is no one form of education that can be taken as optimal for economic development. In addition, the conditions that existed in a society before it embarked on the road to economic development have an impact on the nature of the educational process. Foster's excellent study of the educational system in Ghana illustrates both of these points.[36] During the colonial period, the education of the local population was oriented toward training clerical workers for governmental work. These workers were fed into the system in a rather automatic fashion, and the educational and occupational systems had a close and neat linkage. The education at this period was academically oriented, even though it was designed to fill specific vocations. At the same time, education was the only realistic means of upward mobility for the population. After independence and as the desire to industrialize developed, the traditional form of education remained. More importantly, the population maintained its belief that academic training was the route to the best occupations. This belief corresponds with reality in that the most prestigious positions are obtained through academic training.

At this point there is little difference between the developing nation and those that have passed through the developmental stage. A major problem, however, arises from the fact that the occupational system in a developing society needs people with specific vocational training in both industrial and agricultural skills. Since such training is devalued by the population and since most people in the educational system seek the academic type of education, shortages of trained personnel exist in these important areas, thus inhibiting economic development. While education is an important

[35]Herbert Passin, "Portents of Modernity and the Meiji Emergence," in *Education and Economic Development*, eds. C. Arnold Anderson and Mary Jean Bowman (Chicago: Aldine Publishing Co., 1965), p. 419.

[36]See Phillip Foster, *Education and Social Change in Ghana* (Chicago: University of Chicago Press, 1965).

prerequisite for development, perfect coordination between societal needs and the form of the system itself does not exist.

The case of the developing nation serves to illustrate the nature of the relationship between occupations and the educational system. Education is a prerequisite for development, even though in and of itself it does not insure development.[37] At the same time there is apparently no one best form that the educational system should take in such areas. Anderson has suggested that in developing countries a *loose* connection between education and occupations is more valuable than a close one, since the latter builds in rigidities which would inhibit growth in the long run. He suggests that a diversity of types of schools is probably the optimal arrangement.[38]

Evidence from the developing countries indicates the importance of education at relatively low levels of industrial and technological development. For societies with rather fully developed technological systems, the importance of education is heightened. At the same time there is not a perfect correspondence between the occupational system's needs and the educational system's output.

The nature of the relationship between the educational and occupational systems is one of mutual dependence. The occupational system essentially relies upon the educational system for its supply of personnel, while output of the educational system is consumed by the occupational system. This reciprocal relationship, which has grown in strength, contains a number of strains, which prevent it from being viewed as one of total harmony. A major strain, which has existed over a period of time, involves the nature of those who attain the educational prerequisites for many positions in the occupational structure. Increasing proportions of the population are attaining high school and college educations, indicating the growing need for such education, At the same time, there are questions regarding whether those most qualified attain the educational level for which they are best suited.

Data from a number of sources suggest that the distribution of the population into the various educational levels is not closely related to potential educability. Intruding into the relationship between academic potential and academic attendance is the important factor of position in the stratification system. A. E. Halsey, in a summary of studies in this area, reports that social class still plays a role in determining who shall go to college. While the social class variable has perhaps diminished in importance in recent years, it

[37]Anderson and Bowman, *Education and Economic Development*, p. 345.
[38]Anderson, "The Impact of the Educational System on Technological Change and Modernization," p. 264.

still operates. The lower an individual's position in the stratification system, the less his chances for attaining college entrance or high-school graduation. Since these two educational benchmarks are important criteria for the occupational system, this suggests that the occupational system is not receiving the potential that it might under a system of actual educational equality. The data Halsey reports holds the learning ability of the subjects, as measured by standard intelligence tests, constant so that even if learning ability is in any way differentially distributed across class lines, the relationship between ability and its realization in the educational system is vitally affected by the stratification factor.[39] Findings such as these, which have been repeated in a variety of social settings, raise important moral questions as well as those raised in regard to the occupational system.

A related study by William G. Spady suggests that while the general level of educational attainment has increased, the impact has not resulted in any real occupational upgrading.[40] Noting that today a son must obtain more schooling than his father to achieve the same level of occupation, Spady finds that the rate of college attendance for the sons of poorly educated fathers has actually decreased over time. The people in the bottom strata of society are more disadvantaged than in the past, according to this analysis. This pattern is particularly evident for the Negro. For those above the bottom level the potential for educational attainment has increased. Spady attributes these patterns to the norms and values of the various status levels. For all but the lowest level, the value of at least a high-school education is quite well diffused. If this pattern for the lowest level persists, a perpetuation of poverty is most likely. For the occupational system this implies a continuation of unemployability for a segment of the population. The relative size of this segment will continue to shrink, but it is probable that the extremely poorly educated will soon be outside of the occupational system, except as recipients of the products and services of those in the system.

The amount of education received and its distribution in the population has important implications for the occupational system and society as a whole. Perhaps of greater importance is the nature of the education received. It is apparent that the educational system does not articulate perfectly with the needs of the occupational

[39]"The Sociology of Education" in *Sociology: An Introduction,* ed. Neil J. Smelser (New York: John Wiley & Sons, Inc., 1967), pp. 427–33.
[40]"Educational Mobility and Access: Growth and Paradoxes," *American Journal of Sociology,* LXXIII, 3 (November, 1967), 273–86.

world. Two basic factors are operative. First, the educational system is itself not a cohesive whole. Wide differences exist between schools on urban-rural, central city-suburb, Negro-White, and regional axes. The output from the various patterns emerging from these different dimensions will vary widely. The programs, practices, and intents of the different educational levels are often not well articulated. Graduate and undergraduate education is often not well coordinated nor is the relationship between secondary and higher educational institutions.

Adding to this less than perfect state is the fact that educational programs may be quite different from what actually goes on in the schools. James S. Coleman's study of *The Adolescent Society* clearly demonstrates the impact of the social structure imposed by peers on fellow students.[41] The orientation and efforts of students are strongly affected by the prevailing student subcultures. Athletic and social prowess is typically stressed more than academic achievement in high schools. A study of medical students by Becker *et al.* also suggests that peers have an important influence in structuring behaviors and orientations at this level.[42] It would be difficult to make a strong case that the impact of peers is totally dysfunctional for the occupational system, for some of the influences may be very occupationally relevant. At the same time, however, these influences do deflect from the programs established by the schools. Any established educational program is the basis from which peer based behaviors originate. At the same time, it appears that the occupational system is dependent upon the established, rather than the operating, program. This adds an additional discrepancy to the relationship.

At the present time a further example of this form of discrepancy can be seen. The apparently growing amount of dissent among college students reflects a disenchantment with both the educational and occupational "establishments." Although not studied systematically, there appears to be a growing feeling that occupations, particularly those within the business sphere, are less than desirable. If these trends continue, the concept of education as a pipeline to the occupational world will have to be altered. This assumes, of course, that the occupational system remains relatively static. Even a continuance of the present state of affairs would lead to imbalance between the systems.

[41]See *The Adolescent Society* (New York: The Free Press of Glencoe, 1961).
[42]See *Boys in White: Student Culture in Medical School* (Chicago: University of Chicago Press, 1961).

The process through which an individual passes through the educational system en route to eventual occupational placement is not necessarily rational in terms of the individual's abilities and desires nor in terms of the needs of the occupational system. The placement of individuals into the various curricula available at the elementary and secondary levels is often on the basis of his original social class position. Teachers tend to push middle- and upper-class children into college preparatory curricula, while working- and lower-class youths either are not pushed in any direction or are encouraged to enter vocational or general programs. Vocational counseling itself is often restricted to those who receive more education. Many of these who leave high school before graduation receive no vocational counseling. For those in the system, occupationally relevant decisions often are made on nonoccupationally relevant grounds. The decisions in regard to courses taken, and even majors, are frequently made on the basis of the ease or difficulty of the courses, the hours at which they are given, dating patterns, the popularity of a particular teacher, and other factors of only limited relevance. Although the choice of curriculum can be made on rational or nonrational grounds, the choice itself both opens and closes opportunities. Once a choice is made, it tends to be irreversible. Continued education actually sets limits on the potential occupations for an individual. The range of occupational alternatives is probably greatest at the time of high-school graduation. Before that period it is limited by the lack of education. Afterwards it is limited by specialization. The educational system thus serves as a channeling mechanism, wider at some points than at others.

The actual impact of education on occupational choice is difficult to determine given the wide range of variables which can enter such decisions. James A. Davis' findings and interpretations, based on a sample of 33,982 college seniors studied in 1961, are instructive, however. He states:

> the college freshman has already completed 12 years of education and has lived about one-fifth of his life span in a family and community environment that influences his plans; in many cases he goes to college precisely to implement a specific vocational choice rather than to choose a vocation. . . . The college years are not the sole determinant of vocational choice—nor is any span of 4 years—for vocational choice is the result of a continuous decision process over decades, but there is no evidence in our data that the college years do not contribute their fair share of influence. Although our guess is that the last 2 years of high school are the most strategic period of all

for vocational choice, college is not without its effect. Half of the students appear to change their minds or reach a decision during college . . . .[43]

The patterns of change and choice during college, with some exceptions, indicate that people choosing, or changing into, an occupation tend to be like those who have already chosen it.[44] That is, there is a tendency toward homogamy during the college period in terms of the characteristics of those entering various occupations. For example, using the variables in the Davis study, the physical sciences were underchosen by those oriented toward working with people and by Negroes, overchosen by those destined for high academic performance, by those opting for originality, and by students from larger cities, underchosen by Protestants, and over-chosen by Catholics. Education, on the other hand, was underchosen by men and by those wanting to make a lot of money, overchosen by those oriented toward working with people and by Negroes, under-chosen by students from larger cities and by those with high socio-economic status families, and overchosen by Protestants.[45] The fact that in most cases the movement in college is towards homogamy suggests the complexity of the occupational choice process itself and the complexity of the sorting process performed by the educational system. While occupational choice is not a major concern here, it is clear that it is influenced by a whole series of factors. Some of these same factors appear to be operative within the educational system.

The role of education as preparation for and distribution into occupations is indisputable, even if not entirely harmonious in its implementation. An additional component, which adds some more confusion to the relationship, is that it is not clear what is exactly the optimum form the education should take for occupational preparation. The long standing controversy between vocational and liberal arts forms of preparation has actually grown in intensity. At the high-school level, much of the traditional vocational curriculum is clearly outdated. The rate of technological change is such that skills can quickly become outmoded. At this level there is some argument for a more liberal arts approach, since this might better prepare a person to adapt to changes. This is not a clearly demonstrable fact, however, and the exact form such training should take is also not clear. In higher education the same basic controversy continues. There is a tendency, as Clark notes, for specific voca-

[43]*Undergraduate Career Decisions* (Chicago: Aldine Publishing Co., 1965), p. 33.
[44]Davis, *Undergraduate Career Decisions*, p. 44.
[45]Davis, *Undergraduate Career Decisions*, pp. 12–13.

tional training to be put off until graduate school, as in the case of business or education.[46] The rapid expansion of knowledge would appear to make such a shift more necessary. At the same time, the contents of both the liberal arts and vocational programs may not be the best that could be developed in terms of the needs of the occupational system, which in its own right is not ideal.

summary and conclusions

The thrust of this chapter has been directed toward the interplay between the occupational system and the family and educational systems. Although it is correct to say that the systems are intimately intertwined, it is also clear that the series of incompatibilities discussed preclude any assumption of neat and harmonious reciprocity. Instead of viewing the relationships either as harmonious or conflictual, a more appropriate perspective would be that of change. As each system changes, previously existing relationships are altered. These changes appear to induce additional changes in the related system, whether deliberate or not, leading to continued interplay between the systems, but at the same time apparently not leading to a homeostatic condition.

The contemporary family with its nuclear form allows the division of labor whereby the man can participate in the occupational system with its different normative system and the woman can be in charge of most family functions. At the same time the demands for trained individuals, the rising educational levels of women, and the availability of time for women are confronted by the historic discrimination against women, which precludes their full participation in the labor force. The educational system serves as a distribution and preparation nexus between the family and occupational systems. Both aspects are generally compatible with the occupational system, but it is clear that the distributional function does not always permit the most qualified to pass through and that the preparation is less than perfect. Implicit in the discussion of both topics in this chapter was the idea of change. A major component of the change process is technology. Technological developments in the occupational system have an obvious impact on the family and on the education. Technological developments in the last two systems similarly affect the occupational system. The next chapter will focus on technological developments as they affect occupations.

[46]"Sociology of Education," p. 739.

chapter   11

technological change

The topic of this chapter has been a component of much of the previous discussion. The contemporary occupational structure reflects the state of the technology involved in the various occupations. Some occupations, such as engineering or computer programing, are basically technology changing occupations. Other occupations have been created by technological change, while still others have been eliminated or drastically changed. The fact that this chapter is concerned with change, as opposed to simply with technology, is indicative of the nature of the topic. The current condition of technology is change. While the rate of change is difficult to determine, because of the lack of an adequate base measure, it is obvious that an era of industrialization, and even more one of services-human resources orientation, is based upon change built upon previous developments.

Before beginning the analysis of technological change and its impact on occupations, it should be made clear that neither an overly optimistic nor pessimistic view of the consequences of these changes will be taken. A good part of the literature on this phenomenon.

particularly that dealing with automation, views such change as leading to potential disaster, massive unemployment and alienation from work, or as a step toward a quasi-utopian society, full employment and workers who have realized their full human potential. While it is conceivable that either extreme could be reached, the evidence that is available suggests that both positive and negative consequences of change can be identified.

The impact of change has been uneven throughout the total society. When viewed as a totality, the technological impact is most probably near the midpoint; that is, the negative and positive consequences appear to balance each other. If the focus is shifted to the individual, the same general conclusion can be reached. There are many cases of individual tragedy where a person loses his job and his self-respect as a consequence of the introduction of automation or where individuals become unemployable because they lack the skills demanded by the occupational system. On the other hand, others within the system benefit as their skills become highly marketable or their jobs are upgraded with higher intrinsic and extrinsic yields. The position to be taken is thus one of neutrality. The neutrality is not the ethical neutrality of science, even though this is most relevant in such examinations, but rather that of the evidence.

The approach of this chapter will be to look at the nature of technological change, with the focus on the broad topic of automation and then to examine the consequences of changes as they affect occupations themselves, employment, and the individual.

the nature of technological change

It is almost impossible to discuss occupations without considering technological change. Nels Anderson states:

> Technological inventiveness is linked with man's work. It cannot cease unless man in his work ceases to be competitive and no longer tries to find easier and faster ways of performing his tasks. If he manages to take the heaviness out of work, he then feels the need to take the dullness out of it. The inventions that bring satisfaction in work are never sufficient to quench the thirst for still more invention to make work still lighter and more productive and the workday still shorter. Invention makes work increasingly a knowledgeable activity for man and makes the machine more an instrument for his handling.[1]

[1]*Dimensions of Work*, p. 125.

Anderson thus attributes change to the nature of man and implies that it is a continual and inevitable process. There have been periods and places in man's history where change has been opposed and postponed. Nevertheless, change does appear to be inevitable in that change has occurred. At the present time change is really the normal state of affairs. Much of the general impact of change can be discerned from an analysis of the developing countries. These countries do not necessarily pass through the same stages as those which have already industrialized, but the impact of change on occupations in these societies is in general similar to that which has occurred in all societies.

Neil J. Smelser points out that development leads to a differentiation of functions within the total society.[2] Tasks once performed by a single social unit, usually the family, are distributed among many units as occupational and other activities become separated from their traditional basis. Wilbert E. Moore elaborates on this point by noting that the change in the occupational structure during development actually involves five related processes. The first of these is that workers become involved in market participation.[3] Rather than existing on a simple subsistence level, both agricultural and industrial workers participate in the labor and financial markets. This is the same process identified in the discussion of the shift from the extended to the nuclear family, in that the occupation is carried on outside the home.

The second process is what Moore calls "sectoral relocation."[4] This refers to a shift of occupational situs away from subsistence agriculture toward economic production in industry or agriculture. As this occurs there may be heightened unemployment, since many traditional handcraft operations are no longer needed and the workers are not absorbed into the new industrial system. As was noted earlier, such unemployment would not exist during periods of subsistence farming. Moore also notes that this period is one in which marginal service occupations, such as being a car watcher or porter, flourish.

The additional processes during industrialization are the upgrading of skill requirements in the labor force, specialization of occupations, and greater status mobility, both within and between generations.[5] These processes in the industrializing societies are

[2]See Neil J. Smelser, "Mechanisms of Change and Adjustment to Change," in Hoselitz and Moore, *Industrialization and Society*, pp. 35–40.

[3]*The Impact of Industry* (Englewood Cliffs, N.J.: Prentice-Hall, Inc., 1965), p. 62.

[4]*The Impact of Industry*, pp. 63–64.

[5]Moore, *The Impact of Industry*, pp. 65–67.

similar to those that have occurred in societies that have already passed through the period of industrialization. At the same time, some interesting differences do exist between current industrialization and that which took place in the currently industrialized societies. The industrializing societies apparently are able to profit from some of the experiences of the past or are able to incorporate some of the features of modern societies in their own systems. Charles R. Walker has noted: "Even in the early stages of today's industrialization programs, social protection for the wage earner and his family in the form of health and welfare insurance, unemployment compensation, and other such measures must be provided."[6] Thus some of the problems associated with past industrialization are bypassed. This may, of course, decrease the amount of capital available for modernization, but important human values are supported.

While the information from the developing countries is instructive in the analysis of the broad sweep of change which is occurring, the major concern here is technological change in the contemporary Western system as it is related to occupations. The impact of such changes on occupations can be seen from such simple examples as the typewriter and office work, the reaper and farm work, or the washing machine and house work.

Technological change is thus *any alteration in the equipment utilized to perform work*. The emphasis on equipment is included to differentiate technological change from the broader idea of social change, which would involve rearrangements within any part of the wider social structure. This analysis will therefore view technological change as the independent variable, with changes in the wider social structure taken as the dependent variable. This is simply a heuristic device, since the relationship is not unidirectional. A change in organizational structure, for example, could lead to alteration in the technological system through a number of devices, such as suggestions, emphasis on innovation, or accidental discovery. For the purposes of this analysis, however, technological change will be viewed as the starting point.

The nature of this change is almost totally unidirectional. That is, the alteration in the system is toward less physical labor on the part of humans. A simple example of this is the power shovel as a replacement for the hand shovel; a much more complex case is that of the computer as it performs complex mathematical manipulations. While the latter example does involve the use of ideas, the

[6]*Modern Technology and Civilization* (New York: McGraw-Hill Book Company, 1962), p. 338.

basis for the computer is actually physical manipulation of symbols as directed by the human mind. The direction of technological change is towards automation, defined by John R. Bright as any production process that is significantly more automatic than that which previously existed in a given place of work.[7]

A number of forms of automation have been identified.[8] The first is simply the mechanization of conventional processes where transfer machines replace human labor in moving materials along a production process. The moving assembly line, which replaces the effort of lifting materials from work station to work station, is a simple example of this form. A second form of automation is the mechanization of processes in which machines are linked together for continuous production. These machines are supervised by mechanical control devices that are themselves controlled by feedback from the production process. The work of people in this setting is largely that of monitoring the system. The clearest example of this form is the oil refinery where there is almost no direct contact with the product by humans. Another example would be the bread bakery in which ingredients are mixed, shaped, placed in cooking containers, baked, sliced, wrapped, and packaged for delivery without human contact. These two forms can be viewed as the extremes in automated production. The movement is consistently toward the second form.

An important consideration in the possible future applications of automation is whether or not a particular production process can be mechanized and regularized. If the technological system does not develop a mechanized system to begin with, no movement toward total automation is possible. For example, the mail service is only partially mechanized, and a great deal of the work is done by hand, such as the sorting process and deliveries made by individual workers. Further technological developments are required before any movement toward automation is possible. The product or service involved must be regularized in that a high degree of variance does not allow the ongoing process of automation. In the construction of office buildings, for example, variations in terrain, design, and composition preclude automated assembly beyond that involved in some of the components such as windows and floor materials. Private homes, on the other hand, can be produced in a more

[7]*Automation and Management* (Cambridge, Mass.: Harvard University Graduate School of Business Administration, 1958), p. 6.

[8]The following discussion is partially based on William Silverman's "The Economic and Social Effects of Automation in an Organization," *The American Behavioral Scientist*, IX, 10 (June, 1966), 3–8. This article contains a comprehensive bibliography of empirical studies of automation.

automated fashion if the design and location are kept constant. In general it is easier to automate processes dealing with products than with services. Relatively simple services, such as food dispensing or shoe shines, can be provided through vending machines. In these cases the variation is reduced to a minimum.

The third form of automation is the application of computers to paper work. The preparation of payrolls, keeping of inventories, maintenance of insurance policy records, and compilation of airline reservations are performed by computers. As in the other forms, the computers take over functions which have been performed by humans. At the same time the information fed into computers is highly regularized, whether it deals with inventory or human records. Much of the concern expressed about computers reflects the regularization of data about humans and is based on the belief that each human is a unique creature who is not amenable to categorization into regularized patterns. Evidence from history, psychology, sociology, and the other behavioral and social sciences suggests, however, that regular patterns can be identified. The application of the computer to human data is based on such evidence. The computer is essentially like the second form of automation in that materials (data) are fed into a system, processed, and then come out as a finished product. The same principle of the substitution of mechanical or electronic processing for human effort is involved. The implications of the computer in terms of the speed with which information is handled and the greater amounts of information which can be encompassed are probably greater than that of automated production for the occupational and the wider social systems. As in the case of the second form of automation, the introduction of computers requires that the information be handled in a standardized and regularized form, which in turn implies that previously steps had been taken to put the information in such a form.

Computers can also be utilized in the decision-making process. This fourth form of automation has not been as fully implemented as the others, and therefore, its implications are quite unclear. A simple example of this form is inventories. The computer not only keeps inventory records but also decides when to reorder particular items. The decision is based on instructions included in the computer program. A more complex example is the utilization of computers in policy decisions. In this case the probability of relevant future events, their interrelationships, and the probable consequences of the varying possible situations which would arise on the basis of a particular decision must be considered. As in the previous form, the quality of the decision made is only as good as the information fed into the computer. If the probabilities are relatively certain, the computer can make a decision that can be taken as a careful assessment of the relevant factors and that is probably a correct decision if the information fed into the process reflects future reality. If unexpected or unconsidered factors intervene, the decision loses relevance. Here again, the computer is only doing what has been done by humans in the normal decision-making process. It can, however, utilize more information more rapidly than would be the case for humans.

These four forms of automation are based on the same general principle, the substitution of mechanical or electronic energy for human energy. None of the forms actually involve any new way of performing work, in the sense that whatever is being done (the processing of materials or information) has the same operations performed on it. The difference is in the social and technological organization surrounding the work process. The forms do vary in their impact on the occupations affected by their implementation.

the impact of automation on the occupational structure

At the present time it is difficult to be definitive in regard to the topic at hand. Empirical examinations of the impact of automation have largely been case studies. Although informative, these studies provide neither the data nor the perspective necessary for conclusive generalizations. They are useful in pointing to some of the issues involved, however.

The impact on skill levels required by the occupational system varies with the form of automation. Bright, for example, found that the introduction of automated equipment affected the skill levels in factories which utilized the first form of automation.[9] At this level skill requirements may actually be lessened as production work becomes more routinized. The second form also changes the skill requirements. Charles R. Walker, in a study of an automated pipe factory, found that some skills were no longer required, while new skills were introduced into the system.[10] At the same time, new skill requirements were introduced that involved different skills and a greater amount of judgment. A similar finding by Floyd C. Mann

[9]"Does Automation Raise Skill Requirements?" *Harvard Business Review*, XXXVI, 4 (July–August, 1958), 85–98.
[10]*Toward the Automatic Factory: A Case Study of Men and Machines* (New Haven, Conn.: Yale University Press, 1957), pp. 26–29.

and L. Richard Hoffman was that jobs in an automated power plant required more knowledge than jobs in a traditional power plant.[11] The movement is generally from manual to mental skills in this situation. Since there has been the general upgrading of educational attainment in the social system, this shift will probably not be too disruptive over the long run. For the individuals involved, the shift could be quite threatening.

The introduction of computers to speed the processing of information has a dual effect. Routine jobs, such as filing, operation of tabulation machines, or posting and checking billings, are largely eliminated. At the same time the equally routine job of key punching is introduced. There is also generally an increase in the proportion of professional and technical workers in the labor force. The over-all skill requirements are generally higher, but the workers involved are different. Those who held the relatively low skill jobs in the past are seldom moved into the more skilled positions.

The occupational structure is affected by automation in more ways than the direct kinds of impacts just described. Management and administration deal with a changed situation and must themselves change. An important study by Joan Woodward illustrates the consequences of technological differentiation for the management level of organizations.[12] Woodward classified 100 English firms on the basis of their technology. At one end of a rough three-point scale of technological development are firms that produce goods in small batches or units, such as railroad locomotives or ships. At the midpoint are those firms which utilize large-batch or mass production, such as the automobile assembly line or home appliance manufacturer. At the most technologically developed end of the scale is continuous process production as exemplified by the oil or chemical refinery.

The number of levels in the management hierarchy varied directly with the nature of the technology. Those firms with the most advanced technology had the most hierarchical levels. A recent study by Peter M. Blau corroborates this finding and offers some reasons for this relationship.[13] In this case the organizational sample was 254 finance departments of state and local governmental units in the United States. Despite the shift in functions from production to paper work, the same results are found. The major factor that leads

[11]*Automation and the Worker: A Study of Social Change in Power Plants* (New York: Holt, Rinehart & Winston, Inc., 1960), pp. 65–73.

[12]*Industrial Organization: Theory and Practice* (London: Oxford University Press, 1965), pp. 51–53.

[13]"The Hierarchy of Authority in Organizations," *American Journal of Sociology*, LXXIII, 4 (January, 1968), 453–67.

to this relationship, aside from sheer growth in the size of the organization which itself is strongly associated with the number of hierarchical levels, is the fact that automated processing of products or paper is a means of control over the workers involved. This impersonal form of control is based upon the fact that the worker does not control the pace of his work and also can be checked by performance records. Top management thus does not have to be greatly concerned about worker performance. At the same time in the agencies Blau studied, the organizations with the more automated processes also required higher level qualifications on the part of its workers. Blau states:

> Both the automation of the work process and the merit standards that the managerial and operating staff must meet contribute to the reliable performance of duties and help to make operations comparatively self-regulating within the framework of the organization's objectives and management's policies. These conditions reduce management's need to keep close direct control over operations and, consequently, often give rise to major changes in the hierarchy. To wit, vertical differentiation creates a multilevel hierarchy, which usually decreases the number of major divisions whose heads report to the agency director and increases the span of control of these division heads, and responsibilities become decentralized.[14]

Although the concern here is not with organizational change, the implications for the occupational structure within the organizations are quite clear. The positions at the various levels within the organization are given more autonomy in the sense that there is less direct supervision. The impact on the administrative structure is that responsibility is spread throughout the hierarchy, and the top levels have less direct responsibility and the lower levels have more. Much of the work of the lower levels in the hierarchy is involved in communications in that more information is generated and is processed upwards in the organization. The management function thus shifts from supervision to communications and coordination, with an associated shift in skill requirements.

The Woodward study also found that the span of control (the number of persons controlled by each supervisor) varied according to the type of technology involved.[15] Both the unit and the process production systems had relatively low spans of control, while the

[14]"The Hierarchy of Authority in Organizations," 466.
[15]*Industrial Organization: Theory and Practice*, p. 62.

mass production firms had a higher span of control. Blau also found that the more automated offices had lower spans of control. This finding suggests that although the mass production system can utilize fewer supervisors per worker, because of the impersonal control mechanism of the assembly line, in advanced technological systems the process production system reduces the span of control because of the necessity for insuring that errors do not occur. In this production system, errors are extremely costly, given the speed of the total process. Here again the emphasis is not on supervision per se but rather on the knowledge of the supervisor in error correction and detection. In the case of unit production, the employment of many craftsmen also reduced the need for direct supervision. Here the work units would tend to be organized around crafts and particular projects on each unit, accounting for the lower span of control.

Woodward's study also found that the ratio of managers and supervisors increased as the technological level increased, regardless of the size of the firm.[16] This is also related to the problem of error correction and detection with a concentration of personnel in inspection and control functions. Changing technology thus affects the specific functions performed by all levels of the hierarchy. It also affects the skills involved. Herbert Simon has suggested that managers will increasingly be freed from routine work and will have to be increasingly mathematically sophisticated in their analysis of organizational problems.[17] Whether the projection that mathematical expertise will become important is correct or not, it is probable that the greater amount of information available to managers will increase their communications and coordination activities as the data discussed above suggests. It is also probable that this greater amount of information within an organizational system will require more training as a prerequisite for handling information. The increased educational requirements, discussed in the previous chapter, reflect this tendency.

Elmer H. Burack's review of studies of the impact of technological developments on management supports these interpretations.[18] He found that there was a growing importance of technical staffs in automated operations. The requirement of greater amounts of education was also found, with an emphasis on technical

[16] *Industrial Organization: Theory and Practice*, p. 56.
[17] See *The New Science of Management Decision* (New York: Harper & Row, Publishers, 1960), pp. 38–40.
[18] "Industrial Management in Advanced Production Systems: Some Theoretical Concepts and Preliminary Findings," *Administrative Science Quarterly*, XII, 3 (December, 1967), 479–500.

education in many instances. An important finding was that experience became less important as technological expertise became more important. If this trend continues, personnel policies based upon seniority will increasingly come in conflict with organizational needs, as the well-trained young expert is more organizationally valuable than his more experienced superior. At the managerial level the possibility of a form of technological unemployment or underemployment is thus not remote. It is unlikely that the experienced, but technologically unsophisticated manager or executive will be laid off as might be the case with lower level workers. At the same time, however, he may be bypassed in the promotion process and given work less organizationally and personally relevant than might have been the case if the technological system were not developing so rapidly. These last few comments are conjectural; furthermore the organizational systems themselves contain elements that would at least partially block a rapid movement in the directions being discussed. Dalton's findings in regard to line-staff conflicts suggest that in production organizations line operations typically are the locus of organizational power.[19] Since the technological experts typically enter the organization through the staff side, they might well be impeded in the exercise of their expertise. The sheer fact of hierarchical authority, whether in line or staff, also would hamper the efforts of the younger more technologically oriented persons. Thus, while the direction of change among managers and executives is toward the more technologically sophisticated, the change will probably not be abrupt but rather will be one of transition with minimal personal disruption for the older style individual.

The professions also will be affected by technological change. A direct effect is the emergence of new professions, such as the computer programmer or systems analyst. Occupations such as these have taken their place among the professions with great rapidity. For the balance of the professions a situation similar to that which exists among managers and executives appears to be developing. The recent graduate is generally more technologically sophisticated than his more experienced colleagues. This is a major factor in the growth of "continuing education" seminars or meetings for established practitioners in the various professional fields.

A more significant development for the professions may be the substitution of the computer for certain aspects of professional practice. In medicine, for example, some initial diagnoses of pa-

[19]See Dalton, *Men Who Manage.*

tients has already been accomplished by computers. A full-scale application of such an approach would require more sophistication on the part of computers and, more importantly, on the part of the patients, but there is a potential for reorganization of medical practice with further developments in this direction. In the law an important development is the ability of the computer to do much of the work of the law clerk or of many beginning lawyers. The searching and ordering of past cases can be accomplished more rapidly and accurately by the computer than by the fledgling lawyer. This type of routine work will probably become much less important in the preparation of lawyers. It will also involve a reorganization of many law firms and thus of legal practice. For the accountant the advent of the computer has almost eliminated the importance of the corporate audit as a component in the work process. Organizations with tight control systems of their own are essentially self-auditing. According to Paul D. Montagna, one response to this shift of functions has been the expansion of the role of the accountant into management services, such as computerization or planning and assessing the total information system of an organization, and into taxation issues.[20] The traditional function of the accountant is no longer a meaningful task as a result of technological change, and the occupation is shifting to areas where its knowledge can still be applied to areas of uncertainty.

The impact of technological change on the occupational system varies with the nature of the occupation involved and, usually, its place within the employing organization. Despite the variations, which have been described, the most important fact is that changing technology is affecting all occupations from the unskilled worker to the professional. The evidence that is available suggests that the changes will occur at an increasingly rapid rate in the future.

technological change and employment versus unemployment

The impact of automation and general technological change on employment patterns can be analyzed from three perspectives. Gross employment rate changes, case studies of the introduction of automated operations, and analyses of the impact of unemployment on the individual have all been utilized in assessing the conse-

[20]"Bureaucracy and Change in Large Professional Organizations: A Functional Analysis of Large Public Accounting Firms" (Ph.D. Thesis, New York University, 1967).

quences of automation. In this section we focus on the first two types of analyses.

It is difficult to determine exactly what the impact of automation has been from the data on the total employment patterns within the society. The present low rate of unemployment suggests that the forecasts of optimists regarding automation have been correct—the long-run effect of automation will be to *increase* employment. This conclusion is tempered by the Vietnamese war, which has perhaps given the economy a temporary support and falsely increased the employment rate. At the same time, however, employment rates have remained relatively constant over the past decades with the exception of recessions that appear to be unrelated to automation. At present it is thus extremely difficult to determine the impact of automation on gross employment rates.

When a more detailed analysis of employment patterns is employed, some significant patterns are apparent. The decline in the proportion of unskilled and semiskilled workers in the labor force (see Tables 8.1 and 8.2) indicates the diminished demand for this level of worker. At the same time the rising educational level of the total population allows many who would have gone into this type of work to go into other occupations, which have expanded. For those who do not attain the education necessary for such mobility the outlook is bleak in the sense that these lower-level manual occupations will continue to contract. It is at this point that the possibility or probability of a population segment that is unemployable becomes apparent. In both urban and rural areas the likelihood of such continuing unemployment patterns has already established itself.

It is difficult to determine what the employment patterns among office workers affected by automation have been or will be. Since there is a high rate of turnover among the young females, the backbone of this segment of the labor force, and since there is no definitive pattern of attempts to reenter the labor force, the rate of unemployment is difficult to assess. Unless the individuals involved are actively seeking work, they will not show up in the statistics on unemployment. At the same time, of course, the fact that they are not actively seeking work implies they do not feel great need to find employment, and it is thus difficult to make a case for a severe problem in this area. The automation of the office does reduce the occupational possibilities for the unskilled high-school graduate or dropout girl. If this segment of the population does want to be employed, the problems facing them are evident.

When the focus of the analysis is shifted to particular instances of the introduction of automation, more definitive patterns can be seen. In a summary of the general principles operative in these situations Silverman notes that the introduction of automated equipment into a plant or office reduces costs.[21] If the price of the product or service involved is responsive to cost reduction, the price will decline. When this occurs, the demand for the product or service may increase. If the demand increases, employment is likely to increase or at least stay at the same level. On the other hand, when the price of the product or service is not responsive to reduced costs, workers are likely to be laid off in an attempt to further reduce costs. When the demand stays constant, regardless of pricing patterns, workers are likely to be laid off.

Another important consideration is that if employment even stays constant and output is increased, as a result of the automated situation, jobs that normally would have been created as a result of pressures for more output are not created. In this sense automation reduces the potential number of jobs. If this aspect of technological change continues, it is conceivable that the over-all rate of employment will decline *if* additional forms of employment are not developed through demands for new products and more particularly services not previously in demand. This latter point assumes that those persons not hired because of the lowered demand for workers due to automation can transfer their skills to the new situation. If the potential office clerk, for example, can perform adequately in some new service organization, such as a travel agency, the possibility of reduced employment rates is minimized. This assumes, of course, that such new service organizations are in demand. If, on the other hand, the new service organizations are developed but the skills of those workers not hired due to the introduction of automation are not compatible with the demands of the situation, the potential for higher rates of unemployment increases.

Shifting the analysis from these hypothetical situations to actual case studies, we find that employment is generally reduced. In the case of the first form of automation some of the changes are dramatic. For example, in a factory producing automobile engine blocks an automated line can produce an engine block in twenty minutes with forty-eight workers. Previously, 400 men working forty minutes were required for the same output.[22] Another case from the automobile industry shows the same trend. Before automation, 18,000 men were required to turn out stampings for some 755,000 cars. The introduction of automated equipment into this

[21]"The Economic and Social Effects of Automation in an Organization," p. 4.

[22]Gerald G. Sommers, Edward L. Cushman, and Nat Weinberg, *Adjusting to Technological Change* (New York: Harper & Row, Publishers, 1963), p. 13.

process reduced the required labor force to 13,000 men and also raised the output to 2,241,000 cars.[23] In this sort of automation the major reduction in the labor force is accomplished through reduced need for materials handling. According to Bright, some additional personnel are often hired for the maintenance function, but the numbers involved here are generally insignificant.[24]

Studies by Mann and Hoffman of power plants and Walker of an automated pipe mill suggest that the same pattern is evident in the second form of automation.[25] In these cases rather complete automation allowed the organizations to have much more output with substantially less human input. In these cases the automated plants supplemented pre-existing operations and did not result in layoffs, but the pattern of jobs not created remains.

Automation of the office generally occurs in an ongoing situation rather than in the form of a new plant, as in the previous cases. The result is the aforementioned displacement of bookkeepers and clerks. Here the work force is typically reduced through normal attrition. In some cases of this form of automation the work force can actually be increased. Jack Stieber found that an insurance company added personnel after the introduction of computers to the system.[26] Field agents were relieved of much of their paper work by the computerized system, which itself required personnel. In this sense the field agents could concentrate more heavily on their basic tasks leading to a more rational system.

Although case studies, such as these, are not too useful in providing systematic data on the employment patterns resulting from increased automation, they are instructive in regard to the impact on the workers involved. Even if there is no effect on employment rates, automation does affect the nature of the work and thus the workers' reactions to their occupations. For those who are displaced, the fact of unemployment must also be considered.

automation and the individual

Unemployment due to automation or simple layoffs has an obvious impact on the individual and his general social relation-

[23]Harold L. Sheppard and James L. Stern, "The Impact of Automation on Workers in Supplier Plants," *Labor Law Journal*, VIII, 10 (October, 1957), 714–18.

[24]Bright, *Automation and Management*, p. 202.

[25]See Mann and Hoffman, *Automation and the Worker: A Study of Social Change in Power Plants*, pp. 104–9 and Walker, *Toward the Automatic Factory: A Case Study of Men and Machines*, pp. 26–29.

[26]"Automation and the White Collar Worker," *Personnel*, XXXIV, 3 (November–December, 1957), 8–17.

ships, as was discussed in the section on the family. In the case of automation-based unemployment the effects are most severe for the worker whose skills have become outmoded and who had an emotional investment in those skills. Even where job opportunities are available in another community or another organization, the effect on the individual is such that the opportunities may not be realized. The social ties to a particular work group and to kin and friends in a particular community can be such that the unemployed worker may not want, or be able, to adjust to a new employment situation.[27] Since there has not been a high rate of such layoffs, problems of this sort have not been severe for the labor force as a whole. For the individuals directly affected by such unemployment, the problems are severe.

When the various forms of automation and their impact on the individuals involved are considered, both positive and negative consequences can be seen. Studies of the first form of automation suggest that the plants involved are usually more modern than those in the older systems, presenting the worker with a more physically attractive work environment.[28] Further positive effects of automation are that the work is generally cleaner than it had been, is less physically strenuous, and is generally safer. On the other hand, some automated equipment is very noisy, reducing the opportunity for talking and the normal social interaction on the job. Work in the automated factory is more rigidly paced and thus further out of the control of the workers involved. At the same time the work requires more continuous mental attention. This further reduces the opportunity for social interaction. Faunce reports that auto workers reported less physical tiredness but more mental fatigue due to tensions at work.[29] This last point is interesting in that this represents a sort of negative form of job upgrading in that it is the higher status occupations that most often report such mental fatigue. Faunce also found that the workers felt more responsibility in the automated system. This can be taken as a source of more positive job satisfaction.[30] A study of steelworkers, on the other hand, found little change in such satisfaction. The impact of this form of automation on the individual is thus mixed, and neither positive nor negative factors predominate.

[27]Charles R. Walker, *Steeltown* (New York: Harper & Row, Publishers, 1950), pp. 169–80.
[28]See William A. Faunce, "Automation and the Automobile Worker," *Social Problems*, VI, 1 (Summer, 1958), 68–78 and "Automation in the Automobile Industry: Some Consequences for In-Plant Social Structure," *American Sociological Review*, XXIII, 4 (August, 1958), 401–7.
[29]"Automation and the Automobile Worker," p. 70.
[30]"Automation and the Automobile Worker," p. 70.

The more comprehensive, second form of automation has been found to have generally positive effects on the workers involved.[31] The plants are cleaner than standard plants. Safety and plant lighting are also improved. Employment in such plants gives the workers more prestige in the community. Blauner's analysis of a chemical plant suggests that there is little pressure on the workers, since the work process is totally machine paced and cannot be speeded up.[32] Only during emergencies is the work likely to be frenzied. In this plant the workers were not confined to one work area and were free to move around and interact socially. The work rooms were air conditioned as a further positive physical factor. An important consideration in this type of factory is that labor represents a small proportion of the costs of production, minimizing the likelihood of layoffs and maximizing the bargaining position of the workers. Blauner also found that the workers believed that they controlled the work process, which also led to greater satisfaction. Walker found that the earnings of workers in an automated factory were uniformly higher than they had been in standard operations.[33]

The effects of this form of automation are not totally on the positive side of the ledger. There is likely to be an increase in the amount of shift work, since the equipment, both in terms of its cost and nature, must be run 24 hours a day. Since shift work does disrupt normal social life, off-the-job social interaction can be threatened. The family system in particular is adversely affected by shift work. As was the case in the first form of automation, workers feel a greater amount of tension in this type of operation. In this case, work mistakes can be extremely serious, so that the tension potential is increased.[34] Some automated installations require the workers to be physically dispersed over large areas. Communications are carried out by means of a public address system, which does not facilitate close social relationships and can result in lonesomeness. On the balance, however, the highly automated system does lead to positive consequences for the workers involved. Since the work force is relatively small, the contribution of each worker can be more easily seen, and he feels that his own work is important. The nature of the operation demands cooperation and interdependence, furthering the identification with the organization and job.

[31]See Mann and Hoffman, *Automation and the Worker: A Study of Social Change in Power Plants.*
[32]*Alienation and Freedom*, p. 101.
[33]*Toward the Automatic Factory*, pp. 178–81.
[34]Walker, "Life in The Automatic Factory," *Harvard Business Review*, XXXVI, 1 (January–February, 1958), 112.

Office automation is usually viewed as having negative consequences on the individuals involved. The movement is generally toward more factorylike operations, which reduces an important component of the status difference between office and factory. Shift work, for example, is often introduced in order to maximize utilization of the computers.[35] Time clocks and piece-work rates are also introduced at times. Dull and repetitive work, such as card punching and verifying, are commonplace. Since the input to the computer must be accurate, supervision is often more direct and intense.[36] At the same time, some organizations have been successful in building opportunities for job rotation and variety into the computerized system. Some tedious and repetitive jobs are also eliminated, and the workers feel that their jobs have been upgraded. In general, however, the advent of the computer pushes office work closer to that of the factory. The latter setting, of course, moves closer to an officelike atmosphere, suggesting that the plant-office distinction may become quite meaningless over a period of time.

The impact of automation on executives and professionals is generally viewed as beneficial in that more control and rationality is possible in the production, administration, and decision-making processes. Interestingly enough, there is very little evidence in regard to the satisfaction and general orientation of higher-level employees in organizations that have undergone the process of automation. As a general rule, it would appear that those who can adapt to the new skill and operating requirements would be more satisfied than those who are technologically bypassed.

summary and conclusions

Almost all occupations are affected by technological change, either directly or indirectly. The effect can be viewed neither as positive nor negative but rather as a mixture that depends upon the nature of the occupation and its position within the occupational structure. Those occupations oriented toward change are positively affected, although those which rely upon traditional skills and beliefs suffer the most adverse effects. At the same time those occupations which deal with tasks most amenable to change will be most drastically affected.

[35]See Ida R. Hoos, "When the Computer Takes Over the Office."
[36]See Jack Siegman and Bernard Karsh, "Some Organizational Correlates of White Collar Automation," *Sociological Inquiry*, XXXII, 1 (Winter, 1962), 109.

The general direction of the changes which have occurred and which can be foreseen is that mental, rather than manual, skills will be at a premium. The evidence that is available regarding the impact of change is contradictory and inconclusive. On the one hand, some occupations are downgraded and job security is threatened. On the other, some occupations receive more pay and other rewards. Cases of layoffs are contrasted with increased employment within the total system. Occupations are created while at the same time others are made obsolete. Opportunities are expanded for those with the proper amount and kind of education. For those without the educational prerequisites, there are almost no opportunities. The inevitable conclusion from these considerations is that more time must pass and more evidence must be accumulated before trends in the general social welfare or the future of specific occupations can be realistically forecast. Perhaps the only meaningful conclusion is that the kinds of changes described and many not yet considered will continue, probably at an increasing rate.

chapter 12

occupations
and the
political
system

The link between occupations and the political system is at once obvious and obscure. It is obvious in the sense that certain occupations seem to dominate the political sphere; yet it is obscure when the occupation of politician is considered. The exact role of political considerations within the occupational structure is not clear. This chapter will attempt to analyze the relationships between occupations and the political system in terms of the nature and extent of participation by various occupational groups, both as active political office seekers and as members of political movements. The occupation of politician will also be examined to determine if it can actually be considered an occupation and, if so, where it fits within the total occupational system. A final consideration will be the nature of the political process within the occupational system. Here the concern will be the exercise of power as a component of the nature of occupations.

occupations and political participation

Political participation is unevenly distributed throughout the occupational structure. Involvement in politics as a candidate for office has typically been limited to a few specific occupations. Lawyers traditionally have been the most active single occupation in seeking public office, which is rather natural given their training and involvement in public affairs.[1] Some people plan to enter politics through the law and use the latter field only as a steppingstone to a political career. At the more general level Seymour M. Lipset and Robert E. Lane have noted that occupations vary in the degree to which they allow members to be politically active.[2] Time must be available for participation. Intellectual stimulation of the ideas necessary for entrance into politics also varies by occupation. This is particularly evident in the case of political scientists, another occupation which is over-represented in active political life.

As a general rule, according to Greer and Orleans, "persons more educated, higher paid, and with more highly regarded jobs are more likely to be better informed and interested in politics."[3] Lipset suggests that a potential politician must have *psychic* leisure time to devote to the development of ideas.[4] The extremely poor and those with physically and mentally exhausting jobs are unlikely to have the desire or energy to engage in reading, listening, or thinking about things political.[5] This is reflected in the simple act of voting, as well as participation at higher levels.

Indirect support for the idea of the importance of intellectual stimulation and the availability of leisure time can be developed by considering the role of families and individuals of established wealth in contemporary American politics. The Roosevelts, Rockefellers, Kennedys, Averill Harriman, and G. Mennen Williams all exemplify education at elite schools and the probability of freedom to develop political ideas through unencumbered periods of leisure.

[1]For an early discussion of this phenomenon see H. H. Gerth and C. W. Mills, trans. and ed., *From Max Weber: Essays in Sociology* (New York: Oxford University Press, Inc., 1946), pp. 94–95.
[2]See Lipset, *Political Man* (New York: Doubleday & Company, Inc., 1959), pp. 197–98 and Lane, *Political Life* (New York: The Free Press of Glencoe, Inc., 1959), pp. 331–32.
[3]"Political Sociology," in *Handbook of Modern Sociology*, ed. Robert E. L. Faris, p. 824.
[4]*Political Man*, p. 198.
[5]Lipset, *Political Man*, p. 198.

Lipset concludes that the political position of these men, typically some type of non-economic liberalism (in the areas of foreign relations, civil rights and liberties, and urban affairs) stems largely from their education, general sophistication, and, perhaps, psychic security.[6]

To the idea of training and availability of time for the pursuit of political office must be added the idea of visibility. The importance of the mass media at the national and local levels in political campaigns has apparently allowed those who receive a good deal of exposure to the public to become more likely to be active and successful candidates than those who lack such exposure. The most obvious case of this is movie actors who enter the political arena. Cases of football coaches and other figures from sports illustrate the same point. The historical tie between military prominence and political office seeking illustrates the same phenomenon. While such exposure to the public does not in itself guarantee a successful candidacy, it is an asset not possessed by the majority of potential candidates.

Entrance into active political involvement as an office seeker is thus linked to the nonpolitical occupations of the participants. Occupations vary in the degree to which they provide the knowledge background and allow participation. Occupations that demand a heavy and regular time involvement, such as medicine, executive positions, or the whole array of hourly paid work, almost preclude participation unless the individual is willing to forego his occupation and the derivative income during his office seeking campaign. Since occupations are a major basis for the individual's frame of reference, those occupations that do not provide the intellectual stimulation or basic ideas necessary for political activity are unlikely to be sources of political candidates. The exact patterns of recruitment into political activity are not clear, either from the perspective of the motivations of the individual or their place in the social structure.

While the exact motivations for entrance into active political participation are not clear, there is some evidence that occupationally linked factors affect the direction of political beliefs for the politically active. Lipset reports that Republican office seekers and party officials at the local level tend to come from the professional and business-managerial occupations, while the Democrats have a heavier representation of manual and lower level white-collar occupations.[7] Despite this evidence, our knowledge about the proc-

[6]Lipset, *Political Man*, p. 298.
[7]*Political Man*, p. 288.

esses of entering the political arena is quite fragmentary. Much of
what has been discussed above has been a common-sense appraisal
of the existing situation, rather than an appraisal grounded on
sound research findings. This aspect of political activity remains
quite unexplored.

Part of the reason for the absence of extensive research on
politics as an occupation is undoubtedly that it is usually only a
part-time occupation. At the local and state level most legislators
and many administrators have full-time occupations in addition to
their political work. A state legislator, for example, is only committed to his political occupation during that period in which the legislature is in session. This can be a very brief period of time. The
Indiana legislature only meets for 90 days each biennium. While
legislative committees and the important task of campaigning for
office use up a great deal more time, the legislator typically maintains an "outside" occupation. In addition, at least half of the
politicians at any point in time are not employed in political office.
They have been defeated in their bids for office and thus must be
engaged in some other form of activity.

The small amount of research available in regard to politics as
an occupation probably also reflects the fact that a great variety of
behavior can be observed among office holders. Heinz Eulau et al.
have pointed out that "In politics, the skills presumably necessary
for professional success are much less specific [than other
professions]."[8] While the question might be raised as to whether
politics can be considered a profession, the point raised is appropriate. This fact and the rather transitory nature of most political
careers make analysis difficult, which is reflected in the scarcity of
available information.

Some components of the political occupation have, however,
been identified. In their analysis of state legislators, Eulau et al.
found that the level of competition between parties was a major
variable in ordering the career patterns of the legislators. In states
in which there is active and close competition between the major
parties and the parties themselves are well organized, the following
tendencies were found:

1. state legislators will have had some prior governmental experience, on the local level and in a
   legislative or quasi-legislative capacity;

[8]"Career Perspectives of State Legislators" in *Political Decision Makers*,
ed. Dwaine Marvick (New York: The Free Press of Glencoe, Inc., 1961), p.
229.

2. state legislators will have held party office or done party work at the local level;
3. state legislators will view the political party as a sponsor of their legislative careers;
4. state legislators will appreciate the opportunity given them by the political party in promoting their candidacies;
5. state legislators will not perceive interest groups and/or friends as agents sponsoring their careers;
6. state legislators will value the possession of particular skills thought relevant to a political career;
7. state legislators will have legal training and skills;
8. state legislators will not see opportunities to combine their private and political careers;
9. state legislators will not stress "opportunity" in general as a factor facilitating their careers;
10. state legislators will not look upon their political careers as a means for achieving personal—selfish and/or altruistic—goals;
11. state legislators will be committed to their legislative careers insofar as they plan to run for their seat again;
12. state legislators will attribute their continued commitment to their legislative careers to their "personal involvement" in the legislative job.[9]

Despite the small sample involved in this study, it does suggest that, under the circumstances of political competition and party organization, the idea of a political career has some meaning. In other cases, however, involvement in the state legislature is likely to be opportunistic, with little thought given to a continued level of activity in political office. At the same time it is difficult to generalize from this study of state legislators to other political office holders at higher and lower levels. Aside from the fact that they tend to come from the more advantaged occupations our knowledge of the occupation of politician and the occupational backgrounds of politicians is very limited.

The findings discussed above and an analysis by Peter H. Rossi suggest that part-time involvement in political office is the situation most likely to lead to nonofficial considerations being taken into account by office holders.[10] The part-time mayor, councilman, or

[9]Eulau et al., "Career Perspectives of State Legislators," pp. 259–60.
[10]See Rossi, "Power and Community Structure" in *Political Sociology*, ed. Lewis A. Coser (New York: Harper & Row, Publishers, 1966), p. 138.

legislator is more likely to respond to pressures from his regular occupation and other outside interests than is the full-time office holder.

Turning from political office holding and seeking to political activity in the form of voting, patterns similar to those discussed above are found. Higher rates of voting are found among businessmen, white-collar employees, government employees, commercial-crop farmers and some skilled blue-collar workers. Lower voting turnouts are evident among unskilled workers, servants, service workers, and subsistence farmers.[11] The factors affecting voting behavior are generally similar to those affecting political participation as discussed above.

The direction of voting behavior similarly is occupationally linked. Higher status occupations tend to be more conservative or Republican, while lower status occupations tend to be liberal or Democratic. These patterns have persisted over time. This general tendency is modified, however, by several specific variations. Among the professions, those engaged in intellectual pursuits are likely to be oriented to the left.[12] Alford attributes this orientation to the fact that these professions have no direct link to the dominant economic interest groups, while "entrepreneurial" professions, such as medicine and law, do. The latter type of professional is much more likely to take a conservative political stance.[13] Alford also notes that civil servants who are in a similar position in regard to the economic system are also likely to be oriented toward the liberal side. Another variation, to be discussed in detail below, is the tendency for some lower status occupations to be heavily involved in rightist social movements. Despite these fluctuations from the general pattern, occupational status is a fairly good predictor of voting behavior.[14]

Some additional confusion is introduced into these patterns by changes occurring in the social system. As the general level of prosperity increases, a trend toward more conservative voting would be predicted. At the same time, however, the rising educational level of the population would lead to a prediction of greater identification with liberal positions. In addition to these occupationally based considerations in the voting process, particular

[11]Lipset, *Political Man*, p. 184.
[12]See Lipset, *Political Man*, pp. 310–43 and Robert R. Alford, *Party and Society* (Chicago: Rand McNally & Company), p. 36 for discussions of this phenomenon.
[13]Alford, *Party and Society*, p. 36.
[14]Alford suggests that this pattern will increase in importance as religious and regional bases of differentiation diminish in importance. *Party and Society*, pp. 316–17.

issues, such as war and peace, domestic issues, and the differential attractiveness of candidates, have a great impact on specific voting patterns in specific elections. Over time and across national lines, however, the occupationally based factors remain important.

An interesting exception to the generalizations discussed above is the political movement. Groups drawn to such movements have much in common. In his analysis of political extremism to either the right or the left, Lipset has noted that "Extremist movements have much in common. They appeal to the disgruntled and psychologically homeless, to the personal failures, the socially isolated, the economically insecure, the uneducated, unsophisticated, and authoritarian persons at every level of society."[15]

In viewing the same phenomenon, Kornhauser is more occupationally specific. He suggests that the small businessman and the marginal farmer tend to join movements of the radical right. Also likely to go in this direction are newly wealthy individuals, usually from the business sphere of society, who are not accepted by the established upper class. Turning to the left are workers in isolated industries, such as miners, farm laborers, and maritime workers and longshoremen. Intellectuals who do not have ties to any corporate body, such as universities or colleges, are also likely to move toward the radical left. Cases of this would be writers or artists who work on their own.[16]

Participation in such mass movements is based on much more than simple occupational membership. The occupation does, however, set the conditions under which a person lives and thus contributes to his political orientation. Norbert Wiley's insightful analysis provides some indications of the reasons for this form of political participation.[17] As discussed in Chap. 5, Wiley notes that there are three dimensions of the class system: "(1) the labor market, which is the source of the conflict among occupational and property-owning groups, (2) the credit or money market, which is the basis for the conflict between debtors and creditors, and (3) the commodity market, which is the basis for the conflict between buyers and sellers, and landlords and tenants."[18] There are thus three axes of potential conflict and three bases upon which identification with others can occur.

[15]Lipset, *Political Man*, p. 174.
[16]Kornhauser, *The Politics of Mass Society* (New York: The Free Press of Glencoe, Inc., 1959), pp. 185–219.
[17]See Norbert Wiley, "America's Unique Class Politics: The Interplay of the Labor, Credit, and Commodity Markets."
[18]"America's Unique Class Politics: The Interplay of the Labor, Credit, and Commodity Markets," p. 531.

Wiley suggests that part of the reason that the United States has not had political activity divided along simple class lines is the fact that most people occupy positions (occupations) inconsistent in terms of these bases of conflict. The majority of urban industrial workers, for example, have been concerned about wages and working conditions and less concerned about the credit or commodity market. During the 19th century the workers did not unite with farmers in a socialist movement, despite the fact that both were evidently disadvantaged. From the perspective of this analysis, while both were disadvantaged, the disadvantage was along different axes, and each group would desire a different form of political action. In the case of the isolated worker in mining or farm labor, the inconsistency between axes is minimized. Both the credit and commodity markets are out of his control, and there is often a clear and common enemy who can be identified, the company and its store or the farm owner and his housing and low wages.

Wiley uses a different, but persuasive, interpretation of persons attracted to the radical right. He suggests that it is those people with inconsistent class attributes who are especially prone to support right-wing groups. The small businessman and marginal farmer both fit this category in that

> . . . while both make their living by selling, they also do capital buying from powerful sellers, and their incomes are often affected as much by buying as by selling. In addition, they are often heavily in debt and may be employers of labor, at least sporadically. Both groups, consequently, are afflicted with economic cross pressures and cannot identify with either big business or labor unions.[19]

The same general explanation is used for the emerging orientation toward the extreme right among manual workers. Here the growing amount of capital investment in real estate and the possibility of holding two jobs put the worker in the property-owning group while on the other axes he is among the disadvantaged. The inconsistency, which follows, thus leads to the right-wing involvement, according to this interpretation. From the perspective of this analysis, members of occupational groups that do not show this inconsistency should take a more moderate political stance. This is consistent with the available evidence.

Involvement in politics is closely related to the individual's

[19]"America's Unique Class Politics: The Interplay of the Labor, Credit, and Commodity Markets," p. 536.

position in the occupational structure. The relationship is not as clear as some discussed, such as with the educational or stratification system. At the same time the relationship may well be stronger than has been indicated, because of the lack of research into the area.

Political activity or involvement in the power system at the local or national level is not, of course, limited to the types of activity discussed above. A whole series of studies has suggested that a great deal of power is held by individuals not in public office. Robert S. and Helen Lynds' *Middletown* and C. Wright Mills' *The Power Elite* stand as major contributions to the knowledge of the realities of power at the local and national level.[20] The Lynds identify a family that, without holding public office, controls much of the activities of the community in which they own the principal industry. Mills' work, although severely criticized on methodological grounds, nonetheless has gone relatively unchallenged in its insistence that leaders of government, industry, and the military exercise a tremendous amount of influence in decisions that affect the total society. This influence is above and beyond that which is contained in their official positions. Although a wide range of motivations, from conspiratorial to extreme altruism, have been and can be attributed to the holders of such unofficial power, the fact remains that such power is part of the political system.

In order to obtain a more systematic perspective on such power systems, a large number of investigations of local communities have studied the power system as it operates at the local level. The literature, which has developed from these studies, is confusing in the sense that there is no consensus whether there is *a* power structure at this level. Despite this confusion, there is consensus that the power factor does operate outside of the official governmental channels.

Much of the lack of consensus over the nature of the power system is attributable to the methodological and conceptual approaches taken in the analyses. Sociologists have generally utilized a model of communities which involves a monolithic stratification system leading them to conclude that the power system takes the form of a unified system.[21] This is coupled with a reliance upon the

[20]See R. S. Lynd and H. Lynd, *Middletown in Transition* (New York: Harcourt, Brace & World, Inc., 1937) and C. Wright Mills, *The Power Elite* (New York: Oxford University Press, Inc., 1956).

[21]See, for example, the works of Floyd Hunter, *Community Power Structure* (Chapel Hill: University of North Carolina Press, 1953) and the discussion by Delbert C. Miller in *Power and Democracy in America*, eds. William D'Antonio and Howard Ehrlich (Notre Dame, Ind.: Notre Dame University Press, 1961).

use of informants asked to identify community influentials. Since the informants are given lists of supposed influentials, it is inevitable that the same names will be mentioned time after time, leading to the identification of a monolithic power structure.

The alternative perspective is largely taken by political scientists who do not begin with the same assumption about the nature of the stratification system. They also focus on decisions made in regard to specific issues rather than trying to identify a single elite system.[22] The methodology involved is to determine the leadership in the decision-making process in regard to a series of community issues. The findings from these investigations generally identify a pluralistic power structure in which more than one set of individuals emerges as important holders of power.

While much of the literature on power within the local community is taken up with the debate between advocates of these alternative approaches, the important point for this analysis is that there *is* such a structure. In a sense it does not matter whether this unofficial power structure is monolithic or polylithic, since holders of such unofficial power have been identified as important in the decision-making process. Their influence is felt through their support of or opposition to issues such as zoning ordinances, school bond issues, and the creation of civilian review boards for police. While their influence over official office holders undoubtedly varies widely by community or state, they do wield power.

When the occupational characteristics of the members of community power structures are examined, the same conclusion is reached as was the case for those active directly in politics. They are better educated and have higher status occupations. In general the specific occupations appear to be somewhat different. Lawyers do not dominate the system. Instead, the power structure is made up of leaders from the central interests of the community. In an industrial community, for example, power is held by executives from the major industries, whereas in a diversified community more segments of the community are part of the structure. The major factor in the composition of the community power structure appears to be the position of the individual in the general social structure. Occupation thus again becomes a major determinant of the involvement in the power system.

The relationship between occupations and social power is more complex than simply being a one to one relationship between

[22]See, for example, Robert Dahl, *Who Governs?* (New Haven: Yale University Press, 1961); Raymond E. Wolfinger, *Readings in Political Behavior* (Englewood Cliffs: Prentice-Hall, Inc., 1966); and Nelson W. Polsby, *Politics and Social Life* (Boston: Houghton Mifflin Company, 1963).

position in the stratification system and position in the political system. Certainly stratification and power are related, and those at the bottom of the stratification system also have the least power and vice versa. At the same time, particular occupations emerge as important in the political process, while others at the same level do not. The position of lawyers can be contrasted with that of medical doctors. The latter occupation is essentially apolitical in terms of either official or unofficial political power. At the same time other occupations, such as labor union official, can emerge as important in the community power structure, while the local sports hero can be elected sheriff. The nature of the occupation appears to be a critical variable in determining official or unofficial political participation. While occupations are intimately related to the stratification system, occupational considerations appear to outweigh stratification factors in determining political involvement.

power and politics in the occupational setting

This final section deals with a topic that has already been touched upon in a number of places. The power variable is central in the relationships between professionals and other members of the organizations of which they are a part. Staff-line conflict can similarly be approached from the power perspective as can the attempts on the part of skilled workers to maintain their monopoly over their market. The emergence of new occupations in the services-human resources era raises power issues for the occupations and organizations involved. The establishment of professional licensing and professional schools is often accomplished through legislative acts. This in itself requires the exercise of political skills on the part of the professions involved.

While aspects of the political are found throughout the occupational system and must therefore be included in any analysis of the system, the most direct impact of political considerations on occupations is found within the organizational setting. Since contemporary occupations are organizationally based, the power systems within organizations vitally affect the occupations themselves. The concept of power is central to most organizational analyses. Etzioni, for example, utilizes compliance (a consequence of power) as the basis for his analytical framework for organizations.[23] The manner in which organizational participants

---

[23]See *A Comparative Analysis of Complex Organizations.*

comply with the authority system becomes the basis for a classification system and the analysis of behavior in organizations. Blau and Scott note that authority, as a form of power, is basic to organizations.[24] Some form of power hierarchy is inescapable in organizations, even in the most democratic or collegially based system.

The most occupationally relevant consequence of the power system within organizations is the simple fact that the members of occupations behave in ways prescribed by the organization. Whether or not the control system is tight or loose, the behavior generally conforms to organizational expectations. Similarly, the power contained in a position is itself determined by the organization. The power of the executive is essentially given to the position and the incumbent utilizes that which is available. He may extend or diminish that power by his own actions, but the basic parameters are preset. In the conflict situations, which have been discussed previously (professional-organizational or labor-management), the positions of the participants have been set by the organization. Alterations in the organization that are a result of the conflict restructure the power positions of the participants, but even this restructuring is within the organizational context. The power position of one occupation *vis à vis* another is thus largely determined by the organization.

In addition to organizationally determined or formal power, the relationships between occupations can also be affected by the power granted expertise. Richard L. Peabody has pointed out that acknowledging professional competence, experience, or ability in dealing with other people gives the person acknowledged power over the acknowledger.[25] This type of power, which he labels functional authority, generally supports formal or organizationally derived power in the organizational setting. Outside of the organizational setting, as in the case of the private practitioner in the professions or the skilled worker, this form of power dominates. The important consideration here is that the power factor operates from either or both of these bases, ordering the relationships between occupational incumbents.

There are two major exceptions to these generalizations, which should be noted. The first is the fact that at times persons in relatively low positions in an organization can hold more power than their position would indicate. David Mechanic has pointed out that the secretary, for example, can gain quite a bit of power through her

[24]*Formal Organizations*, pp. 27–28.
[25]"Perceptions of Organizational Authority: A Comparative Analysis," *Administrative Science Quarterly*, VI, 4 (March, 1962), pp. 463–82.

control of information, work flow, and individuals.[26] She may permit some people to see her boss and not others and may do the work of some people before that of others. While this form of power could be reduced by rigorous application of the formal rules, the fact is that this type of situation is quite common. A secretary can exert much more power than her position in the organization would predict. In most cases, however, such power can only be exerted until the formal rules are strongly enforced.

The second exception is when the formal or functional authority system is questioned and threatened. Student power movements among university students affect the power relationships between themselves and university officials. Labor-management confrontations can alter the prerogatives of either party. The power system is thus not immutable. The dynamics of interaction between occupational groups in and out of organizations alters the power relationships both formally, in the case of organizationally derived power, and informally, in the case of relationships between occupations outside of the organizational setting. Each new power relationship does, however, structure future interaction.

summary and conclusions

This final chapter has been in many ways a capsule version of the theme of the entire book. Occupations serve as a major link between the individual and the society. Knowledge of the occupational system provides a basis for prediction about the participation of individuals and groups in the wider social structure. It is thus not surprising to find that certain occupations are more likely than others to be found active in the political system, both in terms of official office seeking and involvement in the regular political processes and through mass movements of one sort or another. Similarly the nature of the occupation allows prediction of the distribution of power in the occupational system.

The rather tentative conclusions reached in regard to the political system and its relationships with the occupational system also illustrate another important point. There is a great deal that is not known about the relationships that have been the focus of the entire discussion. While many of the conclusions have a solid empirical base, many others were hypotheses, which must be examined in the light of evidence as it becomes available.

[26]"Sources of Power of Lower Participants in Complex Organizations," *Administrative Science Quarterly*, VII, 3 (December, 1962), pp. 349–64.

In this chapter on political power and its relationships with occupations there has been little indication of the shift to the services-human resources era, which probably reflects two related considerations. First, the shift in emphasis away from industrialization is not yet complete and has not permeated the total society. The increasing reliance upon experts at all levels of government does indicate some shift toward the services-human resources emphasis, but the shift is not complete in most areas of political life. A conspicuous exception is the growing power of professionals and specialists of all sorts in the occupational setting. Here the movement seems to have been accomplished. The second consideration is linked to the subject at hand. The political scene is one of power. The power system is perhaps one of the most conservative in society in terms of its rate of change. Since power holders by definition have the power to maintain their position, it is less likely that change will occur as rapidly in this sphere as in many other segments of society. If the general discussion has been correct, however, this change should increasingly be evident in political life.

This chapter has illustrated a point implicit throughout the entire book; the occupational system is a major structuring element for the total social system. From the discussion in this chapter, it is evident that occupations form a better basis for prediction of the involvement of individuals in political life than does knowledge of the stratification system. While the stratification system can serve as a general predictor of behavior, the occupational system is probably a stronger basis for prediction. As was discussed above, occupations are the major source of placement in the stratification system. At the same time occupations do more than make this simple, but vital, placement. They provide the individual with skills, knowledge, values, opportunities, and limitations reflected in his total involvement in social life. Specific occupations themselves have characteristics which reflect more than their simple placement in the stratification system.

Our discussion of the occupational system began with the idea that changes in the total social system are reflected in the condition of contemporary occupations. The shift of occupations to the organizational environment and the growth of services-human resources oriented occupations with the related decline in importance of strictly production occupations has profoundly affected the manner in which an individual relates to his occupation. Motivations, training, and reactions to occupational life are influenced by these changes. The type of work that once might have been very satisfying may no longer be so, because of the different type of motivations people bring to their work. The same occupation may no longer receive the kind of rewards it did in the past. New organizational requirements, restrictions, and opportunities confront many previously "free" professions. For the individual, therefore, the occupational system is one of change.

The discussion of types of occupations is indicative of the changing social structure. The proportion of the labor force in the various categories ebbs and flows as societal demands and occupationally generated factors shift over time. The lines between the types of occupations themselves blur as more occupations professionalize and white-collar and blue-collar work becomes less differentiated. The requirements for entrance and success in the various occupational types have changed as the general educational level demanded is continually upgraded. Social skills, in the broadest meaning of the term, are becoming increasingly important throughout the occupational system.

The chapters in this last section have dealt with the relationships between the occupational system and the total social system and have illustrated the close relationships and points of disharmony that exist. They have also illustrated the dynamic nature of the relationships. The changes in the occupational system mean that the stratification system also is changing. The kinds of work that are regarded with high or low prestige shift over time. The manner in which an individual can be socially mobile has been drastically affected by the organizational and services-human resources emphases. At the same time, the central fact remains that it is through the occupational system, in terms of where a person is born and where he enters the system, that mobility is possible in the contemporary situation.

The relationships between occupations and the family, education, technology, and the political environment all reflect the level of over-all societal integration. As we have seen, there is not total integration. In every area discrepancies exist. Rather clearly the adjustment of one discrepancy, by whatever means, leads to new arrangements which further affect the level of integration. As the educational system might change to prepare students to deal more adequately with occupations in a period of technological change, resistance to such change might emerge from the family and political sectors. The fact that resistance to change does exist is itself indicative of the interlocked nature of the components of the social system.

The occupational system is a major basis for order and change within the total social structure. The place of occupations within the social order has been the main theme of this book. An equally important theme has been that the social order in turn affects the occupational system. This interaction between the total system and its occupational component exists in a number of directions and at a series of points within the system. This dynamic interaction leads to the conditions and the changes within the systems themselves.

index

Faunce, William A., 366
Foremen
  characteristics of, 218–22
  conflict and marginality, 221–28
  desirability of position, 225–28
  as potential managers, 228–29
  supervisory role, 222–25
Form, William, 6, 11n, 37n, 128–29,
    158, 160, 199, 218–22, 242, 315
Fortune, editors of, 141–43, 154–55
Foster, Phillip, 344
Freidson, Eliot, 107–8
Friedman, Georges, 54, 238
Fromm, Erich, 53n
Funeral directors, 80

Geer, Blanche, 76, 85n
Gerth, H. H., 371n
Gerver, Israel, 242–44
Ghana, education, 344
Glaser, Barney G., 115n
Glassworkers, 210–11
Gold, Ray, 251
Goldner, Fred H., 162–63
Goode, William J., 71n, 76–77, 186
Gouldner, Alvin M., 173n
Government employees (*see* Officials)
Greenwood, Ernest, 73–75
Greer, Scott, 371
Gross, Edward, 75–76, 178n, 194, 211n
Grossman, Joel B., 90n
Guest, Robert, 50–51, 54, 219, 227–28,
    241, 244n, 245
Guzzardi, Walter, Jr., 148–51

Hage, Jerald, 61–62
Hall, Douglas T., 145
Hall, Oswald, 129–30, 132
Hall, Richard H., 28n, 81–90, 93n,
    121–27
Halsey, A. E., 345–46
Hamilton, Richard F., 216–17
Hatt, Paul K., 295–96
Haug, Marie R., 90n
Hauser, Phillip, 18, 32
Heydebrand, Wolf V., 122–23
Hoffman, L. Richard, 357–58, 365,
    367n
Hoffman, Lois W., 328–29
Hollingshead, A. B., 148n

Homans, George C., 128n, 192–93, 194
Hoos, Ida R., 196–97, 368
Hopson, Dan, 119–20, 129
Hospital administration, 80
Housewife, as occupation, 6, 336–40
Howard, David M., 135
Howton, F. William, 186–87
Hughes, Everett, 5, 110n, 131–33
Hunter, Floyd, 378n

Industrial revolution, 12–16
Informal work groups (*see* Peer
    structuring)
Inkeles, Alex, 48–50

Jackson, Elton F., 135
Janitors, 251–52
Jennings, M. Kent, 170–71
Job dissatisfaction, 53–65
  alienation, 53–62
  and automation, 366–68
  factory work, 53–61
  role conflict, 62–65
Job satisfaction, 47–53, 61
  and automation, 366–68
  executives, 51–53
  factory work, 48–51
  international, 48–50
  social interaction, 193–94
Johnstone, Quintin, 179–20, 129

Kahl, Joseph, 17, 175, 253n
Kahn, Robert, 62–65
Kammerer, Gladys M., 173
Karsh, Bernard, 194–95, 368
Kassalow, Everett M., 176–77, 198–99
Kilpatrick, Franklin P., 170–71
Klein, Viola, 328–31
Kornhauser, Arthur, 60–61, 252
Kornhauser, William, 81n, 113–16,
    376
Krauss, Irving, 44–45, 314

Labor force, changes, 18–21
Ladinsky, Jack, 97–98, 132–33, 311
Lane, Robert E., 371
La Porte, Todd R., 116